The Game Goes On

When a man grows old and his blood runs cold
And his body no longer stands true –
When it bends in the middle like a one-string fiddle
He can tell you a tale or two

Jim Eyre

WILD PLACES
ABERGAVENNY

WILD PLACES PUBLISHING
PO BOX 100
ABERGAVENNY NP7 9WY, UK

First published 2007

Caving is a potentially dangerous pursuit. The inclusion of stories in this book, whether relating to incidents underground or on the surface, and whether linked with caving or otherwise, should not be taken to suggest that the activities involved are recommended to the reader.

Indeed, any reader who attempts to emulate the exploits described in this book is warned that these may not be conducive to continued good health. Neither the author nor publisher accepts any responsibility for any accident or damage, however caused.

MEASUREMENTS
Both imperial measurements (miles, yards, feet and inches) and metric measurements (kilometres, metres) are used in this book. Generally, older references originally contained imperial measurements while European cave surveys have, for many years, used metric units while those of the Americas have favoured distances recorded in feet. Within the context of each section, therefore, this book balances the measurements of older eras and those of latter times, particularly with consideration to overseas expeditions. While this introduces a mixture of imperial and metric distances within the narrative, it retains the feeling that would have prevailed at the time.

To convert measurements, a close approximation can be obtained by multiplying metres by 3.3 to obtain feet, or dividing feet by 3.3 to obtain metres. The imperial pound weight can be converted to kilograms by dividing by 2.2.

British Library Cataloguing in Publication Data
A catalogue record for this book is available from the British Library

ISBN 978-0-9526701-7-9

Design and origination by Wild Places Publishing, Abergavenny
Printed on CPI Matt, an acid-free paper manufactured from
    sustainable sources
Printed in the United Kingdom by CPI, Bath

Contents

Dedication

Writing an autobiography that almost
covers a lifetime can be a soul-searching
experience that briefly enables one to relive
and share sometimes embarrassing adventures
with complete strangers. At the same time, it has
proved almost impossible to describe in print the
tenderness and selfless love I experienced during my
second marriage to a delightful, beautiful and loving lady.
I wish to dedicate this book to Audrey, who came into my
life just when I needed her and stayed for 26 years, charming
everyone she met.

Author's note

To those dedicated and bemused readers who found
themselves stranded in deepest Yugoslavia when my previous
book, *It's Only a Game*, came to an abrupt end in 1964, I owe
an apology; well, two apologies, because here is the other half of
the life and times of Jim Eyre.

Acknowledgements

Special thanks go to the photographers who gave permission
for their pictures to appear in this book – they are credited on
the page (all others are mine).

The extract on p81-2, taken from an article by Pete Livesey
published in *Crags* in 1979, is reprinted by kind permission.

I would also like to thank all my friends, acquaintances and,
especially, cavers who, over the years, have enriched the tapestry
of this book by their presence in my life, no matter how fleetingly.
My thanks also go to the health and safety inspectors for not being
there at all.

Last but not least, my thanks to Judith Calford and Chris Howes,
who had faith in the project and have brought it to a successful
conclusion.

Foreword

WHAT'S THE POINT of living in a country that's being systematically wrecked by a rampant, ravaging establishment worshipping the God of Safety? 'Our first priority must always be public safety.' Yeh, right! Well, my first priority is to plant a good, solid northern boot up your bum, you whining, afraid-of-being-sued lackey of the meddling classes! Regrettably (for me), 'Ers' got in first. This book, like its predecessor *It's Only a Game*, is a glorious romp through a world where 'un-PC' meant that you had just run over a policeman, paedophiles were only sad objects of mirth to lusty, pimply teenagers engaged in rites of passage behind the bike shed, and 'safety' was a curious concept relative to the number of points of contact with rock, water or reality.

Readers of the first part of Jim Eyre's grand masterpiece autobiography will be delighted to learn that this second offering continues his narrative seamlessly and in a similar vein. Either volume can, of course, be read on its own; taken together they constitute an anthem to our indomitable British potholing spirit.

Within these pages I can re-live my mad old days, spent largely underground accompanied by people of very questionable sanity; guys who caved wearing sunglasses or who diverted water *into* pots to make them 'more interesting'. All ladders less than one hundred feet (thirty metres to you, young reader) were routinely free-climbed with not a bolt or deviation in sight; it was a case of straight down with the water as a matter of course (pun).

Bluddy luxury! 'If you weren't 'ard, you shouldn't've come,' as the actress once said. But, even in those halcyon days, travelling from Bonnie Scotland to the Yorkshire Dales, I lived in awe of Jim and his escapades, some recounted with side-splitting gusto in national caving magazines.

There were, of course, degrees of madness and hardness. For example, I drew the line at climbing million-foot-long wire ladders from a surface wracked by thunderstorms. There Mr Eyre and I parted company – as indeed did he with the ladder when lightning struck it – although, actually, we very seldom crossed paths at all. Still, here – surely – was a worthy role model. Alas, my attempts at emulation resulted monotonously in me hurling myself down vertical drops, with concomitant rearrangements of my skeletal frame and regular employment for the rescue teams, of which Jim was an important component.

During the swinging sixties we occupied identical but parallel universes, scrambling and sloshing along countless brown, scalloped passages all over the Dales and I can identify completely with the adventures recounted herein. As technical innovations revolutionised British caving, its exponents began exporting their talents across the globe from the deserts of the Middle East to the jungles of New Guinea. Here was a whole new arena for lunatic behaviour, gaily documented by Jim who played no insignificant part in it – no change there then!

There are those to whom life presents strings of Fortean oddities, possibly as some form of survival test. Jim Eyre is one of these people. You or I could walk down the

High Street quite uneventfully, but if Jim were to do so a Thomson's gazelle would fall on top of him. That is what makes this book such compelling reading.

Some thirty years ago I introduced my indefatigable caving partner Eric Glen to Jim, who took him to Iran. Eric was then probably the hardest caver Scotland had produced, but his achievements paled into insignificance as the Jim Eyre Road Show fumbled its way across the Persian deserts. Typical of their courtship was a night spent at the Northern Pennine Club's headquarters at Greenclose, where a water-throwing contest flooded every room and sleeping bag, eventually driving us to set up camp in the garden. 'Bugger oi,' quoth I. 'Are all the NPC completely mad?' Evidently so. Certainly, Eric was changed for ever by his foreign experiences.

Ah well, that was then. Sadly, we all grow older, but I strongly suspect Jim could still see a lot of us off underground – he certainly can from any bar of your choice!

Jim is a great character, a giant among potholers, a living legend and I am proud to call him friend. The great epic contained within these pages will make you drop your jaw, miss a heartbeat or two and undoubtedly suffer from aching sides. I know you will enjoy these memoirs and if you find any parts dangerously un-PC, regard them as sterling blows for eccentricity *and* common sense. 'The moving finger writes, and, having writ, reaches for a pint.' That's my boy!

Alan L. Jeffreys

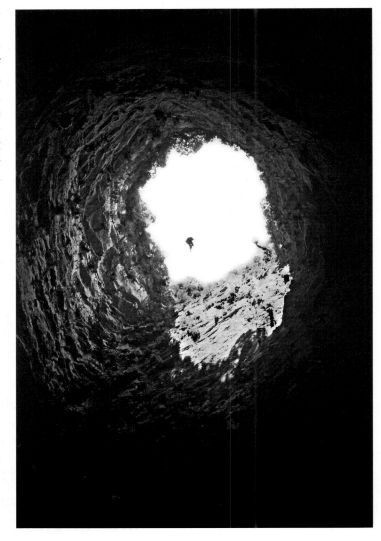

The awesome 1,100 foot (333 metre) deep shaft of Sótano de las Golondrinas

Chapter 1

The Game Goes On

ALL POTHOLERS ARE BLOODY DAFT . . . but some are dafter than others and I struggled frantically, clawing at loose mud and rock as I tried to escape from the massive slab of rock sliding towards me, looking more like a sarcophagus lid inscribed 'Here lies Jim' with every split second . . .

The avalanche of mud and stone funnelling into the lower reaches of my latest dig extinguished all the fervour I had developed for reaching the mythical Leck Fell Master Cave as, like Felix the cartoon cat, I scrambled clear just as the two-ton slab slammed into position, sealing the cavern below for ever – and almost me with it.

With muddy water and stones swilling down the crumbling walls of my favourite dig I dragged myself up onto the heather-clad moor, then one side of the man-made hole detached itself and slid into the crater like a giant, rock-studded mud blancmange, taking me back down again.

'Sod this for a bloody sport,' I yelled as, knee-deep in mud, gravel and water, I surveyed the wreckage of my fine excavation with its promise of 'caverns measureless to man' now reduced to a shallow bomb crater and a rapidly filling pool.

'Here lies Jim'

It was a Shakespearean tragedy. After months of work following a cold blast of cave air down a narrow cleft, we had removed tons of fill and had at last reached the promised land – all that lay between us and an enticing chamber were two round boulders. I had removed one, which crashed into the cave below, and given the other one a mighty heave with the crowbar when, to quote a young lady I know, 'the earth moved'. So here I was, standing on a mist-shrouded, windswept moor in the pouring rain with my buddies, mourning the loss of several slings, one caving ladder, digging ropes, two buckets and nearly the club president.

'Bollocks – I'm taking up golf,' said Dave.

'Me too,' muttered Tom as we slowly made our dejected way

down the fell, now transformed into a quagmire after four days of incessant rain, and onto the fell road which was running with water from the overflowing peat bogs, turning it into a miniature river.

'It's a good job we're not underground,' said Mick dolefully, surveying the flooding bog-cuts and streams that flowed through the heather and down the numerous shake-holes. 'I'll bet Lost John's is booming.'

It was, and so was the Craven Heifer in Ingleton when we arrived later that evening. Packed solid with walkers and cavers, hazy with moisture from wet clothes and ciga-rette smoke, a warm fuzzy smog wrapped in a jangling cacophony of sound as the pianist tried to compete with raucous laughter and the clatter of the one-armed bandit.

Another one-armed bandit appeared through the blue fag smoke like a latter-day buccaneer – it was Dick the Potter. 'I heard you were trying to bury yourself today, Jim – too tight to pay for a proper funeral? What you 'avin'?'

News travels fast in the caving world. The cavers were like old washerwomen: gos-sip was exchanged and beer poured down throats, and the noise levels increased as we steadily became pissed. Then Jack Whitfield, the landlord, who had just answered his phone, shouted: 'There's a callout, Jim – three lads trapped down Little Hull Pot.'

'Bloody 'ell!' I gulped down the rest of my pint and shouted: 'There's room for four in the back of my van.' The bar almost emptied as we headed for our vehicles, for in those days – September 1965 – most cavers in Yorkshire were also members of the Cave Rescue Organisation. Cavers first and foremost and, as only cavers can rescue other cavers, cave rescuers when we had to be.

ELEVEN P.M. ON A SATURDAY NIGHT was not a good time to call out a cave rescue team, as there was a good chance that everyone would be less than sober. How-ever, to cavers trapped below ground that point would be purely academic – better to have some piss-arsed hard man breathing stale beer fumes over you as he fastens you in a stretcher, than wait for some sober citizen who hasn't a clue what he's doing to turn up. Rucksacks and cavers piled into the backs of vans or jumped on the pillion seats of bikes, and the drunken cavalcade was off on a mission of mercy, cursing the silly bastards who had gone caving on such a foul day, yet willing to risk life and limb to rescue them.

Hurtling through a black night in torrential rain along narrow, twisting fell roads is pretty good for the concentration and, peering through the fogged-up windscreen, I vaguely made out a bike in the ditch and a van surrounded by the wreckage of a drystone wall as we drove past through a sheet of water that obliterated everything, including the next corner . . .

I felt a quick judder as I left the road and the sickening crunch of my front right wing as I fought with the steering and pulled up. The back doors flew open; two figures materialised and wrestled with the wing before twisting it off and chucking into the ditch, then they jumped in the back again, slammed the doors and shouted: 'Away you go, Jim.' I turned right onto the rough moorland track, which consisted of two water-filled ruts. I slammed the box into bottom gear and, engine screaming, the van ploughed up the one-in-three track, throwing muddy bow waves before us as we bounced through the deep holes. I felt physical pain with each bang of rock against the van's sump as it skidded and slewed from side to side, scraping against the gate-post as we reached the moor itself.

I pulled up, a steaming wreck, behind the shooting hut next to the CRO Land Rover and a police car. I didn't look at my van, for I was sure it was mortally wounded, but began to strip off and struggle into my wetsuit.

Reg Hainsworth came over. 'We've called out two fire tenders from Settle and Skipton – do you think they'll get up the track?' We could only wait and see.

From previous experience gained during a flood callout to Little Hull Pot in November 1963, we knew that the entrance crawl would be submerged under several feet of water. It would be impassable without building dams and employing high-pressure pumps to divert the floodwaters; I had painful recollections of a flood diversion hitting me squarely in the back and almost washing me over the big pitch, so at least we knew where not to make the diversion.

The two fire tenders had appeared by the time we changed and we watched them inch their way between the gateposts before we helped manhandle the pumps up the fell, which now looked more like a flood plain.

There was no sign of the pothole, just a swollen stream running into a large flooded area before it overflowed down the fellside. It was hard to believe that somewhere under all that fury of running water lay the entrance to a cave containing three shivering cavers huddled together, entombed 200 feet below, water pouring in around them and crashing down the pitches with sounds like peals of thunder as the walls of the cave vibrated with the noise.

Sandbags were filled, dams were built and trenches were dug as the firemen laid hoses across the moor and put the heavy-duty pumps to work. Soon the pumps beat out a steady pulse that was shredded by the gusting wind and, in lulls, muffled by pouring rain, emphasising the life-and-death struggle that was taking place. Men fought, knee-deep in mud, cursing:

'I could be curled up in bed cuddling my sexy wife, instead of freezing my balls off with you lot,' said Harry. 'Shovelling mud into fuckin' sandbags with a fuckin' hangover – all for some bloody daft cavers.'

Two more fire tenders were called out from Skipton and Silsden and, slowly, the water level dropped and the dripping roof of the cave appeared. Eventually, there was enough airspace to allow us to enter and a group of cavers carrying ladders, ropes, telephones and cables was soon grunting and splashing along the low confines of the 150 foot entrance crawl.

Ahead, I could hear a heavy force of water roaring and realised before we reached it that floodwater was entering from another subterranean route. When I emerged from the crawl, all I could see of the first 70 foot pitch was a foaming mass of brown floodwater crashing into space. I could just make out the end of the ladder belay that held the trapped cavers' ladders, which thrashed around in the maelstrom below; it was awesome.

We had to shout to each other to be heard over the noise and, as we cast about looking for somewhere to rig the first two pitches together, I stuck my head and shoulders into a tight, washed-out shale band against the roof and saw a route that continued around the edge of the large chamber 130 feet below. I don't know whether I was fired up with adrenalin or Newcastle Brown Ale, but I tied on a lifeline and pulled myself onto the ledge, which was about twenty inches wide and eighteen inches high; it was devoid of any holds and sloped ominously towards the edge of the drop.

Cautiously, I advanced, feeling desperately for handholds to prevent my body rolling towards the seething water and black space below. It was a remarkably speedy way of honing my powers of concentration and my questing, clinging fingers felt for the slightest deviation in the smooth rock before I inched my way around the lip and reached a recess and a broad ledge that overhung the large chamber. I untied the rope and belayed it, enabling more of the team to use it as a fixed rope and quickly join me with the ladders. Then, with the pitch rigged well away from the waterfall, two of us descended and soon located the trapped cavers.

The looks of total amazement we received when we suddenly materialised at the bottom of the flooded pothole was reward in itself; the three lads looked as though they were seeing ghosts.

'What?'

'How?'

'Where the bloody 'ell have you come from?'

They peered at us as though we were two of the three wise men.

'Where's the other one?' asked one of the lads.

'Up there in heaven,' I answered, pointing up the pitch. Handing him the rope, I said, 'Here, tie on and you can join him.'

It was breaking daylight when we reached the surface to see ten lines of fireman's pumping hose snaking across the moor to Hull Pot. It was still raining heavily – small lakes had appeared everywhere – and the rescued lads were hastily hustled away by the ministering angels of the ambulance service, promising to keep us in free beer for months.

Straightening out our crumpled and battered vehicles, we slithered down the track at 5 a.m., realising we never would have managed to get up it if we had been sober.

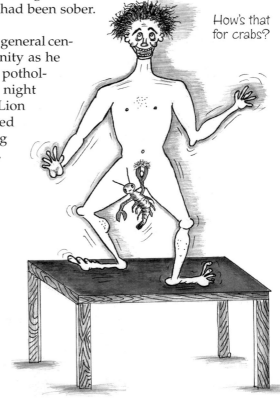

How's that for crabs?

OLD BOB HARDY also agreed with the general census of the much-criticised caving fraternity as he turned to his wife Nellie and said, 'All potholers are bloody daft,' as their convivial night out in the snug confines of the Golden Lion was rudely interrupted by a wild-eyed youth wearing a silly grin and nothing else. He came clattering down the stairs, streaked past the couple and ran the full length of the public bar, before jumping onto the table under the window. He then grabbed a plastic lobster from the table decoration (which was designed to encourage customers to want a meal) then hung it from his genitals by its large plastic claw (which was designed to put them off) before shouting: 'How's that for crabs?'

There were loud shouts and cheers from the locals before the naked youth was pounced upon by two young ladies wearing surgical masks, large wellington boots, surgical operating gowns and nothing else, as was revealed when the gowns flew open at the back. The sight of two nubile bums jiggling up and down as the 'nurses' cajoled their 'patient' to 'get back upstairs and back on the operating table, for we haven't finished with you yet' brought more cheers from the local farmers. When the laughter died down, Nellie said, 'Wasn't that young David from the Northern Pennine Club?'

'Yes lass,' answered Bob, 'it's their club dinner – the daft buggers are re-enacting his operation; he only got circumcised last week.'

'Oh – I thought it looked funny,' said Nellie. 'I'll have another Jubilee Stout.'

THE SWINGING SIXTIES was a wild era when British caving was on a roll. The Yorkshire Dales were full of odd caving characters and 'political correctness' was only something Guy Fawkes had tried to achieve, when Scruff and his girlfriend Minge set up house in a rock shelter in Trow Gill. Every other day Minge used to make the six-mile walk to Clapham Station to fill her rucksack with coal to keep the home fires burning, while Scruff sat at home conversing with his monkey. It picked livestock out of his beard as he tried to convince passing walkers that he was a holy man from Cleckheaton who had renounced all worldly goods and 'could they spare ten pence for some more holy water?' – neglecting to add that it could only be obtained at the New Inn under the trade name of Tetleys.

Some of the old boys in the village almost drooled to death

To drop out of modern society was to be a pot-holer, live in the Dales and discover vast cave systems during the day and tell everyone about it in the local pub at night. So reasoned a certain Mister Duckworth, who convinced the vicar of a small Ribblesdale community that he was a born-again Christian and he and his girlfriend would love to help out with his parish.

The vicar, a kindly man, looked at the small, hairy man with thick glasses and false teeth and gave permission for the two 'born-again Christians' to live in the crypt, providing they cleaned the church windows occasionally. Within no time at all, our two intrepid entrepreneurs had built up a window cleaning business which became very popular when the young, sexy girlfriend, clad in the briefest of micro-mini-skirts, began cleaning the top windows. They soon received lots of orders from the old boys in the village, some of whom almost drooled to death at the sight of the exposed buttocks wriggling around – two heavenly globes of airborne erotica expertly manipulated by a wizard of the wash-leather, who seemed to be able to wiggle both ends at once.

During those heady days it seemed to be a well-known fact that cavers and climbers were all closely related idiots, who did strange things when not engaged in falling off crags or becoming stuck in holes in the ground – and it wasn't just confined to the North. During my travels around the different caving areas of Britain, I found this strange pattern of behaviour existed everywhere. Different characters jealously guarded their reputations of being hard or crazy, and it used to be good fun when you entered the local cavers' pub to try to spot the local headcase.

It was just like the old western films when the locals heard that 'there's a stranger in town'. All eyes would be upon you as you entered the back room bar, and everyone would stop talking as the local hard men weighed you up as you made that long lonely walk to the bar, looking at you through eyes narrowed to slits.

'Where you from, stranger?'

'Lancaster.'

'Do you have business in town?'

'Yep – going potholing.'

'Hmm – done much?'

'Yep, done a bit.'

'The caves are hard in these here parts – here, drink this, you're gonna need it.'

You ended up with a load of new friends who set about trying to drink you under the table before dragging you off to their 'club hut'. This was a pseudonym for a rural slum, where you would spend a night of *nessum dorma* before being dragged out the next day and forced through the worst cave in the area to see if you were as hard as the grapevine said you were.

Later, emerging bruised, battered, and bewildered, half-drowned and completely knackered, you found you had been accepted into a new circle of cavers who would be friends for life. It would have been easier getting into the Freemasons!

That was how I met Reg Howard.

Reg fitted the part of those strong, silent types that crop up in westerns. He didn't drink as much as the rest and he didn't say much either – he was a man to be wary of. He had ginger hair and a ginger beard and, in between, two small gimlet eyes which scrutinised me intensely before he spoke.

'Fancy a trip to the Mendips?'

'Yep,' I answered.

I had heard of Mendip as being a funny sort of odd caving area where holes appeared in farmyards, everything was waterlogged, there were no big holes and everyone spoke funny – and the local cavers pursued a sport known as free-diving.

A group of us decided to meet Reg and his buddies from Southampton Caving Club at Priddy. We set up camp and met a couple of local cavers who took us through a pitch black night to the local pub. I was bemused when we stopped at a huddle of darkened buildings, where one of our companions knocked on the door.

'I thought we were going to the pub,' I said.

'This is it,' I was told and was shown a sign swinging overhead that I couldn't read in the dark. The local banged on the door again. We heard shuffling footsteps slowly approaching and I looked up again at the faded sign where I could just make out 'Sylvester Speed, prop.'.

'He doesn't live up to his name, does he?' I muttered, as the footsteps shuffled to a halt on the other side of the door.

'Yes?' queried a shaky voice.

'Are you open?'

'Yes.'

'Can we come in?'

Long pause.

'Well . . . I suppose so,' and there followed the sound of bolts being withdrawn, chains being unhooked, more muttering, another pause and then the sound of a giant key being turned in a giant lock. I burst out into uncontrollable laughter as it immediately reminded me of *The Goon Show* and I half expected to hear to hear Min as yet another bolt was withdrawn.

The door eventually creaked open and a stoop-shouldered, grey-haired old codger beckoned us in and carefully closed the door behind us. A large room, embellished with dark oak beams and a stone-flagged floor, was sparsely furnished with a few tables and chairs. A roaring fire blazed in the centre of an enormous fireplace, bordered by two large, wing-backed forms, one of which contained another grey-headed old codger.

'Good evening,' I said.

'Aar,' he replied. I guessed that conversation was going to be limited. We ordered drinks, old Lurch shuffled off to the nether regions and, after what seemed like an hour, returned with a tray of half-empty glasses that was slopping with spilled liquids. I followed him back to the bar and carried the rest. It was a good pub for teetotallers and we had an early night – in fact, I think he asked us to go at nine o'clock because he had a promise on.

The next day we discovered the Queen Victoria inn and the beer flowed fast, the sun came out and Reg and his mates turned up. I had forgotten all about free-diving or 'sumping' as they called it on Mendip and, during a hazy boozy evening, Reg began brainwashing us with the joys of Stoke Lane Slocker. There, entry to the further reaches depends on passing a section of totally submerged passage – a sump – by simply holding your breath and struggling through. We just laughed it off.

We were still laughing the next day until we suddenly realised we were at Stoke Bottom Farm and Reg and his crew were leading us towards the cave. Reg kept assuring us that we would like it and no one had ever drowned there – yet. I looked at my trusty companions, Jim Newton and Colin Thwaites, whose normally ruddy faces had been turned into a sort of pale puce by the beer of the night before and I could see that, like me, they were not overly enthusiastic.

It had rained hard during the night and the muddy stream was in spate and just lapping the cattle grid. In response to our worried enquiries Reg assured us that it was quite safe, unless the cattle grid was covered, 'and there's a good inch yet'. This cheered us up no end.

We approached the cave entrance which, apart from being almost underwater, was surrounded by flood warning signs. We were dutifully reading these, which informed us of the number to ring when we became trapped in the cave, when our leader dived through a mass of boiling water and froth and disappeared. We very reluctantly slithered after him down this plughole of an entrance and realised how spiders feel when they are flushed down the sink.

The small, tight passages that followed were very restricted and, after crawling and wriggling half-immersed in the diesel-laden water which splashed over us, we felt sure that we had passed the dreaded sump; we were wrong. Reg and his two clubmates suddenly stopped and the fact that we were lying prone, almost submerged in the water behind them, did not seem to cause them much concern. I listened intently to Reg's voice as it drifted back over the roar of the stream.

'Go on, Brian, you've been through before!'

He was answered by some peculiar gasping noises and a quavering voice which burbled something like: 'It wasn't as deep last time.' Ah – it's too deep, we're saved, I thought.

'Here, Ron, you go in,' said Reg.

'But Reg . . .'

'It's easy – you can't go wrong,' interrupted Reg. 'That's it – take your helmet off – lay down. Yes, you'll find your head will go underwater, but don't worry.'

The sounds of someone drowning came to my ears, then a voice much mellowed by water: 'Why don't you go first?'

'I can't,' said Reg. 'I've got to get this lot through – if I don't keep my eye on them they'll be off out!' This lack of faith hurt my feelings more than our leader's boot, which was pressed firmly on my outstretched hands.

After a while we were allowed to emerge from the wet crawl into a small chamber, where it was a relief to stand up. Jammed together in the constricted space we could see a narrow, water-filled cleft leading to the sump itself, and our leader talking to a helmet that floated on the water. We listened intently as Reg, still talking to the helmet, said earnestly: 'You'll have to take it off!'

A few bubbles came from underneath the helmet and then a hand reached up from below the water and removed it, exposing two bloodshot, panic-stricken eyes and a pale, dead-looking nose. Just below the nose two rock projections closed in underwater, hiding what lay beneath. I gazed at this disembodied horror in silence as I watched it bubble and blurt its way about in the water while its eyes tried to convey a message to us. Suddenly, the head sank a few inches and floated majestically along the cleft for a few feet before emerging in the sump pool where it floated freely, puffing and blowing vigorously.

None of us had ever seen a phenomenon like this before and we marvelled at the strange performance as we peered into the narrow, water-filled confines where, much to our amazement, we could see *two* heads bobbing about in the water. Reg spoke to

A hand reached up from below the water

one of them: 'Feel under with your hand.' The head, which answered to the name of Ron, did so and looked up at his leader in great expectation.

'Can you feel the airspace on the other side?' asked Reg.

'No,' said the head.

'Oh, well, it's there,' responded our leader, casually. 'Two or three feet and you're through – away you go, Ron.'

At this point I couldn't see what was happening because one of my fellow 'hard men' was blocking my view as he gazed intently at the drama being enacted below. 'Bloody hell,' he said. 'Bloody hell – did you see that?'

He knew I hadn't.

'I'm not going in there, oh no, that's not for me!'

These ejaculations came from my fellow caver Colin, who turned to me with an incredulous look and repeated, 'Did you see that?' The two disembodied heads, which had been gaily floating about in the water, had vanished without trace and a cold shiver ran down my back.

'If this is the Mendips you can stuff it,' muttered Colin as we watched Reg slide into the water and remove his helmet, allowing his head to sink between those two awful prongs of rock which threatened to grasp his neck and wring it like a chicken. We received similar, frenzied eye movements to those emitted by the other heads, before he sank almost out of sight, leaving only his ginger thatch above the surface. It looked like a small, animated coconut mat as it sailed along the tight cleft to the sump, where Reg rose from underneath looking, if anything, a trifle wilder than before he had submerged.

'Next,' he shouted. To me, semi-submerged in a miserable little cave that seemed like a sinking submarine, this was more like an invitation to commit hara-kiri and I made sure that Colin, whose common-sense Yorkshire judgement I could rely on, was next. Jim and I watched with interest as Colin tried to insert his plump body into that narrow waterlogged cleft and, as we expected, he became stuck underwater. By an amazing stroke of luck one nostril was above water

when this happened – otherwise all would have been lost, at least from Colin's point of view. I have never seen so much effort put into one nostril and Colin's respiratory organ swelled to twice its normal size as a frantic underwater struggle took place.

Eventually, he freed himself and emerged at the sump a trifle blue in the face, but still fairly sound,

I have never seen so much effort put into one nostril

as we realised when he swore at length in his favourite Yorkshire dialect. We listened in rapt admiration at the string of strange nouns and verbs that rolled glibly from his musical tongue. Our leader spoke to him quietly and persuasively for several minutes, until finally Colin calmed down and looked at Reg glassy-eyed from behind glasses opaque with mist and froth. Reg placed a hand on Colin's head and thrust him out of sight underwater.

'Hell, he's drowned him!' I thought.

'Next,' said Reg.

I experienced the same feeling I used to have when going to the dentist as I lowered myself into the cleft. I removed my helmet and found that by sinking almost out of sight and holding my breath, I could just squeeze past the two prongs of rock. I joined Reg in the sump and looked casually for the way on – there was bound to be a crack, an inch of airspace, a lightening of the water, bubbles . . . Something? Instead, I looked at wet, slimy, solid-looking walls, three candle stubs, one used flashbulb, two empty cigarette packets and an inch of diesel oil that floated on the surface of the dark brown water.

'Now Jim, feel under with your hand,' said Reg. I felt the wall continuing down under the water and, by crouching until my chin was submerged I felt an arched roof. Having a fairly active imagination, I also began feeling for hooked projections and other hidden devices that could trap me underwater.

'Right, found the passage? There's nothing to it, I'll push your head under and the others will catch you on the other side.' Having said this, Reg was about to place his hands on my helmet and dispatch me into oblivion when I was restrained by the sound of drowning coming from behind us. It was Jim Newton, stuck fast in the cleft with his mouth underwater, trying to cough water out of his lungs. Two things made this difficult: he couldn't breath in as his chest was trapped in a deflated position and every time he opened his mouth more water rushed in. In fact, all he succeeded in doing was making small gurgling noises and expelling spouts of water through his nose.

I found this diversion quite a relief but, unfortunately, Jim was soon freed from the rock's embrace and Reg was once more able to turn his attention to a most reluctant sumper to be – me.

'Right,' he said, 'feel through.'

I crouched in the sump again and waved an arm in the passage beyond, in the land of Neptune.

'You'll feel a hand,' said Reg.

I felt nothing except my legs going numb and a small sinking feeling in the pit of my stomach. 'They've gone,' I said and listened intently for voices from the other side. In fact, for all we knew they could really be on the other side – spirits flown.

'They'll still be there,' said Reg. 'How do you know?' I asked.

'Well – er – they will be . . . Feel again.'

'This is bloody ridiculous, standing up to me neck in bloody water waving me bloody hand about,' I muttered.

'Stick your leg through,' said Reg. Glad of a change, I thrust out a leg and waved it about furiously, but apart from cramp nothing happened. Reg placed his hands on my helmet and a most determined look came in his eyes.

'Er, just a minute,' I said.

I broke water on the other side

'Can you feel them?' he asked.

'No, but I think my bootlace is undone.'

Suddenly, a ghostly hand grabbed my leg. 'They've got me,' I gasped, and just managed to take a breath before Reg thrust my body underwater.

The rock scraped against my helmet and the brown water swirled round me like a shroud as I followed my leg. All sense of direction, time and feelings were lost in that brief flurry, until I broke water on the other side, lying on my back and thrashing furiously with my arms and legs, supported by Ron and Brian who were laughing uproariously at my unorthodox appearance. I was in – I had passed through the submerged portals into a watery tomb. I took stock of the slimy, black walls as I stood up, still neck-deep in water that was cold, black and threatening. I felt like a man buried alive.

'Where did I come from?' I asked, and was shown the darkest, deepest, most insignificant corner of the chamber.

'Down there,' said Ron. I watched him and Brian crouch chin-deep, feeling for the next victim. After a long wait, Brian suddenly grunted, 'Got him,' and a flurry of bubbles broke the surface. Ron and Brian heaved up a floundering figure that spluttered and threshed about like a man having a fit – it was Jim, his one good eye wildly rolling around in his head.

'Bloody 'ell – whose fuckin' idea was this?'

Reg soon followed and we thoroughly explored the cave beyond, oohed and ahhed at the formations and tried to whistle jolly little tunes, but our spirits weren't quite in it and we were soon back at the sump. Our leader said: 'It's easy going back, but don't try and swim through.' When I asked 'Why?' Reg offered me a piece of chocolate and drew my attention to some formations.

'What do you think of those?'

'Er, nice – what happens if you swim through?'

'Well, there's a submerged passage that continues past the airspace on the other side and if you don't come up in the right place . . . Here, have another piece of chocolate.'

Ron took up his position carefully and somewhat unnervingly began undertaking deep breathing exercises before disappearing underwater. We spent some time discussing whether he was through or just quietly drowned, before Brian felt about down below and suddenly his eyes glazed over before he too vanished. There was something terribly sinister and final about the silence that followed. Then Reg suddenly was gone.

Jim, Colin and I realised that we were now guideless. We pointed Colin in the general direction of the watery disappearing act and he grunted and made an impressive dive in the direction of the sump. Unfortunately, he didn't dive deep enough and rammed his head into the cave wall before resurfacing, coughing and floundering his way out of control round the chamber. This didn't do much for our confidence.

'Feel for a hand,' I said.

Colin almost submerged as he groped beneath the surface of the murky water. Suddenly, without so much as a goodbye, he vanished and after a lot of bubbling the surface of the water stilled. Then, several seconds later, a huge gush of displaced water welled up and I rushed forward to feel for the drowning body of my friend. Ah, my groping hand encountered a leg and I pulled furiously. Strangely enough, the leg kept kicking my hand away. Didn't he want to be saved?

I reached through again and the leg kicked my hand away for the second time. I had a discussion with Jim – should I grab the leg and go through, or grab the leg and pull Colin back? Little did we know that three men were jammed in the restricted sump pool at the other side and Colin was desperately trying to stop me coming through.

Jim and I waited a while before I tried my hand at underwater trout tickling again. The leg had gone, presumably Colin had gone with it and, waving my hand about some more, my outstretched fingers suddenly encountered another hand. It was like shaking hands with a cold, wet and clammy ghost. I took a deep breath and crouched down into obscurity, emerging battered and bewildered a few seconds later, minus helmet and spouting water from every pore.

Reg's homely face was a thing of beauty as he desperately tried to prise his fingers loose from my rigid grip. 'Nothing to it, Reg,' I chirped, and began cracking jokes and whistling cheerful little ditties as we waited for the lone soul who was still in the sump. Reg felt about underwater.

'Ah, got him. No, he's let go again. Now! Blast, he's let go again!'

It appeared that Jim was reluctant to join us but, eventually, he was dragged to the surface, coughing and spitting and swearing.

'What a bloody 'ole'!

EVERYTHING ON MENDIP WAS STRANGE to us, brought up as we were to find caves and potholes on moorland tops or fellsides. As we popped down holes in car parks, next to slurry tips, under local cafes, public lavatories, village halls and by the roadside, it seemed a bit like cheating or trying to break the world depth record in Holland.

'Tain't natural,' said Jim.

I agreed and, later, when we ensconced ourselves in the Hunters' Lodge Inn, we found that Mendip cavers 'tain't natural' either.

The crowded bar was filled with smoke, noise and what looked like space cowboys from the *Red Dwarf* series on telly; there was so much long hair about that we kept tripping over it. Cavers whose beards touched the floor conversed with girlfriends who could have been a cross between Cousin Itt from the *Addams Family* and an Old English sheepdog, but within no time at all we mastered the language – 'Oo, aar' – and when we supped some of the local scrumpy, we soon realised why they talked funny.

My brain cells had become really zapped by the time I bumped into the local god-father, who was called J-Rat although I couldn't understand why because he didn't seem like a rat, more like a friendly mole – a *Wind in the Willows* type you could take home to meet mother. He spoke a kind of Ancient Briton and was just the sort I could imagine leaping about naked, covered in woad.

After a couple of pints with J-Rat I became curious about the strong thread that was fastened to his lapel with a safety pin, the other end of which disappeared into his mouth.

'Ah,' he said when I asked him. 'It's me mates' idea,' and then he slurped another gulp at his pint.

'Yes, but what's it for?'

'Well,' said J-Rat, peering into my eyes with the look of one who is about to impart some news of importance. 'It's me false teeth.'

Mendip cavers
'tain't natural'

'What? Are they tied on?'

'Well, sort of,' answered J-Rat.

'And what've your mates got to do with it?' I asked.

'Well, they got sick of putting their hands down the U-bend in the bogs and feeling for 'em every time I spewed up, so they tied 'em to my jacket and now when I spews up, they just get ejected and swings in the air and I can pop 'em back in my mouth when I've finished.'

With that he gave me a beaming smile and hotfooted it for the gents. Oo, aar . . .

THERE IS NOTHING WORSE FOR A CAVER than to be trapped in darkness, shivering with cold while listening to the seemingly interminable drip of water. With foresight, could I have avoided the situation I now found myself in? Was I really to blame?

I asked myself these questions as I waved my arms to and fro in an effort to warm up my chilled body which had cooled rapidly in the damp confines of this cold, clammy place where water dripped from the ceiling, ran down the walls and the wet, cheerless stone echoed the hollow dripping of water. Did anyone know of my plight? I wondered if people in the world outside were aware of the poor shivering wretch who awaited rescue?

I thought I heard a noise and listened intently, but a cold shiver ran down my spine when I realised that I was mistaken. However, there was a different note in the sounds about me – the dripping water was coming faster, beating a staccato note on the cold, unyielding stone. I became aware of a splashing and gurgling and the strange throaty roar of water under pressure.

I suddenly sensed an urgent need to escape from these claustrophobic confines as the sound of running water increased and spray lashed my face and arms. Water rumbled and spurted about me and I felt the icy grip of liquid splashing against my ankles. Feeling my way along the rough walls, I recoiled from a powerful jet of water that seemed to block the way, the slimy rock beneath my feet offering no hold. I retreated and worked my way along the other wall, which bulged around a corner. Damn, if only I could see.

The roar of water grew louder and I heard a sullen gurgling as the siphons filled. Becoming desperate, I fumbled my way around the corner. At last, I could see lights and I rushed down the short passage and hurled myself at . . . an iron grille!

MY PREDICAMENT had been brought about by a potholing trip to Derbyshire. Three of us had driven to Manchester late one Saturday night to pick up another clubmate who was arriving on the bus. After the usual couple of pints and one for the road we eventually arrived at the bus station, and while my wife Rose and Ron Bliss were looking for our missing member I was left in charge of the vehicles.

Suddenly, my stomach was attacked by weird stomach bugs that were left by the great plague and are still fornicating in the vats of Derbyshire breweries. With a breathless sprint that would have done justice to an Olympic hopeful, I hastily departed in the direction of the toilets, clutching a coin in one hand and my trousers in the other. Being late at night, the place was in total darkness. I rushed in, fumbling frantically for the nearest cubicle and, discovering that they were all wide open, dived for the nearest and shut the door.

Almost immediately I heard a muffled shout and a metallic clang. I wondered vaguely what it was, but my mind and body were taken up with other things; I had sat on a wet seat.

Sometime later I emerged, light of step and full of good cheer. Imagine my surprise when I found the entrance barred by an extremely strong, well-built, closely woven latticework of exceptionally fine English steel. After shaking this contraption furiously for several minutes, I was convinced that although British workmanship and standards are generally on the decline, there is one thing in which we stand aloof from other nations: the technique of manufacturing strong, no-nonsense, burglar-proof bog doors.

There now follows a tale of woe. England, it seems, is the only place in the world where you can get trapped in a public toilet – because other countries don't lock them. However, in England, if one is unfortunate enough to be placed in this situation, one must not attempt to attract attention by referring to this fact, by either shouting or waving at passers-by.

I broke this unwritten rule – I shouted at a passer-by. He stopped, stared, muttered 'Hooligan' and stormed off. I waved an arm through the lattice; someone in a passing bus waved back. I retreated into the dark, wet confines and lit a fag while I reviewed the situation. Whichever way I reviewed it, I was the fall guy. I imagined the head-lines: 'Potholer trapped in public loo' or 'Exposure case in men's toilet'.

Should I call out the Cave Rescue Organisation? I decided against this as it wouldn't look too well in the incident report. 'Incident 99: rescue of J. Eyre from gent's bog. Mr Boardman states that due to extra gripping it is dangerous to enter Manchester toilets after 11 p.m.'

I crept back to the iron lattice and coo-eed at an old lady who was walking past. She let go with an ear-splitting scream and almost fainted. Then, before I could beat a hasty retreat, I was spotted by other passers-by.

''Ere, Bert, there's a bloke in there trying to assault that old lady,' shrieked a young lady to her fiancé.

I wisely stayed in the shadows until Bert had gone, then ventured out of the dark recesses and was immediately spotted by a small boy. 'Eh – Mam, there's a feller int' gent's bog,' and he dragged his mother over to the grille. I began trying to explain to her what had happened when a small crowd swiftly gathered. I felt a real pillock, like an exhibit in a fairground sideshow.

'What are you doing in there, then?'
'Trying to get out.'
'Ow did you get in?'
'Walked in.'
'Ow did you open the gates?'
'They were open.'
'Why did you shut them?'
'I didn't.'
'Oo did?'
'I don't bloody know.'

This question-and-answer game went on for some time until it was suddenly inter-rupted by raucous laughter from the fringe of the crowd as my mates returned. Rose fell about laughing with tears streaming down her cheeks. The three of them made no

'You know, Alf . . . you might think I'm pissed, but you know what, Alf . . . I can see a bloke in 'ere . . .

effort to come up with anything practical, but just stood there enjoying to the full the spectacle of the club's president entertaining the locals, which received a round of applause when the small boy offered me some of his peanuts. Two drunks rolled up.

'Eh, Fred . . . you know what? Fred . . . *hic* . . . they've got a bloody wild man in there. Bloody maniac, they've 'ad to lock 'im up in the . . . *hic* . . . house.'

His mate peered through the grille and his beer-laden breath drifted over me in a noisome cloud. With his bloodshot eyes inches from mine, he made a pronouncement in the serious way that drunks have.

'You know, Alf . . . you might think I'm pissed, but you know what, Alf . . . *hic* . . . I can see a bloke in 'ere . . . *hic* . . . Hello,' he said to me, 'can you let me in – I want a piss.' I retreated back into the shadows and lit a fag. I could take no more.

Eventually, Rose and Brian reappeared, followed by a police constable, three bus inspectors, and several bus drivers and conductors, all with beaming smiles.

'Now, me lad,' began the constable, who burst out laughing.

'What's the joke?' I asked gruffly.

'The attendant's gone home and taken the key with him,' answered the constable.

'Where's he live?' I asked.

'The other side of Manchester,' yelled Bliss. 'He went on the last bus!' And with that Bliss collapsed with mirth while I once again retreated into the dark privacy of the cubicles and sat down ruefully on another wet seat, lit another fag and contemplated on the great minds that reason that public toilets shall be locked and barred after 11 p.m.

After an interminably long, cold wait I heard the rattling of the grille and a gruff stentorian voice boomed out.

'Are you still in there?'

'Of course I'm still in here,' I muttered as I shuffled into view while the grille slid open, ready to tell the bog attendant what I thought of him. But I changed my mind when I saw him – for an irate bog attendant is a wrathful thing to behold, especially one that's been dragged out of bed and driven across Manchester.

'Why did you lock me in?' I demanded.

'You must have sneaked in when my back was turned,' he said.

'You should warn people,' I said.

'You didn't want to pay,' he said. 'Causing a public disturbance – you should be locked up.'

'I have been!'

Have you ever felt like pushing a public lavatory attendant down one of his own U-bends?

MY ORDEAL OVER we returned to Derbyshire, the land of interesting pubs and folklore to fit every occasion. There were pig-stuffing contests, ox-roastings, wellie-throwing competitions and special events to be celebrated, like the hanging of a local saint or the discovery of a local virgin (this one, unfortunately, has been discontin-ued). The following day we went down Giant's Hole, which is not as big as the name implies; indeed, it is decidedly small near the entrance where, at that time, to gain admittance cavers were forced to submerge themselves in eighteen inches of water in a passage nineteen and a half inches high.

In fact, while my companions had to submerge, I had a secret weapon – my broken, flexible proboscis. I discovered that by lying on my back with my body underwater, I could insert my nose in a crack in the roof and, by propelling myself backwards with-out making a ripple, I could enter the cave without suffering the traumatic effects of near drowning.

Unfortunately, jealousy is a strange thing and when my better-looking, snub-nosed companions inside the cave saw this strange, fleshy protuberance sailing majestically along just above the waterline like some peculiar periscope, they gave vent to their feelings by throwing rocks into the pool at the end of the tight section. The resulting waves swamped the nose and its submerged owner, and it sank with all hands.

Apart from this incident we had an enjoyable caving trip and Saturday evening saw us, slightly bedraggled with mud behind our ears, heading for the back room of the Eagle, the nearby cavers' hangout. The local characters were in there: Wingnut, Sloppy, Icarus, Ginger, Shep, Reg and Ron (these last two being our cave guides from Stoke Lane), plus several others.

After a good evening with lots of beer supped, I woke the next morning with a hangover and the trots, to find that Rose and I were members of the British Speleolo-gical Expedition to the Cantabrian mountains of north-west Spain. What quietly started out as a modest expedition then snowballed beyond the realms of reality and by the time of our departure it had become an attempt on the world's depth record.

I was visited by a reporter from the *Daily Express*, who posed me for photos while loading and unloading the van, listened intently to all I told him, then published a photograph of Rose with half a column all about her and sod all about me. The piece was accompanied by headlines that stated: 'Nymphomaniac cooks for forty cavemen' (or something similar).

The expedition had also become a big scrounge and firms were conned into parting with several hundred pounds' worth of items that ranged from Rolex Oyster watches and waterproof cameras to boot polish. The leaders received the watches and cameras and I was given some boot polish, but Spain now beckoned us onward.

The leaders received the watches and cameras and I was given some boot polish

Chapter 2

Spanish Explorations

THE CANTABRIAN MOUNTAINS cover an area of approximately two hundred miles by sixty miles and run along the northern coast of Spain, west of Bilbao. The peaks of the central group, the Picos de Europa, rise to eight thousand feet and contained several deep but blind potholes which had been explored by three Oxford University Caving Club and Derbyshire-based expeditions during the period from 1961 to 1963.

Mike Walker had been a member of these expeditions and he was subsequently contacted by a Spanish caving group, Grupo Espeleológico de Peñalba, with information about a number of large, active caves which they had not been able to explore fully. This was our aim, to push the unknown depths of these new systems.

In late July 1965, Rose and I drove to Buxton and loaded up my van with caving equipment and boxes and boxes of toffees and chocolate. 'We've had them given to us and they'll be okay for the natives,' said Wingnut as he heaved in another box.

Travelling through France during a hot Continental summer, the small Ford van was transformed into a mobile oven and its two sweating occupants were threatened by an avalanche of melting chocolate that began oozing out of the boxes. We tried eating it and giving it away, but slowly it spread and we were only saved from being turned into two chocolate soldiers by the cooler air of the high mountains of Spain. I was driving on a minor road heading for León when we came across a motor scooter lying on its side in a ditch, with a young woman bent over the prostrate form of a young man.

I stopped and we hurried over. The man was unconscious and the woman distraught; she spoke little English and he was in need of medical attention, so we chucked a load of stuff out of the van and between us laid him out in the back with his wife watching over him as we drove back towards the nearest town and a hospital. I had driven about twenty miles when the body in the back began groaning and moaning and his wife gestured me to stop.

Rose gave him a drink and gradually he came round. I explained we would take him to the hospital for a check-up, but he refused and said he would be alright, so, rather reluctantly, I drove back to the scene of his accident. We helped him out of the van and, as he could barely stand and looked awful, I sat him down and gave him more water until he seemed a little better. As the shock wore off he became quite talkative. His name was Ricardo, his wife was called Maria, we had just 'saved his life' and we must come to his house. I managed to start his scooter and he climbed astride it and promptly keeled over.

'Hospital,' I said.

'No, no, no,' said Ricardo and I began to wonder if we had done the right thing. He eventually managed to balance the machine and insisted that we followed him, so we kept Maria with us and traced the unsteady progress of the scooter as it turned off the road and headed up a dirt track.

For eighteen miles we followed Ricardo perched precariously on his wobbling scooter, along dirt tracks and dried-out stream beds until we came to an adobe village. The only adobe villages that I had ever seen were in Wild West films, produced 'way down in old Mexico'. It was like turning the clock back several hundred years.

As I pulled up, the van was surrounded by villagers and Rose made good use of the chocolate and toffees, before we followed Ricardo into his house while Maria told all the villagers how we had saved Ricardo's life!

Inside the humble dwelling a plain wooden table and a few chairs took up the centre of the living room and a small chest of drawers stood against one whitewashed wall, while a cabinet bearing plastic saints stood against the other. An old lady was dragged from a bedroom and we were introduced as Ricardo's 'saviours'; she crossed herself and kissed our cheeks as several villagers wandered in.

We were invited to sit at the table – someone produced a bottle of cognac and we were each given a tumbler-full. Ricardo then addressed everyone and he and Maria spoke voluble praises about how we had saved his life. We drank the old brandy, which had obviously been kept for a special occasion, then I thanked everyone and stood up to leave. It was an optimistic gesture – I was gently pushed back into my seat, my glass was refilled and a ham that was hanging from a hook in the ceiling was taken down and placed on the table in front of us.

Jim with Ricardo and his family
Photo: Rose Eyre

This was clearly a special ham, saved for a very long time for a *very* special occasion. It was covered in a sort of green mould mixed with fly droppings, some of which were still in the process of making more and, apart from appearing completely mummified, it also looked most unappetising. Ricardo appeared with a knife, Maria appeared with two small plates and all the villagers looked on with smiles of adoration as Ricardo cut the ham and gave us several small portions each. It tasted like raw bacon that had gone off. I smiled at Rose and muttered, 'This is bloody awful.' Our hosts smiled blissfully, unaware of my remarks. I smiled back and said, 'Bueno,' then muttered to Rose, 'Eat it quick and let's blow.'

We forced down the ham and swilled it away with the brandy. There were smiles of approval, more ham appeared on our plates and more cognac appeared in our glasses; I realised why no one had helped the Spaniard out of the ditch – it entailed a certain amount of inebriation and a possible case of food poisoning. Several cognacs later, so drunk that I could hardly walk, I drove the van slowly out of the village with fond farewells ringing in my ears, turned in the wrong direction and ended up in a remote farmyard with an unconscious wife, a thumping headache and heartburn from the indigestible ham.

Twenty-four hours later, covered in dust, we drove up a steep dirt road through Felmín and came to a steaming halt in a small polje where Reg Howard was busy stirring a huge bowl of porridge-like soup over an open fire. After noticing a couple of fag ends floating around in this exotic mixture, we declined the offer to dine and made ourselves busy sorting out our gear.

Mike Walker, the expedition leader, was worried and our tame *Daily Express* reporter was growing restless, as several expedition members had been here for five days and had not found anything of significance. We were beginning to think that the Spaniards had overrated the area.

Some members of the Grupo Espeleológico de Peñalba were camping with us, so a few of us questioned them about the caving possibilities in the area. We managed to persuade two keen lads to join us on a recce into Sima Grail, which, apparently, had been explored by the Spaniards to a ledge at a depth of 360 feet and was still going deeper.

Loaded with ladders and ropes, my enthusiastic team was soon reduced to a wet, soggy, mutinous bunch as we slogged uphill on the spur behind the camp in temperatures that hovered around ninety degrees Fahrenheit. After a thousand feet of steep foot-slogging we found the shaft partially concealed by the wild karst outcrops. The entrance was fifteen feet by twenty feet in size and slightly undercut, but the shaft opened up lower down.

I now discovered that the expedition electron ladders were crap; they seemed to have been made by out-of-work celebrities. The rungs on wire ladders should be plugged, but these were unfinished, badly made and lethal – some rungs were merely held on by a nail stuck through the wire! Others had been coiled and epoxy resin poured over the ends of the rungs in an effort to seal them, which resulted in the rungs being stuck together.

With the ladders strung end to end I climbed into Sima Grail, thankful that I had a good lifelining team as the final ladder was still stuck in a coil and I had to kick the rungs free, rung by rung, before I could reach a steep slope of guano at a depth of about 200 feet. I left the ladder and climbed down another thirty feet through a narrow letterbox into a small passage that ended after a few feet at another pitch.

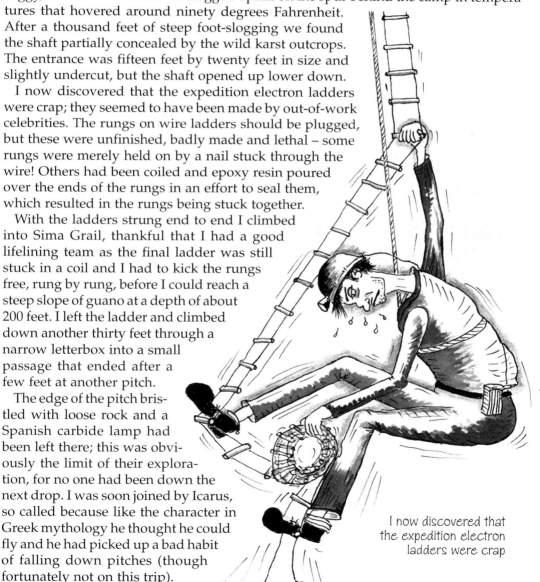

The edge of the pitch bristled with loose rock and a Spanish carbide lamp had been left there; this was obviously the limit of their exploration, for no one had been down the next drop. I was soon joined by Icarus, so called because like the character in Greek mythology he thought he could fly and he had picked up a bad habit of falling down pitches (though fortunately not on this trip).

I now discovered that the expedition electron ladders were crap

'Bloody hell, Jim, those ladders are crap,' he said before helping me dispose of the loose rock. The next pitch was 85 feet deep and then there was another twenty to gain a small chamber blocked by calcite. Three of us, plus a young Spaniard, spent some time clearing out the blockage until we revealed another shaft below, but explosives were needed to widen the approach so we decided to leave it alone.

The total depth we had reached was only about 350 feet and was nothing like the description that Mike had been given, so we wondered about the validity of the Spaniards' other claims. The young lad helping me to clear the blockage could only speak a little English and obviously didn't understand our swear words. He caused a riot when later, back at the camp, he approached me with a puzzled expression on his face.

'Jeem,' he asked, 'what ees thees fuk?' My wife, who was standing nearby, was, like Queen Victoria, not amused.

A volcanic plug dominated the doline and, just beyond, stood a cluster of small adobe buildings, one of which – according to the faded 'Cantina' sign on a loose board above the door – was the local pub. Inside, the single square room formed a small bar above a raised step-like section of the earthen floor. A large, greasy, apron-clad character, with a rugged face highlighted by the harsh light of a fizzing carbide lamp, served drinks. Folded shutters framed the open holes that served as windows, looking out onto a dark Oxford blue night sky splattered with brilliant flashes of light from the myriad stars that twinkled in the clear atmosphere. Three rickety tables and a handful of chairs completed the picture.

A couple of characters in large brimmed hats slouched in one corner, smoking small black cigarillos and watching us with interest as we approached the bar. The silhouette of a mule appeared, framed in the window against the sky, and a fat Spaniard entered the room; he flung an animal skin onto the bar top. A muttered conversation in Spanish took place as the bartender filled the skin with vino from one of the barrels. The man paid his pesetas, muttered 'Gracias, señor' and a greeting to us, before he slung the vino-swollen skin on his shoulder and carried it to his mule. Heaving it across the animal's back, he shouted 'Adiós amigos' before riding off into the night. I was fascinated – it was unreal. Just like the beer when we tried it!

At the equivalent of two pence a gallon, I suppose the beer was value for money, but it was like drinking gnat's piss and we soon discovered that the other barrel behind the bar contained cider. I hadn't known that they drank cider in Spain, but this was a local thing and you had to have been born in the area with the stomach of an alligator to be able to drink it. Added to this there was a special way of doing so, as was demonstrated by the locals later in the evening. The bartender poured the flat-looking liquid into a jug, then one of the locals stood on the step in front of the bar, held an empty glass behind him at hip height, stood stiffly in a matador stance and poured the contents of the jug over his shoulder into the glass. He proudly showed us the bubbles he had created and assured us that this was the only way to drink Spanish cider.

Everyone became soaked as half-drunken cavers tried to perform the feat and found out, aerated or not, that the cider still tasted like battery acid and dealt death blows to gringos' intestines, especially as these were already weakened by the Spanish beer. Several cavers hurriedly departed outside, with clothing soaked and stomachs heaving. The floor was soon swilling in cider and we realised what the step was for as more and more cider was tossed, willy-nilly, over shoulders and into protesting stomachs.

Wingnut (Antony Huntingdon) arrived and decided that his carbide lamp was better than the bartender's, so we had a contest where each tried to outdo the other. By pumping vigorously at the lamps, five-inch-long white flames were produced from the spluttering carbide containers.

With experience, we realised that the Spanish beer was incompatible with British stomachs and the Spanish cider was suicidal. What then of Spanish vino? Ugh! Coloured vinegar! However, we discovered that if it was diluted with 'gaseosa' (Spanish lemonade, and a lovely word), it made a palatable drink. 'Vinogassyoso' thereby became the in drink for us gringos, which at one penny for two gallons wasn't bad.

THE LARGE ENTRANCE of the impressive river cave of Valporquero lay quite near the camp. It was one of the main objectives of the expedition, but it had been agreed that a full exploration would only take place in the company of our Spanish hosts, and only a few had arrived. I became fed up with waiting and persuaded John Carney and two keen Spaniards to join me in a swift recce into the cave.

The impressive entrance was 25 feet high and 130 feet wide; a wide, shallow stream flowed sluggishly into the fern-covered opening. With a cave mouth this size we were able to walk for a considerable distance in daylight. Pockets of plants and mosses grew in the cool atmosphere on the dappled roof and high on the walls, down to a sharp delineation where winter floods had swept all clean.

More and more cider was tossed, willy-nilly, over shoulders and into protesting stomachs

The large entrance passage, 300 feet long and 115 feet high, contained a floor of large boulders and began to descend fairly steeply for another eighty feet. Another steam entered here and flowed through a low section while, overhead, large calcite gours formed a petrified staircase to an upper gallery.

John and I started to climb this, but were asked to wait by Ignacio and Annisimo. We watched in astonishment as they took off their large rucksacks and began climbing into sweaters, long johns and enormous waders, all the while leering at us and jabbering away in Spanish. John and I were only dressed in light caving gear and this seemed to be the source of their amusement. 'Newmonico,' said one and they both burst out laughing.

After a long wait our two intrepid cavers were finally dressed like deep-sea divers and we climbed into a large, high-level passage containing huge flowstone formations and began making our way through a series of chambers. The struggling Spaniards were soon sweating profusely and the only thing that cheered them up was the sight of a three-foot-deep pool that stretched across the passage.

'Ah, Jeem,' they jeered. 'Newmonico, newmonico,' and were amazed when the two of us just splashed our way through. They stood with their mouths open as they waited for us to be struck down with this dreaded Spanish pneumonia, which must occur instantly if you have wet feet.

The calcite barrier began to descend towards the sound of a roaring river and we climbed down the flowstone gours and scrambled over small climbs, which eventually led us to the roof of a large chamber. Another short climb took us into a lower passage where a sizeable stream plunged over a 25 foot pitch into a wide river passage below. This was brilliant caving.

I found a good rock belay and we laddered the pitch, then waited for our two friends to arrive. When they did they were lathered in sweat and developed looks of abject horror when they saw the wet pitch. They cautiously approached its head and peered over at the ladder which disappeared under the spray. Ignacio shook his head: 'No, no. It is not descended. It is very dangerous.'

I tied on and, lifelined by John, climbed down. It was not bad by wet pitch standards and, by kicking at the wall, I kept clear of the main force of water and descended in heavy, monsoon-type rain.

The cave below was really impressive. I landed on the edge of a forty-foot-wide lake and traversed to a rock bridge, leaving John to sort out the two Spaniards. The lake, deep and blue, curved around the corner and out of sight. I was concentrating on climbing across onto a boulder slope when I heard a tremendous shouting above the roar of the water. Turning round and looking back at the pitch, I could see flashing lights and a figure swinging to and fro underneath the waterfall. It was a particularly memorable sight. Arms and legs waving, the figure uttered several high-pitched 'Santa Marias' before being lowered by a cursing Carney.

I sat on the slope and laughed at Annisimo, who clung to the wall below the waterfall, terrified out of his wits, while John heaped curses on my head.

'Eyre, you're a sod! Fancy leaving me with these two comedians!'

John was next heard telling Ignacio what to do as I climbed the boulder slope and rounded the corner. More shouting suddenly ensued – then even louder: 'Jim, come back – quick, for Christ's sake!'

John sounded desperate. Hanging onto the wet, loose blocks of the rock wall, I retraced my steps. Back at the boulder slope, I looked across at a dramatic and even more memorable scene. A very wet, bedraggled Annisimo still clung stoically to the rock below the pitch. He was looking up at his mate, an even more dejected Ignacio who was fiercely embracing the ladder about fifteen feet above his head, doing an imitation of a statue in a fountain. John, under some stress, was holding the wretched Spaniard on the lifeline; Ignacio was clamped rigidly to the ladder and refused to go either up or down. The water cascaded off his body and into his waders – now completely full and expanded with water which spilled over, making a liquid ballet skirt that partially veiled the grotesque, swollen rubber legs below. Every now and then Ignacio's mouth would open like a stranded fish and he would come out with the now familiar refrain of 'Santa Maria, Santa Maria.'

The situation was funny, but required immediate action. From my position I could see a climb leading onto a traverse which would bring me out above the pitch. When I appeared behind John, he looked at me in astonishment. 'Bloody 'ell, where have you come from? Here, give me a hand on this rope!'

Together we heaved on the rope. Nothing happened; Ignacio, with his watery ballast, was immovable.

'Down!' I yelled, leaning over the pitch. 'Go down!'

'Assist – assist,' moaned Ignacio.

'Down – down – *GO DOWN*,' I yelled. All I heard in reply was several Santa Marias and four Hail Marys, before Ignacio repeated his familiar refrain: 'Jeem. Assist – assist!'

Santa Maria

John and I made a superhuman effort and managed to pull him bodily up a couple of rungs, then Santa Maria suddenly came to our rescue by ripping the fastenings on Ignacio's waders, causing them to collapse and let out the water. Thankfully, we hauled him to the top of the pitch. I had been simply heaving on the rope, while John acted as a belay with the rope around his back. As the blue, mottled features of the Spaniard appeared at the brink, I let go of the rope to move out of the way. Ignacio looked at me in stark horror, threw one hand up in the air and made the sign of the cross with the other.

'Jeem! Santa Maria – assist!' he yelled, and would have fallen off the ladder but for John who still held him on the lifeline. Together we dragged him over the edge like a landed fish and, after lying there gasping for several seconds, he picked himself up and hurled himself at John, who turned several shades of pink when a slobbering Ignacio began kissing him.

'Bravo, bravo Meester John, you save-a my life . . . Bravo – *muchas gracias, señor,*' and a grateful Ignacio began kissing John on both cheeks and saying, 'Bravo, I love-a-you.'

It was disgusting. If Carney had been a woman, he would have surrendered his virginity at the top of that pitch. Instead, the spell was broken when the victim of the Spaniard's amorous intentions told him to piss off and go and kiss Jim. Ignacio declined, saying: 'No ee-a-try to keel me! But you-a-sava my life,' and began kissing him again.

This hilarious and romantic episode was cut short by a thin, wailing cry from below: 'Jeem, Jeem – assist – newmonico.'

Oh dear – in the heat of the action we had forgotten Annisimo. I threw the end of the lifeline down to the shivering figure below and cursed quietly as he looked up at me and waved the rope end.

'Jeem, Jeem – fix.'

Bloody hell – he couldn't tie a bowline! I snatched at the rope, pulled it up, tied myself on, had a quick word with John and climbed down to poor Annisimo, who by now was grey-faced and shivering violently. 'Ah, Meester Jeem,' he began with the amorous enthusiasm of his mate, reaching out to grab me by the shoulders. I spun him round. 'Sit,' I said, and assisted him on to his backside. I then began pulling off his cumbersome waders, much to his astonishment – for a moment he tried to resist, but gave in when he saw the look on my face.

Divested of his rubber covering, Annisimo stood shaking on his thin, long-john-clad legs, looking for all the world like a stork with frostbite. I tied the lifeline high up, under his arms, wrapped his waders round my neck and climbed back up the ladder, then John and I heaved Annisimo up the pitch with a speed that had him hardly touching a rung.

Divested of his rubber covering, Annisimo stood shaking on his thin, long-john-clad legs

'Bravo, Jeem,' he yelled as he came over the edge and rushed at me with his arms open wide.

'Get lost,' I yelled. 'Go and cuddle Carney!'

THE FOLLOWING DAY we thought that we had waited long enough for the main bulk of the Spanish speleologists and decided to explore Cueva de Valporquero without them. Loaded with ladders and ropes, six of us headed into the cave, leaving the rest to follow.

Continuing from our furthest point, fortunately without our wader-clad amigos, we climbed down a large calcite barrier to a chamber over 200 feet long and almost 70 feet square. The stream emerged from among boulders to be swallowed by a low passage at the far end, which soon opened into a fine stream passage; it was well decorated with dazzling white flowstone and stalactites that covered the roof.

After 300 feet a 65 foot climb dropped into a larger, canyon-like passage where the roof soared to at least 150 feet above our heads, only vaguely discerned by our most powerful spotlight. We almost ran along this 650 foot-long canyon, splashing through the shallow water and finding it hard to believe that the cave was unexplored.

The large passage ended in a collapse where giant chunks of limestone blocked the way on. The stream flowed beneath the rock pile; we climbed upwards towards a dark expanse and found ourselves in a 300 foot-long upper series of caverns, 70 feet high and disappearing into darkness on either side. They were festooned with large calcite formations and huge stalactites that hung from the darkness like the curtains of some giant theatre.

As we progressed over flowstone and calcite barriers containing deep pools of clear, jade-green water and calcite crystals that sparkled and shimmered with reflected light, we came across a hole opening onto the stream below. A delicate climb and traverse led us back down to the water, which issued from a low, wide crawl. We headed downstream, where the volume of water increased, the passage narrowed and the water deepened, forcing us to swim. The passage widened again, resuming its former large dimensions, then the water increased again as the passage steepened to form chutes and cascades.

It was like an underground water park, as we 'yahooed' and laughed while sliding down cascades and swimming across pools that became larger and deeper where a huge calcite barrier formed a gour dam. Alternately swimming and walking, balanced on the rims of the gours, we eventually reached the edge of the obstacle.

Reg and I stood in amazement, looking at the vastness before us while the others caught up. The huge natural dam of massive, beehive-shaped flowstone continued down in a series of giant steps to a large chamber, 200 feet high. Each giant 'beehive' held back large, deep pools; we rigged a rope and slid down the first bit, climbed and slid the next, then slung another rope on the last drop of 75 feet to slide under a waterfall and land with a splash in the deep lake below.

This was exhilarating caving and, with adrenalin flowing, we slid, climbed and almost fell in our haste to follow the vast underground river. The cave passage increased in size with the roof towering 260 feet above us, while ahead calm lakes beckoned us on.

This was caving par excellence – Valporquero was proving a classic wetsuit caving trip and, thinking of Ignacio and Annisimo in their fishing waders, I could well understand why the cave hadn't been explored; this was not the place for fly-fishing. We swam across four lakes, each held back by large flowstone barriers, one above the other, and by swimming and climbing we reached the last drop that brought us to a hundred-foot-wide sombre chamber where the water sank among gravel banks in a huge sump. My spirits fell as I watched Wingnut poking around, looking for a way on.

Suddenly, he gave a shout as he found an eyehole in the wall above the sump. Soon, we were thrusting and struggling our way up fifteen feet of slimy, vertical, water-polished walls. At the top the passage made a U-turn and descended vertically to a tight bend through a pool to another vertical climb, where a narrow rift dropped into a large daylight chamber in the side of the Torío canyon. It was an amazing and exhilarating experience; we had passed through an ancient, now-drained siphon which was probably the original resurgence. This was unfortunate from a speleological viewpoint – millions of years ago what otherwise would have been a major cave system had been terminated by the Río Torío when it carved out the canyon, bisecting the cave.

The next question was should we return through the cave or should we try to make our way over the top. We opted for the latter and, after a sweaty, very tiring journey, we wished we hadn't. Hours later, carrying our wetsuit tops, we struggled over the crest of the hill overlooking the cave mouth. All the villagers and the rest of the Spanish cavers were standing at the entrance. According to Mike, who translated from a distance, they thought we had been swallowed by the cave, never to return.

Quietly, we approached the concerned villagers from behind. Then one old dear turned around and beheld the wetsuited gringos. She screamed, crossed herself and cried, 'Santa Maria,' as she thought we were ghosts. I thought, 'here we go again', just as Anissimo and Ignacio came rushing up with open arms crying: 'Ah, Meester Jeem, Meester Steve.'

THE NATURE OF THE EXPEDITION changed after the exploration of Valporquero. Splitting into smaller groups, we moved further afield using the Land Rovers. Spain, of course, is the land of fiestas, and we must have hit the fiesta season as every village we entered was the scene of singing and dancing. If we stopped we would be invited to join in, plied with drinks and goodies, and informed of 'caverns measureless to man' by local shepherds.

Chris Shepherd, one of our team, was an ex-boatswain of a youth-training ship. He was a good caver and a decent bloke until he had a drop to drink, then he turned into a miniature Mike Tyson and plonked people on the nose. Even his best friend Tim, as he tried to stop Chris plonking someone else, had his own nose modified.

Perhaps because I was older, perhaps because I already had a broken nose, or perhaps because I had a rapport with fellow drunks, whatever the reason or whatever state he was in, it seemed Chris would listen to me. Even so, when I laid down the law I would look into his small, expressionless eyes and gauge his reaction, always keeping an exit open for a quick retreat.

We became good caving mates on these forays into the heart of the Picos, and Chris and I worked quite well as a team, always being the first to descend the numerous potholes we discovered. Chris and Wingnut were frustrated rally drivers and took those Land Rovers places even mules wouldn't go, and we produced amazed looks when we drove into some of the more isolated villages. In one they fetched an old lady out of bed to look at us, as she had never seen a car in her life – she had also never seen a Wingnut before and when he stood before her, resplendent with an open mesh plastic potato bag on his head, she thought he was a Martian.

We visited one small village in our quest for caves and naturally called in at the local *cantina* to ward off dehydration. It was also a sort of general store and when we asked the owner if he had anything to eat, he promptly went out and killed a sheep! While his wife cooked it, we all became merry on cherry brandy and vino, then bought a pair of soft Spanish boots and a straw hat each. The whole bill came to the equivalent of forty pence a head!

While there we learned of an unexplored hole called Sil de la Columbina in a nearby mountain, so the following day we persuaded a local shepherd to show us the entrance. Loaded up with gear, we followed the man who was wearing an ill-fitting suit, a beret and unlaced, smooth-soled shoes that were several sizes too large. Even so, he took us up a grade IV climb which was so difficult that most of the party had to make a long detour.

At the top, 1,500 feet above the valley, he pointed out a doline which shelved away into an open shaft twenty feet in diameter. We lobbed a couple of rocks down and it seemed about 200 feet deep.

Rose with Wingnut wearing a plastic bag on his head
Right: The group preparing to tackle Sil de la Columbina. Photo: Mike Walker

Soon I was climbing down the ladders, but at 110 feet I stepped onto a steep rubble slope which ended in a boulder choke. This was a disappointment; however, as I slowly worked my way back up to the foot of the ladder I discovered a passage leading to another pitch.

Chris and another of the lads had by now climbed down and were quite nonplussed about how I had vanished into thin air. After we met up, we descended the pitch I had found and it headed into a series of old, dry caverns before becoming partially blocked by a large calcite flow. A climb revealed a high chamber and a T-junction that dropped into another rift with more pitches. It was a strange place with no air currents; bone dry, it led down several pitches, along passages covered with gypsum flowers and flowstone to a spiralling tube that issued great gusts of air. Some time was spent hammering there, trying to enlarge the tube to allow us access, but explosives were needed and were duly brought in.

After more work we were ready. All that could be seen at the top of the pitch was a battery and two wires leading down to our charge. The terminals were connected and the cave vibrated with the force of the detonation. We had removed enough rock to enable us to squeeze through a short way and another charge was required before we could thread a ladder down into a cavern that was beautifully decorated with calcite curtains, crystals and flowstone.

From here, a large water-worn passage plunged downwards at an angle of seventy degrees to another 100 foot pitch that led after a few feet to a further 55 foot pitch which dropped over some impressive formations into the centre of a breathtaking chamber, literally coated with brilliant white stal. The way on was blocked and that was the end of what had promised to be a fine cave.

Jim on Columbina's entrance pitch. Photo: Mike Walker

The expedition made a few more discoveries before it was time to go, but before we left for England we were taken to the León Sporting Club. Here we were wined and dined most regally by our hosts, some of whom apparently belonged to the Spanish aristocracy and arrived with beautiful señoritas poured into slim sheath dresses which left soft brown skin overflowing at various points.

They gazed at us with black, slumberous eyes and smiled sweet smiles as sensuous wet ruby lips drew back from sparkling teeth, matched only by the jewels that dripped from their ears and flawless necks. One beautiful woman looked deeply into my eyes, smiled and turned to her boyfriend and said:

'Scruffy looking lot of sods, aren't they?'

'Scruffy looking lot of sods, aren't they?'

Chapter 3

The Maeshafn Affair

AT LONG LAST, our self-imposed task of resurveying, describing and analysing the intricacies of Ease Gill Caverns was finished – or as finished as any sort of work such this can ever be; even as we took down the large table on which the survey had been laid out, new passages were being discovered.

As we handed the survey over to the Cave Research Group we had every reason to be proud of the fact that a small group of working class lads had completed this complicated survey, without the backing of any specialised training or fancy degrees. We had succeeded in this tremendous advance in British speleology with what Dr Jack Aspin called 'the classic account of a most remarkable cave system'. *Lancaster Hole and the Ease Gill Caverns* was published a few years later and, even today, it remains a fairly unique book of reference and a lasting tribute to the memory of Peter Ashmead, who died shortly after it appeared in 1967.

With its completion, some members of the Red Rose Cave & Pothole Club experienced withdrawal symptoms – they could now go caving without me nagging them to help with the survey, and I too was pleased to remove the millstone of Ease Gill from around my neck. No matter how fine a particular experience is, repetition can make it lose its appeal – a bit like a sex maniac locked in a room full of naked virgins, he's bound to get fed up sometime . . .

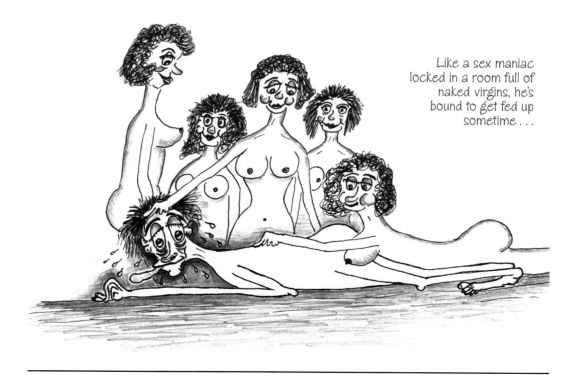

Like a sex maniac locked in a room full of naked virgins, he's bound to get fed up sometime . . .

MY HORIZONS BROADENED as I undertook other projects and carried on my eternal search for another master cave or bottomless pit. Strangely enough, I was soon offered one. I was about to become an extra in a great mystery play called The Maeshafn Affair.

At 2.30 a.m. on Wednesday 30 September 1964, I found myself under police escort driving down the M6 motorway in thick fog, going on an errand of mercy to search for two youths who had gone missing while 'potholing' in North Wales. After a blow-out which caused some delay, we eventually arrived at Mold police station and caught a couple of hours' sleep before being assembled at daybreak, along with every caver in Britain – or so it seemed. The chief constable of the region had never experienced a cave rescue before and he was obviously a man who did not believe in half measures – this man could have organised D-Day!

As the sun came out, a giant convoy of cavers' cars and bikes were escorted to nearby Maeshafn, a small village of ex-miners' houses where an amazing sight met us. It was like a scene from Exodus: a mass of people extended as far as the eye could see. There were soldiers, policemen, cavers, yobs, sightseers and people of all descriptions, and I half expected to see Charlton Heston appear. Instead, we had a lesser version of a crowd controller, our newly elected CRO chairman who, instead of standing out above the throng in flowing scarlet robes (as Charlton Heston would have done), dashed hither and thither as he organised this and disorganised that. His well-modulated voice was enhanced by a new toy he had acquired, an electronically boosted loudhailer.

Now, Mike Hollingworth had one of those voices that goes down well on *Listen with Mother* or as an announcer on the *Antiques Roadshow*, but amplified by several decibels it could remove loose teeth fillings.

A group of us were about to flee the scene when the noise ceased. A large crowd of people detached themselves from the main group and followed Mike into a small building, which soon filled up. Standing on the fringe of the crowd outside, we could

We had a lesser version of a crowd controller

hear our chairman explaining how voices had been heard in a nearby shaft – he then, strangely, despatched groups into the surrounding wilderness to search for the missing youths. This seemed rather odd to me, not being as bright as Mike, and I shouted from the doorway: 'Has anyone been down this shaft?'

This brought a remarkable silence and everyone turned round. Our vociferous chairman looked at me as though I was a gift from the gods. A greasy smile appeared on his face.

'Ah Jim, just the man. Would you like to have a look down the shaft? Great, get your team together and report back here.'

I was immediately grabbed by three reporters and several cavers who patted me on the back, and as I found myself the centre of attention I had a strange feeling that I had said the wrong thing. Slowly, through the hubbub of conversation, I became aware that my innocent question meant that I had just volunteered to go down the Great Grosvenor Shaft.

I was introduced to a mining engineer who once worked in the mine, and he led me through the crowded room to a blackboard. Pinned to this was a sectional survey of the Grosvenor mine, showing a vertical shaft of 979 feet bisecting several levels. After a numbing mental calculation I said, 'But that's nearly a thousand feet.'

'Yep,' he answered, 'you could say that.'

I informed the other members of my team and, to a man, they all volunteered to serve on the lifeline. By this time I had recognised several 'tigers' from other clubs – who also volunteered to man the lifeline.

The word went round and as I approached other groups of cavers, they rapidly dispersed as though I was suffering from the plague, the pox or some other contagious disease. I became a respected but lonely figure who was followed everywhere by a small crowd of reporters and locals waiting patiently for the spectacle of a man falling down a bottomless shaft.

I suddenly experienced the urge to urinate and slipped quietly behind a tree, doggedly pursued by my entourage. Not wishing to miss anything, they watched intently the 'man urinating before falling down bottomless shaft'. Eventually, I was led towards a

Man urinating before falling down bottomless shaft

grim-looking, stone-rimmed, fifteen-foot-wide shaft surrounded by a barbed wire fence and dominated by a crumbling engine house that overlooked the village.

My followers had now become quite a crowd. They watched in awe as I crept under the wire and looked down the shaft. The top fifteen feet were lined with stone, which suddenly finished when that section met undercut walls of clay and shale that ominously overhung the dark shaft. It dropped sheer into the blackest, most terrifying hole that I had ever seen. The knowledge that it was almost a thousand feet deep did nothing to lighten my spirits and, when a small boy handed me a rock, they slumped even further. The rock fell into oblivion with no sound of it striking anything solid – we only heard grim, taunting echoes as it ricocheted off the shaft wall, until the faint rumbling ended altogether in a deep silence broken eventually by the small boy, who said, 'It goes to Hell, mister.'

As I stood there savouring the rapidly growing urge to hotfoot it back to Lancaster, everyone else was galvanised into action. The most motley collection of caving ladders had been assembled from different caving clubs, scrapyards and museums and these were now being lowered into this bottomless pit by a carefree bunch of cavers. Some of the ladders were made out of piano wire and sweat stood out on my brow when three ladders appeared that were constructed with copper rungs, which looked suspiciously like domestic heating pipes. Then someone suggested putting a couple of the better ladders at the top as 'it would look good on the photographs'.

By this time I had ceased to care, as I knew in my crafty scheming mind that there were no lifelines long enough. But no, some bright sod had thought of this and along came the RAF mountain rescue teams with a pair of five-hundred-foot drums of full-weight nylon. My fate was sealed.

Just over seven hundred feet of ladder had been lowered down the shaft. I knew it wouldn't reach the bottom so I informed everyone that I would try and swing into one of the lower levels. I put an extra wire belay on the ladders and climbed over the edge, encouraged by the stalwarts manning the lifeline.

The television cameras began to whirr – it was the moment Wonder Caver had been waiting for. 'Hold it!' shouted his commanding voice and out of the crowd stepped a figure clad in dazzling white pristine overalls festooned by a string of brand new karabiners which glistened in the sun. It was the star of the show, a local 'expert' who had been making regular appearances on the telly and featured in every version of every newspaper.

He advanced towards me. The sun flashing off his new white helmet, glittering 'krabs' and white attire made me blink as the cameras left my homely face and zoomed in on this handsome yobbo. Eventually, suitably posed with one foot on the coping stones and flashing lots of pearly white teeth at the cameras, he thrust a drawing of the shaft at me and said, 'Here is your plan.'

He was like one of those characters in 'Allo 'Allo! who says, 'I shall say this only once.' I really did say something only once – I think it was 'piss off' as I began climbing down the taught ladders.

After fifteen feet the stone 'topping' finished and the undercut walls appeared, just as they were hacked out all those years ago by bygone miners. The ladders swung free past this point and I made good progress, looking carefully for any loose boulders that could be breaking free from the shale walls, but they looked reasonably safe and I continued down at a steady pace until I came across the first horizontal galleries. I shouted into them as I passed, with inane comments like: 'Are you there?' If someone had answered 'No', I would have fallen off the ladder!

At 330 feet the shaft was blocked by rubble from the engine house, which I stepped onto. Unknown to me at the time, it was simply resting on some old car bodies that had been thrown down the shaft. I climbed off the poised blockage into a muddy level and signalled the surface, whereupon a telephone was lowered.

After a brief wait, during which I partially explored the old mine level and noted a few clog marks in the red mud, I returned to the shaft and saw a descending figure silhouetted against the distant skyline. When he arrived, I found out that it was a young Pete Livesey, a budding hard man who had just begun making a name for himself in the caving and climbing world. Clad only in running shoes, jeans and a T-shirt, Pete joined me as we tentatively searched the foul-smelling level, clambering past rotting timbers and 'run-ins' where the walls were disintegrating.

Frantically grabbing at the rungs as they sailed past, I left behind my trouser leg

In places, more miners' footprints stood out in the mud; it was almost as though we had entered a tomb. Further on, evil-smelling water a foot deep gave off bubbles of gas as we sank almost knee-deep in rotten timbers and mud.

'Looks like one of those bad air jobs,' remarked Pete casually as though he was discussing the weather while we both gasped for oxygen and I was thankful when we came to the final collapse. It was obvious that no one had been down the mine since it was abandoned and the voices that had been heard must have been the product of an overheated imagination, so we returned thankfully to the shaft and breathed deeply of the clean air.

I tied on the lifeline and Pete rang the surface. One minute I was casually talking to Pete, and the next I was doing an imitation of Bugs Bunny as ten stalwart men heave-hoed on the new nylon rope. I suddenly became airborne in a mighty leap that left Pete scratching his curly mop in confusion, looking at the space I had recently vacated through his steamed-up glasses. 'Perhaps it was something I said,' muttered Pete as I grabbed the ladder fifteen feet above his head.

Then the elastic qualities of the rope took command. Wham! I was plucked off the ladder; it was like being in a catapult and I was airborne again, frantically grabbing at the rungs as they sailed past. I left behind my trouser leg when it caught on a rung, and I was then literally running in space with a split mini-skirt on one side and a torn, flapping trouser leg on the other, trying to keep up with the frantic bastards above. It was no good shouting 'Whoa,' because by the time they heard it I was off on another 'giant leap for mankind'.

It was the fastest ladder 'climb' ever and I hit the surface running. The cameras whirred as the reporters asked, 'Was anybody down there?' and 'What happened to your leg?'

This was the start of a cavers' eisteddfod and a press field day, when the descent of the shaft became the source of many headlines and stories: 'A third of a mile of steel ladders lowered into giant thousand feet shaft . . . At 10 a.m. Jim Eyre and Peter Livesey descended . . . soon their voices were lost in the rumbling echoes of water but for a little while longer they relied on whistle signals, until even these could no longer be heard . . . Shortly before mid-day they signalled to the crowd by field telephone that they had reached the bottom.'

Various other groups also hit the headlines, as 'clues' were followed that led to old mines and a couple of small caves, though the searches generally ended in pubs. A freshly opened pea tin and a partially consumed packet of lard began a new investigation (we thought that if this is what the lads were living on we would soon find them by following a trail of loose bowel movements). A broken branch near another shaft provided another lead, and a Bolton team was reported as being 'half-way down a five-hundred-foot shaft on a hundred weight of ladders'. Two local children caused the hunt to switch to another village, where they had apparently seen the missing youths.

Norman Thornber – a well-known caver (in 1934 the Cave Rescue Organisation was formed in his house and Norman later wrote some of the first caving guidebooks, *Pennine Underground* and *Britain Underground*) – stated that 'there were more than three hundred caves and mines to be searched.' It also appeared that a special winch was being brought from Matlock and that 'Dr Nigel Harper, the national authority on cave rescue medicine, would be arriving during the night.' Then the focus was suddenly switched again, when two sets of footprints were found alongside two apple cores on Moel Findeg, a nearby thousand-foot-high mountain.

We were popping in and out of the small caves like rabbits – it was crazy. A swift look round a short cave was followed by a swift pint in the local pub or a visit to the lovely ladies of the Women's Voluntary Service, who looked after us like heroes. We never had it so good. Old mates shook hands, old adversaries glared at each other, the weather was sunny and warm and the beer flowed freely, and all sorts of 'experts' appeared in response to frantic press reports.

As the day drew to a close, our lamps were recharged on a National Coal Board mobile charger, and we were all billeted in various establishments. Our group struck lucky – we were sent to a large girls' boarding school (perhaps that should read as a large boarding school for girls) in nearby Loggerheads.

After a fine meal, we were given directions on how to locate our dormitories without finding the girls by mistake. Following these explicit instructions, and led by Jim Newton who gets lost anywhere, we therefore ended up marching en masse into a girls' dormitory. Followed by squeals, giggles and loud bursts of laughter, we made a hasty and embarrassed retreat.

The next day began as before, with (as he phrased it) our chairman 'putting everyone in the picture', but confusing us more. We continued inspecting all the remaining shafts in the area, with contests developing among the different groups as to who could bag the most descents. More and more time was spent in the pub as gullible reporters plied us with drinks so that they could hear the most ludicrous stories we could invent.

On the surrounding moors, five hundred soldiers and several fell rescue teams were thoroughly combing the area. A toffee wrapper was brought in: 'It was still warm when I found it,' said the young soldier. Immediately, the massive search took another direction and Mike rushed around 'putting everyone in the picture'.

In between making frequent telly appearances and hobnobbing with the VIP's, Mike was fast creeping up on Wonder Caver in the popularity stakes. To combat this, Wonder Caver suddenly announced that he knew of another cave. Once again he was the star attraction, but as it turned out to be fifty feet long it was not of sufficient attraction to us shaft-baggers, so we continued supping ale.

I knew I had had enough when into the pub rushed a little old Welsh lady, complete with fancy hat and pinny. 'There's a bottomless pit at the bottom of my garden,' she said to me in a breathless Welsh accent. 'And,' she continued, 'I heard voices.'

This was it. We clambered into two Land Rovers and raced neck and neck along the narrow road, until our driver took a short cut through a garden and up a back lane to Widow Twankey's cottage. She had arrived before us and was just dismounting from her broomstick.

'You've just run over my lucky black cat,' she said, 'I'll put a spell on you.' Lucky for us the cat was only bruised and she only gave us a bollocking – in Welsh, mind, so we don't know what she said – but it sounded rude!

We investigated the bottomless pit at the bottom of the garden and it turned out to be a twenty-foot-deep dry well. Ah well, at least it was opposite another pub.

No one carries money in caving gear but, luckily for us, our guardian angels appeared in the shape of two reporters, one from the *Daily Mirror* and the other from the *Daily Telegraph*. These unlikely bedfellows turned out to be quite good chaps; they swallowed everything we told them, while we swallowed everything they bought us.

Meanwhile, back at Maeshafn, Mike's map, pinned on the wall in his temporary HQ, now looked like a Second World War offensive breakthrough by the Allies. Yet another red pin was added to denote yet another cave (which wasn't one, really – it was an old drift mine, but some Birkenhead Boy Scouts had spent all night digging at a fifty-year-old blockage and it was a shame to discourage them).

Mike, with the devious skill of a budding politician, had made Wonder Caver his right-hand man; on telly they formed a marvellous team – their usefulness was a matter of debate, but they looked good. A bit more of this and they would have had a job for life on television guest shows.

Somehow, after our doing all sorts of deeds of daring and not coming to a sticky end, our gallant chairman decided that we should be despatched down this horrible Boy Scout mine. We knew that all mines are just holes in the ground surrounded by loose rock – and having already experienced sundry near-disasters in some of the looser shafts, we became rather cagey when we found that several more mine levels lay directly overhead.

Some groups of cavers were already in the place and the rumble of falling rocks and shouts of 'Below!' became commonplace, until one of our group was struck a glancing blow by a rock that must have weighed two hundred pounds. I think it was about this time that we decided that the most experienced cavers (us) should explore the higher levels, as we were not likely to knock down as many rocks and we could shout 'Below!' much better than anyone else.

It had been apparent to most of us for some time that we were risking people's necks in vain. Watching folk digging frantically at a fifty-year-old rockfall, I pointed out the error of their ways and then recognised cavers Gordon Batty and Colin Green, who informed me that 'this is a new Northern Pennine Club dig and these nice little Boy Scouts are helping us.'

On the way out of the 'cave' I found an old, rusty hammer and absent-mindedly chipped away at a few rocks. A policeman at the entrance saw the hammer in my hand and rushed over.

'Where did you get that?' he asked.

'In there,' I answered.

'But,' he said, 'it's been used,' and much to my amazement he carefully wrapped it up in newspaper and zoomed off on his motorcycle to see the chief. In a short time we were surrounded by police cars, sergeants, soldiers and reporters: I had evidently found something important, as one of the missing youths had a geologist's hammer with him when he went missing.

'Ah,' I said, not wishing to upset them by explaining that it was an old cob hammer, umpteen years old, and that it was me who had used it. Once again I appeared in print: 'Lancaster painter finds vital clue in search for missing boys.'

Later, we were told not to take any more risks. Then we heard a car had been stolen. Then, eventually, the two missing youths were arrested in Weston-super-Mare.

The little village of Maeshafn now contains an estate of modern houses. I wonder how many have fairies at the bottom of their gardens. Or a bloody great hole, just waiting to swallow up Uncle Alfie as he's digging his potatoes.

Chapter 4

Greece: Into the Abyss

IN 1963 AN OXFORD UNIVERSITY botanical expedition returned from a particularly bleak area of the Greek Pindus Mountains. Although they hadn't discovered any square daisies, they brought back reports of a huge chasm on a barren plateau, six thousand feet above sea level and situated in the centre of the ancient province of Epirus.

Huge caverns feature prominently in accounts in Greek mythology. One is the enormous cave of Acherusia in the Pindus, sometimes said to be the home of the Moirae or Fates. These three grim sisters struck dread into the hearts of men, controlling all the events around them as well as their lifespan. Clotho held the distaff of the thread of life and spun life's events, Lachesis measured out the thread and chose life's destiny, and Atropos cut life's thread.

The Fates were considered beyond appeal and it was just my luck to be thrown against these three ladies in a sort of blind date with destiny, when circumstances over which I seemingly had no control involved me in the exploration of this mysterious cavern. Strangely enough, it lay in the same area of north-west Greece as the mythical Acherusia.

We seem to have a visitor

The Greek shepherds who lived on the mountain called the chasm Provatina, or Place of the Sheep. It was said that a rock hurled down the shaft took eleven seconds before it struck the bottom and I suddenly had the urge to dash off to Greece to, somewhat unwisely, challenge the Fates. It was a decision that must have delighted old Lachesis, as events and happenings from that fateful day have ever since played a powerful part in my life. They have not always been pleasant and have never been under my control, so perhaps I should dedicate this book to Lachesis, a crafty old bird who's kept my life from being dull.

I began to make plans for an expedition to Provatina and was putting together a team of good cavers when I received an offer to join some Derbyshire cavers who were also arranging a trip. The organiser was Ken Kelly, of whom I had never heard, but the leader was a bloke called Frank Salt, who had just been down the Gouffre Berger in France, so I reckoned he would be alright. According to the invitation, the team was well equipped with two thousand feet of ladders and ropes, a specially designed winch, radios, two Land Rovers and one minibus, plus fifteen cavers.

Kelly (his surname quickly became his nickname) paid me a visit and warning signals rang in my head, but old Lachesis told me to ignore them as I listened to this young, short, stocky character with a flattened nose and more than his share of Irish blarney. After this initial encounter things became rather vague and it grew harder to pin Kelly down to any concrete facts about the expedition; numerous letters passed to and fro, all ending with the same answer to my queries: 'Everything is organised.'

THREE WEEKS BEFORE WE WERE DUE TO LEAVE for Greece in 1966, while returning from a caving trip on Casterton Fell, Rose and I had a head-on collision with a Land Rover. Both vehicles were written off and Rose was badly injured.

The following weeks were fairly grim. I needed a vehicle for my painting and decorating business and, as a stopgap, bought an old banger – a Morris van – for £45. It smoked furiously and was minus a first gear, and take-off involved leaping forward in a series of jerks like a ruptured frog making its first jump.

The expedition seemed out of the question, but Rose, who was a fairly tough cookie, insisted that we stick with it. No sooner was this decision made when a postcard appeared through the letterbox. 'Meet Bridger and Thomas at Victoria 10 a.m. Sat' – it was signed by Ken Kelly.

I rang up Kelly to find out which Victoria: Queen, bus, or train station? And who was Thomas?

Lachesis, a crafty old bird who's kept my life from being dull

'Oh, can't miss him,' breezed Kelly. 'Looks like that fellow Hoss in *Bonanza* on telly.'

Two days later Kelly rang me up. 'Big crisis – pack your gear and drive down to Buxton. Everything depends on it!'

Throwing all our kit into the back of the old van, we hit the road and limped slowly towards Buxton, followed by a cloud of thick, blue smoke. Kelly's postal address was wrong, but we eventually tracked him down to The Four Feathers, where he welcomed us with open arms and a cry of 'What yer 'avin?'

Kelly now unfolded his tale of woe. He and his buddies (who I hadn't yet seen) had all lost their driving licences, these having been taken away from them by the strong arm of the law due to various offences, leaving Rose and me as the only current licence holders, apart from Alan Thomas. We didn't have any more vehicles and we would have to hire a Land Rover from a nearby garage. 'Don't worry, he's a big mate of mine,' Kelly said.

This was a disaster. 'Where are all the other members? Where are the two Land Rovers? Where is the minibus? Where is all the equipment? What the bloody hell is going on?' The questions flowed from my tongue.

'One Land Rover is on its way to Greece, via Italy,' said Kelly, 'and – er – Frank Salt can't come.'

I had another pint. The expedition was a dead duck before we even started, but Kelly had booked a ferry crossing and provisions and, as he had stated, everything now depended on Rose and me.

Using my licence, I signed for a well-travelled Land Rover at what seemed an exorbitant price, drove it away, then promptly drove it back when I discovered that it had no spare wheel and no tools, jacks or starting handle. Kelly had no spanners, of course, so I emptied the old Morris of my tools and stuck them under the front seat. Kelly's house was nearby and some of his mates arrived and began loading up the Land Rover with mysterious packages and bundles. Two of them staggered out of the house with a monstrous iron drum. A hefty iron base plate followed, then several lengths of three-inch pipe and a motley collection of bits and pieces of iron, together with a large coil of wire and a massive cast-iron seat.

I stared at this weighty pile of ironware in amazement.

'It's the winch,' said Kelly. 'Me dad made it!'

Three iron sheer legs that must have weighed half a ton lay buried in the long grass in Kelly's front garden. Two, then three of the lads struggled to lift them, and I thought this seemed a good time to tell them about a Land Rover's limitations.

After a heated argument we dispensed with the sheer legs and the cast-iron seat. Even so, by now I was quite worried by the lack of ladders, ropes and food supplies; apart from the ladders and ropes I had brought from the Red Rose Cave & Pothole Club, there didn't seem enough to do a moderate Yorkshire pothole, let alone the deep chasm of Provatina. However, with the vehicle loaded, Kelly unfolded his plan.

It seems there wasn't enough room for everyone. Surprise, surprise! Rose had to take some of the lads to Luton in the van, while I drove the rest in the Land Rover. We hung around for another member who had gone up the road for an injection (he was never seen again), then Kelly suddenly remembered that he had left some 'bang' under his bed and rushed upstairs to retrieve it. He reappeared clutching a brown paper parcel. 'It's weeping,' he shouted, his face as white as a sheet, and dashed across the road to a nearby millpond where he carefully lowered it into the water, tied to a brick. Our organiser hastily scribbled a note for the missing member, Ginger: 'See you at Dover 11 p.m.' and we were off. Well, as far as the motorway, where I discovered that the Land Rover wouldn't steer with the front wheels off the ground and we had a puncture to boot.

The hefty winch drum, sitting on the open tailgate, was moved inside, the spare wheel fitted and, with Rose driving the overladen, clapped-out old van, stinking of burning oil, we eventually reached Luton and pulled up in a cloud of thick blue smoke at the Bridger residence.

Ron Bridger's father looked at us, then at his favourite son, and said in an awed voice: 'Greece! You'll never get to Greece – you'll be lucky if you see Dover!'

We then helped him remove his chestnut paling fence, I ran the van into his Brussel sprouts, the fence was replaced and he kindly offered to run Rose and Ron to London to meet Alan the next day, while the rest of us carried on to Dover. Driving through London I achieved the ambition of most motorists when I drove the heavily laden, seemingly invulnerable Land Rover erratically around Hyde Park Corner, its bits and pieces of iron bars and other equipment sticking out like the knives on Boadicea's chariot. I swapped lanes without signalling, just for the sheer joy of watching everyone scatter.

At Dover I proceeded with Kelly to the embarkation desk and discovered he was not in the Automobile Association or Royal Automobile Club, he possessed no travellers cheques or foreign money, had no personal insurance – and no insurance for the vehicle – and carried no maps. It seemed to be a case of 'turn right at Ostend'.

Ten minutes before embarkation, two of the lads decided to head off to look for some fish and chips, then Kelly went looking for them. The miscreants returned after we had driven onto the boat and Kelly was held by customs officials, who were reluctant to let him go. Unfortunately for us, they did, and we rushed straight to the bar as we sailed across the channel on a Ken Kelly-organised mystery tour.

At Ostend, Kelly took over the Land Rover and I moved into Alan's new Morris. We drove off into a foul night, with torrential rain almost obliterating the road, so Alan and I took turns at driving. At daybreak we reached our first rendezvous at Karlsruhe, where we pitched camp and waited for the slower vehicle. It arrived in the late evening, Kelly having experienced trouble buying the green card insurance, a necessity at that time and one that was not helped by the fact that all the documents were in my name. However, as in all things Kelly was unperturbed and, as we left the following day, he shouted: 'See you in Skopje.'

The fine day gave way to a cloudy evening and, passing through Austria, we encountered more torrential rain so we decided to drive on into Yugoslavia. It was nearly midnight when Alan, dulled by lack of sleep, drove his protesting Morris 1100 up the Wurzen Pass. Once through the border, I bought some petrol coupons and took over the wheel, intending to drive to Ljubljana and a campsite. However, the weather was so atrocious that again we moved on and continued throughout the night. Eyes heavy with fatigue, I drove along the most monotonous and dangerous road in Europe, the Yugoslavian Autoput – a thousand miles of badly contoured, narrow road with barely enough room for two vehicles to pass, as various lorries testified. They lay with their wheels still spinning, upturned in the steep ditches on either side of the road, surrounded by their spilled contents and each with a driver sitting in resignation waiting for daybreak.

This was one of the worst journeys of my life. The dead straight road consisted of large slabs of concrete which had subsided, cracked and buckled, causing the car to rock up and down. At a steady sixty miles an hour, which was all I dared, I soon lulled everyone to sleep. They were awakened occasionally by my evasive action, producing squealing tyres when I tried to avoid lorries that blinded me with their headlamps as they hurtled towards me, forcing me to play blind man's bluff with the six-foot ditch and several tons of metal, which I knew wouldn't stop if it hit us.

The only thing that kept me awake was a Yugoslavian 'road calming' device, which consisted of cobbled sections of road situated at the bottom of hills and on the approach to towns. The cobbles, unlike ours back home, were the size of rugby balls; when you hit those at sixty, boy oh boy did you wake up! The noise, and the car vibrating as though it was going through the sound barrier, almost reduced Alan to tears. 'My car, my car – oh, my car,' he could be heard muttering while still fast asleep.

Zagreb, silhouetted by flares from the oil refineries, passed in the night. Eyes dry and prickling with fatigue while eyelids were heavy from lack of sleep, I had to slow down while Rose applied a cold, wet cloth to the back of my neck to keep me alert. Gradually, the black night turned to dawn and the sun rose and blazed from a cloudless sky as we reached Skopje, the scene of a devastating earthquake the year before. We finally put up the tents and fell asleep.

After waiting twenty-four hours for the Land Rover to materialise, we presumed that Kelly had either broken down, been arrested, killed himself or driven past us as we camped. We drove on into Greece and the joys of the Katara Pass dirt roads. In those days the term 'road' coupled with 'Greece' could mean anything from a mule track to a farm track, especially in the mountains. Greek mountains seemed to be the most unstable in Europe, consisting of shale, breccia and huge boulders, and continually being beset by avalanches and landslips.

At one point I was slewing the car round the vicious hairpin bends when my headlamps angled into the night sky and failed to illuminate the road. I stopped quickly and Alan jumped out – he informed me that the front wheels were perched on the edge of a hundred-foot drop. Everyone climbed out and I cautiously backed down to a newly excavated junction. Everyone had just squeezed back into the car when two black shapes came bounding out of the darkness, eyes and teeth gleaming evilly in the headlights. With these two large dogs growling viciously, tearing at the windows and snapping at the tyres, I hastily moved on. It was a macabre experience as we moved down the road in a cloud of dust, with these black hounds of Satan jumping and clawing at the rear windows.

Another seventy miles of mountain road like this lay ahead and, whenever anyone needed to answer the call of nature, he had to be bloody quick. Poor Ron had the trots – in more ways than one after we had stopped for him on one occasion. He disappeared behind a thorn bush but almost instantaneously reappeared around the other side, clutching his trousers and running like hell from four huge dogs that were snapping and slavering with their large pointed teeth inches from his pink bum. Rose opened the door, Ron leapt in and Rose slammed it shut in the face of a wild fury of bloodshot eyes and gnashing teeth.

We tried to ignore the smell until we could kick Ron out somewhere safer. At four in the morning we came out of the mountains above a large lake where, far below, we could see the twinkling lights of Ioannina, and on the campsite we found a grimy

Land Rover, four recumbent bodies and a Union Jack. Kelly had made it. I was astonished.

THE FOLLOWING MORNING our organiser went looking for camping gas, which – as everyone except Kelly knew – was unobtainable in Greece. We were henceforth reduced to two petrol stoves. Kelly then disappeared to organise our military permits while we had a look at the town, which was crawling with military personnel.

Ioannina is a very old town that comprises a fascinating mixture of east and west, but all the armed soldiers produced a tense feeling about the place. Our organiser returned with the permits and we parked Alan's car in the army headquarters, then Ken ferried us up to the village of Papingo.

Turning off the road in the Land Rover we followed a limestone track which led into the mountains – real mountains now, not like the shale monstrosities we had driven over previously. The scenery became magnificent as we skirted the deep limestone cleft of the Vikos Gorge, a tremendous gash which slices through the stupendous mountain massif of white and gold limestone cliffs, its precipitous walls towering upwards for several thousand feet to the triangular summit of Astraka.

The wide expanse of the plateau above looked like a setting for Conan Doyle's *Lost World*. It was broken by five huge gullies that swept along deep, jagged recesses in the face which, as we turned a corner in the track, we could see continuing down, four thousand feet to the very bottom of the Vikos where, faintly through the deep shadows, we could see a shimmering river. It was magic!

Climbing the spur ahead, we pulled up in the village in a cloud of dust and engine fumes; we had made it. The village comprised well-built houses of local stone and paved streets that straggled up a hill behind an ancient church, whose typical bell tower and cloisters were shaded by large trees growing around its cobbled courtyard. Beyond, in a single-story building, stood the local store and post office, painted blue, a favourite colour of the Greeks. We were soon surrounded by villagers while we unloaded.

We were granted use of the local Greek Alpine Club's building and the church cloisters, and Rose soon had us organised as, Primus roaring, we began to make a meal.

Ron was clutching his trousers and running like hell

A grizzled old Greek came up, followed by a beaming Kelly, and pulled a hunk of dead sheep from his sack and threw it on the cobbles. He then produced a chopping block and an axe and, under Rose's instructions, he hacked off a piece of raw meat which went into the pressure cooker. Heap quick, as they would say in Wild West films, for we were starving.

Later that evening we enjoyed a few drinks with the locals and then, led by Kelly, who seemed to be like a magician producing surprises out of a hat, we went up the village street to a taverna where we met Lefteris, the local representative of the Greek Alpine Club.

We stayed late, enjoying the hospitality of free drinks – which proved too much for our local interpreter, for he ended up talking to Lefteris in English and to me in Greek; it didn't matter, for all drunks speak the same language.

The next morning we loaded our few ladders and ropes onto our backs and hired a young lad as a guide, before setting off to have a look at the mythical abyss of Provatina. Our guide was named Dimitrios, which means Jim, so we swapped names and I became Dimitrios and he became Jim, much to his delight.

As we struggled up the mountain in blast-furnace temperatures, the men were soon separated from the boys and the party began straggling all over the mountain. A red-faced, puffing and blowing irrepressible Kelly brought up the rear, stopping every few minutes to take a swig at his plastic water bottle which, unlike ours, contained red wine. This, he had been assured, would cure his hangover from the night before.

After two hours' slogging up steep scree followed by an almost vertical climb leading to the shoulder of one of the gullies, which dropped away almost two thousand feet below us, we eventually reached Provatina. At the top of the gully, a small cliff face on the left curved back into a large recess. As we approached, a black expanse fifty feet high and eighty feet wide stared out like an empty eye socket in a huge skull. I could sense the vast dimensions of the shaft as I approached the thinly bedded limestone at the cave entrance. The edge of the slabs fell away like a steep broken staircase for twenty feet, before pausing at a small ledge then plunging vertically down a yawning abyss a hundred feet across and eighty feet wide. It was as terrifying as the mouth of hell.

Someone threw a rock down and we instinctively drew back as, six seconds later, a dull rumble issued from below. I decided to look down the shaft to see how the winch should be rigged. After a brief rest in our eagle's eyrie, where the panorama of the Albanian mountains and the plains leading towards the Adriatic were spread out below us, I began sorting through our pathetic selection of ladders. Apart from the Red Rose ladders, which were fifteen years old, the rest were extremely suspect, of varying designs and had a pedigree that stretched down a long line of bastards. However, the two lifelines were good.

At long last we had the pitch rigged and I looked with interest at the fifteen-year-old splicing on the top ladder. There was nothing to belay to, so I anchored the ladders to a loose rock that sat on the bedrock, with instructions: 'If that rock moves, sit on it!'

My caving boots had been packed wet; now, having been cooked in the sun for several days, they were curled up, fossilised and unusable. I borrowed Malcolm Smith's boots, the only ones available without hook attachments that would have caught on the wires of the electron ladders. They were several sizes too big, made of soft rubber and canvas and were more suitable for use on a beach than for climbing ladders. As I was changing, we discovered that the telephone had been damaged, so I would have to rely on voice or whistle signals. This could be my lucky day!

I changed into my caving gear and was soon sweating profusely in the heat. My mouth felt dry and, after I tied on the lifeline, I took a long swig from Ron's proffered bottle, before climbing gingerly over the edge of the platform and down the jagged rock edges to the small ledge twenty feet below.

I paused and looked down the massive shaft before me. It was immense – for several seconds it lay beyond my comprehension, an enormous pit dropping sheer with walls bearing no cracks or joints but only shallow flutings in the smooth, polished limestone. It descended down and down into infinity. The opposite wall plunged to a ledge several hundred feet below, where an indistinct patch of dirty snow still clung, left from the winter storms.

It was a magnificent shaft, so uniform and clean were the walls. The gargantuan opening, a hundred feet across, was illuminated by strong sunlight streaming into the misty depths, which gradually became vague, sombre and overpowering as they gave way to the darkness.

The ladders hung flush against the smooth wall, their wire sides as taught as iron bands. I tried to push them away from the face in order to place my feet on the rungs, but Malcolm's baseball boots, too large and too soft, curled off the alloy rungs and left me with no foothold.

Unable to push the ladder out from the rock owing to its weight hanging below, I made my way slowly down the ladder with most of the strain taken on my arms, my feet continually slipping off. Looking at the airy void below my floundering feet, I was thankful for the taught lifeline held by those above.

I suddenly noticed an alloy rung hooked on a small rock projection – it was the end rung of the bottom ladder, which had somehow snagged while being lowered and now held a giant loop of five hundred feet of ladder that could slip loose at any second; this could be catastrophic. I reached out, pulled the ladder free and was almost dragged from my hold as the sudden weight threw me sideways. Unable to do anything else, I gave a warning shout to the surface, let go of the loose end and clung firmly to the ladder as I waited for the severe jerk that could throw me off or break the belay.

The jolt came within seconds. The already taut ladders stiffened further as the shockwave vibrated through the wire, and I experienced a sinking feeling when the ladder moved downwards – the loose rock that the ladders were belayed to was being dragged towards the shaft. Then it stopped.

After our panic subsided, I continued down until, at a depth of 140 feet, I swung clear of the smooth wall, which finished abruptly at an overhang. This left me suspended in the centre of the gigantic shaft, swaying gently on spidery ladders that suddenly seemed so fragile.

I stopped, held tight on the lifeline, as I gazed in fascination at the smooth, grey walls, still a hundred feet apart. With beautiful symmetry they funnelled down into an obscure gloom, the ladders hanging like a pale cotton thread in the centre until they were swallowed by the vastness. I had been down many large shafts, but never had I experienced anything like this colossal elliptical well. I continued climbing down the swaying ladders like a man in the grip of a terrible compulsion, stopping now and again to look around.

A black recess opened in the left-hand wall and I peered at a concealed inlet, then another opening in the opposite wall came into view. Earlier, Alan had conducted a not very scientific and ultimately unsuccessful attempt to plumb the shaft using what was left of our telephone cable with his nife cell on the end, and here the metallic glint of the light caught my eye where it rested on a jagged outcrop, surrounded by the remains of the cable.

Like everything else, it was out of reach. By now, thoroughly dwarfed by my surroundings, I began to experience a tremendous exhilaration as I realised that I was the first human being to descend into this mythical Acherusia, the home of the Moirae. I could now make out the indistinct floor, 150 feet below. Steadily climbing downwards, towards what looked like the base of the shaft, my thoughts were interrupted by a faint shout from above: 'Only twenty feet of rope left, Jim.' This brought me back to reality and, after another look down to where I could see the end of the ladder swinging free, I looked up at the far away oval of daylight and realised I was a very long way from the surface.

I shouted 'Up, up!' and felt a reassuring tug on the lifeline as I began the long climb out of the cool depths to the searing heat of the plateau. Gasping for breath, with a throat so dry that I could hardly speak, I regained the sunshine and described the shaft to the rest of the interested team – still little realising how monstrous the shaft really was.

WE LEFT THE EQUIPMENT AT THE HOLE and worked our way down the mountain, suffering from pangs of hunger for we had eaten nothing since the night before – plus which we were fairly dehydrated, having run out of water. An hour and a half later, with aching legs and rumbling bellies, we staggered into the village store and drank its entire stock of beer. Kelly turned a red, perspiring face to me: 'Fancy egg and chips?' he asked, and then we all watched with great amusement as he tried out his own peculiar form of Greek – which ranged from 'Oofs, pom frits' to 'Crispo eggo' – and laughed at the variety of objects that the uncomprehending proprietor offered in return.

'Eh, Ken, try clucking like a hen,' someone shouted. Kelly did, with instant recognition by the shopkeeper, who beamed a large smile and produced eggs, potatoes, frying pan and a small stove from behind his diminutive counter. Within seconds he had egg and chips gently frying.

The village store rapidly filled as villagers drifted in, eager to learn of our discoveries. Soon, we were full of booze, eggs, chips and bonhomie as we chatted in pidgin English to a small boy, who translated it into Greek for the older members of the community. They fumbled with their prayer beads and listened intently to every word, occasionally replenishing our empty glasses.

In spite of all this hospitality, we decided to turn in early – all except Kelly, that is, for he had to organise the 'donks' for the morning. Unfortunately, this involved a great deal of bartering for these beasts of burden over many glasses of wine and our organiser eventually staggered past our abode in the small hours. In a flat, off-key voice he sang the latest hit to reach Buxton, 'Red Sails in the Sunset', as he headed for the cloisters, where he threw himself onto the stone flags and lapsed into blissful oblivion.

I slept fitfully and became slowly aware of another sound, the faint clip-clopping of mules coming up the cobbled track and entering the churchyard. The door of the hut had been left open and against the faint lightening of the aperture, a shadowy figure of a man muttered softly in a Greek voice. Hastily, I woke Rose and went around the cloisters to awaken the others.

The four unsuspecting mules were covered with back-breaking loads, especially the poor beast that received the bulk of the winch. It looked at a bleary-eyed Kelly with a hurt expression on its face; so did the rest of us when we discovered we had nothing for breakfast! The expedition was fast becoming a survival course.

High up on the mountain, on the shoulder of the scree slopes beneath the gully, Todero our donkey man halted the mules while we unloaded our personal kit and food, then Alan, Tony Banks, Rose and I started to carry it to the Katathigion refuge. We had been given the key by Lefteris, the Greek Alpine Club representative, for use while we were on the mountain. It was a new building with a steel door and shutters, which had obviously been built as an army blockhouse for use in the long-running war with Albania, the mountains of which stood out clearly a few miles away.

Our organiser on his gallant steed, followed by Rose

We soon reached the refuge, which stood on a col between Astraka and Gamila, with a commanding view of the barren limestone valleys below. Our accommodation was luxurious: bunks complete with expensive blankets, a Calor gas stove, toilets and showers awaited us. Unfortunately, the water tank was dry, as we discovered after an hour's work on the hand pump only produced a kettle of very oily water contaminated by red-lead paint and putty.

We sent a volunteer to a spring further down the mountain and waited for Kelly, Ron and Tony, who were struggling up the escarpment with more equipment. The rough terrain had proved too much for the mules and they had to be offloaded. The next morning, after a night disturbed by a black, hooded figure that kept appearing at the open windows, silhouetted against the night sky. I woke early and was immediately assailed by the man, who turned out to be a mountain shepherd bringing us a gift of either goat's or sheep's milk in a smelly old tin. I gave him some cigarettes and thanked him, and wished he would go away because he stank of dead goats, stale urine and BO – which is not surprising, because he lived and slept with his animals all summer, only coming off the mountain in winter.

After a meagre breakfast we went in search of the equipment, which was now spread over the shoulder of the mountain below the buttress, and spent a hard day ferrying heavy loads on our backs up to the hole. The winch sections gave the most trouble. The drum itself was lashed onto Alan's pack frame and, assisted by two people who held him upright, he staggered upwards over the rough terrain that led to Provatina. Alan certainly lived up to his nickname, Hoss. I carried the broad, thick, iron base plate, which wasn't too bad until I fell over. Lying there, flat on my back and fastened to the plate, I couldn't rise again and floundered with my arms and legs waving in the air like a stranded turtle while I shouted for assistance.

There was a certain danger in carrying these excessive loads on this part of the mountain. We were directly over the gully, which dropped for two thousand feet – anyone losing their balance and rolling would almost certainly have gone over the edge and been killed.

Kelly began drilling holes in the thinly bedded limestone at the cave mouth, then we packed it in for the day and wended our weary way back across the mountain to the refuge.

The capstan winch at Provatina. Photo: Rose Eyre

On the fourth day we rigged a tent on the platform and from then on our hand-drilling continued in the shade. Kelly eventually placed three bolts and we erected the capstan-type winch.

'There you are Jim, safe as a row of houses,' he said while proudly surveying his handiwork. I rocked the winch to and fro and the bolts pulled out!

There followed an interesting discussion on the merits of the drilling and the winch. I was full of dark thoughts as I stood watching Kelly drill deeper holes. It was the first time I had seen the winch assembled and, although I was not an engineer, I could see the design concept was wrong.

At long last the winch was ready in all its glory. There it stood, a vertical windlass with three galvanised pipes projecting horizontally from the top and a handbrake at the base. Of one thing I was sure – whoever was lowered down Provatina on that contraption was not coming back up, and as sure as hell, it wasn't going to be me.

Ron was almost
decapitated as he tried
to reach the brake

I decided it needed a test drive, so we packed a kitbag with rocks and secured it to a pack frame. Kelly suggested we fastened this onto the winch seat (which had miraculously reappeared since I chucked it out at Buxton), but I argued that the seat would catch easily on any projections. My protest was in vain and the hefty cast-iron seat was made even heftier by the weighted bag and frame, and the whole bulky ensemble was hurled over the edge.

The effect was rather alarming.

From the capstan the winch wire strained upwards to a pulley above the cave mouth, which threatened to come out of the wall, though it never did. Then it stretched in the opposite direction to another pulley, before disappearing over the brink. With a tremendous noise the weighted seat clattered its way down the shaft and the arms of the capstan winch flailed around like a berserk windmill. The whole thing rocked on its base and Ron was almost decapitated as he tried to reach the brake, which he only succeeded in doing by crawling on his stomach towards the rocking, spinning monster.

The brake worked and the contraption juddered to a grinding halt, while the frightened screeching of choughs echoed from the cliff face as they wheeled high overhead, disturbed by this strange intrusion into their domain. I suggested that we should try winching the weighted seat back up to the surface, but was again outvoted by enthusiastic cavers carried away by their success in dropping a load of scrap iron down a hole. Just to prove it wasn't a fluke, they decided to lower it to the bottom.

Alan and Malcolm took hold of the galvanised pipes that served as arms and began walking briskly round as they paid out more wire. I watched with interest as their healthy, sun-tanned faces slowly turned green, induced by the rapid circular motion. This looked like an emergency, so someone applied the emergency brake before our two winch men had time to go completely dizzy and spin off down the shaft as two airborne whirling dervishes.

The emergency brake consisted of a ratchet that engaged into slots on the top of the drum. This locked on perfectly, but it had a slight side-effect – it caused the whole winch and centre column to unscrew from its base plate!

We had to hope that we didn't experience a real emergency, because the emergency brake was an emergency in itself. Now was the time to try to winch the weighted seat back up, but no, the rest of the team was intent on breaking its own record of 'lowering cast-iron seat down hole'. Manual lowering continued until the seat hit some floor or ledge.

The lads were quite pleased with this achievement until they tried to winch the seat back up, when they found, as I had suspected, that it could only be raised for a few feet before the wire became taut and immovable. The winch ground to a halt in spite of all our efforts. The pulleys were in the wrong positions and the wire disappeared into a groove it had worn in the rock.

After a lot of exertion, continually raising and lowering the seat, we managed to lift the weight some fifty feet before the wire bit deeply into the coil on the drum and again everything ceased to function. There was too much friction everywhere. It was obvious that the winch was useless and I cursed the fact that I hadn't been able to properly assess this 'expedition' before leaving Britain. However, there we were with the seat down the hole, and we had to be thankful there wasn't a man sitting in it.

This was a package holiday with a difference!

'Where do you want to go?'

'Down the deepest hole in the world.'

'Certainly sir. Single?'

We now had to think about how to retrieve the junk suspended in the shaft – though sorely tempted, we couldn't merely walk away and leave it dangling as a monument to our folly. We locked the winch 'mechanism' and I lifelined Kelly onto the ledge above the shaft while he hit the snatch block open with a hammer.

Their healthy, sun-tanned faces slowly turned green

The wire whistled down the hole, the weighted seat fell and the winch rocked on its base as the wire tightened again to the tune of a terrific clatter that echoed from the depths. We tried to winch the seat up again, but it was hopeless; someone would have to go down the shaft to ease the tension on the wire.

I suggested to Kelly that as the winch was his brainchild, he should go down. He turned white and almost fainted.

I looked around at the others, but the only positive response was: 'Can't we just cut the wire and sod off?'

Jim about to descend Provatina. Photo: Rose Eyre

Once again I put on Malcolm's boots and climbed down to just above the overhang. There was one small, sloping foothold of three inches, so I shouted up for the team to secure my lifeline while I pushed the wire away from the walls – then they were to try to winch on my instructions.

Clinging to my airy perch, I pushed the taut wire outwards and the winch lifted for a few feet before the wire tightened like a steel bar and it started to vibrate as tensions built up. 'Stop!' I yelled. While in the Navy I had seen wire cables snap and I knew the consequences. 'Lower.'

With my back against the rock while clinging to the ladder, I placed both feet on the wire and pushed, forcing the weight far below to pendulum. 'Up!'

It worked – we would gain a few feet before it jammed again, whereupon I had to repeat the process. This was very tiring and, after frequent rests (which, hanging on my hands, weren't really refreshing), I was relieved to see a vague shape start to materialise in the gloom below.

As it was slowly drawn up to me, I gazed in horror at the biggest bunch of bastards that I had ever seen in my life. The ladders were wrapped around the bloody cast-iron seat, in which the bulky kitbag sat like some headless nodding body looking down at the loops of ladder being dragged up with it. What a bloody mess!

The winch wire jammed again and I yelled up to lock the winch while I tried to sort it out. I struggled to free the tangled ladders, but it was hopeless; it was worse than the original Gordian knot. I decided that all I could do was to lighten the load. I could just reach the canvas kitbag and fumbled with one hand to attempt to unfasten it from the seat, but after a struggle I worked at a tear in the bag instead and managed to enlarge it and began pulling rocks out.

Heaving large stones down a deep shaft is an unnerving experience when one stands on the surface – here, balanced on sod all 130 feet down, it was terrifying. As I threw rocks into space, I could see them falling until they seemed to dissolve. Several seconds later a deep boom echoed up as they hit the floor.

By the time I was halfway through the bag, I had become used to the several seconds' interval – but was suddenly shaken out of my senses by a very deep, sonorous boom – it didn't belong to any of *my* rocks, surely!

'What the bloody hell was that?' My blood froze. Where the hell had that come from?

When I stopped shaking, I started throwing rocks in different directions until once again I produced that same deep sonorous boom. It seemed to come from the very bowels of the earth – and the noise wasn't doing mine any good, either, as I realised that I was poised above the deepest hole in the world with a Monty Python crew above. I must be breaking the world record for idiocy.

I suddenly felt terribly exposed – what I had thought was the floor of the shaft was merely a ledge with another enormous drop beyond. I carried on with my task, feeling – apart from being completely knackered – bemused and not a little scared at such profound depths. It was beyond my comprehension.

Much later, I climbed out and surveyed the massive mound of snarled up ladders – I cursed Kelly and his winch. Alan and Malcolm volunteered to bivouac for the night by the hole, but the rest of us hurried back to the refuge before nightfall.

By now we had been five days on the mountain, tramping back and forth between the refuge and the cave. What little food we were surviving on was almost finished and we were getting thinner by the minute. Everyone was completely frustrated by the lack of organisation that had placed us in this position and feelings were running high.

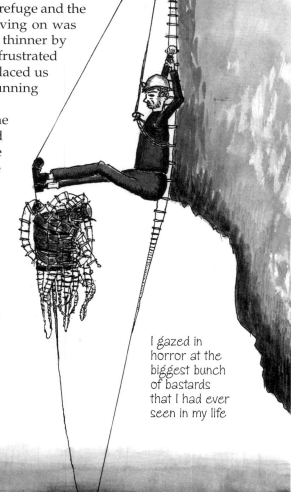

I decided that I would go down the shaft as far as our equipment would allow and, if the intervening distance between the ladders and the ledge wasn't too great, I would fix on the winch wire and allow myself to be lowered the remaining distance, hoping that they could get me back up again. This was obviously the reasoning of a madman and it demonstrates the level of exasperation I had reached.

Back at Provatina we found that Alan and Malcolm had examined the ladders and found that two were damaged, though they were still marginally safer than some of the undamaged ones which seemed to have been designed in a scrapyard.

'Connect everything together with all the crap at the bottom,' I said. The chair was estimated

I gazed in horror at the biggest bunch of bastards that I had ever seen in my life to have bottomed at 570 feet – the ladders totalled 520 feet. Fifty bloody feet short – what a bloody farce!

I went to the extreme of desperation by fastening all the belay wires together to gain a few more feet. I joined our two longest ropes end to end and attached a piece of cloth over the knot to avoid it snagging, then tied on the lifeline and clipped the end of the winch wire to my sling – I would it pull down with me as Alan paid it out.

Soon I was descending into the shaft for a third time, though this time in my own boots – they had been softened by sacrificing some of the drinking water. The climb down was uneventful, my attention concentrated on keeping the winch wire and lifeline from tangling. As I descended into the cool depths I was now becoming used to the airy vastness of Provatina and I was soon clinging to the last and very fragile-looking ladder. I looked dolefully at the loose end, which thrashed about some fifty feet above the ledge. I climbed down to within a few rungs from the end – I had never felt so intensely angry and frustrated in my life.

Experimenting with the winch wire, by shouting up to Tony (who was on the twenty-foot ledge, relaying my faint signals to the others) I managed to get the wire to tighten, but not lift my body weight. The bloody thing really was quite useless. After a lot of confused shouting and trotting up and down on the last few rungs of a madly thrashing ladder, I began to feel the strain. I looked at the inaccessible ledge below. It seemed to be made of earth and sloped steeply downwards to a dark, canyon-like opening on the north-western side of the pitch, which was now approximately thirty feet by twenty feet. This seemed to be the head of the next frightening drop, which was probably over seven hundred feet deep according to our estimate based on the 'boom-delay' of the rocks I had previously dropped.

So here I was, suspended almost halfway down a thirteen-hundred-foot abyss, the deepest known hole in the world. I was almost suicidal with desperation and seriously toyed with the idea of being lowered the next fifty feet despite the problems of making a return, for in my mind fifty feet was nothing. I cursed the lack of equipment, I cursed the bloody useless winch and I cursed the ladder I was clinging to as the rungs began to slip down the wires. I looked at the thin, rope-cored wire and the suspect splicing with its copper binding, and suddenly all notions of doing a one-way Peter Pan act on the end of the winch wire were rapidly dispelled and sanity returned.

As I fought my way on the swinging ladders back up the height of Blackpool Tower, I looked at the mysterious opening below and saw three vague figures, then heard a cackle of laughter from the Moirae. I swore to return.

Chapter 5

The Tragedy of Mossdale Caverns

THE CRAVEN HEIFER WAS PACKED. A thick fog of cigarette smoke filled the room and you had to shout to be heard above the babble of voices. Cavers and their wives and girlfriends jostled shoulder to shoulder in the small bar as people struggled past with drinks held above shoulder height to prevent them being spilled.

In 1967 the Heifer in Ingleton – with its popular landlord Jack Whitfield and his wife Mary – was the local Mecca for cavers, a dynamo of gossip and club activities and happenings. We had just returned from a good trip down Notts Pot and were discussing the possibilities of the high-level series going, when Dave Adamson, one of the Leeds lads, came over and enquired about my forthcoming return to Greece, which I had asked him to join.

'Oh, we're well organised. Jim Farnworth's made a brilliant winch – are you still coming?'

'I'm not sure if I can make Provatina yet – it all depends on my exam results. If I don't get through, I'm in trouble,' Dave replied, 'and we're still pushing Mossdale. Why don't you join us next week?'

Mossdale Caverns, with its low but extensive network of flood-prone passages, was the scene of significant pushing by several young 'tigers', but the constant threat of flooding unnerved me.

'I'll tell you what, Dave, that bloody hole frightens me to death,' I replied.

'Oh, you're alright if you watch the weather – it's perfectly safe. See you next week if you change your mind.' Dave went over to his clubmates and I never saw him again.

I HAD ALWAYS STEERED CLEAR of Mossdale Caverns and I was not alone, as it struck fear into the hearts of many cavers. Situated above Wharfedale on Grassington Moor at 1,400 feet above sea level, the cave entrance is a miserable cleft at the base of a low, limestone cliff face some 50 feet high and around 250 feet long. Mossdale Beck, the largest stream in the area, drains a wide expanse of fell and sinks in this restricted, horizontal joint in the base of the scar. In spate, the stream can turn into a swollen cataract which soon floods the cave and has been known to submerge the entrance under ten feet of water. Add to this the fact that the cave below extends for three miles, with almost all of its passages being only a few feet high and most becoming submerged after even moderate rainfall, and you have a potential killer.

Mossdale Beck resurges at Black Keld on the edge of the River Wharfe three miles away and 750 feet lower. This is the lure that has drawn many cavers into the inhospitable confines of Mossdale Caverns, in an attempt to find the large system that many believe must exist below; taken to its potential limit it could be one of the deepest in Britain.

Unfortunately, cave exploration is the most enigmatic pursuit on the planet. The known part of Mossdale Caverns is situated in thinly bedded Yoredale limestones and shale beds, above the Great Scar Limestone where the large cave system must lie. To reach this Great Scar Limestone the stream has cut through the thinly bedded series above, and this is the spur that draws cavers into Mossdale's wet, dripping crawls in search of this elusive connection.

In the 1960s, with young, hard, wetsuit-clad cavers, Mossdale was a challenge to be met, following in the wake of such hard cavers as Bob Leakey – who, during a lengthy solo exploration of the flood-prone passageways, covered himself in mud to preserve his body heat and calmly slept for a few hours before continuing. Mike Boon and Pete Livesey explored the cave even further in 1963, working their way through the low, dripping limestone passages, in rock coloured almost black by the constant flooding where the cave's development was restricted by the impervious layer of sandstone and grit which floored the passages. Following in Leakey's footsteps, they rediscovered the high-level chambers at the end – dark, sombre places with roofs of collapsed shale bands and walls slimy with peat deposits, washed in by floodwaters which, even here in the highest part of the cave, reached right up to the faraway roof.

To date, the rewards offered by a cave of this nature had therefore been sparse, and the consequence of failure was catastrophic. There are cavers who cannot see danger and there are cavers who can see danger and choose to ignore it; other cavers are very aware of the danger they face, but tend to underestimate it and think they can handle it. Mike Boon, an exceptional caver, remarked on his Mossdale trip with Pete Livesey: 'We changed and paddled over the shrunken beck to the entrance, each with a heavy bag of carbide, food and spare electric lights. In view of all the tales we were ready for twenty-four hours down the cave, longer if it flooded.'

This was probably the attitude of the young cavers who were resurveying and exploring new sections of Mossdale in their search for the hidden caverns beyond. After several skirmishes and near-flooding incidents, some of them were becoming less respectful of the ever constant flooding threat and were beginning to descend the cave in uncertain weather conditions. They had unknowingly started to play a game of Russian roulette with nature – a game that could only have one outcome.

Saturday 24 June 1967 is a date that will be etched on the memories of cavers for generations. It dawned grey and ominous; the weather forecast was poor and halfway through the morning a grey drizzle swept over the fells, increasing in intensity to a steady downpour as the day wore on. Mossdale Caverns was about to enact a terrible revenge for the contempt shown towards it.

On the bleak, windswept Grassington Moor the cold drizzle drew a wet clammy curtain across the limestone crags where Mossdale Beck swirled sullenly before sinking into the base of the exposed rock of the scar. At 2 p.m. ten wetsuited cavers slid through the tight, debris-covered crack. Six of them would never see the light of day again.

By mid-afternoon the light drizzle had turned to rain and, high on the upper slopes of Grassington Moor, tiny rivulets and streams started to swell. Peat bogs began to overflow into age-old drainage channels that converged into Mossdale Beck. At 5 p.m. four of the party decided to return to the surface, leaving the other six to push on with their exploration.

The rain increased slightly, but the water levels both in the cave and on the surface had not noticeably risen as Jim Cunningham, John Shepherd and two women, Morag Forbes and Colette Lord, surfaced. Unaware of the tragedy that was building up, three of them returned to the Happy Wanderers club headquarters in Kingsdale, leaving Morag to wait for her fiancé Dave Adamson and the others, periodically checking on the entrance.

The rain steadily increased. On Morag's second visit to the cave she was horrified to find the surface stream swollen and the entire area in front of the cliff face awash under a sheet of water, submerging the entrance. The frightened young woman ran and stumbled for two and a half miles across the sodden moor to reach the nearest farm, where she raised the alarm.

At 11.10 p.m. the Upper Wharfedale Fell Rescue Association was told that five men were trapped by floodwater in Mossdale. Immediately, a full callout ensued and the Cave Rescue Organisation was also alerted. Just before midnight my telephone rang – it was the CRO. 'Jim – some cavers are trapped in Mossdale.' I went cold, hearing little else of the message.

Very early in the morning, when I and other members of the rescue teams arrived at Conistone, we were informed of the seriousness of the situation and ferried up to the hole in Land Rovers and farm vehicles, which soon churned the saturated hillside into a morass. Mossdale Scar was the scene of a desperate struggle to divert the flooding beck away from its natural sink, the entrance to the cave. When the first rescue teams had arrived at 1.15 a.m. this was under four feet of water, part of a large lake that swirled in front of the scar under the continuing rain.

Mechanical excavators were pressed into service and teams of men had been working to dig a diversion channel while the excavators piled up an earth dam. At 2.25 a.m. the first rescue team was able to enter the cave, but surfaced less than an hour later to report that there was froth on the roof and the lower passages were submerged.

The rain stopped briefly and the dark grey, scudding clouds rolling across the moor lifted slightly on the scene of over a hundred men toiling waist-deep in the peat-stained floodwater that eddied sullenly through the muddy basin below the grey, shattered scar. It was a scene reminiscent of a First World War battlefield: semi-liquid mud covered everything, teams of men, stripped to the waist, slogged away at the diversion ditch and the ten-foot-high dam was strengthened as the water pressure behind it increased.

*Building the dam during the rescue attempt at Mossdale Caverns
Photos: Fred Winpenny*

The noise of mobile pumps beat out a staccato symphony against a background of rushing water, diesel engines and the metallic s▪rape of shovels. Pulsating lengths of fire hose stretched everywhere, spewing water away from the sink so that it fanned out across the churned-up moor and flowed into the valley beyond.

Water ponding behind the dam. Photo: Fred Winpenny

We had a briefing from Reg Hainsworth and Len Huff, the rescue leaders, then stripped off and changed outside the food tent, the grim atmosphere lightened only slightly when one of the lads overbalanced and his bare backside made a brief appearance through the open flap of the tent. My wife Rose, who was gently stirring a large pan of hot pea soup, promptly gave the spotted bum a playful slap with the alloy ladle, forgetting that it was very hot. The spotted bum vanished as the owner leapt up in the air, clutching his burnt regions with a look of complete amazement on his face.

At 12.40 p.m. a search party reported that the water in the cave was beginning to diminish and we watched and waited while a secondary dam was strengthened. I looked at the fourteen cavers who were in my team; most were clubmates of the trapped cavers. I then looked at the surface workers, whose numbers had increased to almost two hundred, many digging with their bare hands, and I felt proud to belong to such a fraternity of people who were prepared to go to any lengths to help their stricken comrades.

Our task was to try to reach Far Marathon crawl, a name which speaks for itself. If conditions were suitable, we were to continue into the further reaches of the cave to the high-level caverns near the end, where it was possible the trapped cavers could have avoided the flood.

At 1.35 p.m. the white-haired figure of Reg Hainsworth approached us.

'Have you got your lads ready, Jim?' he asked in his usual quiet, fatherly manner.

One by one we descended into the narrow, evil, dripping crack, overlooked by the earth dam which held back many tons of floodwater, some of which sprayed over its lip in the wind. Easing my body into the tight, wet confines, I was soon forced to lie flat-out, crawling through passages still dripping from being submerged a few hours previously. I am not religious, but in this instance I wished that I was, so that I could pray for the dams to hold.

We eagerly pushed through the restricted passageways to the Assembly Hall, where we stood in a hushed group as we sorted out which way to go. Both alternatives looked grim: both were low, forbidding apertures that steadily dripped water from ominously clean ceilings. Someone thought they heard a shout and we listened intently. The cave was as silent as the grave.

'They'll be making their way out, Jim,' said one of the Wanderers.

'Yes,' agreed another. 'Once the water level dropped they would make a move.'

'Probably been sitting it out in the high-level caverns,' said another optimistically. I couldn't answer.

We pressed on through the restricted cave, hemmed in by black walls and ceilings with the flood debris of grass and heather jammed in cracks and joints. There were no stalactite formations or rock sculptures, or anything resembling a normal cave; this was a dead world, an underground sewer which was made more oppressive by the unnatural silence created by the dams that prevented the normal sound of flowing water.

'Do you think they're okay, Jim?' asked one of the lads. I sought a reply. I had come to the conclusion that if the trapped cavers were alive, they would be working their way out by now and we would have met them. I had a horrible feeling that they had all perished, especially when we entered the more restricted crawls. 'I think you had better prepare yourselves for the worst,' I said, hoping against hope that I would be proved wrong.

In this last section a change came over the team, as slowly it began to penetrate their numbed minds that their mates could be dead. By the time we reached Far Marathon, the atmosphere of death seemed to be with us. I knew the extent of the crawls and had a grim foreboding of what lay ahead.

'Six of us will go on from here while the rest of you wait here,' I said, but before I finished talking seven or eight cavers had pushed past so I stayed with the rest, trying to ignore the tears that some of these hard cavers were quietly shedding. After what seemed a long time I entered the crawls with two others to find the cause of the delay. We crawled some distance on our hands and knees, then heard voices and met the others who were returning.

'Go back Jim, go back. They're all dead!' said Tony Waltham.

The shocked, ashen faces of the group told all and, when the rest were informed, some broke down and wept openly. I considered trying to evacuate the bodies but, with shocked and tired rescuers and a cave liable to flood again, I quickly dismissed the idea. I realised it would be a major operation to get one body out, never mind six.

A telephone party had rigged a line into the cave and when we reached them I phoned the surface with the grim yet not unexpected news. It was 5.20 p.m. when I spoke to Reg and he told me to extract my team as quickly as possible; I sensed the urgency in his voice, so I got the lads moving without appearing panicky. When we eventually reached the surface, relieved faces told us all we needed to know. I later learned that another cloudburst had sent more floodwater down the valley, where it had poured over one of the dams and threatened a collapse. This was only prevented by using one of the mechanical diggers to shore it up. Once we were out of the cave the weather became worse and during the night heavy rain caused the swollen beck to breach the dams in two places.

The forward team had found five bodies strewn along the restricted confines of Far Marathon passage, parts of their wetsuits and equipment having been torn off by the force of the flood that hit them. Considering that at the flood's height the level of the surface pool was ten feet above the entrance, the pressure of water coming down those restricted passageways must have been tremendous and the unfortunate cavers would have been hit with the force of a liquid battering ram. Death must have been almost instantaneous.

However, one can only guess at the sheer horror experienced by these young men as they felt the blast of displaced air and heard the thunder of the approaching flood. Jim Cunningham and John Shepherd, who were with the original group and had surfaced with the two girls, had shown tremendous courage in returning with my team to look for their comrades.

Jim then suddenly realised that although five cavers had been reported trapped in the original callout, there were actually six in the group. Five dead cavers had been identified by their friends who found them, but the sixth – John Ogden – was still missing. Had 'Oggie' been able to reach somewhere out of the floods? Did he remain alive in the cold, dark depths of Mossdale?

On Monday, in spite of the obvious dangers, several more search parties were organised, but ominous thunderclouds built up and at 2 p.m. the teams were withdrawn from the cave without finding the missing sixth caver. Could John still be alive? Most of us doubted it, but there was always the slim chance that he could have escaped the catastrophe that had overwhelmed his companions, or been washed down the submerged passage to an air pocket. No one could relax until we knew.

Another team tried to enter the cave but the weather worsened and the stream rose four feet in half an hour, so the group hastily exited as once again a dam breached. The main earthwork was now ten feet high and fifteen feet thick, while the secondary dam around the cave entrance, built to allow men in the cave extra time to escape, was six feet high and six feet thick.

The situation seemed hopeless, yet we could not give in and a desperate long-term dig was started at the nearby Black Edge Pot in the vain hope of reaching a high-level inlet in Rough Chamber in Mossdale. Use of a heavyweight drill was offered at the cost of fifty pounds an hour, but it was turned down as impractical as it weighed fifty-six tons and obviously could not be transported to the site.

On Tuesday the 27th several search teams were able to re-enter the cave and, eventually, at 3.10 a.m. on the Wednesday, the last search party led by Brian Boardman located John in a narrow side passage adjacent to three of the bodies. Brian had to crawl over these in order to see up a narrow, silted-up passage, where he noticed a pair of boots and a white helmet, by which he identified the missing caver.

The weather again deteriorated and heavy rain began to fall. Later in the day, after a meeting between the police, the coroner and representatives of the rescue teams, it was agreed that the bodies of the dead cavers could not be brought out without appreciable risk to others. The decision was taken to abandon their recovery and seal the cave entrance.

It was an unsatisfactory ending after all the tremendous effort that had gone into the rescue, but it was the only sensible decision that could be taken at that time. The cave was sealed and the dams destroyed.

The traumatic effect of the Mossdale tragedy numbed the caving world for years. However, such is the bond between cavers that several clubmates re-entered the cave during more settled weather and dragged the bodies of their dead comrades out of Far Marathon and buried them in a high-level chamber in the far end of the system, away from the raging torrents that had destroyed them.

A plaque in their memory was placed over the entrance, and Mossdale Caverns was left in sombre isolation with its brooding cliff face a permanent tombstone to the six young cavers who perished: Dave Adamson, Geoff Boireau, Bill Frakes, John Ogden, Mike Ryan and Colin Vickers.

Chapter 6

Donner und Blitzen:
The Wrath of the Gods

THE LOSS OF SIX YOUNG CAVERS, who were in the forefront of British caving, deeply affected the caving fraternity – some cavers were so traumatised by the horror of Mossdale that they gave up the sport altogether. However, life goes on, and at the other end of the caving spectrum we had Buxton's answer to Biggles. Nine days before the trauma of Mossdale he had burst into print, having persuaded the *Daily Express* to back another expedition to Provatina, as a result of which I experienced a mini-trauma of my own. With my 1967 expedition in the final stages of readiness, my breakfast was totally ruined by that familiar face grinning back at me from my morning paper, complete with lurid headlines proclaiming that seventeen Derbyshire cavers were going to attempt to break the world's depth record.

After a few days my blood pressure returned to normal – once it was reported that the Derbyshire-based group had managed to get a couple of men down to the ledge and found that the next pitch was between two hundred and three hundred feet deep, though strangely enough that they hadn't attempted to descend it. So, it took a team of seventeen men, two reporters, a new winch and lots of hullabaloo to gain an extra fifty feet that could have easily been reached the year before with an extra fifty feet of ladder. *C'est la vie* . . . It sells papers, but I wonder how much a foot that cost.

The chaos of the previous year seemed to have rubbed off on me and, thanks to a clapped-out Land Rover with crap tyres and no brakes (the expedition money that should have paid for improvements had been used for something else), we arrived in Ioannina two days late. Since I had obtained my permit from the Greek embassy in London, there had been a military takeover by the country's generals and, unfortunately, my man was on the wrong side. When I gaily waved my permit at the senior officers in the military headquarters, I was treated with great suspicion, almost arrested and told to report to the police. I drove across Ioannina to the police station and was again treated with suspicion, this time by a group of hostile police officers who spoke no English and did not intend to go to night school to learn.

Several hours later, after telephoning Athens, they informed me that the area was closed. I would have to obtain permission from the colonel who was commander-in-chief of north-west Greece, so I returned to the military HQ – where I was refused admission. Defeated, I returned to the camp, but the next day again presented myself and again received the same hostile treatment. By this time I was becoming severely pissed off and demanded to see a more senior officer. After a lot of arguing, I managed to see a bloke with a lot of pips on his shoulder, who spoke some English.

'You must see the colonel – report here tomorrow at 9 a.m.'

Another two days wasted. Eventually, I managed to see the big man, at which time I wondered if I should impress him with my Navy record. Then I thought better of the idea.

The colonel examined all our passports and gave me a large glass of orange juice. When I told him how much happier the people looked under the new regime, he shook my hand and wished me good luck. Three days' frustration were over and, much later that day, we finally established camp on the Astraka plateau adjacent to Provatina.

THE FOURTEEN CAVERS on the expedition came from different clubs, but our training meets had welded them into a good working unit and, within a day of our arrival, the camp was organised, the entrance shaft laddered and the lifeline winch assembled and bolted in position.

The Farnworth 'Oxfam' Mk I winch was a piece of engineering genius, a far cry from the quixotic nightmare of the previous year. Jim's winch comprised a light alloy drum mounted horizontally on a light Dexion frame, incorporating a brake and other safety features – unlike the Kelly winch, it worked both ways: up and down. It could be dismantled into two carrying loads and reassembled in a matter of minutes, it had no gears and was two-manpower (using handles). A thousand feet of seven-by-seven-strand, one-ton galvanised steel wire completed the ensemble, with a backup lifeline for emergencies plus 2,200 feet of ladders and lifelines. What could go wrong?

Little things, it transpired, like the fact that when I made the initial descent, the speech diaphragm fell off the telephone and that I landed, not on earth as I surmised the year before, but on a steep slope of ice and snow, lightly dusted with earth and bird droppings for effect. It sure fooled me, as I went hurtling down the seventy degree slope before the winch lifeline yanked me to a stop, hanging onto the ladders which, helped by a coil of spare ladder on the end, had slid at an angle and left me hanging over the next drop.

A faint detached voice kept telling me . . .

A faint detached voice kept telling me to press the button as I hung on the edge of the void, struggling to pull up the end of the ladder and hook the surplus to the wall. I couldn't stand on the steep ice slope without crampons, so I informed the men above to send down a digging tool and crampons, and to pull up the Spunstron rope which I then untied. As soon as I released the tension on the rope, being new it spun wildly,

Jim descending the massive shaft of Provatina and (right) the Spider, showing the steep ice field and lower trench
Photos: Pete Faulkner

wrapping itself around the telephone cable and the winch wire. The telephone cable snapped but, fortunately, the tangled mess slid up the winch wire without fouling it. I had the feeling I was being watched and I'm sure I heard a voice say in ancient Greek: 'Another cock-up – these Brits are a load of head bangers.'

In view of the expected delay I returned to the surface. Later, with a new telephone diaphragm constructed from the top of a food tin, Chris Shepherd descended armed with a digger, an ice axe and crampons. After an hour or so he returned to report that he had dug a trench in the snow slope and that the next pitch seemed to be very deep: 'About a thousand feet!' This seemed incredible and everyone tried to convince him that he must be mistaken, but Chris remained adamant. 'It's bloody deep.'

The following day a team of four was sent to clear the lip of the lower shaft, establish lifelining trenches and drill holes for the rawlbolts. At this depth the funnel-shaped shaft is approximately one hundred feet by eighty feet in section. Steep banks of frozen snow converge on the narrow neck of the funnel, which drops sheer into its continuation – it was in this dangerous lower section of the funnel that the expedition had to work. It was very exposed: there was no cover from any debris that might fall from above, and everyone had to be belayed as any slip would be fatal.

We excavated a major trench against the east wall, which afforded some slight protection, but the second working position, on the lip of the next vertical, was completely exposed. With snow hissing down the slope from the diggers above, men working here were under constant tension, especially after noting the tremendous time lapse before the faint thud of fallen snow echoed from the depths. The trench lengths were kept to a minimum to reduce the risk of an avalanche.

This dangerous place was reminiscent of the exposed ice field on the north face of the Eiger, and we christened it with the same name: the Spider. Four men had just returned up the pitch after completing several hours' work when the winch lifeline started to twist and kink, even though it was kept under tension. I had feared this might happen and for months previously I had tried to obtain a special non-rotating cable, but found the price prohibitive.

A dangerous kink had developed near the Talurit (the eye-shaped end of the cable, secured by a metal ferrule) and work was abandoned while the damaged wire was cut off, the wire unwound from the drum, reversed and rewound, and the remaining Talurit on the other end was connected to a dismantled pulley block with a swivel neck. Improvisation thus saved the day, though the amount of twist that developed in the wire was demonstrated on every ascent as the swivel block kept up a continuous spin on the top hundred feet of the shaft. Without the swivel the wire would soon have become unusable.

Examining the kinked wire
Photo: Pete Faulkner

The following day we were ready for an assault on the next drop and some of the tackle was lowered in readiness for the second shaft. At about three in the afternoon the weather became threatening; it was obvious that we had upset the Gods as the first of a regular series of thunderstorms began to form over the mountain. In spite of dire predictions by our weather expert, I decided to head down and supervise rigging the next pitch, especially as I would be the one going down it.

I descended the ladder into a hive of activity and landed neatly in a trench that was three feet wide, eight feet long and four feet deep. Several bolts had been placed on the left-hand wall and two on the lower lip, which had by now been cleared of overhanging snow. The telephone rang and Bill Holden answered it – he was informed that a storm was imminent, then he suddenly dropped the instrument when he received an electric shock.

The ominous rumble of thunder echoed down the giant shaft and we hastily lined the others up into our overcrowded position, though not before two more lads received shocks from the metal ladders. We were told that the ladders and winch wire were being pulled up, as they would act as a giant lightning conductor – not that it would make much difference as we were already in one. A shaft this size, situated at an altitude of six thousand feet, would send out a column of ionised air many hundreds of feet into the sky and attract electrical discharges like a politician attracting backhanders. We were in a dodgy situation – we just had to hope that we weren't going to be cooked.

The light began to fade as we watched the ladders going up. We felt strangely isolated as we stood in the cramped, icy confines of the trench, waiting apprehensively while the ominous rumbling increased in intensity until the huge shaft reverberated to the thunder of the storm outside. It acted like an enormous amplifier as the sound echoed round and round, punctuated by noises like cannon fire that seemed to shake the very walls and rattle past us into the depths.

The daylight filtering down the shaft faded completely as a tremendous crash vibrated through our bodies. It was quickly followed by another, and lightning illuminated the top of the shaft with an eerie blue light, silhouetting the frightened birds that wheeled high overhead. The crescendo increased and we all felt very

vulnerable, perched as we were some six hundred feet down the world's deepest shaft on a snow ledge that could avalanche or be washed away at any time.

Jim Farnworth stood next to me, chain-smoking his home-made cigarettes. 'Do you think we'll get out of this, Jim?' he asked, as another explosion of blue light hit the shaft above us.

I didn't answer, as I was hastily hooking my karabiner back onto the wire belay bolted to the wall. Some of us had unclipped, to avoid conducting any electrical discharge, but I noticed that one by one we had all reclipped, preferring an electric shock to being swept down the shaft if the snow moved.

Gradually, we discerned a faint lightening to the sky, as the rumbling diminished and the storm moved on. The telephone crackled to life and Jim Newton answered it, receiving another electric shock and the message that the ladders were being lowered. He clipped on the winch wire and began the long climb to the surface.

After an interminable wait the telephone informed us that he was up and the winch wire was coming back down, with the end in a weighted bag to stop it snagging or going through the rungs of the ladder: 'Please bring the bag up.'

Bill Holden, then Chris Shepherd, made their way out. By this time Jim Farnworth and I noticed that the light was fading once more and we heard a faint rumbling as the winch wire slowly appeared, ghost-like beside us. Jim fastened on, I rang the surface and they began assisting Jim up the ladder while informing me that the weather was again threatening.

Something was wrong with my light; it had probably become partially discharged in transit and it was now reduced to a dull yellow glow. I switched it off, hoping to conserve what little I had for the climb out, when I heard a slithering noise and switched on just in time to see the end of the winch wire, encased in a brown canvas bag, come to rest below me on the snow slope. This meant I had to climb down and retrieve it without a safety rope. It was only a few feet, but with my light nearly out and the ladder sliding around on the steep snow, I couldn't afford to think about making a mistake. I was very relieved when I grabbed the wire and hastily clipped on before climbing back to the trench to ring the surface.

I have never been up a ladder so fast in my life – it took me all my time to keep pace with the men on the winch. The haste was understandable, for the storm was upon us again and with lightning cracking at our heels, we speedily left the vicinity of the shaft and headed for our tents.

MUCH LATER THAT EVENING the storm rolled away behind the peak of Astraka and a small group of us sat in our delightful little meadow, discussing the day's events, high above the mundane world. Idly, I watched a small cotton-wool cloud roll up the valley below. Without warning it suddenly increased in size and rushed up the gully to envelop the camp in a cold, clammy fog that reduced visibility to a couple of feet. It seemed to me an evil omen and, coupled with the storm that had appeared out of nowhere, it made me feel vaguely uneasy.

I crawled into my sleeping bag and lay there for some time, unable to sleep as I wrestled with the problems that now confronted the expedition. The lower part of the shaft was of an unprecedented depth, much deeper than anyone had anticipated, and the shaft as a whole was deeper than any natural shaft known in the world at that time. Had we enough equipment? Was the snow slope safe? What could we use for communication? Dare I fix the hand-winch onto the Spider? Had we enough time? Thoughts like these turned over and over in my mind, until the long night passed and I awoke to a glorious day.

In this beautiful spot I soon forgot my worries and helped Nigel Beattie sieve all sorts of weird life from our drinking water. I sent the first working party down the hole with instructions to clear as much snow and rubble as possible away from the edge of the next drop and start putting the ladders down.

After a short interval, I climbed into my harness and once more descended the frail-looking electron ladders that threaded gossamer-like down the airy vastness of this huge shaft. No matter how many times I climbed into its depths, it was always a thrill and today was no exception when I landed in the familiar surroundings of the trench.

Carl Pickstone, our more scientifically minded member, informed me of two facts: the temperature of the snow was at zero degrees and could not be considered safe and, to cheer me up even more, he had made some serious timing studies using some large stones. The ten to eleven seconds free-fall from the Spider indicated that the lower shaft was well over a thousand feet deep.

I was faced with the unpalatable fact that trying to descend a drop of this magnitude, while working from an unstable snow slope without proper communication, had all the makings of a disaster. Again I toyed with the idea of lowering the winch to the Spider; this would give us a thousand feet of lifeline, but would also leave us extremely vulnerable if anything went wrong. If our soundings were correct, the Abyss of Provatina was a natural shaft of between fifteen hundred and sixteen hundred feet. It was a bitter irony, as it had always been my ambition to discover something like this – but now that I had, how the hell did I get down it? Oh, how those Greek gods must have been laughing.

Jim in the trench before descending the lower section
Photo: Pete Faulkner

We had plenty of ladders and ropes, so I decided to descend into the lower shaft in the hope of finding a ledge big enough to work from. After checking that my lifeline team and ladders were safely secured, I edged my way over the lip of the menacing Spider.

The lower shaft lay at right angles to the upper shaft, like a massive underground canyon twenty feet wide and eighty feet long. On my left the roof soared out of sight into an aven on the northern side. Below, the walls, smooth and fluted and glistening in my light, receded after a few feet and the ladder swung clear in space.

A blast of cold air chilled me as I slowly climbed down the swaying ladders into the black, airy void. I looked up at the menacing lip directly above my head, which held back tons of loose snow and rock. Receiving shouts of encouragement, I continued down.

The shaft gradually began to bell out and the clear, cold air gave excellent visibility. A piece of snow and a small rock hit me on the shoulder as I willed myself not to look down, but only to concentrate on climbing. We had no telephone communication and every so often I shouted to the men above on the Spider. Their answers became fainter as I descended further, down and down into the elongated rift.

Looking below, I could see the silver thread of the wire ladders disappearing into nothingness, smooth fluted walls in front and behind – to the sides and below, nothing but a black space. I heard a faint shout from above and a whirring noise as a rock whistled past. I looked down again: nothing. I continued climbing.

It was obvious from the symmetrical shape of the shaft that there wasn't going to be a ledge of any description. I had changed my Nife cell and I therefore had a good headlamp, which in that situation could pick out anything up to two hundred feet away. There was no sign of any break in the smooth walls; below, the end of the ladders thrashed to and fro, and beyond that an inky blackness conveyed an impression of great depth.

A faint shout came down, then a couple more rocks. I stopped near the end of the ladders; we had more, and lines to go with them, but this was only a look-see. I heard another shout and felt a tug on the line as I experienced a moment of truth that this lower, gigantic abyss would be an extremely arduous and dangerous shaft to tackle on ladders. I was a long way down, but there was no sign of the bottom. I slowly became aware of falling water, another faint shout and a *fierce* tug on the lifeline. I took a last look downwards into the centre of the earth and then climbed back up, head and shoulders hunched against the snow and spray falling around me.

While I was in the lower shaft another storm had approached the mountain, it had begun to rain and I was therefore greeted with relief by the men shivering on the snow slope. Considerable time had elapsed since we entered the hole. With only three men having returned up the ladders and the rumble of the storm becoming more threatening, the surface team was working in relays to bring us out before the full fury of the storm hit.

It proved to be touch and go. The storm was on us just as I reached the surface, and two men were still to come up. We worked in a torrential downpour, taking turns on the winch handles as we listened, awestruck, to deep booming noises as water swilled down the shaft and washed snow off the higher ledges onto the Spider, before thundering down the lower shaft to where only a brief hour before I had hung on a slender ladder. Luckily, everyone emerged unscathed. The last man, soaked to the skin, was literally dragged away from the edge of the shaft just as lightning struck within feet of the winch with a tremendous crack that almost stunned us.

The gods were really angry that we had dared to violate the depths of Acherusia and the violence of these Greek thunderstorms was truly frightening. As we watched the vivid white-blue lightning strikes fracturing the rock around the entrance to Provatina with ear-splitting claps of thunder, we could almost smell the brimstone and treacle while we huddled in our tents, wincing at each tremendous bang.

But we made bold plans for the morrow – we weren't going to let this piddling little hole beat us!

THE FOLLOWING DAY we began measuring out the ladders and ropes for a final bid. The day seemed heavy and our weather expert, Dave Stevenson, drew my attention to some clouds building up over the Adriatic. Three men had already descended to the Spider and lowered a plumb line for 685 feet into the lower shaft, finding what we assumed to be a ledge at 1,285 feet from the surface. We were weighing up this controversial information when the sky darkened, lightning gashed the sky and it began to rain heavily. I swore and said, 'That's it, start de-laddering.'

Working frantically, we retrieved all the tackle from the Spider and brought two of the underground team to the surface as the storm intensified. The last man to leave the Spider was struggling, so the winch men put extra effort into their work.

The climber was wearing a commercial harness, one of several which had been donated to the expedition. It had a built-in shock-loading factor in case of a fall. The tired caver missed his footing near the top of the shaft and fell backwards – he was a big, heavy lad and the harness was probably designed for lightweight 'spider men' because we heard a sudden tearing sound as the stitches around the D-ring attachment point parted and the harness immediately lengthened by two feet, accompanied by screams of horror from the unfortunate lad. He thought his end had come, but he ended up dangling in space on the end of the winch wire to be wound in bodily, like a landed fish, by the winch men. They thought it was highly amusing.

As they were being removed from the top shaft, the ladders caught on something; after several unsuccessful attempts to free them, I tied on a lifeline and climbed into the hole to ease them past the flake of rock that was snagging them. All was going well when in an instant the wire ladders flickered with an eerie bluish glow and a tremendous bang thundered in my ears as lightning struck the cave entrance. Simultaneously, the men on the surface were thrown about like rag dolls and I was hurled into space.

Luckily for me, Russell Cox had tied my lifeline to a rock while he gave me a hand on the ladders, or I would have had a very spectacular end. As it was I swung across the shaft, held firmly on the taut rope until I hit the right-hand wall, where I clung to the rock face like a limpet.

A sickening silence came after the impact, followed by a woman's hysterical screaming as four white faces peered down the hole at the space where I had been, and another white face peered up from where I was. One man was slightly burned and the rest of us were badly shaken by this incident. We were forced to abandon everything until the next morning and we sat in the comparative safety of our tents, watching lightning strike at the head of the shaft with monotonous regularity, producing a cannonade of noise. We listened to the torrential rain drumming on our tents as the storm raged well into the night.

The following morning we discovered that we had been visited

Four white faces peered down the hole at the space where I had been

by a nocturnal burglar, who had stolen three boots from outside the tents and a watch from the cookhouse. We decided to ask for the time from the first three-legged shepherd we met.

So ended our early forays into Provatina and we returned from our tussle with the Greek gods with burnt fingers and scorched trousers – but once again I vowed to return.

BACK HOME, after convincing Rose that I would stay away from the thunderbolts of Zeus, I was engaged in painting a large metal frame on the roof of a high building on Morecambe promenade. Boldly emblazoned on the frame was the message STAR CAFE and boldly clinging to the letter S was a suicidal painter who had climbed a fifty-year-old triple extension ladder, which was now bent like a banana, and another ladder which he had tied to the top. Three painters were holding the bottom of the ladders, while lots of holidaymakers with funny hats watched intently from benches and deckchairs on the seafront.

'Eh, Mavis, look at yon chap up there – ee must be bloody mad,' said one old codger to his wife.

'You wouldn't catch me up there,' said another old dear. Probably not – especially in the next ten minutes, because the sky suddenly darkened and the mother and father of all thunderstorms hit Morecambe. A gale sprang up and the promenade miraculously cleared; even the three painters holding the foot of the old wooden ladder vanished, leaving the ladder spinning on one leg, lashed by waves sweeping over the seafront. Lightning flashed and thunder crashed and there was not a soul to be seen, save a solitary figure clinging desperately to the letter S on the Star Cafe roof with his hair standing on end and sparks coming out of his ears as the letter S flashed on and off.

PROVATINA WAS UNIQUE in the annals of speleology and was going to be extremely difficult to crack, as well as being dangerous to explore using current techniques. We had demonstrated that a 600 foot ladder climb was no problem, so a second of 685 feet should be no problem either – *if* a safe working platform could be established on the Spider. However, this was a big 'if' as the kink in the shaft at the Spider would hold snow from the heavy winter falls and there was a strong probability that this would always pose avalanche problems.

This extraordinary shaft required extraordinary equipment. A winch with a special non-spinning cable was required, and a foolproof communications system, before anyone could reach the known 1,285 foot level and descend further with any degree of safety. The engineering know-how involved, and the probable cost, made financial backing essential, so once again back in England we printed good publicity sheets and posted these wherever and to whomever we could. Some considerable backing came from interested firms, but there was still insufficient money in the kitty when suddenly I had a stroke of luck.

The Guardian was offering a £2,000 bursary to budding explorers. I sent in a summarised report on the 1967 Provatina expedition and our plans for a return in 1968. I made it to the shortlist and was invited to London to meet the panel of judges, which included such distinguished people as Sir Vivian Fuchs, the leader of the Commonwealth Trans-Antarctic Expedition which made the first crossing of the Antarctic (2,100 miles) in 1958, George Greenfield, who was the literary agent for Sir Edmund Hillary and Sir Francis Chichester, and Sir Miles Clifford, chairman of the British National Committee on Antarctic Research and a vice-president of the Royal Geographical Society. After meeting these illustrious people and other gentlemen, I was very impressed by Sir Vivian Fuch's keen observations and the mini-skirted secretary who led me up the steep flight of stairs. I came away elated.

Meanwhile, back in the depths of Acherusia, Lachesis was working to wipe the smile off my face. Ken Kelly was organising another expedition and wrote to me asking me to join. I did not answer, so he rang me up and said he had this fantastic winch and that Ken Pearce (a well-known hard caver of the time) was joining his expedition.

The following evening Ken Pearce rang me to say that Kelly had asked him to join his expedition, and had informed him that I was going. I put him straight. I received several more communications from the inventive Kelly, including an invitation to inspect his new winch, so I travelled to Derbyshire to look at the opposition. I was received with open arms – it was amazing that a bloke who had almost played a part in my demise could be so friendly.

'Ow you doing, Jim? You're looking good – what yer 'avin?'

Much backslapping and pouring beer down my unyielding throat ended with me looking at his winch – along with two carloads of reporters! Kelly the consummate salesman had struck again, and I quickly informed all and sundry that my name was Joe Bloggs and I was only looking.

The cavalcade followed Kelly's van on a tour of Derbyshire as he went in search of a suitable mineshaft on which to try his winch. Several stops and much poring over maps resulted in many consultations with farmers, during which

Rose in Kelly's Rocket and the metal contraption about to be lowered down the mineshaft

times I adjourned to the nearest pub.

Eventually, the concourse pulled up in the vicinity of two mineshafts. Kelly marched forward and tested them for depth by throwing in rocks. One seemed about 150 feet deep and the other forty feet deep. 'Ah,' said he, indicating the shallow one, 'this seems to be just right.'

Kelly and his mates dragged out some builders' scaffolding from the depths of his van and soon erected this over the small shaft, which was six feet in diameter, and fixed a pulley wheel on a bulldog clip to a crossbar. Then, with a flourish, Kelly unveiled his secret weapon and from the depths of another van he dragged out an incredible capsule that looked as though it had broken free from some fairground attraction.

Eight feet long, cylindrical with a point at each end and painted red and green, the metal monster looked like Britain's answer to the space race. It took my breath away. A wire grille in the centre opened to reveal a cosy little seat for one. It had to be some sort of elaborate joke . . .

'Well, what do you think?' asked a buoyant Kelly, as he stood back in admiration.

'You're not going down Provatina in that?' I gasped.

'Yeah, isn't it great?' answered a beaming Kelly as he fastened the hauling wire on with a bulldog clip. I pointed out the obvious danger of rope-cored wire and bulldog clips, and the spinning tendency of hawser-laid wire and other points . . . I just didn't want the bloke to kill himself. In the meantime his mates began assembling a petrol-driven winch, which was a far cry from the capstan monster that had nearly decimated the crew of the expedition that I had been on and looked a reasonably sound job.

Kelly's Rocket was hoisted up and swung over the mineshaft. The reporters converged as Kelly stepped into his metal capsule, closed the wire-mesh door and immediately vanished into the bowels of the earth with a blood-curdling yell as his weight lifted the winch off the ground.

It was unbelievable. There was Kelly down the hole, with his winch upended and jammed under the pulley above his head, surrounded by reporters with flashing cameras. The winch was eventually dragged back to earth and weighted with several large blocks of stone, then after a great deal of struggling a pale-faced replica of Kelly was retrieved from the hole.

This was just the curtain-raiser. After a lot of fiddling about and technical examinations, telephones were connected and Kelly and his second in command checked these by talking side by side.

'Are you there?' asked the captain of the spaceship *Enterprise*.

'Yes, come in, I can hear you,' answered his first mate from two feet away.

The winch started and the capsule was launched with a bottle of beer – one thing about Kelly, he does things in style. I then had a most beautiful experience of watching the capsule, spinning madly, being lowered down the shaft – the lower it went, the faster it spun.

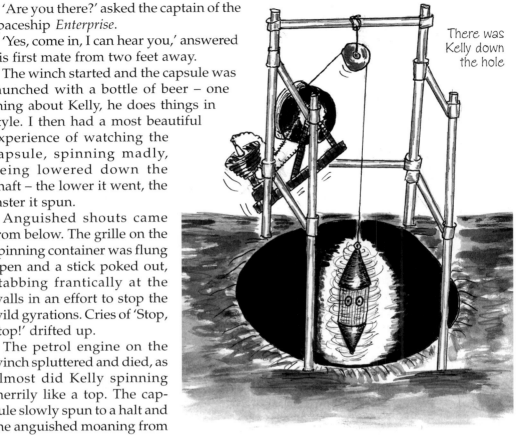

There was Kelly down the hole

Anguished shouts came from below. The grille on the spinning container was flung open and a stick poked out, stabbing frantically at the walls in an effort to stop the wild gyrations. Cries of 'Stop, stop!' drifted up.

The petrol engine on the winch spluttered and died, as almost did Kelly spinning merrily like a top. The capsule slowly spun to a halt and the anguished moaning from below ceased. Ah, but only for a moment, for then the capsule slowly started spinning the other way, gradually increasing in speed until once more there was frantic poking with the stick and cries of 'Get me out!'

By this time I was on the verge of hysterics at this performance. The winch was restarted but, just as Kelly and his Rocket were about to be retrieved, the clutch went and Kelly was stranded, halfway down his forty-foot mineshaft, slowly gyrating and moaning in his 'Flash Gordon's trip to the moon lookalike tin container' until his staunch companions winched him back up by hand.

I imagined this procedure repeated down Provatina which, it had to be admitted, was slightly larger than a forty-foot-deep mineshaft. Kelly would have been spun-dried into the remnants of a human prune before eventually coming to a horrible end, to be found later on some history programme on television: 'Caged prune found in Greek cavern has human genes – was it an early spaceman?'

Eventually, Kelly emerged from his trip into inner space, pale, perspiring and a shadow of the man that went down, but undaunted. Nothing would change him and once again he made the headlines in the *Daily Express*: 'Kelly's Rocket capsule may beat deep cave.'

There followed an exaggerated account of Kelly 'enjoying a luxury ride to the bottom of a 200 foot mineshaft', stating: 'It's marvellous: this is potholing in style.'

Another classic quote continued, 'Other attempts to explore the depths of the 5,000 foot cave spiralling into the heart of Mount Astraka have failed. But this time Kelly and his team think they can make it by descending the first 1,500 feet in the capsule.' The finest quote of all was: 'Kelly, whose caving exploits would give most men nightmares, said: "We need one or two modifications, and there is a bit of spinning."'

You can say that again! This intrepid group of cavers and their publicity machine were years ahead of their time, for they had discovered the art of spin long before Tony Blair and his New Labour government had left school.

ALL THIS PUBLICITY in the press, and my own expedition report, was attracting all sorts of adventurers into the arena. Apart from being chased by Greek gods who were determined to zap me, I found I was also being chased by the army.

A Captain Kim Brook had been touring the Dales looking for me and the word had gone around my fellow cavers that I was a deserter from the army. I then received a letter from a Major Geoffrey Morris informing me that, because he had 'loaned Kelly four members of the 16th Parachute Brigade and equipment for the 1967 attempt', he was qualified to send an army expedition to Provatina – as he put it, 'for an engineering exercise'.

This really annoyed me. Here we were, struggling to raise funds by our own efforts and along come the bloody army, with sod all else to do except ride on the back of our achievements and pinch Provatina while financed by taxpayers' (and my) money! Why couldn't they find a bloody war to fight?

Old Lachesis began working overtime on my thread of life – the silly old sod started putting knots in it. Things began happening fast. I was unofficially informed that I was being awarded the £2,000 bursary – this was great news! Then, within days I received a telephone call from John Bright-Holmes, the managing director of Eyre (no relation, more's the pity) & Spottiswoode, joint sponsors of the bursary, asking me to go to London. There I met the panel of judges, who informed me that owing to Kelly's interest in Provatina and the effect it could have on the outcome and the book I would be writing, they were withdrawing the award.

I closed the door behind me and cursed Kelly and cursed the panel of judges. But a bigger disaster was to come, for the Parachute Regiment had added to their battle honours by bottoming Provatina, finding it completely blocked at a depth of 1,326 feet. I had mixed feelings as I read a report from Captain Kim Brook, with an apology for 'pinching' the hole and an explanation of the mystery of the depth of the second stage of the shaft, which was 720 feet.

In spite of my deep disappointment at not being the first to see the bottom of Provatina, I realised that the army team had saved me a lot of disappointment, expense and embarrassment of the sort that happened some years later to the second Ghar Parau expedition to the deepest cave in Asia. In 1971 a British team explored a difficult pothole to a depth of 2,350 feet, to be stopped by a small pitch where they ran out of equipment. A large and expensive expedition was organised for the following year and the small pitch was descended, but the cave only continued for 150 feet before it became impassable.

This must have been a bitter blow and illustrates the enigma of cave exploration. In Provatina our soundings had reached the bottom and not a ledge as had been suggested. The army had dropped and timed stones from the Spider and received the same eleven seconds to impact, but later concluded that there was a distorted echo which had thrown out the figures.

The men of G Parachute Battery (Mercer's Troop) Royal Horse Artillery (what an astounding name for a parachute company!) had spent four days hauling stuff up from Papingo to Provatina, plus an incredible nine days dragging up the winch. Talk about using a sledgehammer to crack a walnut!

The machine they used was built in 1928, weighed half a ton and was powered by a 750cc twin JAP engine. To take it up the mountain, the winch was placed on a sledge and the wire towed out and secured to a rock or a tree, then the winch wound in the wire and gradually towed itself up the slope. It overturned several times and pulled large rocks from the ground; there was also 3,000 feet of cable, weighing 500 pounds, trailing behind the winch. Reading the army report and being familiar with the rough terrain, it was indeed an 'engineering exercise' – and some.

When the team reached the cave, the soldiers spent another day winding on the cable after cutting off the damaged pieces that had done the hauling. Army engineers fixed plates and rawlbolts on the walls over the cave entrance and other cables were attached to these to give a rigid structure that enabled the pulley to be placed directly over the centre of the shaft. They fastened the cable to a helicopter air-sea rescue boatswain's chair using a ball-bearing swivel hook, then an engineer was lowered to the Spider and brought up again.

As I had pointed out, communication would be a problem and I thought the army would have had enough technical know-how to have sorted this out, but they hadn't. Another man was lowered to the point I had reached, about 400 feet down the second stage of the shaft, and was hauled out again when his radio ceased to function.

Eventually, they fastened another pulley on the Spider and one of the team sat in the boatswain's chair to be lowered the full 1,326 feet, without communications but with instructions that he would be given fifteen feet of slack and ten minutes, and then be pulled out again.

After two days of hoisting bods up and down, they realised there was no way on at the bottom – which was fortunate, for it doesn't require much imagination to wonder what would have happened in an emergency, such as the cable snagging or the winch breaking down. It would be interesting to know what the army plans were for retrieving a man stuck in mid-air without communication.

However, the 'engineering exercise' was a success. The team measured the floor of the shaft (110 feet by eighty feet) and described it as being covered in snow, ice and huge rocks. One storm hit the mountain without doing more than giving one unfortunate fellow, who was in the hole, a thorough soaking (army-speak for being almost drowned).

This heavyweight expedition, with its mind-boggling logistics, can be contrasted to an American visit just five years later. That team used a new technique when Wil Howie, JJ Jones, Bob Osburn and John Pollack walked up from Papingo and, with only two ropes, abseiled in and prusiked out of Provatina taking a mere six and a half hours for each two-man round-trip.

FROM 1966 TO 1973, descents of Provatina illustrated a watershed in cave exploration. During this period electron ladders were found to be impractical for use on the really big drops that were being discovered around the world, and winches left an awful lot to be desired. In the late 1960s American cavers perfected a different caving technique when a new, immensely strong, non-stretch, non-twist rope was developed, together with a sophisticated method of rope-walking that revolutionised caving and consigned winches to the scrap heap.

All except one, that is, for, as the army was returning from Provatina, they passed what looked like a rebel army going in the opposite direction. It was Kelly and his Brigands, so called by Pete Livesey who had been flannelled, bribed, coerced or cajoled to join yet another Provatina expedition – complete, of course, with a *Daily Express* reporter. He had written a report about these gallant adventurers leaving England to embark on yet another attempt to bottom Provatina, hoping to descend an astonishing 5,000 feet in Kelly's Rocket, which would really have amazed the sun worshippers down at sea level, while in the same article reporting that 'a team of paratroopers from Aldershot delved 1,350 feet into Provatina to find their way blocked by a small underground lake and a fall of boulders.'

This must rank among Nobel prize-winning articles for journalistic doublespeak, describing a group going to explore a cave and a group who had already explored it, both in the same report!

The saga ended with Pete (hard man, athlete, caver, climber, but not 'Kelly-proof') allowing himself to be lowered – not in the famous Kelly Rocket, but in a parachute harness – to the bottom of Provatina. The following is an abbreviated account taken from one of Pete's articles written for *Crags* climbing magazine in 1979 – they are some of the funniest – sometimes fanciful – stories ever written:

THE FIRST WHISTLING NOISE made a sharp crack on a boulder a few feet away and I was showered in shattered bits of jumar. I moved slowly, not knowing where in the darkness; my lamp was probably the second whistle and crash, followed seconds later by others. Descendeur, krabs – and finally, with a great 'vroomsh', came the transmitter, a beautiful and expensive squashed mass of bits.

I sat down again and groped around on the floor for something, anything – any piece of gadget, modern and reassuring, that would save me. My fingers lighted on a dead bird, and another, then a smashed microphone with no lead.

'Livesey calling Wallamboola base, Livesey calling Wallamboola base, come in, please.' Silence, not even the chirping of dead choughs. Silence!

As I sat there I pondered – quite logically I thought – the chain of events that had got me into this position. It had all started about three years before, this fatal fascination of mine with sliding down ropes; now

Entrance to Provatina

snow and ice on ledges

The Spider, 600ft

Blackpool Tower, 518ft

1,326ft

here I was, 2,000 miles from home sitting on a rock 1,300 foot underground in a dark icy cathedral, staring up at a pinpoint of light that was the surface of a mountain somewhere in a military zone on the Albanian border. How ridiculous.

Twelve months ago abseiling had seemed the obvious way to descend this unexplored shaft in Northern Greece. Expeditions were rushing out in the summer to attempt a descent, so I tried to persuade John Sheard to come with me on a 'phantom' trip a month or so earlier. We would tie all our climbing ropes together and abseil down, then learn how to jumar to get out. Unfortunately for me he wouldn't come, and I was forced into joining the only team heading for the hole that was short of men: Kelly's Heroes, a group of brigands and mercenaries from Whaley Bridge . . .

The plan was beautifully simple: hire a big van for the day in Salford, pick up a *Daily Express* reporter in London, drive to Greece borrowing money from the reporter for petrol on the way, go to the blood-bank in Thessaloniki and sell eight pints of this reporter's blood – which would pay him back for the petrol, keep him out of the way and finance the rest of the expedition.

The rest of the plan, which they hadn't told me about, was to bribe the Greek Army with a crate of whisky, steal a fleet of donkeys, pack into the hole and then lower me down it on a 2,000 foot length of something akin to barbed wire. They were then either to leave me down there and collect a load of money from the *Daily Express*, or get me out and sell all my blood in Thessaloniki for the journey back.

As I sat there on my boulder pondering which plan the loonies above were about to adopt, a great avalanche came rumbling down the shaft – yes, avalanche! – and there 700 feet above was Shaun the Irish mechanic, leaping about on a 50 degree icefield stuck to the wall of the shaft, having just cleared it of snow to make a ledge for himself. Shaun was crazy, but he could improvise a winch from three empty tins of SAS spam, a bayonet and a donkey. In fact, he just had done.

You see, when I'd been lowered down and had reached the bottom, I hung all my gear on a krab on the end of the barbed wire as I wandered around letting my eyes get used to the dark. The radio wouldn't work and the tension was off the barbed wire, so the team on top had naturally assumed I was dead (as this would bring in more money from the *Daily Express* anyway) and begun to haul the wire back up.

I had turned round just in time to see my sack just leaving the ground and had to run for it, leaping up just far enough to grab the trailing waist strap of the sack. At about 15 feet above the floor I had begun to ponder the wisdom of this course of action, and by 17 feet 6 inches I had let go and dropped back down. My sack and harness had snagged on the way up, shredding on the rock and spraying me with the contents. When the tattered remnants arrived on the surface their hopes were confirmed, and the Irish mechanic descended for a souvenir – an arm or a leg or something.

This light-hearted tale leaves out the fact that Pete was stuck for almost three hours in the freezing depths in lightweight clothing, while Shaun O'Neil was lowered to the Spider to guide the winch wire back down.

With that delightful story of country folk, the saga of Provatina ended – though Lachesis, the weaver of life's events, had not finished with me yet.

Chapter 7

A Glimpse Behind the Iron Curtain

CAVE RESCUE began to take up more of my time because caving suddenly became more popular as new clubs were formed, and more education authorities seemed to think it a good idea to cut down class sizes by sending kids into the great unknown with a couple of dozy teachers.

We undertook an occasional rescue practice when things were quiet, just to keep us on our toes. Unfortunately, sometimes the practice rescues turned out to be more thrilling than the real thing, as in Rowten Pot when some of our hauling team became a little too enthusiastic and literally plucked our stretcher-bound victim out of our hands before we were ready. He suddenly shot skywards, with Phil Papard hanging onto the foot stirrup doing a trapeze act, swinging underneath a very vocal 'body' which wanted to know 'what the fuckin' hell' was going on as they both swung over a 130 foot drop. It was not a good day.

We eventually retrieved our airborne duo, gave the surface team a bollocking and started again. This time the stretcher was on number one rope and our team doctor John Frankland was on the other, climbing the ladder guiding the stretcher.

The lift out up the eighty-foot daylight pitch began smoothly enough, with John and his patient getting along quite well, when something happened. They must have had a row or something, because they suddenly parted company and John did an imitation of Superman going backwards as he was abruptly pulled off the ladder by a badly placed lifeline team. He pendulumed across the wide shaft, away from the ladder.

Seen from below, John looked spectacular and each time he pendulumed across the skyline, his language became more interesting. Not to be outdone, the 'body' – no longer being held in John's loving embrace – also began to pendulum in the opposite direction, until we had two celestial bodies orbiting across our line of vision like human weights on a giant cuckoo clock. As a controller I should have known what was happening, but I hadn't a clue why John had unexpectedly left his post and gone walkabout in space.

The bloke in the stretcher wasn't too happy, either, and a string of asterisks came hurtling down on our heads. '******** stupid *****! What the **** is going on?'

The poor sod was encased in bamboo in a new neoprene bag, which had arms but no holes for hands (as rescuees don't need hands), and he seemed to be trying to fly, looking like a fat seal in his neoprene hood, with large staring eyes and flippers flapping wildly. John, on the other hand, was making wild lunges for the ladder each time he pendulumed past, but kept missing.

The situation was eventually resolved by the seal – er, 'body' – who, fed up with flying solo, eventually caught hold of John with his flippers as they were passing each other and held him in a loving embrace, refusing to let go until John managed to grab the ladder and normal service was resumed.

There were no videos in those days – it would have made an interesting educational film as it was the first time a 'body' had ever rescued a doctor, and it could have been shown to budding cavers to encourage them to take up other sports that had proper rescue facilities.

Fortunately, this Keystone Cops performance was a one-off and the following evening – 3 November 1968 – we were called out for real to yet another accident down Ireby Fell Cavern, a wet, flood-prone pothole that so impressed the original explorers that they named the pitches according to the nursery rhyme: 'Ding, dong, bell, pussy's in the well'. In this case it wasn't a pussy in the well, it was a member of Orpheus Caving Club who had just climbed back up the final pitch, Well, untied his lifeline and slipped off the traverse at the top. He fell thirty feet, fracturing his right femur and kneecap.

Over half a mile from the entrance, in a tortuous cave 300 feet below ground, is not the best place to have a break like this. The Cave Rescue Organisation was alerted at 4 p.m. and prepared for a long rescue. The first team entered the cave at 5.30 that afternoon, splinted the casualty and began the evacuation, while a second team concentrated on rerigging the pitches and diverting water away from the entrance pitches.

Owing to the awkward nature of the cave and our previous experiences, I organised a changeover system. A group handling the stretcher through a problem area could hand it over to another group waiting ahead, which had already rigged the next difficulty, with the teams switching places in roomier sections and on pitches. This considerably speeded up the rescue.

He looked like a fat seal

We started off with a complication on the pitch where the casualty had fallen. Heavy water was falling over the pitch, which had very limited headroom so that we were forced to raise the stretcher vertically and then swing it into the horizontal, low, hands-and-knees-sized passage at the top. This difficult manoeuvre was accomplished by two men clinging to the wall on the other side of the pitch and raising the foot of the stretcher as the men in the crawl pulled it into the small stream passage. There were only inches to spare and, with water spraying round us, the casualty was eventually dragged into the passage beyond.

From here, half a mile of restricted, twisting passages lead to a notorious constriction known as the Keyhole. As the passages become lower and more confined we looked for an alternative route which would enable us to move the stretcher past the obstruction.

The Keyhole section consists of a long crawl which changes to a narrow rift leading into the keyhole-shaped section above, with yet another horizontal crawl through its widest part ending in a drop into a roomy chamber below the series of entrance pitches. For a fit caver, this section provided acrobatic sport with lots of grunting and thrusting, but it was fun; for an injured caver in a stretcher, it was impossible.

Luckily, we discovered a narrow, vertical rift that bypassed the worst parts of the Keyhole series and broke into the chamber twenty feet higher, beyond a rock flake. This was our only chance – it was a gamble, but worth a try, as the alternative meant removing the suffering casualty from the stretcher and dragging him through the restrictions without its protection, causing more distress and pain.

We spent some time rigging the alternative route; the stretcher was a tight fit in the rift, but we managed to pull it clear and then lower it and its occupant out over the chamber with fixed guide ropes, before pulling it down at an angle across to a broad ledge and thus miss the wet constrictions below. The gamble paid off: the patient remained conscious and remarkably cheerful during these aerobatics and from there, thanks to our teams having diverted water from the pitches, it was a straightforward haul. The stretcher was passed from one group to another and the casualty reached the surface at 11 p.m. on a bitterly cold winter's night just over five hours after the first rescuers entered the cave. It was a brilliant team effort.

WITH THE SWINGING SIXTIES drawing to a close, we heard that something had gone wrong with the honours system – an MBE had slipped through the net and was being awarded to Reg Hainsworth, a founder member of the Cave Rescue Organisation and our leader and guiding light for almost forty years.

I could imagine the faces in Whitehall when they found out their mistake: 'I say, who is this chap? He's not a civil servant, or a pop star, nor even a footballer. After studying his portfolio, I'm sure he's not a gay thespian, or a spy or a bent politician – what do you make of it, Humphrey?' 'What, he spent forty years saving peoples lives? That's not what the honours system is designed for – this man hasn't even paid a penny bribe as far as I can make out. Heads will roll!'

Anyway, our Reg had been awarded the MBE and we were all pleased to see a medal going to someone who had actually earned it, as well as recognition for the CRO. With typical modesty Reg said: 'CRO isn't a one-man show. I know they have given the MBE to me, but it's a tribute to all the lads.'

Good on you, Reg, I thought as I dusted the blank space reserved on the top of the piano for my 'gong' and replaced it with a picture of Karl Marx because I knew Whitehall wouldn't make the same mistake again. Even a suave friend of mine, who reckoned he was in for the big K, downgraded his expectations to a mention in the local paper.

Anyway, we had other perks, like shrimp sandwiches . . .

The police had asked the CRO to look for an elderly fisherman who was overdue from a fishing trip, and at first light we started searching the missing angler's fishing haunts. After looking along a few miles of river bank, the team found the man's body; he had died peacefully from natural causes.

A group returned to base for a stretcher, leaving 'Hopkirk' and 'Henpot' to stay with the body, to make sure no one pinched it. The morning was developing into a lovely summer's day, and Henpot eyed the wickerwork picnic basket next to the body.

'I'm bloody thirsty,' he muttered. 'I wonder if there is any coffee in there.'

'The lid's open,' said Hopkirk, 'I'll have a look inside. Bloody 'ell, a flask of coffee – and guess what?'

'What?' asked his mate.

'Shrimp sandwiches!' exclaimed Hopkirk.

'Cor! I love shrimp sandwiches,' said Henpot. 'They'll soon go off in this heat – and he won't need them,' he continued, gesturing towards the body. And so the shrimp sandwiches and coffee promptly disappeared down thankful gullets.

A few minutes later, along came the stretcher party, two policemen and another angler.

'Yes, he was just lying there when I found him. I was about to phone the police when I met you lot coming for the stretcher,' said the angler as he picked up his picnic basket. 'Pity about the old gentleman – never mind, it's a good way to go. I'll do a bit of fishing now and enjoy my shrimp sandwiches; my missus makes a lovely shrimp sandwich.' He departed slowly along the river bank, while Henpot and Hopkirk rapidly sidled off in the opposite direction.

RESCUING DEAD ANGLERS (and live angler's shrimp butties) illustrated how much the CRO had evolved into a local troubleshooter and general emergency service for the area. Now, apart from being a cave rescue team, much of our time was taken up by fell and mountain rescues and all sorts of other emergencies, ranging from helping to retrieve the driver of a lorry that had crashed down a steep embankment and came to rest on the Settle to Carlisle railway line, to an even stranger happening when we were called out to rescue several firemen who had been hit by an avalanche on Ingle-borough!

Our most regular customers, however, were animals, which seem to have a strange affinity with holes in the ground and keep falling down them. Perhaps they are reincarnated potholers – especially sheep, for they – like lots of potholers I know – are covered in wool, have a very low IQ and a particularly gormless expression on their faces.

After my close relationship with Phoebe (our ship's mascot on HMS *Cadmus*; see *It's Only a Game*), sheep seemed to figure prominently in my life, and none more promi-nently than one particular big, woolly monster that hurtled towards me behind a massive pair of curly, lethal-looking horns.

The snag was that we were both temporary residents on a eighteen-inch-wide ledge that clung to the open shaft of Cow Pot, forty feet above the floor. Me, the CRO's good Samaritan rescuer of fallen sheep, and the giant tup which classed all good Samaritans as socialist busybodies and was determined not to be rescued. Many of us do foolish things in our lives and I had taken off my safety line and advanced towards this poor injured animal with the rope end in my hand, while making sweet, reassuring noises like, 'Here kitty, kitty.' Well, 'Here sheepy, sheepy' didn't sound right. Anyway, it seemed to do the trick for the animal jumped upright, gave me a baleful look and advanced towards me at the speed of a runaway train, its outside legs skidding in space and the menacing horns giving real meaning to the term 'battering ram'.

To loud cheers from above, I swung on the rope as I leapt into the air and opened my legs farther than they had ever been opened before. Even so, the tip of one horn sliced off a piece of trouser leg as I landed, straddled across the broad woolly back which began bucking wildly as the demented animal tried to throw me off.

Hanging onto that broad, woolly arse, I could only guess what the other end was thinking (correction – sheep don't think) and, as I bounced up and down, my only consolation was that my reluctant steed was most unlikely to have heard of Japanese kamikaze pilots and therefore was most unlikely to try to emulate them. However, I was wrong and I ended up grimly hanging onto the rope with my legs tightly crossed in a desperate scissor grip around the sheep's neck which, together with its front legs, was now in space.

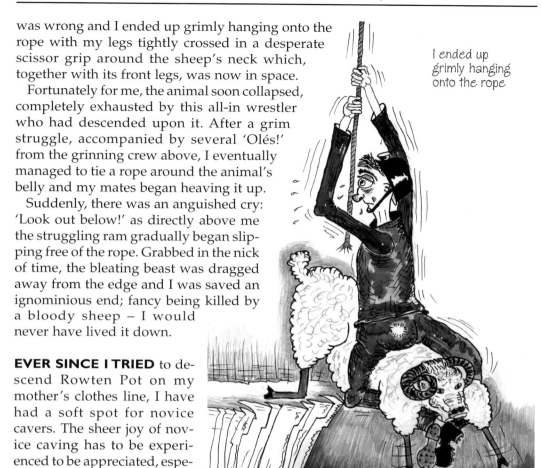

I ended up grimly hanging onto the rope

Fortunately for me, the animal soon collapsed, completely exhausted by this all-in wrestler who had descended upon it. After a grim struggle, accompanied by several 'Olés!' from the grinning crew above, I eventually managed to tie a rope around the animal's belly and my mates began heaving it up.

Suddenly, there was an anguished cry: 'Look out below!' as directly above me the struggling ram gradually began slipping free of the rope. Grabbed in the nick of time, the bleating beast was dragged away from the edge and I was saved an ignominious end; fancy being killed by a bloody sheep – I would never have lived it down.

EVER SINCE I TRIED to descend Rowten Pot on my mother's clothes line, I have had a soft spot for novice cavers. The sheer joy of novice caving has to be experienced to be appreciated, especially on home-made ladders, for there is nothing stranger than a caving ladder made by novices; this is conceptual art at its finest. I have seen ladders made out of barbed wire with the barbs hammered flat and bits of firewood used as rungs, I have seen pieces of sweeping brush handles threaded through a single rope, and I have seen ladders that looked as though they were knitted by someone's mother-in-law.

However, three young novices from Blackburn were justly proud of their home-made ladders, which were a definite improvement on the above examples for they were constructed of wooden rungs strung out at fifteen inches apart on thin, three-sixteenths of an inch nylon – still crap and totally unsuitable for experienced cavers, but great for our enthusiastic novices who managed against all the odds to reach the last pitch in Disappointment Pot. There, one youth got into a bit of a tangle when one foot went through the ladder and he was suspended upside down, surrounded by the flimsy nylon cord and ladder rungs.

Young John was obviously made of stern stuff as, hanging upside down, he took charge of the situation and shouted to his lifeliner above for a tight rope while he took one hand off the ladder to untangle his foot. Unfortunately, his mate thought John had asked for slack, and this caused John to lose grip with his other hand. He fell further, ending up suspended several feet above the floor of the pitch, enmeshed in a nylon cobweb beneath a waterfall.

To quote our young hero: 'On finding myself upside down, I did not panic . . . there was no great pain in my right foot, although it was becoming numb. I then tried, with the aid of my lifeliner, to pull myself upright; this failed and probably tired me out as I tried to do it several times.'

Things were now looking grim, until his other resourceful mate Stephen – who was below – took hold of the bottom of the ladder and dragged it to one side of the chamber where John, still upside down, tried to obtain a grip on the wall while the youth above was told to release the ladder. To quote John again: 'Unfortunately, the lifeliner couldn't release the ladder with my weight on it, so Stephen managed to lift my weight off the ladder by climbing up the wall and getting his back under my body. When this was done, the ladder came down and I flopped on to the rock next to Stephen. I had been approximately ten minutes upside down, suspended under the fall of water.'

The ladder was hauled back up the pitch and rebelayed, but John was now too weak to climb out. At 7 p.m. the CRO was called out by the victim's two companions, who had left him alone with his thoughts where he was to remain for another five hours because twelve inches of snow had fallen on the fell and bogged down the rescue vehicles.

The pothole was reladdered with a strong party and, after lots of hot drinks were poured down him, John was eventually talked out of the cave and became a mini-celebrity as he was depicted in a cartoon which adorned the front of Newcastle University Caving Club members' T-shirts uttering those now famous words: 'On finding myself upside down I did not panic.'

ADVENTURES LIKE THESE are being removed from society by those pathetic denizens of that ancient edifice that goes under the misnomer of the House of Commons, whose laws remove slides and swings from children's playgrounds and ban village fêtes because they are 'dangerous' or sell off school playing fields in case someone trips over a dandelion.

Fortunately, there are still people in our green and pleasant land who treat politicians with the contempt they deserve, for what is life without a little risk?

Richard and Graham's thoughts were far from the Whitehall warriors as they pottered about on the fell in the shadow of Ingleborough, investigating little caves and dark crevices in the limestone with the aid of their trusty torches.

Climbing down into the quarry-like hole of Bar Pot, they discovered a gap among the rocks that beckoned them on. Then, much to their delight they found a rope ladder hanging down the first 45 foot pitch. Full of excitement, the two youths – who were deaf and dumb – climbed down into the chambers below and, after conversing in sign language, they decided to explore further.

The top of the 110 foot pitch which they encountered was roomy; it bore a stout-looking rope ladder that hung invitingly down the shaft and, being fairly strong lads, our two heroes followed each other onto the swaying ladder and began to climb down. Richard and Graham were two-thirds of the way down when members of the group which owned the ladders, from the White Rose Pothole Club, reappeared in the chamber below and shouted up a warning to the two intrepid explorers. Of course, being deaf they could not hear what was going on, but one of the White Rose cavers must have been waving his arms about because Richard, being fairly polite, took his hands off the ladder to answer him and promptly fell off, knocking Graham from the rungs below him. This caused Anne, another White Rose caver, to faint with shock. It was like a game of underground snooker with Richard going in-off Graham and potting Anne in the process.

When the CRO arrived to retrieve the casualties, we found it was a difficult mess to sort out. The two youths were unable to tell us who they were or where they were from, and when we got Richard stuck in the tight bottleneck at the top of the entrance pitch he couldn't tell us which bit was stuck so we had to work on the decibel system: the loudest howl denoted the most pain, after which we could adjust him accordingly.

The White Rose caver who caused the accident has sworn never again to wave at a deaf and dumb caver who is climbing a ladder and, if he does so in some forgetful moment, his girlfriend has promised not to look.

AFTER GAZING LONGINGLY at the mountains of Albania from across the Greek border during my attempts to descend Provatina, I had developed an urge to visit this forbidden country. Finding that it was impossible to obtain a visa to enter this strong-hold of Maoist communism, I turned my attention to Bulgaria, another delightful coun-try, and managed to arrange an invitation to join an international caving expedition.

The Bulgarian caving scene was almost a closed shop, as far as British cavers were concerned; well, as far as anyone was concerned really, because in 1968 the iron curtain had not yet been lifted, only wafted a little to one side. I was informed by one Ing. P. Radochev that the expedition would be exploring caves in the Balkan mountains near Lovec, eighty miles north-east of the capital, Sofia. This seemed a good opportunity to see a bit more of Eastern Europe, so I decided to drive through Czechoslovakia, Hungary and Romania before visiting Bulgaria, and then return to England.

Unfortunately, I was unaware that the Russian Army was also thinking of visiting Czechoslovakia – it's a pity they didn't experience as much trouble as we did at the border, or they wouldn't have bothered. I had been warned beforehand about the excessive red tape, but even so I was surprised at the number of forms to be filled in, all in quadruplicate with a photograph on each. This caused a bit of a problem because my wife Rose and I only had three spare photographs each, so the situation required some native cunning. We fixed the photographs on six forms and I carefully removed an old, faded photograph from an out-of-date French camping carnet which I found in the car. Then we played the photograph game.

Rose stuck the old photograph on a form using nail varnish and handed it over. The official stamped it and handed it back as Rose pushed the other forms at him, while I removed the photograph from the still soft nail varnish and stuck it on another form, which Rose handed over with the next batch, and we went through this procedure at three check points before being allowed through.

I drove through a pretty, undulating landscape of picture-book farmland and dense forests, before Rose noticed a small sign nailed to a tree denoting a campsite. Dusk was falling, so we followed the direction of the painted arrow. This took us along a deeply rutted track for several miles, through a thick, black, impenetrable forest before we reached a small clearing and a very small green hut festooned with loudspeakers, out of which blared the metallic tones of a cockney voice singing 'The Lambeth Walk'. It was completely surreal – a bit like a crazy dream.

Three small tents were pitched in the clearing and I half expected the 'mad hatter' to emerge. However, they belonged to some Dutch people who informed us that the hut was a bar – but that it was closed and a Russian invasion was imminent! Rose and I left at first light and I was soon driving through Prague. Hurriedly and rather carelessly, I drove into a tunnel which was reserved for trams coming the other way, one of which I met.

The single, dazzling headlight bore down on us, accompanied by the deafening clanging of bells. I hastily slammed the car into reverse and ricocheted off the narrow tunnel walls as, gearbox screaming, we shot back out of the tunnel two feet ahead of the tram and the wildly gesticulating figure of its driver, who was swearing at us and obviously intent on running us down.

I swung the Morris Oxford round, still in reverse, hit a bollard, changed gear and drove around the large paved square, past the ornate buildings and the crowds of people standing around waiting for something to happen, who looked at the white estate car in amazement. They were expecting a Russian invasion, not a chase scene fugitive from a silent movie.

I saw a road leading out of the square, then I saw a 'No Entry' sign. Sod it! I drove past more amazed onlookers, took the first junction and drove quite blindly down all sorts of quaint streets, away from the apprehensive atmosphere of the city centre. Rose was becoming excited: 'Where are we going?'

'Hungary, I hope,' I replied as I found a major road signposted Brno and turned onto it.

The road was obviously a major route, but it was strangely deserted and ahead I saw the squat earth-coloured shape of a Russian tank, spewing diesel smoke and heading towards us. I turned off the main road and drove down tree-lined avenues, past large houses and, working by instinct and the position of the sun, headed roughly eastwards until we once again chanced upon the road to Brno. I drove non-stop towards the nearest Hungarian frontier post, having decided to postpone my tour of Czechoslovakia until the Russian Army had returned home.

Entering Hungary posed the eternal problem that is ingrained in communist countries: bullshit, bureaucracy gone mad, three men doing one man's work and six pieces of paper where one would do, all handled by officials who have had their brains removed and couldn't care less about anything.

After having our passports examined and filling in fistfuls of forms, I visited the currency exchange desk, but it seemed that the official wouldn't exchange any currency until the correct amount had been entered into my passport and that I had to return to the passport desk. This I did and explained to the chappie that I wanted to change some money, told him how much and could he please enter it in my passport for his mate in the other cubicle. He looked at me over his rimless glasses, held out his hand and said: 'Money.'

'I haven't got any – your mate won't let me have some until you stamp my passport,' I exclaimed.

'No money, no stamp,' said the man. 'Go.' He pointed at the other desk. I marched across and stuck a fistful of notes under the official's nose and said, 'Change.'

'Passport,' he said, then flicked through it and said 'No stamp. Go,' and pointed to the other desk.

I was in a Catch-22 situation and I tried about four times, then lost my temper and gave both officials a loud bollocking and kept thrusting my passport under their noses, waving fistfuls of various currencies. This was a mistake, as they both studiously ignored me, which made it worse – I needed the money and I wasn't going anywhere without it.

I shoved my way to the front of the queue and kept banging on the counter with my passport and money. 'Change! Change! Change! Change!' I kept shouting the words. Suddenly, with a shrug of his shoulders, my money was changed, a receipt stuck in my passport and both were handed back without a word. I was flabbergasted. We left this madhouse, jumped into the car, drove a hundred yards and were flagged down by a soldier waving his rifle at us and made to park alongside several other cars.

Rose and I watched several soldiers conducting a search of people and their hand luggage, before poking around inside the cars and ending by giving the predominantly rear-engine car bonnets a mighty thump with the butt of their rifles to make the terrified owners open them up. Then all their suitcase contents would be strewn across the road while the soldiers had great fun holding up flimsy underwear and making a pantomime of sniffing at knickers while the poor females almost died of embarrassment.

Now it was our turn. Two soldiers walked around the car, looked underneath, looked closely at us as though we were Bonnie and Clyde, then one approached the bonnet and gave it a mighty thump with his rifle. I pointed at the obvious luggage in the back of the car, which was an estate. He ignored this and banged on the bonnet even harder. I flipped the catch and opened it to show the very surprised young soldier an engine. He consulted his sergeant, who was also surprised to see an engine in the luggage compartment. They both glared at me as though I was guilty of some conspiracy. Thrusting a bristly chin close to mine, the sergeant looked at the stuff in the back and said in a voice like rasping sandpaper: 'Any guns, ammunition?'

'No,' I answered, wishing I had. 'Go,' he said, pointing in the general direction of Hungary, which by now I was completely unimpressed with.

This bureaucratic circus had confused me and I possessed more Hungarian currency than I needed. Consequently, when we arrived at the Romanian border and tried to change the Hungarian notes, I was refused and informed that Hungarians do not change their own currency. However, I needed the cash in usable form so I purchased a large bottle of Hungarian booze with Hungarian money and proceeded to make myself very drunk and disorderly. By constantly harassing the clerk at the exchange desk, while waving my currency form, passport and money at him and telling him I was broke, as well as reducing Rose to tears, I was eventually offered some dollars and marks. It was a poor deal, but the best I was going to receive and it was better than sod all.

Romania proved to be a complete contrast – it was friendly and extremely colourful after the drab conformity of Hungary, the only hazards being the huge Pacific-type locomotives, complete with cowcatchers and brass bells, that suddenly shot across the road almost without warning. The traffic police also leapt out at you without warning, banging on your windscreen with small lollipop signs, meaning either that you were travelling too close to the car in front, or that you had overtaken a tram, or that you were about to knock down a policeman waving a lollipop sign.

At Ploiesti I pulled up for petrol at a filling station literally surrounded by oil wells, where I found that petrol cost more than anywhere else on my travels. Crossing the Danube on a pontoon bridge, we finally entered Bulgaria, drab and forbidding and more communist than Russia. The only splash of colour was in the propaganda posters, which depicted smiling peasants with brawny arms shouting slogans in a strange language.

The grim aspects of the country, with its sullen, openly hostile people, made us feel quite depressed as I drove down the low-lying Black Sea coast in search of somewhere to put up our tent – as in all communist countries, it is forbidden to camp anywhere other than on an official camp-site. Rose spotted a sign with a funny looking wigwam on it, which differed from other camp-site signs but we presumed it meant the same thing. It didn't, for it represented a sort of Bulgarian Billy Butlin's, a small village of tiny wooden cabins with high-pitched roofs which resembled large dog kennels. On making enquiries we were told it was a holiday camp for the workers, but we could pitch a tent for one night.

Romanian peasants in the fields and a shoe sale in the market – the shoes were made from old car tyres

After getting organised, we spent an enjoyable evening watching our neighbours arriving, the men looking uncomfortable in cheap, ill-fitting suits and flat caps, with the women clothed in dark, loosely fitting peasant-type dresses and wearing headscarves. Everyone carried old battered suitcases, which they placed outside their designated dog kennel before going into the surrounding woods in search of dead bracken and straw with which to make a bed.

We realised how fortunate we were as they unpacked their cases and revealed sparse and pitiful belongings, specially chosen for their once-in-a-year, few days' holiday. I lit the stove and Rose put on the pressure cooker, which caused an immediate sensation as no one had seen such a strange invention. We were soon surrounded by our fellow campers, who advanced timidly, nearer and nearer, until Rose let the pressure off and subsequently vanished like a she-devil in a cloud of steam. The bystanders immediately fled in terror back into their dog kennels, though we sensed them peering at us from gloomy interiors, convinced that we were from another planet.

Our nearest neighbours eventually emerged and Rose gave them something to eat and a cup of tea. It was impossible to converse with them, as the young couple was very shy and every time I smiled at the young lady she began giggling and hiding her face in her hands. I always seemed to have a strange effect on young women.

The car, tent and camping equipment caused great interest, but eventually the people gradually drifted away once more. Later, watching the clouds turn gold and red in the setting sun, Rose and I walked along the almost tideless shoreline. It was a beautiful evening and, slowly, above the hiss of the shingle being rolled to and fro by the lazy swell, we became aware of soft, sensuous music.

The steady rhythm of guitars led us on, drawing us – like the effects of the Pied Piper – away from the beach towards a small wood, where the glow of firelight flickered and shimmered between the trees. As we approached we could see vague figures circling the fire, dancing slowly in unison, swaying delicately to the haunting music, first to the right and then round to the left, before completing a full circle. For some time we stood on the edge of the clearing, unobserved, taking in the scene as men, arm in arm, slowly executed intricate steps around the fire while the women, dressed in colourful traditional costumes, formed a larger circle around them, clapping steadily to the beat of the music.

Gradually, people became aware of our presence. We were invited into the circle of dancers and, much to my embarrassment, Rose and I linked arms with the men and slowly circled the flames to the age-old strumming of guitars that seemed to draw us back in time to an era before humanity was created. We were alone with the last flickering glow of the deep red sunset, primeval music and the soft surging of the timeless sea.

SOFIA WAS A COMPLETE CONTRAST to this peaceful Black Sea scene. Apart from the hustle and bustle of any modern city, it had the further complications of road signs in Cyrillic and trams which bore down on you from every direction. With Rose trying to decipher each street name from little plaques set high on the walls of buildings, then comparing them with the address on our crumpled letter, and me trying to miss trams and wrong-way roundabouts plus traffic lights cunningly concealed in trees, it's a wonder we found Radochev's address – but we did, and he was out.

I left a note denoting our whereabouts pinned to his door and we made our way to a campsite to the north of the city. We had not been contacted by late evening so, leaving Rose asleep, I took a stroll around the campground and joined some Swiss youngsters in a drink and a sing-song around their fire. Later, returning to the tent, I found Rose suffering from a surfeit of nervous excitement after being awakened from blissful sleep by a large, hairy face which had been thrust through the tent flap to enquire, in a deep booming voice, after 'Meester Jeem Airey?'

After recovering from her initial shock, Rose said: 'I don't know where he is – try the bog.' She then had to explain to someone who didn't understand colloquial English what 'ze bog' was, and the owner of the large hairy face vanished. I hurried to the camp toilets and saw two figures lurking in the shadows waiting to ambush anyone who emerged. One was Radochev, who was the image of all the desperadoes that I had ever seen on the silver screen – in fact, he made some of them seem positively effeminate!

This man was a real Bulgarian bandit: medium height, but very stockily

'Meester Jeem Airey?'

built with powerful broad shoulders and arms like my legs. Extremely dark skinned, with black flashing eyes, thick black oily hair and a heavy drooping moustache, he was a formidable looking man.

'Jeem Airy,' he growled and grasped me in a bear hug which produced the sound of cracking ribs, then shook me by the hand with a huge fist, which guaranteed that I would never be able to play the piano again. He talked volubly through his companion, whom he had brought along as an interpreter, but who could only translate a third of what Radochev was saying. The gist of it was that Rose and I were to meet Radochev opposite the Balkan Hotel in Sofia the following morning and he would take us to the site of the caving expedition.

The next day we ran the gamut of Sofia's one-way streets and met up with Ing. P. Radochev in the cafe opposite the hotel where, after a few drinks, I learned that 'Ing' meant 'engineer' and our new friend was called Peter. He jumped into the back of the car and directed us out of the city, then north through beautiful scenic limestone valleys bordered by imposing limestone escarpments which were very similar to those in the Yorkshire Dales.

After an hour or so we stopped for a meal at a crowded restaurant, though it was obvious there were no vacant places. Undeterred, Radochev shouted at the manager, strode across to an old chap who was sitting on his own, removed him from his seat, grabbed two other chairs and sat down. Bulgarians are not noted for their hospitality, especially towards the English, so I found this gesture rather touching.

To where the old man was consigned with his half-finished meal, I did not know; nor had I time to wonder as, with a sweep of his heavy hand, Radochev dragged the soiled tablecloth from the table, complete with all the condiments, and threw this miscellany on the floor. The manager hastily materialised at Radochev's side wearing a greasy, fixed, obsequious smile as he hastily scurried around like a frightened rabbit. Within seconds we had a new tablecloth, an instant meal and bottles of wine.

I was under the impression that if I had complained about the meal, that particular manager would never be seen again. Obviously, my new buddy was a man of considerable power and that the little badge on his lapel meant a lot. I asked him where I could obtain one – he looked at me and smiled slowly, but his eyes remained impassive.

One hundred miles from Sofia we passed through Lovec, then turned off onto some steep unsurfaced tracks up into the hills. Passing over two very flimsy wooden bridges, which rattled and swayed ominously as I drove slowly across, we arrived at our destination, the village of Krushuna. A few houses were laid out around the perimeter of a large square – the equivalent of our village green, only this was dried mud. Four large posts surmounted with loudspeakers adorned the square, where the sounds of martial music and news bulletins assailed our ears.

Standing by a jeep, the only vehicle to be seen, was a group of men who eyed us with curiosity. Someone then recognised Radochev and we were soon surrounded by the gang. With much handshaking we were introduced to their leader, Peter Tranteev. He spoke a little English and welcomed us to the expedition, then asked us to follow the jeep up a steep track that continued into the limestone hills behind the village.

Leaving Radochev in the local bar, we went up a rough track that grew steeper, V-shaped and was cut by deep, narrow gullies which became increasingly more difficult to drive the car across. On one particularly deep one the car ground to a halt, the front bumper buried in earth and the rear jammed in a similar fashion; the car was too long for the narrow gully and we were left suspended across the washed-out space below.

The Bulgarians saw our plight, left their jeep and walked back. Being well-built lads, they lifted the heavy car across the gully until my wheels obtained purchase – then, following the jeep once more, we drove to a grassy plateau where a circle of tents was pitched. I was instructed to pitch my tent some distance away from the others and we were left severely alone, as though we had the pox or were carriers of some awful capitalistic bug, until late in the evening when we were invited to join the others around the campfire and discuss plans of exploration.

The expedition had just started exploring a nearby resurgence, where a large volume of water came out of a low river cave. The following morning I was invited to help survey Vodopada, the Cave of the Waterfall, as it was later named. The Bulgarians were strictly disciplined and Peter Tranteev instructed me to share a rubber dinghy with two younger members of the team, Tomino and Georgio, who – I later discovered – were both good lads with a great sense of humour.

The Bulgarians' mode of caving dress comprised thigh-length waders worn over ordinary clothes and, apart from the occasional dry-cell lamp, their main form of lighting consisted of large paraffin pressure lamps. They were quite amazed when I stripped off and pulled on my old torn and well-patched wetsuit – it was the first time any of them had seen a neoprene suit and one chap was most concerned that I would die of exposure, so he offered me a sweater.

The cave entrance lay just behind the camp. Overgrown by small trees, it was low and wide, forcing us to crouch as we dragged the dinghies over shingle barriers until we reached the underground river. The prospect that faced us was a river that looked black, deep and cold, and the low, arched roof that stretched away into the gloom was covered in mud and devoid of even the smallest stalactite. It was obvious to me that the cave flooded to the roof in this section – frequently. I hoped it was the dry season.

Standing waist-deep in water, I held the dinghies while my new comrades climbed stiffly aboard their unstable craft with their hissing paraffin lamps illuminating the scene with a strange yellow glare. With three men precariously balanced in each dinghy, we paddled slowly upstream. The splashing paddles and hollow slap of the waves against the lower edges of the ceiling arch echoed down the semi-circular streamway ahead, and was joined by the slap of the small wake of our craft behind us.

No one spoke as the glare of the lamps picked out sharp, jagged fangs of rock that protruded from the cave walls a few inches underwater, reaching for the soft rubber skin of the dinghies like a vampire lunging for the soft white neck of a young virgin. (After all, we were very close to Transylvania, the land of vampires, and Bela Lugosi lived just up the road.)

The passage width increased to twenty feet and the water beneath the boats seemed very deep. I was glad that I was wearing a wetsuit, for a ripped dinghy would be fatal for my shipmates, who would be trying to swim in boots and waders full of water. The roof of the cave lowered until we were forced to lie full length in the dinghies. Cramped as we were, we found this manoeuvre extremely difficult, as the paraffin lamps had to be held over the side and almost in the water, making it difficult to paddle. The dinghy I was in began to drift under the low roof near the walls. I slid over the side and propelled the craft back to the centre and on to a roomy chamber, where beautiful calcite draperies glistened, high in the roof – a welcome sight.

Shouting came from behind – the other crews were having trouble in the low section, so I swam back and steered them through to join their mates, who had beached on a large calcite barrier that had grown across the passage. It blocked the river with a natural dam of deep gour pools which cascaded down from the river above. We lifted the dinghies to the top of the barrier, where the river flowed sluggishly from a low opening; however, after a few feet the roof lifted revealing large stalactites glistening with a pale phosphorescent glow above our heads, and the roomy river passage ahead was liberally decorated with white flowstone and lovely pendants. My two companions became quite excited and kept shouting to their comrades behind of the wonders that lay ahead.

As we paddled onwards I noticed a lot of flood debris sticking to stalactites high overhead, some of it quite fresh. I pointed out this and other flood signs to Georgio and asked him about the frequency of flooding and rainfall in my broken pidgin English-cum-French-cum-German, Serbo-Croat and Esperanto slang, which invariably gets results on difficult occasions. But all I received in reply was, 'Ees good, eh Jeem?' so I gave up and kept alert for any sign of the water rising or any increase in the sound of running water, but mainly made mental notes of high areas. The three dinghies sailed along several canal-like sections, illuminating the walls and flickering water in a yellow, friendly glow from the hissing paraffin lamps as we dispersed the eternal blackness that had reigned ever since the first trickle of water had found its way underground through a crack in the limestone.

After each of these canals a calcite barrier held back the river where the roof lifted and at the top of these natural dams the cave roof came within inches of the water. These bits were difficult to pass and caused great delays, as each rubber dinghy had to be partially deflated and pulled through on a line with one man at a time lying full-length inside each craft and the cave roof almost scraping his face, while I towed them to a ledge before the dinghy was pulled back by the others.

This part of the cave had quite a draught and wetsuits are not made for hanging about in. I was beginning to feel the cold and I almost envied the Bulgarians, wrapped in their thick woollen sweaters, until I realised they were all wet through and several were shivering violently. Once past the barriers, the nature of the cave changed and the river widened considerably to form a chain of small lakes, but still the roof remained ominously low and was festooned with small, ugly mud stalactites in the centre, before dipping into the black, cold water on each side.

We proceeded slowly upstream, each dinghy surrounded by a halo of vapour from our wet bodies. The scene had a surreal appearance and the vapour fogged our vision until we seemed to be floating in black space on a limitless sea. The roof lowered to within a foot of the water and the leading dinghy, with two men in it, inched its way through carefully, until one side jammed half underwater, forced down by the dipping roof. There was a muffled exclamation, the sickly rasp of rubber scraping against rock, then an almighty splash and frenzied yelling as their light was extinguished. I quickly swam to their aid and dragged the two floundering figures into a roomy section ahead, where they stood waist-deep on a submerged ledge while I retrieved the sinking dinghy and oars. Their paraffin lamp had gone to the bottom and so too would have our luckless friends, but for the proximity of the chamber.

I found a ledge above the water and we climbed up, dragging the semi-deflated dinghy with us. The shivering Bulgarians were completely demoralised by this incident; we left them with the repair kit and a couple of hand torches as the rest of us pushed on.

After a hundred feet or so the lakes finished in a low, dismal chamber. We beached the dinghies and crawled over black limestone slabs, looking for a way on. I spotted a low opening where a silent flow of water emerged from beyond. Forcing my way through the narrow slot and along a flat-out crawl, I reached another, larger lake. This gave us a problem. The only way to get the boats through was by deflating them completely, dragging them through the crawl and inflating them by lung power on the other side.

No one seemed very enthusiastic at this prospect but, once the leader said it had to be done, such was the communist discipline that the task was undertaken and we huffed and puffed in turn until once again we all set sail.

This final lake was more impressive than the others we had passed. It was approximately thirty feet wide and appeared to be over a thousand feet long. In its final stage the low, flat bedding of the roof was broken in the centre where a powerful waterfall spewed out of a jagged, four-foot-wide opening. Getting my faithful crew to manoeuvre the dinghy as close to the fall as we dared, I persuaded Tomino to hold me in balance while I reached above me and grasped a couple of good handholds, then pulled myself up.

I climbed a series of waterfalls, which brought me to a fine stream passage which zigzagged up at a steep angle to end in a small round chamber of clean, light-coloured rock. An incredibly beautiful, deep blue siphon pool was the source of the underground river that welled up silently from caverns out of reach. After the drab cave below, this small chamber with its smooth walls and the liquid jewel of a clear, deep artesian well was almost like finding a holy shrine and for some time in silent wonder I crouched at the water's edge, peering into the ever-deepening shades of blue down into the azure depths, knowing that whatever lay beyond in this mysterious world of blue shadows and turquoise water would remain unsullied by man. I reluctantly dragged myself away from this privileged glimpse into a pristine subaqueous world and followed the water as I climbed back down the passage that led to the dark, sombre cave beneath.

I plunged off the lip of the waterfall into the black lake and rejoined the others. Slowly we returned, picking up our two shivering shipwrecked mariners on the way. The repaired dinghy leaked like a sieve and could only hold one man, so to ease the situation I swam or held onto the dinghies in the lower sections, whenever possible leaving the water and traversing in the higher parts of the river passage using submerged ledges which afforded some relief from the cold. In this fashion we returned to the surface after fifteen hours' caving.

I FOUND THAT I WAS NOW ONE OF THE LADS, an honorary Bulgarian caver, as there was a sudden upheaval of tents and, much to Rose's surprise, our abode was pulled down and repitched inside the circle. She was presented with a bunch of grapes.

After a meal we all descended to the village to celebrate a successful exploration. It never ceases to amaze me how easy it is to become multilingual when one has a drop to drink – perhaps there is a secret language known only to drunks, for in no time at all I found myself conversing freely with the Bulgarians and we were soon telling each other stories and regaling caving exploits, accompanied by much waving of arms and backslapping.

We gained this remarkable ability in a very short time by a process of toasting. Each person was supplied with two glasses, one containing beer and the other

Jim's Morris estate at the expedition campsite

some form of nitroglycerine which they called brandy. Georgio shook me by the hand and solemnly toasted the Queen by knocking back the brandy followed by the beer. I replied by toasting their present dictator, then they did impressions of the pop singer Tom Jones, then I did Karl Marx and his brothers, then they did the Beatles (more pop singers) and then I did Gregory Stanovitch (not a pop singer) and then . . . things became a bit vague.

During all this merrymaking it had rained heavily and, when eventually we left the bar and staggered outside, we found the track had turned into a stream. Slithering about in the deep ruts, we struggled back to the camp. A patch of colour – muddy, wet, orange cotton – stood out in the darkness. I picked up the bedraggled material and slowly my befuddled senses cleared as I recognised my tent. Perplexed, everyone looked around at the wreckage of tents and personal belongings which were scattered across the hillside. A few yards further we reached the plateau where only hours before had been an orderly circle of tents. Now, all was desolation and utter devastation. Apart from one tent, which leaned drunkenly on one pole, all the rest had been flattened and redistributed over a wide area. Cooking utensils, clothes, stoves, tables and chairs, food and everything else was half-buried in liquid mud. Several streams flowed sluggishly through the morass and men had to scavenge for their belongings, salvaging anything of use.

We stood silently under the dripping trees while one of the Bulgarians told of the last surveying party, which had left the cave minutes in front of a wall of water and mud that gushed out of the low cave mouth, breaking down small trees and bushes before it hit the camp in a brown, four-foot-high tidal wave and flattened everything, washing tents and sleeping bags away. We began to realise what a narrow escape this had been; anyone caught in the low tunnels and streamways inside the cave would have perished instantly. It was obvious that a heavy rainstorm had taken place many miles away and that the surge of water could have been advancing towards us even while we exploring, those few hours previously. Luckily, though, Rose and I had left our sleeping bags in the car, which is where we spent a cramped night having a blazing row before falling asleep.

The following morning it was still raining as I awoke to an almighty hangover and a sulking wife, but after an hour or so the sky cleared and the sun came out. Everyone began searching for their possessions. The international components of the expedition tended to come apart with this blow – the three Poles, two Hungarians and several of the Bulgarians departed, leaving me with eight Bulgarians to explore a second cave. We spent the rest of the day scavenging for equipment and drying out sleeping bags, blankets and muddy clothes, repairing what could be repaired.

Urushka Maara (Cave of the Turk) lay two miles from the camp, along the escarpment in a cliff face at the head of a valley in a rocky defile. Unlike Vodopada, it was high and narrow and its rift-like entrance gave welcome shade from the sun as we gratefully flung off our heavy packs and rested in the chamber beyond. The cave ceiling and upper walls were covered in bats, a seething mass of grey, leathery bodies waiting for dusk. I asked one of the Bulgarians if they were vampires, but I only received a strange look, so I shut up.

As I was now in favour, I had been given a pneumatic canoe all to myself and, accompanied by three dinghies with two men in each, we set sail up the narrow river passage that lay at the bottom of a rift about a hundred feet deep. The thin, horizontal bedding of the limestone was separated by bands of shale and chert which had been eroded away, leaving razor-sharp edges of water-honed limestone jutting out within inches of the thin rubber fabric of our frail craft.

We progressed cautiously along the narrow streamway, as even the slightest nudge would be enough to send a boat down like a stone, until after a few hundred feet the walls of this underground canyon closed in. Here we had to lift the boats out of the water and climb into a wider section nearer the roof, pulling up the dinghies behind us.

By traversing along ledges we passed the narrow section and climbed down where the cave opened up to reveal a stream passage magnificently festooned with stalactites and white banks of flowstone. We relaunched the boats and paddled our way upstream, past dappled walls and glistening white calcite formations. The passage widened and came to life with the murmuring and splashing of falling water as we passed oxbows and small inlets that sprayed from above.

The paraffin lamps threw shadows into the hollows and recesses, highlighting translucent straws and curtains hanging from the walls, reflecting from the moisture on the rock and from the surface of the stream in a broken pattern of shimmering gold that played in swirling splashes of yellow that danced before us, to suddenly vanish like a will-o'-the-wisp, only to reappear somewhere else.

The sound of falling water became louder and, as we turned a bend in the passage, we encountered a waterfall spraying into a high, circular chamber from the black opening of a passage twenty feet above. The climb up was not too difficult and the stream passage continued via deep pools and canals. Aided by one of the Bulgarians, I heaved on the rope to haul up the first dinghy. It stuck on something and a chorus of shouts matched our next, mighty heave. The shouting turned to cries of anguish, reinforced by the sharp hissing of escaping air as we impaled the dinghy on several large stalactites.

Somewhat subdued, we continued hauling and pulled in a mass of shapeless yellow rubber. Our leader was most annoyed – if I had been Bulgarian, I would have been sacked on the spot, had my union card confiscated and been deported to somewhere nasty where I would have spent the rest of my days digging in a salt mine. When he had finished giving his fellow Bulgarian a bollocking, he turned to me and almost cried when I grinned at him and said, 'Kaput!' as I handed him the remains of his once beautiful dinghy.

However, the lads were very versatile. Out came the repair outfit and I spent a very boring hour watching rubber mechanics at work repairing a three-inch slit. We eventually launched into the stream above the waterfall with two dinghies and one canoe, leaving one dinghy behind in the lower passage. After only a short distance it soon became obvious that we would have to leave the boats as the passage was climbing steeply and the pools and canals, although quite deep and numerous, did not merit dragging the boats over so many obstacles.

Two men stayed with the boats while I and four Bulgarians pressed on up the tortuous passage. We were now in a narrow rift which was inclined at about fifteen degrees off vertical; the walls were about five feet apart, uneven and serrated with viciously sharp rock edges. The passage floor was uneven, with deep pools and underwater ribs of rock, and it was almost impossible to walk at any speed without stumbling over ankle-trappers and falling against the razor-like walls.

We soon suffered from gashes on our hands and I found myself following a trail of blood from the four men in front. Carrying large paraffin lamps, they were easily thrown off balance and, being unable to let go of their lights, they had sustained bad cuts from scraping the back of their hands on the walls. This, and several immersions in the deep cold pools, soon had two of the men in a bad way, shivering violently, while Georgio's right hand urgently needed attention.

We spent some time tearing up a shirt to make impromptu bandages for the worst cuts, before continuing up this merciless passage. After a while two men stopped and began arguing, before deciding to return to the dinghies – it seemed they had had enough, and left the three of us to carry on. The going became even rougher as the rift narrowed to three feet, then we began traversing high above the stream on broad ledges. Soon these petered out and we had to descend to the stream where, using the black bands of shale that trapped our feet and knocked our ankles, we forced our way up some steeply ascending cascades.

The peculiar tilt of the passage seemed more pronounced as the passage narrowed and we staggered about like drunken men as it began to twist and turn, throwing us against the jagged walls time and time again. We rounded yet another sharp bend to find that, at last, this bloody awful passage had come to an end. We stood nonplussed in a small chamber beside a deep blue siphon pool. This was even more magnificent than the one I had discovered in Vodopada, and one of the most beautiful I have ever seen – perhaps it was the black shale that enhanced the colours. The three of us stood at the edge of the pool, knee-deep in water, and peered into its tranquil depths where the dazzling light blue of the surface layers gradually gave way to varying hues ranging from azure to a dim midnight blue with graduations so vague as to be imperceptible. There was no way on except for a cave diver, who alone could plumb those crystal depths into the world beyond.

As we stood lost in reverie a dark cloud spread over the surface of the pool – it was blood, dripping heavily from the ends of the fingers of the man standing next to me. The back of his left hand had been slashed wide open, exposing white bone. It was time for more shirt surgery and, in spite of his protests, I ripped a couple of strips from his shirt and bandaged his badly damaged hand. He seemed more concerned about his shirt than his wound, so to shut him up I promised him one of mine.

We quickly returned along the rift, tripping frequently and staggering into the razor-sharp serrations. Georgio suddenly cursed and was thrown full length as his boot caught on a jagged fang of chert that jutted out below the surface of a pool; protecting his precious lamp, he had gashed the back of his uninjured hand and received a cut to his cheek, but he picked himself up and we continued down the tortuous passage.

My two companions were tired and suffering from exposure due to their inadequate clothing; both were soaked to the skin. They were now staggering more frequently, sustaining more cuts, and I noticed Georgio had begun to limp rather badly, so I stopped him to have a look at his foot. The sole of his boot had been ripped open and the uppers split; his foot was bleeding profusely. More shirt was called for to bandage the foot and tie his boot sole on. It was a paradox: here were two men, suffering from the cold, and I kept relieving them of their clothing by tearing up their shirts to patch their wounds.

At long last we reached the boats where, rather than make my way out slowly with the others, we decided that I should go on ahead and wait for them near the entrance, there being little more I could do to help by staying. I bid the team farewell and at a fair speed I paddled my one-man canoe with the current towards the cave exit. I had gone over halfway and was making good progress along the main river passage when unexpectedly the river divided. I had not noticed this junction on the way in – which way should I go?

I decided on the right-hand passage, which seemed the larger of the two. I have never had much luck at gambling and soon found myself fighting a turbulent mael-strom. I was so busy keeping the canoe upright that I failed to notice that the river had gone from beneath me and I was airborne. The words from the song 'Up, Up and Away' went through my head as I was briefly carried aloft in my yellow pneumatic canoe, sailing through a starless sky above what seemed to me to be an underground Niagara.

Fifteen feet isn't much in the scheme of great subterranean depths, but to me in my blow-up rubber yellow sausage, in the blackness of a cave in a foreign country, for several seconds I was off the planet. Fortunately, the pool below was deep and wide and, much to my astonishment, I made a three-point landing the right way up. I was so exhilarated that I burst out laughing – then the canoe turned over.

Dragging my boat behind me, I swam to a small bank of pebbles and bailed out my trusty craft before circumnavigating the walls and finding no way on. There were a couple of inches of airspace at the largest point between the water and the roof and this, apart from a four-inch-wide crack, was where the water was going.

Then the novelty of the situation hit me. Thanks to choosing the wrong route, I was now trapped in a bottle-shaped chamber, gazing up at a powerful water-fall which poured from overhanging walls, and there was no way out. I was like a bug in a bottle.

I had to climb out. Tying the end of the canoe rope on my sling, I strug-gled up the bulging wall. Four feet from the top I slipped

For several seconds I was off the planet

and again fell into the deep pool. On my second attempt I reached the lip and, thankfully, heaved on a good jug handle in the black chert – which broke and sent me flying back into my watery prison. My third attempt was a success and, after a rest, I began heaving up the semi-water-filled canoe, which was rather heavy until I managed to turn it to a vertical position, when much of the water drained out.

Cautiously, I inched the boat up by the side of the waterfall, but a few feet from the top disaster struck. The powerful jet of water hit the canoe and instantly filled it again. With the rope tight around my back I was powerless: I couldn't lift the dead weight, and I couldn't let go as I had twisted the rope around one wrist.

The impasse was suddenly solved when the weight of water split the canoe open. The rubber fabric parted, the canoe deflated and I shot backwards into the river. I wrapped the wet rubber that so recently had been my trusty canoe around the paddles and tied it in a bundle, which I dragged and towed as I swam and traversed towards the main river junction. There, having found a rock that jutted out of the black, swiftly flowing river, I parked my bundle and dolefully sat on it, hoping that the Bulgarians were still in the cave and would come to my rescue.

When one is sitting in the middle of an underground river, one soon becomes cold. Waiting, shivering amid a cloud of vapour as my wetsuit dried, I realised what it was to be alone in the world. At last I heard a noise above the roar of the water, then a glimpse of light before the dinghies hove into view.

'Ah – Meester Jeem,' said Georgio, and together with his mates he burst into fits of laughter as they illuminated this miserable wet figure sitting on the wreckage of his craft, like a hopped-up Lorelei waiting to lure passing mariners onto the rocks. After the hilarity died down, the wreckage was loaded into a dinghy and I swam till we reached the wider passage near the entrance. There, I clambered aboard one of the boats, which the Bulgarians tied together.

From somewhere someone produced a large bottle of cognac and it was passed from man to man as we gently floated out with the current, singing wild Bulgarian songs.

I parked my bundle and dolefully sat on it

Chapter 8

A Return to the Pindus

DURING MY TWO GREEK EXPEDITIONS I had found two fairly deep shafts in a loose outcrop of tottering pinnacles near the edge of the Vikos Gorge, but didn't have time to explore them. Enquiries among the villagers and shepherds revealed the existence of two other large caverns, one of which was, to quote the shepherds, 'much deeper than Provatina and so huge that clouds formed in its depths'.

A chance meeting with Jean-Yves Vallat, a French geologist who was also exploring the area, verified another large shaft on the other side of the plateau, near the village of Kapesovo, which he described as having an entrance thirty feet wide and sixty-five feet long. Stones thrown down took seven or eight seconds to hit anything, and then ricocheted from ledges for a longer time still.

Jean later sent me a sketch map of the area he had covered and the approximate position of seven other potholes. This could easily form the basis for another trip to my magic mountain – Astraka, in all its moods, seemed to be weaving a spell over me that I found hard to resist (or was it Lachesis, the measurer of life's thread still plotting my fate?).

One wet Saturday night, I bumped into Pete Livesey in the Craven Heifer in Ingleton. I told him that I was planning a return to the Pindus Mountains and asked if he fancied coming with us. After comparing notes and a bit of verbal fencing, I realised that Pete was not being entirely on the level. He kept a sly, enigmatic grin on his face as he asked me a lot of questions about my 'oles, but didn't tell me anything. It was obvious that the crafty sod was up to something.

A week later all was revealed when I received a letter, grandly headed in black print: 'The British Expedition to the Epos Chasm, Greece. Leader: Peter Livesey'. His rather roundabout letter informed me that he and Shaun O'Neil (Ken Kelly's second winch builder) had discovered Epos, which didn't sound like any of the shafts I had information about. Rather than duplicate effort, I was invited to join his expedition, which was scheduled for summer 1969. Secretly relieved to be released from all the work that would be caused by organising another trip, I accepted.

Pete was a genius at innovation and he had persuaded a group of young trainee teachers to join the expedition, promising them visits to historical sights and glorious beaches. 'Cheaper than your usual package deal,' said Pete, carefully neglecting to inform the youthful bargain hunters that they would also be expected to assist as sherpas, lugging stuff up a mountain and lowering and retrieving sweaty cavers on the end of lifelines.

The other novelty was that we were going to be filmed while we broke the world depth record. Within days the peace of my quiet cul-de-sac was shattered by the arrival of a Mini Moke with a blowing silencer. The motley crew – looking like three fugitives from an SS Panzer division but dressed in ex-RAF flying jackets and wellies – consisted of Sid Perou (ace cameraman, director and scriptwriter) and his two assistants, Norman Hinchcliffe and Neil 'Nelly' Antrim. They invaded my lounge, smoked all my cigarettes, drank all my booze and would no doubt have seduced my wife if she had been willing. When all my resources and relevant information on Greece had been drained, like warriors returning with the spoils of war they departed for the wilds of deepest Yorkshire, leaving us feeling that we had been pillaged. I went to the corner store to replenish our depleted stocks, while Rose went to bed.

A TEACHERS' TRAINING COLLEGE in Bingley seemed a most inauspicious place to launch a world depth record attempt, but the two bread delivery vans proclaiming this message with bold posters and lots of Union Jacks stood in front of the building. So, this must be the place.

The Ford vans were large, square, motorised alloy containers with venetian-roller-type pull-down doors and perspex roofs; from the back, no communication was possible with the driver. Peter reckoned this was ideal: put all the cavers in a box, lock them in where they couldn't interfere with the drivers, and let them out for a pee when we reached Yugoslavia.

However, he was outvoted and I had the idea of buying some wooden boards which slotted into the roller grooves, thus enabling us to have the backs open while travelling but preventing things and people from sliding out when we went uphill. The vans proved to be ideal expedition vehicles: the built-in slats inside became shelves and were perfect for hanging up rucksacks, and several packaging cases at the back were used for storing equipment – they also served as beds for the relief drivers. The problem of communication with the drivers was solved by banging on the outside of the van with a stick until a co-driver leaned out of a window and conversed with someone leaning out at the rear.

Once on the road we discovered that not many of us were going to reach Greece alive, as exhaust fumes were being sucked into the vans. We hastily stopped and I had a flash of inspiration. I persuaded John Russom, our resident engineering genius, to turn the silencers to one side while the rest of us had a quick feed of Heinz baked beans. The empty tins were threaded on the ends of the silencers to extend them and, thus modified, we departed for Greece.

Sid decided to film the journey out, so we rigged him with a climbing harness and hung him out of the back of the second van so that he could film the one in front. This worked okay until we reached Bulgaria. I was driving the lead van at the time, breaking our leader's orders by exceeding 60 m.p.h. In fact, I was doing 75 m.p.h., hotly pursued by a grim-faced Livesey with Sid swinging wildly from the rear when we passed two Bulgarian policemen who frantically waved their lollipop signs.

They missed me but detained Pete and his crew, which delayed us while he tried to explain, in Bulgarian, what the hell he was doing exceeding the speed limit and driving like a lunatic with a passenger dangling in space waving a cine camera at everything. The vanload only just missed being arrested and I only just missed being lynched when the much-chastised crew caught up with us, sitting by a roadside cafe supping beer and drinking a toast to lost comrades.

Proceeding at a more sedate pace, with Sid firmly locked inside the van, we arrived in Greece where, apart from a slight delay when a sharp-eyed official noticed that, according to his passport, Jim 'Oxfam' Farnworth was only four years old, things went fairly smoothly. Following Jean's map, we drove up the far side of the Vikos Gorge, until the rough mountain track finished at the small hamlet of Kapesovo at the head of a narrow deep gorge, a subsidiary of the Vikos.

One of the small stone buildings was a sort of general store and pub. Here, while discussing my hand-drawn map with the locals, I discovered that the mysterious hole described by Jean had a name: the Hole of the Married Woman. Local legend had it that many years ago one of the villagers caught his wife being unfaithful. Unlike today, when she would be rewarded with half the house and half her husband's pension plus maintenance payments, they had a better system –

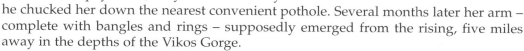

The Hole of the Married Woman

he chucked her down the nearest convenient pothole. Several months later her arm – complete with bangles and rings – supposedly emerged from the rising, five miles away in the depths of the Vikos Gorge.

While I sounded out local knowledge over several ouzos, a deal was forged with the local donkey owner and we were soon the proud drovers of a mule train which wound its way steadily up the side of the gorge towards its head, where we climbed on up to the Astraka plateau.

As Sid and company busily filmed us from various vantage points, we urged the mules up the steep rock. It never ceased to amaze me how these Greek mules kept their feet on the slippery, polished limestone of these old worn tracks. With its iron muleshoes skidding and sending up sparks, my own animal lurched along after the others, stopping every so often to admire the scenery.

As a budding muleteer I decided my beast required a bit of encouragement, so I gave it a little flick with my thin willow stick. Wow! The idiot mule jumped a foot in the air, ran into another mule which fell over, then headed straight for the edge of the gorge with me following hotfoot, closely pursued and being overtaken by the diminutive, grey-headed owner of the animal. The mule was steered away from the brink and I was given a bollocking in Greek and some Anglo-Saxon. My muleteer's wand was taken from me and I was demoted.

'Well, they hit them with bloody great whips in the pictures,' I said.

I soon found that the steady plod of the mules was quite deceiving, for every time anyone loitered to have a look at a promising cave entrance, he had to run to catch up with the mule train.

As we picked our way across the escarpment, my attention was drawn to a craggy knoll and, clambering up, I was rewarded with a panoramic view of the plateau and the black gash of an open pothole. Accompanied by John Green and John Russom, I investigated – the hole was an open rift thirty feet long and only nine feet wide, overhung by shattered rock. It was not too inviting, but I dropped a rock down the shaft. It took four seconds before it struck, then fell further. This tied in with the villagers' description: it must be the Hole of the Married Woman. We presumed that there was another shaft nearby tallying with Jean's description of a pot with an eight-second drop, and decided to explore these holes on our return.

We spent some time poking about, then suddenly realised that the mule train had vanished. We had a rough idea of the route and, aided by occasional mule droppings, we made our way across the undulating barrenness of the eastern plateau. It was a gorgeous day and we could see for miles, in one direction we could just make out the tiny dots of the mule train threading its way through a shallow rocky defile, while in the other our eyes were drawn to another tiny dot on the summit of an adjoining ridge.

John Russom, a laconic Yorkshireman, squinted for a while at the small object and said, 'I think yon shepherd is trying to attract our attention.' We looked into the distance and, sure enough, the tiny dot was jumping up and down, waving its arms.

'Should we go and see what he wants?' I asked and, after some discussion, we headed down an adjoining valley and struggled up on to the other ridge where, surprise, surprise, 'yon shepherd' turned out to be a very excited Sid Perou.

'I thought you were Greeks,' he said. 'I'm lost! Missed half me bloody film, 'aven't I!'

Some hours later we staggered into camp with a despondent Sid, who spent some time trying to persuade a couple of volunteers to take down a tent which had just been erected, repack their rucksacks, go back the way they had just come, then walk back again, empty their rucksacks and repitch their tent. He was told to f*** off, p*** off and, by the more polite, to go and stuff himself.

However, for the sake of the film, Jim and Norman volunteered. A tent and two rucksacks were loaded on their still-aching backs and they slowly made their weary way down the slope until, almost out of sight, Sid, our intrepid film director, waved them back. Sid set up his tripod and aided by Nelly, began filming the two exhausted men staggering into camp.

'This had better be good, Perou,' shouted Jim. Sid just grinned, his eye buried in the viewfinder as he waved them on. Suddenly, the whirring of the mechanism changed pitch.

'Christ!' said Sid. 'I've run out of film!'

'Keep filming,' muttered Nelly out of the side of his mouth. 'If they find out they'll kill us!'

The two actors, unaware that their efforts were in vain, approached slowly.

'Look tired,' I shouted.

'Piss off, Eyres,' was the disgruntled reply. Everyone struggled to keep a straight face as the tent was erected and our two volunteers threw themselves on the ground. Sid and Nelly hastily departed and the rest of us collapsed with laughter.

EPOS CHASM is situated in the centre of a two-mile radius area of low shale banks near the edge of the plateau, where dry streambeds radiate downwards through fine, broken, slate-like debris, like spokes in a bicycle wheel, to end at the hub. Here, a Y-shaped rift lies exposed in the underlying limestone. It is an obvious and potentially very dangerous flood trap in the event of rain, especially the torrential rain of the thunderstorms which seemed to occur frequently in this part of the Pindus Mountains.

The next day, as we began laddering the hole, Dave Cobley slipped and wrenched his back on the green slippery rock of the entrance rift, putting him out of action for twenty-four hours. Our willing band of sherpas ferried all the ladders and ropes to the broader base of the rift where the head of the first pitch dropped abruptly from a white slab of limestone, itself jammed above a black hole that created an immediate impression of space.

Carefully checking the fastenings, Pete and I paid out the ladders, which steadily clicked their way down the shaft and became heavier in the process, until five hundred feet of ladder had been

The plateau edge containing the Epos Chasm. Photo: John Russom

lowered and belayed. Pete tied the lifeline around his waist and eased himself backwards over the drop, and soon the only communication between us was the rhythmic pull of the lifeline as it passed through my hands while he steadily descended at a constant rate – the mark of a good caver. The pull of the rope eventually stopped and a faint blast of a whistle drifted up to let me know that Pete was at the bottom and had untied. I let the trainee teachers heave on the lifeline while I saved my strength in unaccustomed luxury, never having had trained sherpas before.

I lit my carbide lamp, knowing full well that it would either go out or blow up as Jim Eyre and carbide lamps don't go together – I seem to be permanently jinxed with this form of lighting. The end of the rope was passed to me and I tied on, making sure that my lifeline team contained at least one familiar caver's face. Even though our team of youthful helpers was very enthusiastic, you never know – they could have all 'heave-ho'd' together as one man, which is alright on the heave bit, but it's not alright if they let go as one man on the ho bit. I can't help being a cynic . . .

On the first few feet the ladder was pulling at an angle, making climbing awkward. My light, strangely enough, was blasting away like a blowlamp and lit up the magnificent shaft which spiralled down in the clean, white, thinly bedded limestone. This was the first time I had ever been able to see clearly with a carbide lamp and I was not in the least surprised when it suddenly began hissing and bubbling and spurting water out of the top. I turned it down until the bubbling stopped and I was left with a small yellow flame and almost negligible visibility, which is the norm for carbide lamps. This way you're guaranteed that the bubbling, splurting volcano on your helmet isn't going to explode, but you can't see either.

In semi-darkness I fumbled my way down the taught ladder until I reached a small ledge, where I detached a rung hooked onto a small rock projection and the ladder swung round a corner to hang clear. The shaft took on much grander proportions as I made faster progress down the now free-hanging ladder and after some time I heard a faint shout. Looking down, I could just make out Pete's light, glowing like a cigarette end far below. Nearing Pete, I could see we were in an impressive pothole and, reaching the flat, clean rock of the shaft bottom, I stepped off the swinging wire ladder and congratulated him on his discovery. Fiddling with my light again, I gazed upwards, spellbound at the smooth, banded walls of the pitch we had just descended. The striped effect of the narrow bands of dark brown chert, interspersed with the clean, sparkling white limestone that soared overhead, gave the impression of looking through the wrong end of a telescope, up, up, in a narrowing perspective that after 454 feet faded away into darkness.

The area we were standing on was thirty feet wide and fifty feet long and was split by two holes. The larger, twenty feet across, was the obvious continuation of the main shaft. I lobbed a rock down; it fell for over four hundred feet and I drew back from the brink. Apart from a bank of flood-deposited shale, everywhere was sparklingly clean – the place had the fresh smell and feel of a large flood culvert. Water still dripped into crystal-clear pools and, thinking of the huge drainage basin above and the ferocity of Greek thunderstorms, I was pleased to hear the clanking of an ex-army ammunition box containing the field telephone (being cheap and waterproof, cavers used ammo boxes to carry all sorts of kit) as someone carried it down the ladder towards us.

The banded walls of the Epos Chasm
Photo: John Russom

We soon had the tackle down and we laddered the smaller hole which, after 150 feet, took us to a small, rubble-strewn chamber and another pitch. This was the limit of Pete's reconnaissance of the year before when, with Shaun lifelining him on the entrance pitch, Pete had made a solo exploration. We were laddering the next pitch through a slit in the floor when, preceded by an avalanche of breccia, we were joined by two big-footed Yorkshire men: John Green and John Russom, who were bringing in some more equipment.

The next drop of seventy-five feet led into a large rift floored with broken rocks which had fallen off the shattered walls. This was a direct contrast to the rest of the chasm and three particularly large blocks teetered ominously on the edge of the main shaft, which by now we had rejoined. This was an awesome place and was very exposed. The shaft continued overhead, direct to the surface eight hundred feet above us – any falling rocks would explode like bombs on the very spot where we were standing.

There was no other route and we were forced to hang our ladders in the main shaft directly in the line of fire; a rock whistled past us as we were talking and we heard it clattering and booming into the depths. We hoped it had missed our ladders. In typical Sod's Law fashion, we seemed to have ended up with some particularly crappy ladders to use on this, the most dangerous part of the cave, but rather than wait for some decent replacements to arrive, Pete – characteristically – decided to recce what lay below.

Making sure I was safely belayed, I lined Pete as he climbed down the frail-looking 'piano wire' ladders into the huge shaft. After 125 feet he ran out of ladder at a small ledge, where he had to stop. He reported another ledge seventy feet lower down and the shaft continuing. This was great news and we felt sure that we had stumbled on another bottomless pit, though more friendly than the Provatina variety.

Returning to the surface, we found the entrance pitch difficult to climb as the ladders were hooked on small projections which held them taught and at an angle again. When I neared the top of the pitch the taught ladders swung me from side to side, until I could no longer maintain my high-wire act; then they twisted over and I was immediately underneath, swinging by my hands. This is not to be recommended with four hundred feet of space below, so we decided to rerig the pitch the following day.

That evening, everyone was in high spirits. The hole looked good and Pete's curried rice had not yet become monotonous. I later lay outside my tent, savouring the beautiful, clear, starlit sky and listening to the howling of the wild dog packs that frequent this part of the Pindus. Suddenly, my peaceful reverie was shattered as Sid started up his portable generator and began charging his film batteries. Realising that this noise was going to last all night, I cursed the vague figure that bustled to and fro while he fiddled with his bits and pieces under a makeshift shelter. However, I was not the only one watching Sid, for I noticed a very large, particularly evil-looking dog slowly creeping up on him from the surrounding darkness. My spirits lifted.

I suppose, being a mate, I should have warned him – but that would have spoiled things. There was a sudden snarl and a spine-chilling shriek as Sid dived for the nearest tent, hotly pursued by the ferocious animal. Instantly, Sid's guardian angel came to his rescue in the form of a wild Australian, Tom Wigley. Unfortunately, Tom was no knight in shining armour, for in place of armour Tom was clad in a lovely pink skin and, instead of a shield and sword, he clutched a climbing boot in each hand.

For two seconds there was an impasse as Tom glared at the dog and the dog, hardly believing its luck, eyed up Tom's naked body – especially the choice morsel that dangled so tantalisingly close. Tom raised his arm to hurl a boot and yelled a blood-curdling aboriginal war cry – the dog turned and ran with a victorious Wigley in hot pursuit. Flush with success, Tom hurled a boot which caught the dog square on the rump and then, foolish man, he hurled the other – but missed.

I am not sure if that dog could count, but as the boot went sailing past it faltered and looked over its shoulder, then stopped and turned around. I've never seen a dog smile

I've never seen a dog smile before, but this one did

before, but this one did. Tom seemed to freeze in mid-air as he met the dog's gaze which, strangely enough, focused intently on that dangly bit that comprised Tom's willy. Tom cast about wildly for a stone, one hand now clutching his vulnerable apparatus. The dog growled and bounded forward and Tom ran like pink lightning, closely followed by a sex-mad dog, and dived into the nearest tent.

The dog, robbed of its 'hot dog' supper, was driven off by a hail of missiles thrown by an appreciative audience.

The following morning, another team entered the hole to continue laddering while John Russom, Pete and I rerigged the entrance pitch. John fixed two bolts at a small ledge we had christened the Pulpit and we split the top section of the shaft by using three separate ladders, thereby avoiding the problem of them continuously snagging and pulling taught at an angle. Telephones were rigged, more tackle was lowered, and the film crew began to peer over the edge. Sid and Nelly descended to the Pulpit, festooned with lights, batteries, wires and plugs and, strangely enough, a camera (which Sid generally forgets). Somehow, they managed to assemble all this paraphernalia on the small ledge, before lighting up the shaft with a large arc lamp. Sid, tethered to a rope, was soon swinging about in space, wildly filming everything in sight, until Nelly accidentally backed into the arc lamp, which burned his bum, put out the light and finished filming as the bulb blew. Oh, that we'd had a film crew to film the film crew!

A message came through on the phone that the men below were crying out for their leader, so Livesey was despatched into the depths. I received a message that dark clouds were building up and it was starting to rain, so I telephoned the team in the chasm. Luckily, they were on their way out, somehow having run out of carbide. John 'Shep' Shepherd had descended the seventy-foot pitch where Pete stopped the day before, then carried on down another 135 foot pitch which led to another big drop. Epos was going well.

Getting the team up the entrance pitch was very time-consuming and by the time we had everyone out we were fairly tired. We struggled back to camp for the exotic delights of curried rice, where some of us began to develop the awful feeling that Pete had done a deal with a Chinese buddy of his.

Resting after this culinary feast, we watched a violent storm rage over the Ionian Sea. It increased in intensity as it headed for our mountain camp; the heavy black clouds, alive with flickering electrical discharges and loaded with menace, suddenly enveloped the mountain and the storm burst about us in all its fury. Crouched in our tents, every few seconds we saw lightning earth into the plateau with a blinding, sizzling flash of light and an instant tremendous clap of thunder with every strike. My wife Rose was terrified and was convinced that, after my experience in Provatina, I had upset the gods and old Zeus had turned it into something personal. After a mighty bang which shattered the rock a few feet from our canvas shelter, I was inclined to agree with her.

The storm soon passed and we woke to a beautiful day, but had to decide whether an underground camp should be established as we were now over one thousand feet down in Epos and it was still going deeper. What was more important was the fact that the thousand feet totally comprised ladder climbing. Given the nature of the cave and its unknown flooding potential, we decided to send a strong team down with plenty of food and equipment, then push on without an underground base – as it turned out, this was the right decision.

On the surface at the Epos Chasm with (right) Jim in the centre and (below, left to right) John Shepherd, Norman Hinchcliffe, Dave Cobley, Jim Farnworth and Jim Eyre
Far right: Underground in Epos
Photos: John Russom

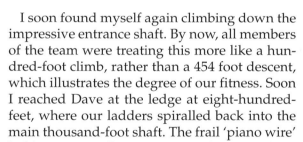

I soon found myself again climbing down the impressive entrance shaft. By now, all members of the team were treating this more like a hundred-foot climb, rather than a 454 foot descent, which illustrates the degree of our fitness. Soon I reached Dave at the ledge at eight-hundred-feet, where our ladders spiralled back into the main thousand-foot shaft. The frail 'piano wire' ladders were still in position in this most dangerous and exposed section of the hole, as in their haste to get down no one had thought to change them.

I cursed and, securely lined by Dave, literally crept over the edge of the next three-hundred-foot drop to find that three of the pencil-thin rungs had slipped, leaving two very thin wires and nothing else. The good ladders were all below.

'This ladder is lethal,' I said to Dave as I looked into the yawning drop. 'Give me a tight line.' I gingerly made my way to a narrow ledge where another set of good ladders had been separately belayed over a sixty-five-foot drop to an exposed ledge, and then a 135 foot drop which led directly to what appeared to be the base of the shaft.

It was here that I met Jim and Tony Waltham, who were surveying and seemed particularly pleased to see me as they needed someone to lifeline them down the next pitch. Before they left, they informed me that I was now standing on the most exposed ledge in the shaft and anything that fell in would inevitably hit the spot on which I stood. I thanked them for this fascinating piece of information and, as I waited for someone to relieve me, I remained on my narrow perch looking at the numerous impact marks in the rock, wondering where the next one would be. That relief someone turned out to be Shaun, who told me that it was raining, so I hastily tied on the lifeline and vacated the ledge.

Stepping off the ladder 135 feet lower down, I landed in a huge chamber with a gully in the floor. At last, I thought, the cave was changing into large horizontal passages. But no, after only a few feet the sloping gully ended above another yawning abyss. It seemed the vertical development would go on for ever.

I approached the group that was lifelining Shep back up from a vertical climb almost the height of St Paul's Cathedral, which is 355 feet. This last pitch ended, incredibly, in a small but deep lake with no apparent way on. Everyone present descended the pitch to verify these findings, while our fearless leader did a hair-raising traverse over the top of the black hole to investigate a continuation, which was also a dead end. It would have been a very dead end if Pete had misjudged his footwork.

Just as I was about to descend the pitch the news arrived that the rain was increasing in strength. At the time, the bottom seemed to be a safer place than being caught where I was in the main shaft, so I elected for a speedy climb with a quick pull up from my team-mates if anything went wrong.

I climbed past jagged flakes of rock which jutted from the shaft walls, making the descent difficult as they snagged the ladder. An ominous shaft lay below and I passed slimy, mud-covered walls; everything was wet and dripping and a slight stream of water began to fall from somewhere above me. I wondered if the hole was beginning to flood, but carried on into the black pit secure in the knowledge that, in any eventuality, the hard group of cavers above would soon have me out. Just to be sure, I checked that my lifeline was securely tied.

Soon, I could make out a black lake and the end of the ladder continuing underwater. Clinging to the ladder, I peered into every recess above the forty-foot-wide lake, but there was nothing. The way on, if indeed there was a way on, lay below the water. I felt a tug on the rope and made my way back up the pitch.

At 1,500 feet this was a disappointing end to the deepest known cave in Greece. Although not among the world's deepest caves, Epos was unusual because, of its 1,500 feet depth, 1,350 feet of it required the use of ladders. An alarming note was struck on our return when the piano wires above Tom's ledge slipped another four rungs; the thin wire had become so badly twisted that a hard jerk would have snapped it. Rather than trust the ladder, with assistance from a lifeline team most of us climbed up the cave wall.

EPOS, LIKE PROVATINA, ends in a bedding of dolomitic limestone, which tends to break down rather than form caves. We therefore wondered if the Hole of the Married Woman, which was higher up the gorge, would break through this dolomitic barrier, so several of us decided to explore it once we had reorganised ourselves, as some of our sherpas wanted to go sightseeing.

After establishing a tourist camp at Ioannina, seven of us took one of the vans and drove back around the mountain to Kapesovo, where we loaded a few ropes and ladders on our backs and trekked to the hole. The thirty-foot-long rift was overhung by shattered rock but, after a bit of work, we established a clean take-off point and rigged the shaft with five hundred feet of ladders.

I tied on the lifeline and slid over the edge, expecting loose walls and ledges filled with shale. I was pleasantly surprised as the rock belled out into a beautiful, smooth, elliptical shaft that left the ladders swinging clear in the centre. The walls of the shaft were typical of the area: striped with narrow horizontal bands of different coloured limestone and, in this cave, these were interspersed with a broader band where the strata tilted at an angle of forty degrees. It was very impressive, and the lower I climbed the more beautiful and symmetrical it became.

I caught sight of a ledge just as my progress was halted at four hundred feet while my lifeline was being extended.

'Hang on, Jim,' shouted John Russom as he tied on another rope. Clinging to the ladders, with no lifeline support for a short time, I waited patiently until I was able to continue to the small ledge, thirty feet below. The weak glimmer of my carbide lamp was not strong enough to illuminate the depths, so I heaved a rock down, which caused surprised yells from above when it landed with a deep boom 250 feet below.

After an easy climb back to the surface, we checked the equipment and found that the long rope had been left in Ioannina, leaving us short of lifelines – we would have to return to collect it. While I cursed and raged, the others under-took a quick trip down the shaft to verify my

The Hole of the Married Woman: the entrance from the surface and looking up the shaft. Photos: Tony Waltham

findings and, as we were so engaged, an ominous black cloud crept stealthily over the mountain behind us. As Norman was climbing out of the hole, all hell broke loose. The sky darkened, the temperature plummeted and the heavens opened in one of the heaviest downpours I have ever experienced in my life, and that includes tropical storms and monsoon rain.

Within minutes, water was swilling down the shaft, taking stones and gravel with it. Just two feet from us, with a tremendous bang, lightning struck the top of the shaft. Cries of alarm drifted up as four of us grabbed the line and heaved poor Norman out while the lightning struck again, splintering a large flake of rock with an ear-splitting crash and we unceremoniously dragged him away from the edge of the shaft. The clouds lowered and we were literally bombarded by lightning strikes while we crouched in a small depression, heads bowed against the almost solid sheet of rain and hail. John Russom had started to de-ladder: 'Let go!' I shouted as a streak of bluish-white light sizzled between us and missed John's left foot by inches while the metal ladders flickered like a badly functioning neon sign. John let go alright, and we hastily backed away from the shaft. 'Bloody 'ell!' said John.

This was shades of Provatina with a vengeance – there must be something in Greek mythology for, each time that I have defiled the virgin entrances to the underworld by my worldly presence, I have been attacked by old Zeus and almost microwaved. With the smell of burning in the air, the physical beating from the rain and sounds like cannon fire as lightning struck around us, we were helpless and completely demoralised in the half-light of the centre of the storm.

Sid and his sidekick Nelly were only wearing shorts and were shaking violently with the sudden drop in temperature. Sid ran to take shelter under an overhanging rock in a shallow gully; he crouched down, seconds before a wall of water obliterated him from view, to emerge moments later spitting, coughing and gasping

'Bloody 'ell!' said John

for breath, as white as a ghost while the dry gully turned into a raging torrent.

Rose began screaming as the storm intensified around us. She started to become hysterical, which is not surprising after seeing the surface team knocked over like rag dolls and remembering that her favourite husband was almost killed at Provatina. Even so, this was not like Rose, for she was fairly tough, though I realised the situation could become more serious – especially as, with every minute that passed, Sid looked more like an exposure victim.

We had a quick discussion, shouting to be heard over the cacophony, and Sid and I loaded as much gear as we could carry, then grabbed hold of Rose and set off for the van, leaving the other four to de-ladder when the storm abated.

Leaving the lads crouched together, the three of us headed into the driving rain, trying to calm Rose every time lightning bounced off the rock.

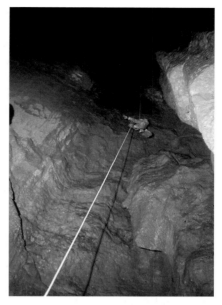

The second pitch in the Hole of the Married Woman. Photo: Tony Waltham

Soon, there was a perceptible lightening of the sky and the worst of the storm rolled over. Shortly after we reached the van, we saw the others approaching and then, driving through storm damage and over washed-out roads, we finally reached Ioannina to find a search party being launched to look for us. The streets in the town had been flooded to depths of several feet and everyone thought we must have come to a sticky end six thousand feet higher on the mountain.

WE DECIDED THAT WE SHOULD RELAX on a lovely beach next to an old-fashioned taverna, so we drove to Thessalonica – it was Jim's idea, because Jim, always broke and hungry, needed the money for the lovely beach and taverna and he had a disposable asset to sell: his blood. It seems that inside Thessalonica's hospital, patients were fading away for lack of the stuff and distraught relatives pounded the streets trying to persuade healthy and well-filled visitors to part with a few pints at £3 per pint, as it was against the prevailing religious beliefs of the locals to donate blood.

Jim had just finished explaining this when a fat lady emerged from the hospital, crying and casting about desperately. 'Ah, a customer,' said Jim and, after making a furtive approach, some money changed hands, the fat lady gave Jim a sly pinch – just to make sure he was suitable – and he was hustled away.

Patiently, we waited. Would Jim be drained of all he possessed and flushed down the drain, to emerge white and transparent like an old used-up condom, to drift for ever on the tides of the Aegean Sea? For this is what befell careless travellers in this part of the world . . .

Suddenly John gave a yell. 'There he is – well, it could be him, only thinner and paler.'

It was indeed a very pale and almost transparent Jim who staggered towards us. He was escorted to the nearest bar, where we helped to refill his valuable body with liquid bearing as much head as the stuff he had just lost.

As he downed his beer in one gulp, we stood back and waited for his face to flood with colour. It didn't. 'Quick, get some more beer down him,' I urged. After another four or five pints, Jim's lacklustre eyes began to sparkle again, his skin lost its grey pallor and the end of his nose began to glow with the faint blush of newborn vitality. This was all the proof the lads needed and several of our hard-up and more adventurous souls rushed to the hospital gate, clamouring to be drained. Alas, it was lunchtime and the market was poor. A helpful young doctor informed us of a sort of 'off-licence' near the docks, where one could sell blood day and night – a kind of transport cafe for passing vampires.

Soon, ensconced in a comfortable, green cane chair in the bar opposite, I drank several beers as I watched the blood retailers go one by one into the large wooden hut. There was a red cross painted on the roof, but it might well have been a vampire bat or a painting of Dracula. A pale ghost of Nelly came staggering out of the door marked 'empties'.

'Bloody sods – they only gave me two pounds a pint.'

He was closely followed by Tom, who looked decidedly ill, and Sid Perou, who had 'reject' stamped on his forehead. Then, surprise, surprise, Pete our superman – who could give six pints without even missing it – also emerged stamped 'reject'.

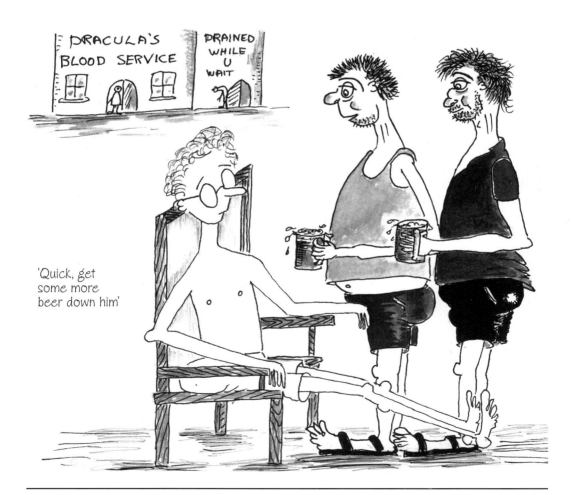

'Quick, get some more beer down him'

'Bloody sods, they said it was no good. Must be too bloody strong for them,' muttered Pete as I bought him a beer.

John Shepherd had to be physically assisted to the bar, as his was a rare blood group and they had taken an extra pint. We were all celebrating Shep's dried-out body when we realised that John Green was missing. 'Oh, he was in a bed by the door – not too good,' said Shep, when the beer reached his brain.

Poor John. When we went to collect him, he was lying on a camp bed where he had passed out cold after only giving one pint, and to add insult to injury they only paid him one pound due to all the trouble he had caused. As we took him away, a white-coated figure emerged. 'Him should see a doctor,' he said.

Leaving the Greek coast behind, we drove through the rough mountain wilderness of Macedonia before heading north. After a hard, sticky day we pulled up at a small shady clearing with a stream for washing and a village with a friendly bar nearby. It was ideal and, after a pleasant evening in the bar (which used to be Alexander the Great's local), we crashed out. It was too warm for tents, so we simply lay down in a circle under the stars. Gradually, the recumbent bodies stopped twitching and grunting and peace descended.

Much later in the night Rose woke to see a shadowy figure crawling towards her, the moonlight suddenly illuminating two staring eyes and white, glistening teeth that gripped an evil-looking knife. She sat bolt upright and screamed and screamed until, slowly, the noise and the fact that I was being roughly shaken woke me from a deep sleep. I looked at the panic-stricken face of my wife and followed her outflung arm, which indicated a figure

'He's here lads, we've caught the bugger'

running into the surrounding forest. I jumped to my feet, clad only in my briefs, and charged after him, just catching Rose's warning: 'Look out – he's got a knife.'

Knowing that there were enough of us to overpower him I charged on, until I suddenly realised that I was in a dense forest with a wild Macedonian armed with a knife and local knowledge. I stopped and listened and heard the sound of heavy breathing.

'He's here lads, we've caught the bugger,' I whispered and crept forward.

I don't know when I first decided that I was on my own; I think it was when I realised that my buddies were making less noise than an Indian scout – and when I whispered to them, I received no reply.

I stood stock still. Not a sound from the cavalry – just faint sounds in the forest ahead. My team had rolled over and gone back to sleep! I was alone in a black forest, semi-naked, barefooted, with a Macedonian version of Jack the Ripper. It didn't look good. If I turned, I would get a knife in my back, so I had to bluff him.

I saw a vague movement to my right, so I shouted something at the top of my voice and ran towards him, making as much noise as I could. Thankfully, he ran off. I woke the camp when I returned and thanked my heroic buddies for their support. Most of them hadn't a clue what had gone on, and the others were too fuddled with drink to care.

We took toll. John Shepherd's watch had been removed from his wrist and his wallet taken from his trousers, which were rolled up under his head. Jim had lost all his money, another had lost his but, fortunately, still had some in a money belt. John Russom, who was staying on in Yugoslavia for a lengthy period and was carrying a lot of money, dived head first into his sleeping bag and found he had been missed. In daylight we searched the area and found Shep's wallet, complete with driving licence and insurance, but no money.

We made a report to the local police, which was very time-consuming but worthwhile, because the theft was considered a slur on the village and the thief was eventually caught. Eighteen months later, John Shepherd received a parcel from Yugoslavia containing his watch.

Chapter 9

Iran

IRAN, NEVER AN EASY COUNTRY TO EXPLORE, suddenly had all restrictions to access eased in 1971 when the Shah decided, with remarkable insight, to celebrate the occasion of the age: the 2,500th anniversary of the Persian Empire. Consequently, while all the world's crowned heads and political leaders attended the flamboyant celebrations, some cavers took advantage of the situation and investigated the ancient country's cave potential.

John Middleton, a very competent caver, had already travelled extensively in the Middle East. He had explored caves in Lebanon, taken part in several French expeditions to southern Turkey, and in the summer of 1971 he became the driving force behind an expedition to the Zagros Mountains in Iran.

My old caving friend Reg Howard was loaning the expedition two Land Rovers and I, ever the opportunist, became a prospective member. Unfortunately, there was a disagreement over who should have ultimate control of the vehicles and Reg and his wife Margaret pulled out of the trip. Being a mate, I felt obliged to stick with them and take part in their own trip to Iran, leaving just before John's expedition. As a result, I missed the opportunity of exploring the deepest and most arduous cave in the Middle East, the 740 metre deep Ghar Parau.

However, such is fate and six months later, while John was organising a team of hard cavers, I was on my way with Reg, sharing the inside of a long-wheelbased Land Rover with three other cavers, three women and three children. Actually, Reg and Margaret's kids could not really be classed as children – aged between seven and twelve, they were hard cases and didn't need a babysitter – more a jailer!

Travelling overland with a heavily laden trailer behind us, we made an uneventful journey to Turkey and the Bosporus, that magical boundary between East and West which is dominated by the minarets and domes of the ancient city of Istanbul as it straddles the Golden Horn and two different worlds. Istanbul is truly a magical city and in the early seventies our senses were overwhelmed by the exotic smells, noise and whirling cornucopia of colour that enveloped us. We felt that we were truly in a foreign land.

My thoughts, which were drifting idly around the old Sultans and their thousand and one nights, were rudely interrupted by Rose, who grabbed my arm roughly.

'Bugger off,' she shouted.

'Why?' I asked.

'Not you – him!' she said angrily, indicating a brown-faced, skinny-looking gent neatly attired in an old de-mob suit who had materialised by her side.

'Don't you like him?' I asked.

'No! I've just been tapped up – he's just given me a touch!'

'Hmm – lucky you,' I said, not quite understanding why my wife should become so excited, at the same time eyeing our dark stranger with apprehension as he sidled very skilfully around to my quarter.

'Ah,' he said, rolling his bloodshot eyes. I recoiled as his Eastern halitosis hit me at the same time as his knobbly fingers stroked my shoulder. 'I make ze English love to your wife for only thirty pounds.'

'Eh,' I muttered, pausing in mid stride.

'Yes – I am very good stud,' said he.

'Well go and **** yourself!' said I, spinning him round on his heels. Mr Anonymous, sensing a 'no sale', rapidly sidled off with his metaphorical tail tucked between his legs.

'Cheeky sod,' said Rose.

Pushing inland we were soon in the wilds of northern Turkey and, once Ankara was left behind, we became aware of a sense of isolation. The distances between petrol filling stations grew greater and the people became distinctively more unfriendly. The roads started to deteriorate as we approached north-eastern Turkey, an area which was then under martial law. It was quite usual for women to lift their veils to spit at us as we passed, and for gangs of shaven-headed youths to bombard us with rocks. We soon became fed-up with this treatment, especially when one of the side windows was broken and young Timothy Howard was hit by a stone.

At the first opportunity we loaded up the vehicle with some good-sized stones and, when we were next attacked, we retaliated. This was considered most unfair and our assailants ran off until they were out of range, where they shook their fists and cursed us.

In this hostile region we soon discovered that to stop for a minor traffic accident was to stop for a beating and I had a lucky escape when, on a very bad stretch of dirt road, I clipped a Turkish minibus. Both vehicles stopped and as I walked back towards the other vehicle, nine Turks jumped out and picked up large stones. I had no choice but to keep walking towards them with my hand outstretched in greeting. I approached the biggest and cautiously shook his free hand, then inspected the very slight, very small scratch in the side of the bus. I spat on my thumb, rubbed over the scratch, polished it off and made a joke of it, then beckoned them over to inspect our broken wing mirror. They looked in amazement at young Timothy, who handed them a packet of English cigarettes, and dropped their stones as I shook them all by the hand before they departed, still muttering among themselves.

Beware of Turks

We had been told not to camp in the open as there was a very real risk of losing our possessions or being shot, so we drove until we found a military barracks. The army was most helpful and we were allowed to camp inside the compound where we were invited to use the toilet facilities, which was great for us but a bit dodgy for the women. Every time the lasses went to the loo or for a wash or shower, they had to go *en masse* to block peering eyes, as soldiers climbed up to stare through windows or under or over doors to receive a glimpse of female flesh.

Peter Lockery took a shower when the ladies had finished, but left somewhat hurriedly followed by a burly corporal, who had a smile on his face. 'That bugger stroked my arse,' said Peter, visibly shocked.

Beware of Turks: no one was safe, as we found out later, when one even tapped me up. Mind you, he was quite myopic.

It was not always possible to reach a military post and, after one day's particularly hard driving over mountain passes on slimy roads made of clay that were slippery after heavy rain, we had made little progress. The day turned into a particularly foul night – we were all tired, and Reg and I were discussing what to do when a heavy, articulated lorry came swinging round the bend ahead. The driver braked and the lorry suddenly veered sideways, heading straight towards us, out of control. Peering through the rain-lashed windscreen at the approaching vehicle, I jammed the wheel over and touched the brakes – and we too were out of control. The Land Rover turned sideways and the trailer wheels lurched over the edge of the mountainside.

More by good luck than anything else, I just prevented the Land Rover's wheels from doing the same thing as the lorry missed us by inches and careened onwards for several yards, before toppling sideways into a large flood ditch. My passengers saw the driver emerge from his cab, white-faced and shaken, before the rain obliterated him.

Our own vehicle continued its sideways slide down the mountain pass, until I managed to bring it to a halt with the trailer still hanging over the edge of a steep drop. We jumped out and found it extremely difficult to stand on the greasy clay surface as we struggled to pull the trailer back on to the road. We succeeded, then resumed our journey down the steeply descending mountain pass at a snail's pace in four-wheel drive. We were shattered and, as soon as we cleared the mountains, we pulled off the road, erected the tents and collapsed into a deep sleep.

The next morning, opening one eye, I basked in the orange glow of sunlight filtering through the tent walls, and for several minutes I lay in a pleasant, half-awake doze. Slowly, I became aware of strange, soft voices intruding on my consciousness. Curious, I leaned forward and unzipped the tent, to be greeted by a throng of people standing patiently by, holding a body on a crude bier. It was not a sight many campers have been greeted with before breakfast! I looked at them in astonishment and they looked

It was not a sight many campers have been greeted with before breakfast!

at my front guy rope, which straddled the hole I had fallen in while putting up the tent. I suddenly realised it was a grave waiting to receive its occupant.

I don't remember saying anything to them (well, what could I say: 'Good morning, nice day for a burial'?). I hastily woke Rose with: 'We're in the middle of a funeral – get up,' then bundled our gear out and dismantled the tent before waking the others. We retreated from the graveyard, which only comprised a few mounds in the middle of nowhere.

We swiftly departed from the newly departed and the multitude of mourners and pulled up, again in the middle of nowhere, to have our breakfast. We were immediately joined by a solitary youth, who seemed to materialise out of thin air. We gave him some food and he left with a huge smile on his face, for he was so sharp that he stole more from us in ten minutes than the whole funeral party could have accomplished in an hour.

Early in the evening we came across an army post, which was becoming a rarer sight, so Reg pulled over and we were invited to bring our vehicle into the gated compound. A young French couple came over to join us and, in halting English, explained how they had been attacked in the night, had their tent and car set on fire and most of their belongings stolen. They had escaped with their money and the clothes they were wearing, to be picked up by a lorry driver who had brought them to the army post two days previously. The officer in charge had been very good and had arranged transport to take them to Ankara and, as we were talking, they were beckoned towards an army lorry. We wished them better luck as they left.

After a clean-up and a meal, Eric Glen discovered a sort of canteen that served beer and possessed a table-tennis table, so we spent a pleasant evening watching Sue Green (our Canadian nurse) and Peter playing table tennis with the soldiers. Sue, being a good-looking lass, soon had the rest of the camp queuing up to play against her, and she discovered that the only way to have a rest was to bring out her guitar and sing some folk songs.

This was not a good move as, unfortunately for Sue, it created an even greater interest. When we turned in for the night, poor Sue was still strumming away like a latter-day Scheherazade, for she was now convinced that as soon as her guitar was laid down, so would she be. 'Don't leave me alone with these lecherous devils, Jim,' was the last sound I heard before I crept into the arms of Morpheus.

WHENEVER I AM NAVIGATING on a long journey, I have an overwhelming urge to try shortcuts and, although I can never recall one being really successful, like an addict I am compelled to repeat disaster after disaster. It took an hour to convince Reg of my foolproof route which avoided the long detour to Tokat – and it took the adopted route only thirty minutes to convince us that we should have stayed on the main road, as thin brown lines on Turkish maps don't necessarily mean there *is* a road. In fact, they don't necessarily mean there is a donkey track.

At two in the morning, almost out of fuel and completely out of patience, Reg pulled off the rutted track into which my route had degenerated and drove across several stubble fields before risking a camp. In the middle of a wilderness at 2.30 a.m. we began erecting our tents and slowly became aware that we were being watched, with interest, by about thirty Turkish men, women and children who studied our every movement. The men, grizzled and weather-beaten, were all armed.

There is, somewhere in mythology, an account where some character scatters a slain dragon's teeth on the earth and they immediately grow into armed soldiers. I'll bet the bloke who wrote that was a Turk, for here people really do grow out of the ground. Why am I so attractive to old grizzly men? Why do they never approach Reg or any of the other blokes?

I asked myself that question as I was approached by the most grizzly of the grizzlies who, detaching himself from the rest, walked towards me, only stopping when the end of his gun barrel was an inch from my nose.

'Er, hello,' I said in my best Turkish accent. 'What can I do for you?'

It was obvious. He slowly looked me up and down and began feeling my trouser leg – he wanted either sex or my trousers. I told him I was homophobic, so he went for the trousers. I was quite attached to my

He wanted either sex or my trousers

trousers but, after looking at his knobbly finger, which was caressing a hair trigger, I decided he could have them. However, anyone who has read this far will have realised that in moments of crisis I always have a solution. I conveyed to the grizzled trouser-bagger that I had a very good pair of trousers on the top of the Land Rover, and he could have them in the morning.

After I levered his grasping left hand off my Marks & Spencer's nylon and cotton, he retreated into the shadows along with his camp followers. 'Phew, that was a near thing,' I remarked, whereupon the old bastard returned clutching a hissing tilley lamp, an armful of blankets and his ancient rifle. Without even a goodnight, he lay the blankets on the ground, wrapped himself in them and, with rifle barrel and one eye pointing in my direction, shut the other and went to sleep.

Tired as we were, there was little sleep in the camp that night, given our armed guard outside. We had left Margaret, Sue and the kids to sleep in the Land Rover, while the rest of us piled into two tents, ready for a quick getaway. At first light I was awakened from a deep sleep by Rose, who whispered that everyone else was ready to move. I rolled up my sleeping bag as Reg whispered from the next tent: 'Ready?'

'Yes,' I answered.

'Right. Go!' shouted Reg, and unzipped his tent and charged out, clutching his sleeping bag, right into an audience of surrounding Turks – who obviously get up much earlier than Brits!

It was like a scene from a slapstick comedy: we milled around, some shaking hands with the Turks and offering them cigarettes while others pulled the tents down and flung them onto the vehicle. My brain was still fuddled from lack of sleep as I grabbed my trouser-bagging friend, shook his rifle-free hand vigorously, then led him slowly towards the Land Rover where I pointed at the roof rack. Climbing up and opening a suitcase, I took out a pair of trousers and waved them at him.

'Go!' I shouted. Reg started the engine and did a Grand Prix start. We shot off in a cloud of dust with rear doors flying open, the tents ballooning behind and me clinging grimly onto the roof rack, waiting for flying bullets, while the Turks stood frozen to the ground in total amazement.

I heard one say to his mate, 'By gum, they're funny buggers these foreigners.'

LEAVING THE WILDERNESS OF TURKEY behind, we passed into Iran after running a gauntlet of red tape, checking visas and interminable waiting. The Persians were a direct contrast to the Turks and a change in the road surface was immediately apparent as we passed through a massive gateway, following the old lava fields that once flowed from nearby Mount Ararat towards the huge limestone cliffs of Maku. These dwarfed the gold-painted statue of the Shah and the houses of the small town, which huddled under the brooding, overhanging walls. We felt that we were in a much more civilised society and it wasn't long before we learned that the Iranians are one of the most friendly and hospitable races in the world. After an hour or so we pulled off the highway and drove a few miles along a dirt track for our ritual of afternoon tea.

As we were getting organised, along came an old peasant with a camel and six mangy cows. From his pack he took out a shabby sheepskin and sat on it while he arranged pieces of animal dung and lit them. From a piece of stiff wire stuck into the ground, he hung a small, blue enamel kettle over the smoking fire and, within minutes, had

produced four chipped, blue enamel cups and invited us to sit down and join him in a tea party. He even produced sugar lumps.

Our genial host never stopped talking and smiling, and the women thought this was wonderful as he even shared his sheepskin with them to sit on. Unfortunately, the tea party came to a swift conclusion when the ladies, who all wore natty little shorts, discovered that they were being infested by lice,
fleas and the other exotic creatures that resided in the sheepskin but fancied a change of address – and, as everyone knows, there is nothing so succulent as a young lady's inner thigh.

Rose at one of our tea parties

There is nothing so succulent as a young lady's inner thigh

As they shot to their feet shrieking, the old boy thought it was a huge joke, especially when Sue had to take her shorts off to shake them out.

Good roads with light traffic and reasonable eating houses took us south past the shoreline of Lake Urmia, a salt lake over 160 kilometres long that smelled of dilute sewage. Still in the Kurdish province of Azerbaijan, we pulled up in the small military town of Mahabad and, within seconds of stopping, we were accosted by a short, chubby, excitable Iranian student named Ali, who spoke fairly good English.

While we stood talking to Ali, an Iranian army officer approached and invited us all to his club for a meal. Iran was becoming better. Soon, we were sitting at tables on a beautiful lawn under strings of coloured lights, being served a fine meal and beer by waiters of impeccable style and manners, resplendent in evening dress. It was all rather embarrassing; all around us were beautiful women with their escorts, army officers in impressive smart uniforms and sparkling with medals – and here we were, dressed like tramps. Many of the Iranians spoke English and were interested, though slightly puzzled, in what we were doing. They were curious as to what was in these caves that merited the long journey out from England.

We were further embarrassed when our host refused to let us pay for our meal and explained that in Iran it is the custom to welcome travellers and offer them refreshments. We thanked him and left. Somehow, when we returned to the Land Rover we found that Ali had become a member of our expedition, as he 'knew where there was a cave'.

The next day, following Ali's instructions, we drove for several hours across rough, sun-baked terrain before reaching a low, rocky outcrop which contained a black opening. The rock was sandstone and the opening was the entrance to a tomb – so much for our new cave guide. Reg cursed Ali, for our trailer had almost disintegrated during the journey and the hard ruts had broken several springs. Slowly, we drove across country to the nearest town – Miandoab – where Ali persuaded the local blacksmith to repair the trailer springs while we went for a much-needed drink in a nearby bar.

Poor Ali, he was very upset over his mistaken interpretation of the word 'cave' and insisted on buying us all drinks. Suddenly he brightened, and I thought it was the beer, but no.

'Ah, Meester Jeem, I know of another cave,' he said.

'Get lost,' I answered.

'No, Meester Jeem, you must listen. It is in the village of my uncle,' and once again Ali unfolded a tale of bottomless holes. Against my better judgement, I at last agreed with the others that we should give Ali one more chance. The trailer repairs would take some time and Ali's uncle lived 'one hour away', so, again following Ali's instructions, we drove south for several kilometres before turning off the road and heading across country towards some low-lying foothills in the west.

After two hours' hard driving up dried-out riverbeds and across parched semi-desert, we reached a small village of square, mud-walled houses and a scruffy old camel tethered to a discarded car wheel. All the occupants and their livestock turned out to greet us in open-mouthed amazement, which soon turned to beaming smiles of recognition when they noticed Ali. The contrast between Ali in his suit and his fellow countrymen in their traditional costumes of turbans and colourful robes was most marked, and we had the feeling that we had driven back a thousand years in time as Ali's uncle appeared and invited us all into his primitive dwelling.

Sitting cross-legged on Persian carpets in the cool interior of the adobe house, we were fed melon, chapattis, meat and rice, which were washed down with innumerable cups of tea while neighbours peered at us and scrawny chickens walked across our floor-level 'table'. Our meal took a considerable time while, through Ali, we conversed with his uncle. When the meal was finished we were led outside into the blinding glare of sunlight, where I almost received a bite from his evil-smelling camel as I followed the others up the bleak hillside behind the village.

In Ali's uncle's village

Ali's uncle pointed proudly to the jagged entrance of a small pothole. It gave off a strange odour. I sincerely hoped that this wasn't the cave we had come to explore, but we cast about for some tackle and came to realise we had left it all in the trailer in Miandoab.

Eventually, Reg found an old piece of half-weight nylon which was slightly older than Eric, our over-imaginative Scot who was overpowered, tied on and lowered down the nine-metre drop.

'Och, it stinks,' exclaimed Eric as he vanished from view down the dark overhang. A few minutes of silence was suddenly broken by a mighty yell: 'Get me oot, get me oot!' Aided by a couple of the villagers, we heaved up our very white-faced Scotsman.

'There's bloody bodies in there,' he gasped. 'Ah'm no going doon there again!' It seemed the cave floor consisted of half a metre of stagnant water and soft mud that bubbled when Eric sank in it, giving off methane gas. Numerous bones littered the chamber and a black opening led on, but when Eric came face to face with a human skull, that was that! Ali informed his uncle of Eric's discovery, and he nodded sagely as he explained that two government tax inspectors had been disposed of in this very hole.

We didn't push the exploration, but hoped that this ancient custom might one day reach England.

As we prepared to depart, Ali and his uncle became involved in a very animated discussion, while the rest of us waited in the Land Rover. At last Ali walked across and approached Reg, because he knew I wouldn't believe him.

'Meester Reg, Meester Reg, my uncle know where there is very big cave.' Reg peered at him suspiciously through his gimlet eyes.

'How far?'

Ali came up with the stock answer: 'Only one hour,' and waved his hand vaguely towards Baghdad.

Much against our better judgement we took Ali's uncle on board, together with his unique brand of body odour which he shared with his camel. Once again we headed west into the great unknown. No one had written travel books about this part of the world, because no one had been there, and with Ali's uncle grasping me by the shoulder and breathing 'essence of Mesopotamian minger' all over me, I would translate to

Reg, 'Left hand down a bit,' while he grimly clutched the steering wheel as we balanced on the edges of gorges or screwed our way up steep inclines of moving sand.

This cross-country driving had us all enthralled and, dodging round rocks, deep gullies and various other obstacles, we zigzagged across the bleak terrain. We followed a barely discernible trail which, at times, caused the vehicle to bog down in soft sand. Several compulsory stops were made while we all jumped out and dug like fury around the buried wheels, patiently watched by a group of sinister-looking vultures who gazed upon us with benevolence – a sort of meals on wheels.

Slowly climbing up from the plain, we experienced several uneasy moments as we began traversing along a rocky escarpment and the vehicle teetered dangerously on two wheels, almost turning over. Reg had just about had enough.

'What about this one-hour drive?' he grunted. 'We've been on the go over two hours now!'

'Ah, Meester Reg, perhaps my uncle think you go faster as crow fly? Soon he say we see cave.'

I had a suspicion that it was Ali and his uncle's chance in a lifetime to visit distant relatives they hadn't seen for years, and as dusk began to fall I had the feeling that we were all on a magic Persian carpet with Ali Baba.

Reg eventually coaxed the struggling vehicle up a steep incline into a narrow, dry valley that led up into some low-lying limestone hills. Rounding a bend, we could see the entrance to a large cave under an overhanging cliff. With a grunt of relief, Reg pulled up and slumped across the steering wheel while the rest of us began unloading and pitching the tents.

'Meester Jeem, Meester Jeem!' Ali's excited cry drew our attention to a large group of fierce Kurds. All wore distinctive semi-turban cloth headgear and all carried rifles and bandoleers, and they didn't look too friendly as they approached. We had been travelling west for nearly three hours and, by my reckoning, this put us uncomfortably close to, if not over, the Iraq border in an autonomous Kurdish region.

We stopped what we were doing as Ali and his uncle were beckoned over – we were immediately surrounded by the armed men and a heated discussion took place. After a long-winded and loud discourse, with voices often raised in anger, Ali came rushing back to us, his face yellow-grey with fear.

'We must go,' he said, and leapt into the Land Rover. 'Quick, Meester Jeem, Meester Reg – we go!' Between us we managed to calm him down; it seemed, from Ali's translation of events, that we had unwittingly driven into the border area between Iran and Iraq and stumbled upon a guerrilla hideout. Ali was trembling, 'They ask me to get your guns,' he said.

'Well, we haven't got any,' answered Reg.

'Ah,' said Ali, his face momentarily lighting up in a crafty grin, 'I tell them you have many rifles and Colts.'

'Bloody hell, you silly sod,' I exclaimed. 'What did you do that for?'

'Well,' said Ali, shamefaced, 'I thought that would make them afraid to attack.'

'Oh yes, armed Kurds afraid to attack three women, three kids and four blokes.' Ali had seen too many cowboy films.

The group of tribesmen had grown larger as we were talking, so Reg and I walked across and started shaking hands with the leaders. We brought out some cigarettes and started making small talk, with much waving of hands. The bloke with the blackest beard said something to Ali's uncle, who said something to Ali, who in turn translated to us.

'Meester Jeem, you must all go to the village in one hour.' Ali followed this announcement with a sharp tug at my shirt and a whispered, 'Meester Jeem, don't go – you will never return!' Ali's fear quickly communicated itself to us when we noticed that Ali's uncle had vanished. What to do? It was an insult to refuse hospitality and if they were going to attack us we could only offer token resistance, so we compromised and told Ali to tell the Kurds that the women and children were very tired and asked to be excused, but that three of us would go. There was some discussion among our wild-looking hosts, before they agreed and departed. Almost immediately, Ali began dismantling a tent.

'Quick, we go,' he shouted, and cheered us up further by pronouncing that we would have our throats cut in the village. He was a great bloke to have around in a crisis. We decided to leave Reg, who was capable of handling anything, in charge of the women, kids and the excitable Ali, while Eric, Peter and I attended the 'terrorist's tea party'. If we were not back by 11 p.m. Reg would break camp and pull out. If, on the other hand, the camp was attacked, Reg was to flash his headlights and sound his horn. All these melodramatic arrangements read like something out of a *Boy's Own* magazine and were totally useless, but with Eric finding skeletons and the general instability of the area, it made us feel better.

I gathered my two trusty sacrificial lambs about me and we advanced into the darkness. Which way? We hadn't even seen a village. 'It's probably near the cave,' I reasoned, so we plodded off to meet our fate. Suddenly, out of the blackness I heard a sound like a slow puncture; there was a pronounced 'Hiss!' and a figure materialised beside me. Something hard pressed against my side – I hoped it was his wallet. Our silent guide led us along a barely discernible track into a deep gorge, where several flat-roofed mud houses clung tenaciously to the sheer walls.

We traversed along the side of the gorge until the only route lay across the top of the houses. As we found ourselves creeping along the rooftops in almost total darkness, Eric – with the Massacre of Glencoe no doubt still fresh in his mind – said: 'It looks a likely place for an ambush,' before promptly disappearing down an open chimney, stopping only when his chin and outspread arms hit the roof.

We heard a startled commotion from below, as they don't believe in Father Christmas in these parts, and a group of figures emerged clutching guns. No doubt they would have shot us but for the presence of our guide, who murmured something in Kurdish – it sounded like: 'Fookin Scotsmen that cannae see.'

After dragging Eric out of the chimney's embrace, we were escorted to the largest dwelling in the village. By the flickering light that came from within, I could see a kind of porch with two wooden cages containing large birds of prey, probably falcons, and a curtained doorway. A rifle playfully nudged me in the ribs and my guide pointed at my feet, so we took off our boots and placed them with the more interesting types of footwear that were lined up on the floor. The curtain was drawn back and we were ushered into a scene that could have come straight from the *Rubáiyát of Omar Khayyám*.

The room was about six metres square. Hanging from the whitewashed walls were several colourful handwoven fabrics, on the floor was spread a beautiful Persian carpet, and sitting cross-legged around the perimeter were about twenty fierce-looking

Eric promptly disappeared down an open chimney

tribesmen in splendid head-dresses, beads and baggy trousers. By the light of a large, ornate, gleaming brass oil lamp in the centre of the floor, bandoleers, knife handles, polished gun butts and gold teeth glistened. In a corner of the room hung another oil lamp and, underneath, dominating the scene, was a magnificent brass tea urn and a small boy who waited patiently.

The room fell silent as the village headman gestured that we join him. Gingerly, we sat down on golden cushions in the places of honour by his side – at the same time noting with apprehension the three men dressed in Western clothing who entered the room and sat nearby. Several young boys appeared and began laying out our meals, while the tea lad scurried round with drinks proffered in small, delicate china cups. Anywhere else, it would have been a fascinating experience, but here, in the wilds between Iran and Iraq, dining in a war zone with persecuted Kurds added a certain frisson to the proceedings.

The first part of the meal consisted of thin, sour, milk-type yoghurt with thick, sour, milk-type yoghurt and rubbery cheese-type yoghurt. This was served with and on chapattis, which doubled as bread, tablecloths, car-wash leathers and nose wipers. The main course was lamb, complete with brains and eyeballs, which I ate. I slid most of the other stuff to Peter

Eric and Peter (end wall, far right) at the tea party

who, being a student, would eat anything. There were no alcoholic beverages and, as I was telling a joke to a one-eyed Kurd, I realised I could have told it much better if I had been drinking something stronger than tea. In fact, I had the feeling that he hadn't got the point at all – he just looked at me with his one eye glittering evilly as he toyed with his knife blade with the end of a horny thumb.

The atmosphere in the room was strained and Eric whispered in my ear that we would never be allowed out of the village. Looking round, I had a similar feeling as subdued conversations and gestures in our direction conveyed that we were the sole topic of conversation. The soft murmur of voices ceased and the room became ominously silent.

'Do you like the Vietcong?' asked a cultured voice. I looked up from my meal at a sallow-skinned man in a lounge suit, who stared intently at me with piercing eyes.

'Dunno,' I answered. 'Never met any,' and continued diving into the sheep's eyeballs with a calmness that belied the fear I felt. For a second or two the silence in the room was oppressive, then someone gave a short laugh and my answer was translated to the others by my questioner. The tension and the prickly sensation at the back of my neck were dispelled. While drinking endless cups of tea we were deluged with questions. What were we doing here? Were we working with the army? What were our occupations? How did we find this place?

Gradually, the questions veered round to Middle Eastern politics and Peter, being a student, jumped in with both feet and began talking about plane hijacks and Baghdad, almost in one breath. Eric turned several shades of green and I sensed open hostility creeping into the faces of the attentive English-speaking questioners. I interrupted Peter's dialogue and told him to shut up as I started fielding the questions that his monologue had raised in the Kurds' minds. Two students and a builder in a restricted area were difficult to explain away, but a painter and decorator?

Question: 'What is a painter and decorator?' How do you explain the skills of paper-hanging to someone who lives in a mud hut?

Before Peter could mention that Hitler had been a painter and decorator, I managed to convey to my interested audience that in this country I would probably be white-

'Do you like the Vietcong?'

washing mud huts. While this answer was being translated and digested, I realised that a mud hut whitewasher would probably earn about one pound a year, so the next question was not unexpected.

'How can you afford to travel from England when you only whitewash mud huts?'

'The huts belong to very rich people,' I answered, not believing the conversation I was having.

'You were sent by the army,' shouted a man who up till then had been quiet. Eric thought this was a good time to go as it was getting late.

'One of us had better go back to Reg. I'll volunteer,' he said.

'My friend is not feeling very well,' I said, not feeling very well myself. 'Could he be excused?' There was some fairly excitable conversation and much arm waving, before two evil characters were summoned from the doorway. One had a scarred face and one had an ominous bulge in his trousers. They beckoned to a very reluctant Eric and he was taken away as the interrogation continued.

It was a long, uphill struggle, but Peter and I eventually managed to convey to the Kurds that we sympathised with their plight and that we were just crazy English cavers who wished to explore their cave. When this fact was at last accepted, we were told that the villagers went into the cave to capture bats, which they ate. Perhaps we misunderstood – there couldn't be much food on a bat and I mused on the haute cuisine of 'bat and chips' and 'bat-in-the-hole' or 'battered bat' as the evening ended on a friendly note.

After shaking hands all around, Peter and I were escorted through the pitch dark back to our camp. In spite of everything, we felt uneasy and the feeling was intensified when I entered my tent and found Rose in a state of fear. Indeed, everyone had been thrown into a panic by Eric's solemn pronouncement that Peter and I would never be seen alive again, while Ali, of course, was convinced that everyone would be slaughtered in the night. We held a council of war in Reg's tent and realised there was little we could do if the guerrillas decided to take the Land Rover and (if they believed Ali) our guns. As Eric had discovered, bodies were soon disposed of in these parts – no one knew where we were and we wouldn't be missed for a long time. With these happy thoughts zooming around in my head, I tried to get some sleep, but could only lie there.

I was brought to full alertness by a rustling noise outside the tent; a dark figure was silhouetted against the flap opening.

'Meester Jeem, Meester Jeem.' It was Ali, and he will never know how close he came to being assaulted. 'They are coming,' he said in a tremulous voice, high-pitched with fear.

I leapt out of my sleeping bag and stood shivering in the cold night air outside. I peered into the surrounding darkness for thirty minutes, before giving up and returning to my sleeping bag. Rose then arrived from the other tent, where all the women and kids were sleeping together, and first she, then Ali, would awaken me as things went bump in the night. With this treatment, I was soon reduced to a nervous wreck and, bowels rumbling, I had to make a sudden dash outside.

Clutching my pink toilet roll, I rushed up the barren hillside behind the camp and there, in the gloom, I was suddenly confronted by a menacing figure crouching ahead of me. I could see a hand raised . . .

'Give me some paper, I think the bastards have poisoned us!' It was Eric, who had also experienced an attack of the trots, and the two of us squatted side by side in a howling gale, festooning the hillside with streamers of pink toilet paper as the wind carried everything away.

Feeling cold, miserable and quite drained, I later crawled into my sleeping bag and fell into a deep sleep. A blood-chilling roar awoke me with a start and I sat bolt upright, thinking that perhaps it was the figment of a dream, and listened intently, trying to distinguish any strange noises above the flapping tent and howling wind. A loud, deep roar suddenly overcame all the other sounds and I knew I hadn't been dreaming. I was aware of Rose, sitting erect next to me saying, 'What was that?' We could hear deep growling and another spine-tingling roar, then the tent flap flew open as Ali landed prostrate before us.

'Meester Jeem, Meester Jeem, there is a tiger!'

'A what?' I yelled. By now all was commotion – screaming women and shouting kids, as everyone sprang out of their tents. We heard the roar again; it seemed to be coming from a smaller opening above the large cave mouth.

'It's probably a mountain lion,' said Peter, 'although Persian tigers are still supposed to exist in isolated regions.'

'It is in there,' said Ali, flashing a torch at the hole and looking expectantly at me. I had never tackled a mountain lion, so we decided to leave Ali on watch to warn us if the animal took a stroll in our direction, while we tried to catch up with some sleep. Oh, what a night – first guerrillas, now bloody tigers!

I lay with eyes prickling from lack of sleep as I listened to every faint noise: the faint growling from the cave, a rattle of stones rolling down the hill, the whistling wind and the eerie howling of a wild dog or wolf, which was picked up and answered by others until mournful cries came from all around. I closed my eyes, but sleep wouldn't come. In my imagination I began reliving all the western films I had seen where Apaches surround a beleaguered wagon train, calling to each other in the night.

'Meester Jeem, Meester Jeem, they are here, present yourself.' Ali's warning shout brought me to my feet. What are 'they'? Tigers? Apaches? Guerrillas? My bemused mind couldn't cope and I crawled out of my tent, clutching my weapon – a sling,

'Meester Jeem, Meester Jeem, there is a tiger!'

threaded with three karabiners. I looked around for tigers, terrorists or whatever was going to attack us. Nothing could be seen.

The black night had given way to a greyish, pre-dawn light. Ali grabbed my arm and pointed at a vague shape that was moving towards us from behind some large rocks. It turned out to be a person holding something and, as he saw us watching, strode purposefully towards us with hand outstretched. What was he holding? Was it a gun?

It was a head-dress containing six eggs. The Kurd greeted us and presented us with this gift from the village. The sun's rays slanted down the valley, illuminating the grey faces of our group and washing away the anxiety and fears of the night, before warming us as we enjoyed breakfast.

THE CAVING GEAR WAS UNPACKED, the dinghy was inflated and we were watched with interest by the villagers, especially when we began to put on our tattered wetsuits. There were many willing hands to help us carry the dinghy and other gear down the thirty-metre boulder slope into the cave entrance, where a beach of fine gravel and sand sloped steeply into a clear, deep blue river which curved away out of sight along a passage eight metres high and six metres wide. Eric and Sue took the dinghy, while Peter, Reg and I swam.

The water was surprisingly cold and I swam downstream, away from the others, for a considerable distance before the roof lowered to a deep sump. Returning upstream, I followed the rest of the group for two hundred metres to a large chamber fifty metres high and sixty metres wide. A rock peninsula jutted into the lake and several routes led off. It was a relief to get out of the water when we beached the dinghy and we climbed up a mud slope to the higher levels, where Reg made a surprising discovery: steps cut in the mud. He received an even bigger shock when he shone his light upwards and it revealed a pyjama-clad leg and a bare brown foot, which had just appeared through an eyehole in the cave wall.

Soon we were confronted by three grinning villagers. The leader, clutching an old, smoking oil lamp, was the village headman – grinning even more broadly, he shook us by the hand in a kind of Stanley–Livingstone greeting. The wizened character waved his hand at the cave roof and our lights picked out large swarms of bats; he gestured that they did indeed use them for food. The roof of the cave was obliterated under a moving mass of small, leathery bodies, and my open notebook was soon covered in a fine drizzle of bat droppings and small fleas that rained from above.

After poking around in the higher levels, we quickly realised that the barefoot villagers had been everywhere, so we returned to the river. This flowed from a high, narrow passage across the lake – Peter and I swam into this, but after some distance it gradually narrowed into a tight cleft, though it widened underwater. Two other inlets feeding the lake also sumped, again with sizeable continuations underwater.

We rejoined the others, where our pyjamad buddies began gesticulating frantically and pointing up into a dark recess in the roof, which we had missed. A short climb took us into a large passage that continued over the river and past the two sumps we had encountered. Then, one of our guides directed us back into the water – it seemed that he was as keen as we were to find out where this river originated.

The river passage became a canal – it was very deep and, after swimming for eighty metres, we reached a T-junction where each branch sumped. Here, in a recess, we found some bones which Peter declared were human; not being a bone-ologist, I couldn't disagree, but whatever they were – human or animal – they must have been washed here from another opening that led to the surface. How many kilometres away that was we would never know.

After exhausting all ways on at river level, we climbed back into the dry chambers and passages and, sending Sue and Eric out in the dinghy, we followed a well-trodden trail of barefoot prints to a daylight rift, which involved a tricky twenty-metre climb, the last bit overhanging, that brought us out to the hillside above the cave. Looking down, we were surprised to see two army vehicles and a group of soldiers holding rifles pointed at a very white-faced Eric and Sue, who were standing by the dinghy facing a very irate officer who was shouting and waving his pistol. The villagers had been herded into a group and were guarded by more troops. Of the armed tribesmen, the lounge-suited guerrillas and Ali's uncle, there was no sign.

Suddenly, a shout went up as we were seen and several rifles were trained in our direction, so we climbed down towards the uniformed figures. We were berated by the officer and hustled out of the area at gunpoint, without being allowed to pack or even deflate the dinghy. One minute we were caving, and the next – still in wetsuits – we were driving across the desert landscape, shadowed by a section of the army. Which army it was, we never found out.

Once alone, we stopped, changed and packed everything away, before returning to Miandoab, to find that the blacksmith had repaired the trailer springs by the simple expedient of welding all the broken pieces together into a solid block of metal. He thereby ensured that they would never break again – and also made certain that the trailer would be shaken to bits on the first rough road.

WE SAID OUR GOODBYES to our stalwart guide, Ali, and headed south for Kermanshah and the Zagros Mountains. When we eventually came upon the city I was struck by the backdrop of jagged limestone peaks, our original objective. I could smell cave country and, after noticing several risings where, in spite of several months of drought, water still flowed sluggishly from the base of the limestone, I suggested that we stay a few days and examine the area's cave potential. However, the amateur geologist in our team explained that the area around Kermanshah 'was not conducive to cave development' and I was outvoted.

How wrong can you be? A short while later, John Middleton's expedition proved all the experts wrong by discovering Ghar Parau, an isolated cave near the summit of Kuh-e Parau, an impressive 3,357 metre peak that dominated the area. John's team explored the cave to a depth of 740 metres via twenty-five pitches, making it the deepest cave in Asia. Luckily for me, his expedition took place a few weeks after we had left the area and, remaining in blissful ignorance of the doings of his intrepid band, I was spared a nervous breakdown. The best cave discovery in Asia, and we drove past it!

From Kermanshah we headed eastwards towards Hamadan to investigate the caves at Sar-Ab and Ali-Sard. Reaching Hamadan, we again left the road and drove across the semi-desert landscape, which soon put paid to our much-maligned trailer – one tyre blew out and the solid iron of the welded spring shook the other parts to bits. We pulled up in a cloud of dust and opened the trailer to find that the sugar, dehydrated potatoes, powdered milk, cheese, jam and various other goodies had been in orbit, ending up enmeshed in the caving ropes like some sort of sticky modern sculpture. It was now a large spaghetti ball that would have made us a fortune at that future edifice, Tate Modern. Saatchi would have been delighted with it.

Our creation – 'Wotafuckinmess' – was removed from the wreckage and we salvaged what we could, then fastened the remains of the trailer on the Land Rover's roof rack before moving on across the rough, arid landscape of low hills and dried-out river-beds. At each small village the mud dwellings would disgorge their inhabitants as we approached, and the Land Rover would be surrounded by groups of boys and men in turbans while the women in their colourful costumes, some veiled, would linger shyly in the background. The headman would introduce himself with much shaking of hands and beaming smiles, welcoming us into his house to accept his and the villagers' hospitality.

These kind people plied us with fruit, a sort of chapatti, rice and lamb and, of course, innumerable drinks of tea served in delicate china cups, complete with large sugar lumps which one was expected to dip into the tea and suck. These meals play a great part in Iranian custom and cannot be hurried. Indeed, why should they be? Where else can one sit cross-legged with neighbours on a beautiful Persian carpet where chickens walk across the 'table'?

Several villages lay on our route and at each one we received the same treatment, and in each one we had to send one of our women to search for Timothy, whose blue eyes and blonde hair attracted the darker Persian ladies like a magnet. He was always discovered surrounded by adoring females, who stroked his hair and held his hands as though he was the reincarnation of a Persian god. He would eventually be retrieved wearing a self-satisfied smile on his ungodly features, clutching fistfuls of goodies that had been heaped on him by these lovely ladies, who didn't realise what a little sod he could be.

If I had a wish, it would be to be transformed into a blue-eyed blonde and be deposited among these beautiful Persian women – although not at Timothy's tender age.

It took several hours of hard driving before we arrived, with an overheated engine, at the foot of a range of low-lying, ochre-coloured hills, mottled with dark splashes of green where indistinct olive groves were dotted along a line where the hills met the sand. Here, there would most likely be water resurging from the caves. Suddenly, the Land Rover gave a lurch and the engine revved, accompanied by the smell of hot rubber as the wheels churned into a soft patch of gravel and sand, burying the vehicle up to its axles.

We soon discovered that the ground was a

Wotafuckinmess

waterlogged flood plain, with water issuing from cave openings buried under the sand – and it was just our luck to strike water in the middle of a desert. Despite all our efforts, the vehicle kept sinking steadily until the rear wheels disappeared from sight, and it was obvious that we had a major problem. The vehicle was lightened and, with make-shift tools, we dug two deep trenches behind the rear wheels and lined them with large stones. Reg carefully reversed until the tyres gained purchase, then he accelerated furiously downhill to reach a firm base. After this mishap, we made a long detour to the low escarpment and pulled up in a small olive grove, where a handful of grotesquely misshapen trees gave shade from the scorching sun.

Reg testing a bridge, and Sue, Peter and Rose washing the Land Rover

I was fascinated by these old, gnarled trees and was soon lost in reverie as I wondered about their great age. How many travellers had passed this very spot in distant times, resting on their journey? 'Perhaps even Jesus passed this way,' I mused, when a shout broke into my daydreaming – a cave had been discovered.

Water welled slowly from a rocky outcrop into the remains of an old stone culvert carved by the ancients and, a few metres away, a low opening emitted a howling, ice-cold draught. I peered down into the deep, still water until, clad only in shorts, I was forced to withdraw my freezing body from the icy blast.

'There's a big cave under here, Reg,' I said as I warmed myself in the sunlight. 'It's got to be big with a draught like that,' I enthused. 'Get out the wetsuits.'

The caves near Sar-Ab and Ali-Sard were situated at an altitude of around two thousand metres and have been known and utilised for many centuries by the Persians but, apart from some probes by a local Hamadan group, we understood that they remained unexplored. Putting on wetsuits in a temperature of thirty-eight degrees Celsius was a sweaty and uncomfortable experience, but our discomfort vanished once we were sliding down the low, tunnel-like entrance into Ghar Sar-Ab. We were now in another world of shimmering crystals and blue water that reflected our lights onto a cave roof covered in calcite. Ahead lay a short traverse over deep pools and, beyond that, a long canal passage stretched ahead.

The water in the narrow canal was incredibly clear at the surface, but gradually changed into varying shades of blue as we peered into depths of over ten metres. The roof and walls were completely covered in large dog-tooth crystals that continued into the azure depths, their facets shining even far underwater, such was the water's clarity.

The extent of the crystals suggested that for a long part of the cave's history it had been completely submerged, but some more recent event (an earth tremor, perhaps) had lowered the water table, enabling us to make progress on small, crystal-covered outcrops just above the water. It seemed rather strange, walking on these delicate structures over what seemed to be a deep, blue canyon, an optical illusion created by the complete clarity and stillness of the water. At any second I expected my flimsy foothold to collapse and propel me into space, such was the sense of exposure.

The passage widened and the footholds finished where a small metal plaque was fastened to the wall. Painted black and inscribed with white Persian lettering, it denoted that this was the limit of the exploration by the Hamadan group and that they had dedicated the cave to Omar Khayyám, the ancient astronomer poet of Persia. This made a nice change from Kilroy and it seemed fitting to dedicate such a beautiful cave to such a famous man, who obviously enjoyed life and liked a drink.

Then to this earthen Bowl did I adjourn
My Lip the secret Well of Life to learn:
And Lip to Lip it murmur'd – 'While you live,
Drink! – for once dead you never shall return.'

With this half-forgotten poem in my mind I slid into the clear, still water, swimming along the ever-widening canal, past glittering formations, through small lagoons and lakes that were reminiscent of a miniature subterranean Venice, until the passage branched. I clambered onto a large, detached block and watched Reg and Peter swimming towards me in a kaleidoscope of flashing light as their headlamps reflected from the broken water and bounced back from the white roof. The nature of the cave changed at this point: the roof lifted, revealing loose slabs of rock poised overhead, some of which now lay in the water, with several smaller passages radiating off among the rockfalls.

We split up as we explored each way on, swimming along the narrow streamways and climbing over fallen rocks. Unfortunately for us, the only way forward seemed to be underwater and I lay full length on a flat slab of rock, peering downwards. To me, it seemed a cave diver's dream, a subterranean world of blue light, crystal-clear water, beautiful underwater formations and deep mysterious canyons with eroded walls that threaded through a maze of fallen rocks. Alas, we were not cave divers and, reluctantly, we left Omar Khayyám's dream world and returned to the harsh realities of outside – where there was the welcome smell of stew and veg which Margaret and Rose had prepared.

The next morning we left our peaceful olive grove and drove along the base of the escarpment, passing several risings which still ran in spite of it being the height of the dry season. It gave us some idea of the tremendous volume of water that must be ponded in the hills behind. After driving for several kilometres along the edge of the old, yellow, limestone hills, we reached the village of Ali-Sard, where a large cave (now called Ghar Alisadr) acted as a natural reservoir and supplied a stream of water, even in conditions of extreme drought.

The villagers were astonished by the arrival of the Land Rover, as the only vehicle in this part of the world was a camel. We were soon the centre of attraction for the awe-struck villagers and Timothy was once again whipped away by adoring ladies to the local harem, closely followed by his proud mum, Margaret, and Rose and Sue. The male population swarmed around the vehicle as though it was Dr Who's telephone kiosk, and this was followed by the inevitable meal and cups of tea, so it was some time before we could drive up to the cave.

The collapsed entrance of Ghar Alisadr led us into a huge passage floored with half a metre of glutinous mud. It was a dank, gloomy place, a complete contrast to Ghar Sar-Ab, and we were soon struggling knee-deep as the foul-smelling black mud tried to digest our legs and suck us down. Another, larger passage bisected the one we were exploring and the mud became deeper and slimier as we progressed downwards along large tunnel-like passages that obviously had recently been submerged.

After much cursing and sweating, we reached a steep mud slope that dropped into an evil-looking black lake. Even with the combined power of our lights we could not see any shoreline or walls. It was just a sheet of black water that stretched away on all sides – a most forbidding place.

We could hear the sound of running water and squelched our way along the edge of the lake until we came to a carved, stone-lined culvert which carried water from the lake into a small canal, probably a water supply leading outside. With lamps hardly piercing the gloom, we could make out more tunnels extending beyond our vision as we continued the traverse, but our muddy beach soon finished and black, slimy walls forced us into the lake. Clinging to angular projections in the wall, we groped our way along in chest-deep, bitterly cold water.

In the lead, I felt myself being pulled down by the mud, a most peculiar feeling when water reaches to your chin! I was aware of panic rising and, with difficulty, worked my legs free. Frantic splashing and strangled gargling noises from behind informed me that Reg was also having trouble, so we took to swimming.

Eventually, I was left on my own as the others returned for the rubber dinghy. I swam carefully from ledge to ledge, keeping close to the walls and taking care not to splash my carbide lamp, as I had no wish to be plunged into darkness – I would have become disorientated in seconds.

Weird rock pinnacles rose from the depths like the black, corroded teeth of some giant sea monster waiting to devour me, and I experienced a sense of relief when I heard a distant shout and saw a pinprick of light in the darkness behind. I stood on a submerged pinnacle, hypnotised by this faraway glow-worm suspended in the Stygian gloom as it flew from side to side. Slowly, it turned into a will-o'-the-wisp and grew larger and brighter, until it metamorphosed again into Peter, spinning around in an inflated inner tube, looking for all the world like a Martian on a flying saucer as he skimmed towards me, contained in a misty halo of light.

The lights of the others appeared and slowly this macabre cavern came into view. A flat roof ten metres above our heads extended across an area of roughly four hundred metres by fifty metres. Numerous jagged, eroded fangs of rock hung down to continue underwater, while others had dissolved into black swords of Damocles hanging menacingly above our heads. Other fangs reared out of the black water in weird distorted shapes, like weathered ice formations sandblasted with black granite. We were in an enormous phreatic cavern which had been formed underwater below an ancient water table, with the limestone rock slowly dissolving over millions of years until this huge underground lake had been formed.

Four streamways led off and, borrowing Peter's rubber coracle, I paddled my way across the lake and worked my way along stream passages that gradually narrowed, until I had to abandon the inner tube and swim. Each passage eventually sumped with only a few centimetres of airspace remaining and the roof ominously lowered, so I returned to the rest of the group. They had found a grand exit from the cave, up a series of well-worn stone steps to a large, excavated tunnel leading to daylight and the eighth century. Here, above the entrance portal, was carved the insignia of King Darius I.

BACK ON THE HIGHWAY, heading north to Tehran, the enigma that was modern Iran – with its mixture of the mighty Persian Empire and a twentieth-century dynamic economy – was evident in the fascinating contrasts. Huge lorries roared past camel trains plodding alongside the road, seemingly oblivious to the noise and exhaust fumes, apart from the occasional haughty sneer from the camels.

The Shah of Iran presided over a society that lay under the strict control of an army that was becoming modernised too fast for the ayatollahs, who later would drag the country back into its medieval past. However, our minds were on the present when a mighty 'clunk' came from the gearbox, followed by a lot of jiggling with the gear lever and a string of oaths from our driver, Reg.

The selector had gone and we were reduced to driving at a funereal pace in a low gear. Luckily, we were only a hundred and fifty kilometres from Tehran and on a good road which was almost flat. The other point in our favour was the fact that, at that time, Tehran was the only city in the Middle East that boasted a Land Rover agency. We were going to the city because Margaret had been corresponding with two Iranian geologists, who had supplied her with information and maps of the areas we had been exploring. The plan was that we would pick up Andy and Darius at their offices in the centre of Tehran before driving north to the Elburz Mountains, a promising and practically unknown area with great cave potential.

Carefully picking our way through the flocks of sheep, goats, shepherds and camel trains that were being funnelled onto the road by the presence of filling stations and other low, flat-roofed suburban structures, we were abruptly and painfully dragged into the twentieth century by what seemed to us to be a miniature version of New York. The two broad highways suddenly filled with vehicles driving four and five abreast, with cars passing us on each side and even on the pavement, honking furiously, as we all headed for downtown Tehran, an opulent, flamboyant, chromium-plated, high-rise capital of the Middle East that had gone mad with the Shah's birthday celebration of the anniversary of an unbroken dynasty.

Reg finally found the administrative tower block of Iran Pan American Oil, where a puzzled official ushered our scruffy, unkempt group into the plush air-conditioned interior and we were further directed, after several telephone calls, to Darius' office. 'Our man' turned out to be a pleasant, diminutive gentleman who – after the initial shock – welcomed us with open arms and took us to meet his charming wife before telephoning the Land Rover agent to collect our vehicle. Darius next contacted a deluxe motel on the city outskirts and we were soon installed as guests, lounging around the swimming pool, forcing ice-cold beer down our gullets, while the Land Rover was being looked at. Life was grim.

The dollar and sterling had just been devalued, so to save money Reg struck a deal with the garage owner, who let us remove the gearbox ourselves and replace it after it was repaired. It was a brilliant deal, especially when some of the workforce surreptitiously assisted us and cleaned the vehicle inside and out! You couldn't imagine this happening in Britain.

With the repairs completed, we picked up Darius and his large, bluff extrovert friend, Andy, and left Tehran. This was not without a certain reluctance on my part, for never had I seen such beautiful, smartly dressed women. To think of them today, covered in shapeless, drab chadors – what a disappointment.

Our next objective was to explore two large caves. The only problem was that they were situated halfway up a 350 metre sheer rock face, but our enthusiastic friends were sure that we could overcome a slight obstacle like that.

'There was a similar problem gaining access to the Cave of the Assassins, a few years ago, but Joe Brown soon solved that,' stated Andy, his imagination already fired by the thought of treasure that was there for the taking. I didn't like to disillusion him by saying that Joe Brown's climbing skills and mine were slightly different.

Both Iranians were well educated and spoke very good English – and both liked a glass of beer, which made them fairly garrulous and turned them into excellent guides. Being amateur archaeologists, they brought Persian history to life by indicating historical sights and points of interest. We learned the great potential of modern Iran as we motored by huge irrigation projects, where water is conveyed hundreds of kilometres from the mountains to reach Tehran via great dams and impressive hydro-electric schemes.

Driving across a flat plain as we approached the mountains, I was puzzled by the lack of power in the engine and had to keep changing to a lower gear, until I was down to second to maintain headway.

'It is 2 p.m.,' explained Andy. 'An overspill of cold air from the mountains is meeting the hot air from the plains and causes a strong wind at this time of day – if you went outside the wind would blow you over; it only lasts for an hour.' Even as he spoke, day was turned into night by a giant, circular sandstorm that overwhelmed us and rocked the Land Rover as we crawled past a shuttered village, to which we were assured life would return at 3 p.m.

Sure enough, within a short space of time I was driving under blue skies again with not even the merest zephyr of a breeze. At a point midway between Qazvin and Rasht I was directed along a minor road which wound directly up into the mountains, passing small villages that clung to the steepening slopes, each with its own beautiful area of bright green terracing and small paddy fields. The air became thinner and cooler as we approached 2,800 metres above sea level, and beautiful alpine meadows and pine trees appeared when we reached the summit of the Elburz foothills and our destination. We pulled off the road onto a grassy knoll and unloaded the vehicle.

Directly below us a deep gorge cut the mountain in two and at its head a magnificent limestone peak dominated the scene. An almost vertical rock face swept up the face of the peak and in the centre of this expanse of vertiginous rock, like eye sockets in a huge skull, lay two black openings. These were the caves we had come to explore.

A small village was situated nearby and a steep track led down into the gorge. Darius went to enquire if we could hire a mule to carry the climbing and caving gear the ten kilometres or so to the base of the peak, while the rest of us set up camp. Later, after having eaten, Andy and Darius showed their true worth by building a bonfire and bringing forth two bottles of whisky and several cans of beer. This was marvellous, especially for the two northerners – Eric and me. We had both been raised on beer, but had been without the stuff for several days, as we seemed to have entered a Muslim area where Coca-Cola and 7 Up reigned supreme. Drinking water in the Middle East is a sure way of committing suicide, and lacing it with purifying pills can rot your teeth (as well as other bits); the alternative, drinking litres of fizzy sugar, is anathema to beer drinkers as they develop withdrawal symptoms and blow up with gas. As a consequence, Eric and I had stopped drinking and had reached the semi-transparent stage that kippers go through when they're drying out.

We thanked our two friends for saving our bodies from complete desiccation and had a pleasant evening, until Andy filled us in on the details of the area. It seemed that, once again, we were in a 'hot' area which had been the scene of a student rebellion. In the forest below, six months previously, forty student revolutionaries had been systematically hunted down and killed by the army: 'And over there,' continued Andy, waving his arm casually towards the adjourning forest, 'are tigers.'

Here we go again, I thought, when a faint echo of a deep-throated roar came from below us, causing Eric's glasses to steam up. He grabbed another beer. Andy threw another log on the fire and continued with his narrative, telling us how three men were savaged by a Persian tiger in the last village we had passed through.

A tiger had been seen near the village on several occasions, but no one had taken any particular notice of it until the animal attacked one of the villagers, who fired a shot at it, wounding the creature before it knocked him to the ground. Screaming furiously, the man wrapped his arms around a small tree while the tiger, with jaws gripping him by a leg, tried to haul him into the forest. His cries alerted two men in a nearby field and they attacked the tiger with machetes, hacking at its back legs while it refused to let go of its victim. One leg was actually severed before the beast, enraged with pain, let go of its victim and turned and attacked its tormentors, badly mauling one before running after the other; although severely disabled, it leapt on him, dropping him like a stone. By this time the ensuing uproar and cries of pain from men and beast brought the rest of the villagers to the scene and the animal was eventually shot dead. A short time after the incident Andy had visited the village: one of the villagers had lost a leg and the two others were still in hospital.

The tiger's skin, which was hung up on display, was a mass of slits and holes, which showed how fierce the battle must have been. Even more remarkable was its severed leg bone, where soil had been forced into the marrow when the crippled animal put its weight on its stump. With this pleasant tale in my head, I went to sleep dreaming of three-legged tigers and one-legged men.

The following morning we were approached by a donkey and two guides, who said they would lead us to a point near the caves. However, by the time we had sorted ourselves out, the morning was well advanced and Darius was concerned that we would be walking over rough ground in the heat of the day. Unfortunately, being hard men, we ignored his advice. Standing on the hilltop, we viewed our objective. It looked deceptively near, which dismissed Darius' anxiety and so set the seal on a disaster.

On any expedition into unfamiliar terrain, local knowledge is invaluable, as our guides quickly demonstrated. They took us in the opposite direction from the rockface, down another valley in order to reach the one we wished to traverse, and once we arrived in the valley floor we realised why.

We were taken aback by the obstacles that confronted us. The valley leading to the caves was extremely steep-sided and covered in a thick jungle of vicious thorn bushes which formed an impenetrable barrier, while the overgrown streambed was narrow, full of loose blocks and boulders and entirely unfit for the donkey.

Our guides led us into the thorny jungle but, after an hour of being ripped to shreds, they stopped and said there was no way on and we had to backtrack a long way until the bushes thinned out. To me, the only obvious route was to climb above the treeline and traverse across the steep slope above, so I climbed up the hillside, beckoning the others to follow. The heat was intense but, stripped to the waist, it seemed to have no effect on me. I was already deeply tanned and I was not even sweating. I felt really fit and was soon way in front of the others, in spite of the heavy pack I was carrying. I waited for Darius and he said I should slow down and put my shirt on. I said something facetious and bombed on.

Rounding the top of the thorn forest and dropping down a rocky defile, I wondered how the donkey would fare – Greek donkeys could climb anywhere, so I presumed the Persian one could too.

Soon, I heard a faint shout. It was Reg waving me back: 'The donkey can't make it,' he said, with obvious disgust. I returned. Bodies were strewn all over the place as everyone rested and the two guides looked crestfallen. The donkey, in turn, looked up at the rock slab in front of it with a defiant 'Sod that!' expression on its face.

Having to unload the donkey and share out the extra weight was going to be a killer, and it took some time to sort out the loads. One pack frame was much heavier than the rest so, feeling good, I volunteered to carry it and swap loads with Reg when I needed a break.

After a lengthy struggle, unbalanced by our heavy loads, we reached the dazzling white limestone. By now the sun was blasting heat into the narrow valley, the air was calm and the atmosphere became furnace-like.

I looked up at the cliff ahead. The two caves, although nearer now, were still a long way off – and a new problem appeared. Another deep, incised valley still separated us from our objective. We were two hundred metres above the valley floor and I was loathe to climb down and then struggle back up again. I looked up and saw a traverse that would take us above the caves. Reg, Eric and I struggled towards it with our heavy packs, to be brought to a heart-breaking stop when we found that the rock face we were aiming for was a separate pinnacle of rock detached from the main face, and that we would still have to climb down again beyond it. I cursed and felt uneasy – things were going wrong.

The donkey looked up at the rock slab in front of it with a defiant 'Sod that!' expression on its face

Nevertheless, I decided to climb over the pinnacle, reasoning that climbing down its rear would gain the main face and the traverse. I waited while Reg, lathered in sweat, joined me and I told him what I thought. He told me what he thought, which I can't print here.

However, climbing up, we eventually made it to the top of the pinnacle and by sliding, scrambling and falling we managed to get down the other side, then began a long traverse on blinding hot limestone in an effort to reach the caves. We were now feeling grim, as we had neglected to bring any water bottles. Eric was dropping behind and both Reg and I began to doubt the wisdom of what we were doing, but we carried on, determined.

The rock steepened as I rounded a corner and there below us was the cave, a huge black hole in the cliff. 'We've cracked it,' I croaked, then slowly realised that we hadn't – between us and the cave the rock below was undercut.

Spreadeagled in the white glare of sunlight reflecting from the heated limestone, Reg and I cast about for a route into the cave. The heavy packs made climbing difficult – we were an accident waiting to happen and slowly we bowed to the inevitable as we both realised that we had made a bad mistake in trying to traverse above the caves instead of climbing up from below.

The heat was intense. Eric was a dot far below on the harsh karst landscape, still gamely struggling on. Reg shouted to him and he stopped, confused, as he watched us slowly retracing our steps across that blast furnace of a cliff.

I suddenly felt very weak and ill at ease, my pack instantly increased its weight threefold and my legs began to tremble. Somehow, I managed to follow Reg and climb down to the intersecting gully and slid down wearily while Reg climbed up the intervening spur to look for the others. I watched my ginger-headed mate climb to the top of the pinnacle, while I remained where I had slumped, a lethargic and very uneasy human being. It had not occurred to me that I was experiencing the early stages of heat exhaustion, or that I would become progressively worse.

I followed Reg down off the rock pinnacle, staggering and falling as my movements became slower and more uncoordinated, until Reg realised that something was wrong and stopped to give me a rest. Swapping packs, I gained some relief from the lighter load, but soon encountered the weird sensation of all my strength draining from my body, as though someone had removed a plug.

My breathing became very fast and shallow and I vaguely wondered if I was about to collapse with a heart attack, when my legs turned to rubber and I slid to the ground in a humiliating heap. I heard indistinct voices as Sue and Peter arrived on the scene and, when Reg lifted the pack off my back, I felt a deep sense of shame. I sat crouching with my head on my knees, listening to their conversation. Were they talking about me? The hard man? This abject heap of humanity that despises weakness in others, yet now shows it himself by collapsing after a moderate walk?

'How are the mighty fallen.' I remembered these words from somewhere as I tried to apologise to Sue in a faint croaking voice which released a string of words strung together in the slurred, incoherent senseless ramblings of a drunk.

'He must have some water,' Sue said as she put her arm around my shoulders and sat down beside me.

As Reg dashed off down the track for Darius' water bottle, I realised what special people nurses are. Sue talked quietly to me and reassured me that I would soon recover – I found all this compassion from her and Peter quite embarrassing, and forced myself to stand up until I stood swaying like a drunk.

'Come on,' I mumbled, and slowly moved into a reeling kind of walk for a few paces before once more collapsing to the ground. I had a strong desire to sleep and in a daze felt a water bottle being pressed to my lips. Strangely enough, up to that time I had never felt thirsty but, not having had a drink for several hours, I emptied the container in a second.

The hired donkey and the others had returned down the valley, so it was a case of trying to put one foot in front of the other while supported by Peter and Reg, with Sue giving me words of encouragement and ordering frequent stops when she didn't like the look of me. Someone else appeared with a bottle of water and eventually, after a long, gruelling and embarrassing walk (or, I should say, drag), I was taken to a gin-clear spring. Heaven can take on many forms and this cool pool was mine as I lay down, immersed my head in the water and drank deeply, only stopping occasionally for a breath. Again and again, I took on water like a camel until my distended stomach would hold no more. My dehydrated body soaked up the precious liquid and the dust in my veins was slowly replaced by real blood. Sue later informed me that I had been severely dehydrated, which can be followed by coma and death. I vowed never to miss any liquid again – even Coca-Cola!

Thinking about the extent of dehydration that had taken place, one wonders why I hadn't been completely mummified, for even after gorging my body with water from the spring, drinking several water bottles empty and taking on large cupfuls of water every few minutes throughout the night, as well as drinking eight bottles of 7 Up, I never urinated.

Hyperthermia struck Eric with a form of madness. After he watched Reg and me climbing down the cliff face, he began to retreat along the top of the thorn jungle carrying a pack frame loaded with ladders. To quote Eric: 'This burning thirst was driving me mad and I kept thinking of all the desert films I had seen, where men dig deeply into the sand with their bare hands in an effort to try to find a little muddy water. I imagined my eyes going red and my tongue turning black, when I heard the sound of running water.'

Eric, peering through the dense thorn bushes, detected sunlight sparkling on a stream far below. This sight, it seemed, was too much to bear and he threw himself into the prickly growth and fought and slid his way down the steep slope. He was stopped, bleeding profusely and surrounded by fallen rocks, at the edge of a small cliff. Incredible as it now seems, Eric threw off his pack and jumped down what turned out to be a nine-metre drop, then he rolled and slithered, together with a miniature landslide, to end up bruised and battered lying full length in the greenish, foul-smelling water of a small stream.

He was aware that the water was polluted, but nevertheless he drank as much as he could swallow and remembered little of the rest of his wanderings before he was located by Peter, who discovered him several hours later in a dazed condition. Two of the party, following Eric's instructions, returned to search for the pack frame and our precious ladders, but never found them.

After this episode Eric, of course, became very ill and gave us cause for concern. However, this was in the future and the following morning, after our abortive attempt to reach the caves, an army jeep containing two officers pulled up at our camp. They were very friendly, spoke good English and joined us in a drink of tea while they plied us with questions about our travels. 'Do you ever find any golden artefacts in the caves?' It seemed that removing antiquities was a touchy subject in Iran and before leaving they had a long discussion with Darius in Persian.

Later in the day we drove to a nearby village to visit a local archaeologist, an acquaintance of Andy's. We caught him unawares as we entered his house and Rose later swore that she had seen a glimpse of gold as an object was hurriedly wrapped in newspaper before disappearing under the coat of another visitor, who hastily slipped out through the rear door.

It was all rather intriguing, as more objects were quickly covered over in the half-light at the rear of the room – a touch of Indiana Jones which was no concern of ours.

Eric threw off his pack and jumped down

Eventually we left and found an army jeep parked behind our vehicle in the village square. It was our officer friends, who insisted on buying us refreshments in a nearby cafe. After numerous drinks of 7 Up and lots of tea, I dozed off so missed much of the conversation and I was quite surprised when I was told that Andy and Darius were being arrested! It seemed that they had not brought their identity cards with them and in Iran, especially in an area of unrest, it was an arrestable offence. Even though Andy's father had been a high-ranking officer, it made no difference: they were being taken to Rasht to be held in custody in an army barracks. We could do nothing except break camp and follow the army vehicles which contained our luckless friends.

After a long drive we arrived at a large army barracks and watched the gates clang shut behind the two jeeps. Reg parked the Land Rover near the entrance, but almost immediately an officer approached and told us to move it. I informed him that we were waiting for our friends and gave him the full story. He listened politely, then said he would go inside and make some enquiries. After a long wait the officer returned and said, 'You must go, your friends will be some time.'

'How long?' asked Reg.

'Oh, perhaps two days, perhaps two weeks,' answered the officer smiling sardonically. 'You must leave.'

'We can't,' I said, becoming exasperated. 'We've got all their equipment and personal belongings – besides, we brought them here from Tehran and we can't just desert them!'

'They have broken the law, now you must go,' replied the officer, the smile gone from his face. 'Move this vehicle!'

Reg drove the Land Rover out of the blistering heat to the shade of some nearby trees, while we decided on a plan of action. It was out of the question to simply drive away and desert Andy and Darius. Reg and I, in true British fashion, marched up to the sentry and demanded to see the general. Of course, this was 1971 and the British hadn't quite lost the world's respect at that time. A few years later and the sentry would have kicked us up the backside and told us to 'piss off you British bums'.

However, after a great deal of arguing with the confused sentry – who spoke no English – we caused enough of a commotion to attract the attention of a corporal, a sergeant and another officer. The latter, having ascertained what the problem was, hastily hotfooted his way into the admin building, to emerge red-faced with another more imposing figure with brass bits twinkling on his shoulders. We were informed, with a certain arrogance, that the two Iranians could not prove their identity so were being held in custody.

'Balls,' I shouted. 'It's a load of balls!'

'Excuse?' queried the officer, totally bemused by this strange use of the English language. 'Bolls? What is this bolls?'

'Look, we know who they are, we can prove who they are. I demand to see the general!' I exclaimed.

'It is not possible,' the man said.

'Well make it bloody possible,' said I, my old hatred of the officer class rising with my blood pressure. 'I want to see the general!' The man stalked off, looking as though he was about to suffer an apoplectic fit.

'Eh, calm down Jim, you're going to get us all shoved in clink,' said Reg. It seemed the others thought the same, as they had left the vehicle to watch the strange spectacle of a stroppy British ex-Able Seaman requesting an audience with an Iranian general. It was like Ko-Ko demanding to see the Mikado.

The officer returned with a captain and two armed soldiers. The captain glared at me. 'You are British?'

'Yes,' l said truculently.

'I want all your passports,' the captain said.

'Shit,' I thought as I collected them. The captain scrutinised each one carefully.

It was like Ko-Ko demanding to see the Mikado

'You come with me,' he said ominously, before turning on his heel. He marched off abruptly with me following closely, an armed guard on each side.

With boots clattering on the polished marble floor, he scattered numerous lower-ranking soldiers, who stiffened and saluted at his presence as we walked hurriedly through a maze of corridors. We came to a halt at an armed sentry who stood outside a door marked 'Private', or more probably 'General' or its Persian equivalent.

'Wait,' the captain demanded as, armed with our passports, he entered the room. Standing in the corridor, a skinny, brown, knobbly-kneed individual, clad at one end in a pair of shabby khaki shorts and at the other with a mass of hair and beard out of which peered two shifty eyes and a well-bent broken nose, I attracted many curious looks from passing military personnel. I wondered if perhaps I was overplaying the 'I'm British' bit and I tried to whistle a tuneless, flat version of 'Rule Britannia', which petered out in an asthmatic wheeze as I slowly realised that we didn't rule anything any more.

After a long wait I was ushered into the general's office. A miniature version of Ghengis Khan sat behind the desk studying our passports. 'You are Mister Eyre?' he said with some incredulity as he compared the photograph with the apparition that stood before him. 'How old is this photograph? Was it taken many years ago?'

'Er, no – I need a wash and a shave, sir,' I answered smartly.

'How did you meet Mister Djafar-Zade and his friend?'

I answered at length, giving details of Margaret's correspondence with the Iranians and our mutual interest in speleology.

'Have you ever seen these two men before?'

'No.'

'Well, how do you know who they are?' he asked curtly, his moustache bristling. Warning bells began ringing in my mind as I answered.

'I have been to Mister Djafar-Zade's home and met his wife.'

'How do you know she is his wife?'

'Mister Djafar-Zade introduced her as such, so I presume she is.'

The general permitted himself a slight smile. 'In Iran, Mister Eyre, we cannot presume anything. Now, how can you prove that these two men are who they say they are?'

'Ah, telephone their office. They work for Pan American Oil,' I answered triumphantly.

'We have already done that,' answered the general, 'but the office is closed. Now, Mister Eyre, if there are two employees of the company bearing the same names as our prisoners, how can we be sure that the men in custody are not masquerading under false names?'

'Telephone Darius's wife,' I answered.

'We already have talked to a lady on the telephone, who says she is the wife of Djafar-Zade, but unfortunately it is impossible to identify a person over a telephone wire – wouldn't you agree, Mister Eyre?'

The crafty old bastard.

'Couldn't she read out his particulars from his identity card?' I asked.

'Oh, yes,' said the general, obviously enjoying the interview, 'but what about the photograph? How could she read that? Now Mister Eyre, I have one last question. Have you any documentary proof of the identity of the two men in custody?'

Crestfallen, I admitted defeat. 'No sir, only my word.' The general had a brief conversation with another officer and scrutinised several pages of statements and other documents before returning to me.

'Mister Eyre, you and your friends have been in a politically unstable area in the company of two Iranians who are travelling without identification documents, which is an arrestable offence in Iran. I accept your identity and your other explanations, but what guarantee can you give me that the two prisoners are who they say they are?'

'Only my word, I suppose,' I answered.

'If I release the two prisoners, will you see to it that they are returned immediately to Tehran and that they report immediately to the military authorities with their papers?'

'Yes, sir,' I answered smartly. There followed another discussion in Persian, a soldier departed and later arrived with Andy and Darius, who were quite surprised to see me. The two unfortunate men were given a severe grilling by the general, who then turned to me and said, 'I am going to release these men in your custody. Will you give me your word to abide by a written agreement?'

'Yes, sir,' I answered, obviously relieved that Andy and Darius were to be released. During our conversation a typist had been busy typing out a document which was given to me to sign. It was typed in Persian.

'I can't sign this!' I exclaimed.

'Why not?' queried an officer.

'Well, I can't understand it. For all I know I could be signing up for the Iranian army!' This remark put smiles on everyone's faces and the situation became more humorous when Andy volunteered to translate a copy into English. He sat down and wrote a document literally placing Darius and himself in my custody. It was again a bit like Gilbert and Sullivan and when I read it I almost burst out laughing. Keeping a straight face, I signed it and the Persian equivalent, and so did the general.

'You may go,' he said to Andy and Darius, who thanked him profusely. 'Present yourselves to the authorities in Tehran within twenty-four hours.' I shook the general by the hand and we departed.

RETURNING OUR IRANIAN FRIENDS to Tehran, we headed once more for the Elburz Mountains and the Caspian Sea, aiming ultimately for the UK. It was a route full of surprises, climbing up from the plains in temperatures well above forty degrees Celsius, the narrow one-in-four gradient road suddenly plunged into a tunnel roughly hewn from the rock. Unlit and narrow, the passage twisted steadily upwards at a very steep angle as it corkscrewed its way through the mountain. It was more like a mine working than a road tunnel as Reg dodged minor rockfalls and we all hoped nothing was coming the other way.

A pinprick of light lay ahead and, after several kilometres, we emerged, dazzled and bewildered, into another world. Left behind were the arid mountains and scorching plains, and before us stretched a panorama of snow and trees that gradually merged into green alpine meadows and beautiful limestone hills and gorges.

The abrupt transition from one climate to another was further emphasised by the soft banks of cloud and the light rain that fell in the cold, clear air. It was our first experience of a tunnel linking two such contrasting climates and we felt like Alice must have felt in Wonderland when she passed though the keyhole.

The Elburz had other marvels in store for, thanks to my map and superb route-finding, I was once again tempted to try a short-cut and I directed Reg on a very scenic drive indeed. Everyone was enthralled by the vistas of limestone peaks and valleys that opened before them, except Reg of course, as he wanted to know where the bloody road had gone. I began to experience a niggling doubt that perhaps I had taken the wrong direction, as the track gradually deteriorated into two dry, dirt grooves.

When Reg found out that I had discovered a short-cut, he immediately stopped the vehicle and we all jumped out, spread the map on the bonnet and studied my sugges-tion. There was indeed a route – a very thin, spidery brown line that meandered across the page like the passing of a drunken midge with bowel problems, before it stag-gered over the final mountain range and dropped steeply to the coast. Looking up the key to the symbols, someone discovered that 'brown' ranged from an unsurfaced road to mule tracks, but if we could stay with it we would save a day's travelling and experience the thrill of discovery.

I took over the driving and was soon struggling up a mountain pass on a dirt road with bends so acute that I had to reverse on each one before the Land Rover could be locked round. We had one hairy moment when I missed a gear and nearly reversed over the edge of a fierce drop until, with the wheels kicking dirt into space, I managed to regain control and resumed progress up the long drag before the mountain levelled off onto a beautiful plateau.

If there is a paradise on earth rather than under it, mine would have to be here in this idyllic pasture, where every type of alpine flower seemed to blossom in the lush grass of the rounded hilltop on which we found ourselves. All around us magnificent limestone peaks trimmed the horizon like jagged teeth reaching out of the low-lying cloud and haze. A small chalet-style farm building softened the isolation and an incredible flash of iridescent blue streaked across the meadow as a beautiful blue bird flickered and danced in front of us, before it resumed its dazzling flight and was promptly out of sight.

In the far distance we could see the glistening gold of the Caspian Sea, our target. Ahead of us two men cutting grass looked at us in total amazement, frozen immobile as they watched our approach with incredulity. We stopped and passed the time of day, shook hands, offered them cigarettes and stuck a map in front of their totally bemused faces before their eyes flashed with returning life. Their slack jaws regained control of their speech and both began talking at once, the gist of which was: 'Where the bloody hell have you come from?' The track we were on apparently ended above a vertical cliff. We pointed at the track and our vehicle, waved the map and gradually our two new acquaintances became aware that we were mad.

One of them pointed at the Land Rover, then at the track and emphatically shook his head and did a very good imitation of a breast stroke with his arms, meaning that the track was unfit for our vehicle. This was a bit disconcerting, but Reg, who is descended from a Viking, decided to have a look at what lay ahead – or should I say below. The narrow, rutted track clung to the wall of a cliff face that descended sheer for almost six hundred metres, shrouded below with wisps of clouds which hung around the shattered rock. Reg found a tyre mark – what of, we never found out; it was probably left by a demented unicyclist.

I have often heard the expression 'the point of no return'. Reg took us beyond that as, grasping the wheel, he put the vehicle in four-wheel drive and we edged our way downwards on a journey I have no wish to repeat. It was by far the steepest track I have ever encountered and one side of the Land Rover was permanently hanging over the rocky edge. The hairpin bends were equally as sharp as the ones I had negotiated, but the driving required more skill as it was difficult to reverse on the wet, slippery rock on such an extreme gradient. On each bend the passengers climbed out for safety, while on the straight bits none of the women would sit on the side that overlooked space, so we were continually changing sides.

Reg inched his way down the precipitous track into the mist. This was really grim because, though spared the sight of the awesome drop, we knew it was still there and all eyes were glued on the indistinct outline of the track edge. After what seemed an interminable length of time, the mist began to thin and the track started to level off, until we came to a river and there, looming up out of the mist, appeared a rickety wooden bridge. Was it strong enough to take our weight? By this time Reg was past caring and he drove across the rattling planks to pull up in front of an equally rickety wooden hut, where he leaned over the wheel, drained of energy.

We then noticed a table outside the hut, decorated by a glass jar containing soggy flowers and surrounded by wet, woodworm-riddled chairs. Could it be? Like people in a trance we tried the door; it opened and we went inside. As our eyes became accustomed to the gloom we saw a bar, bottles of beer and a menu card. Eric sat down heavily on the nearest chair and peered wide-eyed from behind his steamed-up glasses.

'We've all died and gone to heaven,' he said.

The owner of the establishment appeared and he too was astonished when we took him outside and gesticulated where we had come from, as that track was only ever used by a specially adapted vehicle. He gave us free beer and soft drinks for the kids. Later, he came up with fried eggs and fritters and, as we sat around our banquet, we marvelled at the wonderful country of Iran. After we enjoyed a final few days on the Caspian coast, we headed for home.

'We've all died and gone to heaven'

Chapter 10

The Seventies: A Time of Change

ONE FATEFUL DAY, when I returned home from a hard day slaving over a hot paintbrush, I discovered I was wifeless. I had departed that morning as usual, seen off by my devoted Rose who had packed me a pie baked by her own loving hands and given me my usual tender kiss before waving me off. She had then buggered off with a shifty-eyed taxi driver of no fixed means and no fixed address.

The owner of pointed, patent leather shoes, a toothbrush moustache, slicked back hair plastered with Brylcreem and a smarmy obsequious smile, he had the look of a wartime spiv. His was a face like a ferret with the flickering eyes of an ex-con; he was one of life's unfortunates who had a wife and seven kids in Middlesbrough and was currently 'shacked up' with a lady in Morecambe. He also bred budgies – hence the name 'Budgie Bill'. Rose had met him while doing voluntary work for handicapped children; he was one of the part-time drivers and would bring the children sweeties. He was 'such a nice man', according to Rose, who introduced him to me one day.

'He doesn't have many friends and he likes you,' she said later. 'Well, I don't like him,' I muttered.

'He doesn't have many friends and he likes you'

'Oh, you will when you get to know him,' answered Rose. And get to know him I did – or at least his bloody budgies, which suddenly started appearing in my garage.

'Just a few, for a couple of weeks Jim, while I repair my aviary,' he said in his whingey voice. 'Oh, you are a smashing couple – I don't know what I would do without you.'

After a couple of weeks I realised that my garage was slowly shrinking – I could hardly fit my car in for the budgie boxes full of screeching birds that lined the walls and the bits of furniture that had miraculously appeared.

Rose explained: 'His wife's thrown him out.'

'But she lives in Middlesbrough,' I said.

'No, not her, the one in Morecambe. He's desperate and I said it would be alright until he gets another place,' said Rose, 'and the police are after him for non-payment of family support . . .'

All that took place a couple of months before and I had seen little of Budgie Bill since then. Now, I was home after a long day's work and, as I made a meal that night, I vaguely wondered where Rose was. It was most unusual that she was not there for, being a good wife, she was always around to look after my every need. I began ringing around her friends and acquaintances, then her relatives and then, as the night wore on, with a numb feeling in the pit of my stomach, I telephoned the local hospitals, thinking she had been involved in a driving accident. Then I tried the police, who said they would make enquiries and keep me informed.

After a sleepless night I checked again – nothing. I sat down and racked my brains, wondering where could she be as I went through lists of old friends, and caving mates' wives and girlfriends. Nothing! Slowly, my numb mind thought of Budgie Bill. Perhaps he knew where she was. I rang the taxi firm he worked for and said I would like to speak to him. 'So would I,' said the boss on the other end, 'the bastard's pissed off with a week's takings!'

I went cold. 'What do you want him for?' enquired the voice on the end of the phone.

'I think the bastard's pissed off with my wife.'

'Well, let me know if you find him,' said the man.

'There'll be no need, because I'll kill the bastard!' I exclaimed. It was ridiculous; I couldn't believe it – there had to be another explanation. Rose and I had shared a good marriage; we were very close, seldom had an argument and had done everything together for twenty-five years. We were the envy of many of our friends. She could never go off with a bum like that!

The following days were a turmoil as I finished the job I was on and made excuses about others, while checking with the police and giving more excuses to relatives and friends about Rose's non-appearance, telling everyone she was visiting a sick relative.

Three days later I had a visit from a police sergeant and a woman police constable, who sat down and had a long talk with me about my wife's vanishing trick. The woman constable asked if Rose had taken any clothes and, together, we made a thorough search and found nothing missing – even the housekeeping money was intact. There was no note, or anything.

'We find this very unusual. A woman running away generally takes something,' said the sergeant. 'Have another look, and in the meantime we'll put her on the missing persons list and make further enquiries about her and her car.'

Things grew steadily worse as my ageing parents kept asking why Rose hadn't been visiting them – she generally called in once or twice a day and they thought a lot of her; 'helping a sick relative' was becoming a bit stale after three weeks. Everyone was enquiring after her. I slowly came to the very painful conclusion that my faithful, loving wife had gone completely mad and disappeared with Budgie Bill.

Why? I shall never know, because I never saw her again.

And Budgie Bill? Oh, I searched for him alright. Every night I toured the taxi ranks within a thirty-mile radius. I even went to Manchester looking for this creep, but never found him.

Eventually, everyone had to be told – they were just as incredulous as I was and could hardly believe it. However, each cloud has a silver lining and my dear old mother, who was very astute, soon developed a nice little sideline flogging budgies to her friends at bingo. I did all the work and she made all the profit. I had been left holding the bird in more ways than one.

Someone once remarked that bereavement is often less traumatic than desertion, pointing out that with the death of a loved one the bereaved is left with memories that will never fade or die. Desertion, on the other hand, causes one to question an erstwhile good marriage, as deceit is a slow poison that spreads its corrosive influence until the happiest of memories become tainted and false.

After the initial shock and the never-ending question of 'why?' which kept recurring in my mind, I became obsessed and carried a cold anger and the need for revenge. The deep feelings that I had for Rose turned to hatred as I trawled the area in search of any clue that would set me on the path of retribution. I kept a machete in the boot of my car on the off-chance that I might come across the 'budgie fancier', so I could slice his balls off. Fortunately, I never found him.

AFTER SOME TIME IN LIMBO, where in my distraught state I became desperate for female compassion, I realised that I needed expert advice on how to attract a woman. I decided to approach the fount of all human knowledge on bird-pulling: Greenclose near Clapham, the headquarters of the Northern Pennine Club for potholers, cavers, men about town and bird-pullers extraordinaire.

For years I had listened to the amorous adventures of my caving club's Casanovas, while drooling with envy into my beer as they gave me blow by blow accounts of wrestling with buxom nymphomaniacs and fighting off virgins who wanted to give their all. Now, being single again, I could join them.

Karate Bill, Black Mike and Sambo were in residence. After they had listened to my plight I said: 'Right – let's go and pull some birds.'

They looked at me in astonishment.

'What? Do you know some?' they chorused.

'No, but I thought you lot did. You're always telling me about the birds you've had,' I said.

'Oh, er, well, er, well. I haven't had a date for six months,' said Black Mike. 'They seem to have gone off me.'

A typical NPC wild bunch of the period: Dave Barker, 'Karate' Bill Pybus and the Duckworth brothers, Little and Big Sambo

'Well, how about all this crumpet at Ingleton?' I asked despairingly. 'What about Sonia Snell and her mate, whatsername, er, Marion, you were always on about?'

'Oh, Marion's up the spout and Sonia's got married to Slug's mate,' answered Sambo glumly.

'How about the local hop?'

'Cancelled – too many drunks – us,' said Karate Bill.

'You must know some women,' I said.

'No,' came the answer in a unanimous grunt.

'What about all these birds you are always telling me about?' I asked

'Lies, Jim,' they said. 'All lies!'

We all retired to the Flying Horseshoes at Clapham Station and got pissed. 'You're all full of bullshit,' I said.

'Yes, we know,' chorused my fellow bachelors.

I decided all was fair in love and war. The sad truth was that if I even wanted to see a young lady again, I would have to keep away from the caving scene for a bit and look for a young lady's habitat – the nearest being the dance halls of Morecambe.

Within no time at all, my luck had changed and I found that young ladies are like buses – you can wait for ever and then suddenly two come along at once. In my case I hit the jackpot, because they were both nymphomaniacs. One nymphomaniac can cause premature ageing, but *two* is a recipe for disaster that no normal man can handle.

I decided to take the two sisters for a ride in the country to see my country estate, namely Greenclose. Karate Bill and Dave were standing in the doorway as I drove up. It was wonderful to see their faces.

'Bloody 'ell, it's Ers with two women!'

'Bloody 'ell,' said Dave, 'it's Ers with two women!'

They looked at me with respect as I presented them to the two ladies, tempered slightly as the two sisters drew nearer, for nymphomaniacs are not always the best of lookers. But there it was: Ers, with not one woman but two and hoping shortly to have only one as Dave began paying rapt attention to the older sister, whom I wished to offload.

After a visit to the Flying Horseshoes, Dave and the older sister fell madly in love while the younger sister and I departed for Morecambe and some strenuous physical exercise. This darkened the rings under my eyes until I resembled a tall, thin panda that had been mistreated.

I received another visit from the police, who wanted to know if I had heard anything from or about my missing wife. I also had a long chat with the police lady, who couldn't understand why Rose had taken nothing and suggested that we conduct another, more detailed search. This revealed that her hair drier and food mixer had gone.

'Are you sure that you never had a dispute or argument of any kind? Where do her relatives live? Do you mind if we look round the garden?'

At this stage I thought that I should mention the strange coincidence of the missing taxi driver, whereupon they both became more friendly and went to Morecambe to pursue another line of enquiry. I went to the fish and chip shop, because nymphomaniacs can't cook.

I HAD NOT BEEN BORN RICH or good-looking, but I've always considered myself lucky – not in the gambling sense, but in dealing with life's problems (which were generally self-made). Somehow or other, I would always escape unscathed to emerge to fight again another day.

Jean, one of Rose's old workmates, invited me to a party, an occasion which proved to be the most important one of my life. Also attending was an angel, a lovely, slim, fair-headed lady with sad, bluish-grey eyes and a beautiful smile. 'This is Audrey,' said Jean, and my new life began.

I knew Audrey's husband Bill casually, having worked with him – both of us were in the building trade – and Audrey had worked in the office of the factory where Rose had been employed; indeed, I soon found out that some years previously she had sold Rose her bike.

By a series of strange coincidences our lives had run on parallel tracks: we had both been married for about the same length of time, Bill and I were self-employed, hard-working and very similar in nature; my marriage had gone, while theirs was tottering. In addition, my wife had gone off with a taxi driver, whereas Bill had suddenly fallen in love with the milkman's wife and, like many men before who had suddenly become besotted, almost overnight he had changed from a faithful, loving husband into a peculiar, almost crazy person who divided their bungalow in two and denied Audrey access to his half – although he 'allowed' her to cook his meals and do his washing. Bill had also told her he didn't love her any more and was going to leave with the milkman's wife, yet this lovely woman still stood by him and suffered daily humiliation because, in spite of everything, she still loved him. It was a case of mutual attraction for two innocent victims and I determined to put the sparkle back into those beautiful, sad eyes.

The milkman's wife suddenly decided that she would not leave her husband and the stress of everything made Audrey's husband worse. Audrey left him to live with her mother – Elsie, a charming lady – who looked upon me as though I was an evil prince intent on spiriting her fair daughter away – which I was. Eventually I did, after much recrimination from Elsie about living in sin (and the fact that 'Bunny', her old boss from forty years previously who kept rabbits and lived two doors away from me, meant that she would never be able to hold her head up again). Dear old Elsie.

It took a great deal of persuasion to persuade Audrey to move in with me, for in those days morals were very different. In the end it was Elsie that clinched it. 'Go on, our Audrey, you might as well – it's wearing him out coming out here every day.'

One morning, while I was out at work, two stolid policemen came marching down the drive of 27 Chequers Avenue and knocked on the door. It was opened by a beautiful, blonde-haired lady who smiled and said: 'Hello.'

The policemen, obviously taken aback, said, 'Mrs Eyre?' You're back?'

'Oh, no, I'm not Mrs Eyre. I'm Audrey.'

'We are still trying to trace Mrs Eyre,' said the sergeant. 'I don't suppose you have any idea where she might be?'

'No,' answered Audrey, 'for all I know she could be under those rosebushes,' she said, waving her hand in the direction of the back garden.

'Oh,' said the sergeant,

'Would you like a cup of tea, love?' asked Audrey, smiling sweetly.

'Er, no thanks – we had better be off,' and the two bobbies marched back up the drive with very thoughtful looks on their faces. 'What do you think Arthur? Do you reckon she was kidding?' asked one. 'Dunno,' said his mate, 'I think it's a job for the special branch.'

During this period of wooing and winning the fair Audrey, I was on my best behaviour and kept away from cavers, who on the whole are an unsavoury lot. I had stopped swearing, washed twice a day and was the epitome of the perfect husband – even though I wasn't one. I had even dropped into the bad habit of taking a drive into the countryside and dining out in some style.

After an enjoyable day showing Audrey the beauties of the Yorkshire Dales, we ended up in the Marton Arms in Thornton-in-Lonsdale, taking great care to go in at the posh end, away from the small rear bar frequented by rough cavers and kept separate by a small serving hatch. Audrey and I were having a pleasant tête-à-tête when I heard a raucous cry ring out above the general hubbub, which chilled me to the marrow.

'There's Ers with a bit of stuff.'

Out of the corner of my eye I discerned Karate Bill's mop of curly hair framed in the serving hatch, but pretended not to notice.

'Jim, Jim!' The loud yell silenced all conversation and Audrey said, 'I think someone is trying to attract your attention.'

'It won't be me, it's probably another Jim,' I said, shifting my chair slightly so my back was to the hatch. Suddenly, I was confronted with my worst nightmare.

''Ello, Jim, and who do we have here?' I looked up at the motley crew that surrounded us. Karate Bill looked like a miniature Marx brother, Barker was grinning like a Cheshire cat, while Cadge was smirking evilly at Audrey and the two Sambo brothers resembled fugitives from a refugee camp. 'Can we join you?' asked Cadge, sitting down next to Audrey.

'No,' I said, 'you're not dressed correctly; you should be in the back room.'

'Are these your friends?' asked the sweet Audrey.

'No,' I said.

'Are you going to introduce us to this delightful lady?' asked Barker in a smarmy voice.

'No,' I said. It was no good, I was trapped and my innocent relationship with Audrey would soon be coming to an end. No one could withstand the onslaught of disgusting behaviour which I knew would soon be unleashed.

I grabbed Karate Bill and whispered in his ear, 'If I get the drinks in will you keep your traps shut?'

Audrey

'Certainly Jim,' he answered in his amiable, angelic way.

When I returned from the bar I found these evil sods clustered around Audrey like wasps around a jam pot and I dreaded what they were telling her. Whatever it was, though, it was making her laugh.

'Have you heard this one?' Barker was saying, before bursting into song in a fine baritone voice, joined by the rest of the barbershop singers as they started on 'The Ball of Kirriemuir'. This became muckier with every verse and was causing me great anxiety for, as it got muckier, I could see they were taking great delight in trying to shock the fair Audrey. Having finished in fine style, gloating in anticipation, they

'Are you going to introduce us to this delightful lady?'

were astonished when the fair Audrey sang another three verses, which were even muckier still.

'Wow,' uttered Barker. 'What a fine woman you have here, Jim.' What's more, he was right!

I later asked gentle, innocent Audrey how she came by such disgustingly funny lyrics, forgetting that her husband had served with the Fifth Army in Italy.

EVERY EASTER the Northern Pennine Club's climbing section would descend on Glen Coe, where we would camp outside the Clachaig Inn and do battle with various peaks, frightening rock faces, snow and ice ridges and gullies. In those far-off days, camping was simply a matter of finding a piece of ground flat enough and dry enough to place a tent on (in Scotland, that meant under less than a foot of water). We ancient Britons and Scots were primitive people who were able to exist without campsites, wardens, toilets and washrooms, but none were more primitive than the residents of a large, battered, red vehicle which boldly proclaimed in large white painted letters on its sides: McBrindle's Sausage Van.

Sitting with Audrey outside my tent one evening, we watched with interest as the van ground to a halt and disgorged what seemed to us to be half the Gorbals' population of juvenile delinquents along with a gorgeous girl with long, blonde hair, clutching a guitar. She had obviously been kidnapped and I half expected her to be tied to the nearest tree to prevent her escaping – but no, the leader of this warlike tribe took her by the hand and said: 'Och away Angie, let's awa tae the fookin' pub,' then gave me a cheery wave and shouted: 'Ar ye alright Jammie – ar ye no comin' fer a drank?'

Scottish hotels were not built for comfort and, later on that evening, we became engaged in the only activity that was suitable under the galvanised roof of the small climbers' bar at the rear of the Clachaig. Soon, our spartan surroundings softened with the effects of Scottish beer, raucous laughter and wild songs, and we discovered that McBrindle's van was the official transport for a group of Glasgow's young tearaways who, under the leadership of Mac Brindle and thanks to some local charity, might benefit from a few days in the mountains. Every year, while most of the previous lot ended up in jail, Mac would try again and bring another group to Glen Coe.

Scottish licensing laws at that time ensured that everyone became severely inebriated, for the bars closed at 9 p.m. and you had to drink fast then vacate the premises fast, as glasses were whipped out of your grasp and forms were tipped up from beneath you by a burly group of bar staff. By five minutes past nine we were deposited outside and staggering the hundred yards to our tents.

One thing was obvious: we weren't going to be cold, for Mac's gang had built an enormous bonfire next to my tent. I pointed out my smouldering guy ropes to one of the lads and he replied, 'Nae problem,' pissed on them and shoved a can of beer in my hand.

There was to be no sleep that night, so we sat around the fire and listened to the lovely blonde girl (who was a Dutch hitchhiker) playing her guitar and singing in a soft, melodic voice which entranced these wild young Scotsmen into worshipful silence. 'Och, Jimmy, she's an angel,' said Mac.

The following day we were up late, there had been a heavy frost, and the McBrindle clan (which didn't seem to have slept at all) was busy foraging for wood in the nearby sparse tree growth, to stoke up the fire. They didn't seem to eat, either, and appeared

They both fired and shot him up the arse

to exist on tins of beer and crisps, which they kept digging out from underneath the two old mattresses that floored the back of the van.

Audrey found her new lifestyle of sleeping on the ground next to neighbours such as these quite fascinating, having previously been used to staying in hotels.

'It's not always like this – it's quite nice when it's sunny and you don't often come across people like these.' I was apologising profusely when Audrey approached one of the lads who, feeling the pangs of hunger, was about to put a tin of beans on the fire. Smiling sweetly, she took the tin off the lad, opened it with our tin opener, put the contents in one of our pans, warmed it on one of our Primus stoves and popped it onto the lad's plate. Craigie looked at Audrey with admiration. 'Och, thanks hen,' he said and vanished into the van.

'Well,' said Audrey, 'it's better than having an exploding can covering us with beans.'

We had some brief entertainment laid on as we were packing our rucksacks prior to setting off for the Aonach Eagach traverse. Several air rifles had suddenly appeared among our neighbours and the lads asked Mac to set up some targets on the hillside. As Mac clambered up the steep slope, I watched two of the lads cock their loaded weapons before shouting to their unsuspecting leader.

'That'll dae, Mac,' and as Mac bent over to place the targets they both fired and shot him up the arse. He leapt in the air with a cry of rage.

'Ye fookin' wee tearawa' bastards – I'll have ye fookin' balls off!'

Dare I leave Audrey near this lot? She assured me that she would be alright – she would take her terrier Tara for a walk, and there were plenty of other people around.

Reluctantly, I jumped into a car with the rest of our team and headed to the top of the glen to start the long traverse. It turned out to be one of those unforgettable days that only Scotland can provide. The sun broke through the early morning mist and sparkled off the foot-deep, hard, frozen snow which covered the higher ground. We kicked our way up the steep slope behind Am Bodach, leaving the classic shape of

Glen Coe curving away beneath our feet. The River Coe flashed gold as it flowed into the small loch of Achtriochtan before continuing to Loch Leven, just coming into view as a blue ribbon of water against the paler blue of the sky. It was good to be alive and, being fit men, the four of us reached the beginning of the ridge in good time.

It was crampon time, for the rock was covered in ice with a layer of snow frozen crisply on top. These were perfect conditions for taking on this classic ridge, the only blot on the horizon being Wilky.

Wilky was one of those exuberant characters that hang around the caving and climbing world, who either have done everything or are going to do everything. Stockily built, red-faced and with eyes peering enthusiastically from behind thick glasses while he forever jumped about banging his hands together, Wilky was always on cloud nine and, apart from being a fairly likeable character, could never quite get his act together. I had just fastened my crampons on when I noticed Wilky pulling out a pair of brand new crampons from a climbing shop bag, complete with price tag.

'Have you tried those on?' I queried.

'No, they'll fit,' answered Wilky, wrapping the straps around his boots while trying to ignore the two-inch gap at the front of each crampon. In spite of words of advice from the three of us that the crampons needed adjusting to his boots, Wilky insisted that he would be alright. 'Anyway, I can climb without these things.'

We set off up the ice-covered rock and within seconds Wilky was in trouble – one of his crampons had come loose and, held by the strap, was swinging from his ankle.

'Jim, Jim. Chuck us a rope,' he shouted. It wasn't desperate, so I directed him to some ice-free rock with big jugs where he could pull himself up.

'Bloody 'ell,' he said as he sat down on the broad ledge.

'You silly sod,' Frank said, 'we told you they would come off.' Wilky busily wrapped the straps around again.

'They'll be alright now,' said Wilky and I led the way up the steeply rising ground onto the crest of the ridge.

Coming out of the cold shade into the dazzling glare of the sun, I could feel the instant warmth and stood for a moment, taking in the humpback of the Aonach Eagach as it undulated in a sweeping curve of ice and snow, like a huge ice-bound whale heading towards the sea.

Moving across the crisp ice that crunched beneath the points of our crampons, I clambered over hard-packed snow which took us to the summit of Am Bodach and the start of the ridge proper. The view was superb and we stood for a while, taking in the miniature figures of climbers dotted on the steep snow slopes of Bidean nam Bian, standing out among the arc of snow-covered peaks across the other side of the broad U-shaped expanse of the glen. Behind us lay the familiar, imposing sight of Buachaille Etive Mor, standing sentinel over the hazy wilds of Rannoch Moor and the road, like a silver thread drawn across the dark peat bogs, heading south towards England.

Continuing over rocks rimed with frost, I came to a short climb down. It was not difficult, though it was severely iced up and there was a long way to plummet if one fell and skidded off the ridge just below us. I uncoiled the rope and lined Jim down. Wilky clipped on and walked towards the edge, stepped out of his new crampons, slipped on the ice and went zooming over the edge of the twenty-foot drop.

It was unbelievably hilarious – a line of crampon prints in the snow that suddenly stopped at two crampons, empty and deserted at the edge of a vertical drop, with their former owner swinging in space below and making all sorts of strange noises. Frank and I were in hysterics and I almost let Wilky go, I was laughing so much. Eventually, I recovered and lowered him into the arms of some other climbers who were also traversing the ridge.

When I climbed down to them, Wilky was receiving a bollocking from a bluff Yorkshireman. 'Silly buggers like you shouldn't be allowed on a mountain. Hast tha no bloody crampons?'

Jim climbing on the Aonoch Eagach ridge. Photo: Jim Newton

'Yes,' says Wilky, 'they're up there.'

'Bloody amateurs,' said the Yorkshireman.

'I'm a potholer, really,' said Wilky with a demeaning grin on his face.

'Aye,' said the Yorkshireman, 'tha'd be better off down a bloody 'ole in't ground – it'd save us burying thee.'

Luckily for us and Wilky, this chance encounter proved to be a good thing, for one of the climbers had a crampon key in his pack. Wilky's new-found Yorkshire admirer said, 'Sit thee arse down there,' and adjusted his crampons for him. 'That'll cost thee a pint if tha gets down with out killing theesel',' he said as we moved on.

Although it was only just over 3,000 feet high, being on the ridge was like walking on the roof of the world. Not for us the massive Himalayan peaks – our roof of the world, though much more modest, was less threatening and we strode along, breathing the clear mountain air, with the warm sun brushing us with an agreeable glow. Sheets of ice glowed silver against the panorama of snow-covered peaks and dark valleys that swept northwards like a rumpled tablecloth towards the looming mass of Ben Nevis.

Ah, Scotland, bonny Scotland. On a day like this, with heavy gear stowed away in the rucksack, invigorated by the sun under a cloudless azure blue sky, heading along a ridge steadily curving towards Sgorr na Ciche that was silhouetted like a woman's breast against the backdrop of the deep, blue sea lochs of Leven and Eil, what could be better? With these marvellous conditions we soon made up for our late start and, as the sun dipped low, we traversed around the horseshoe beyond Sgorr nam Fiannaidh and headed for the edge of the ridge which overlooked Signal Rock and the lower end of the glen. Soon, we were back at the tents. The sausage van was there, but many tents had gone. So had Audrey, probably taking Tara for a walk, I thought.

As Jim and Frank drove up the glen to pick up Frank's car, I wandered across to the Clachaig for a swift pint before a meal. There at the bar stood Audrey, surrounded by Mac's gang. Mac spotted me entering the bar.

'Och, Jammie, yor wee wifie is a fookin' lovely woman.'

'Aye. Ye can fookin' sae that again,' chorused the ginger-haired urchin who had shot Mac with his airgun.

'Aye, and her wee scabby dog is fookin' great fun too,' said another, shoving an ashtray full of beer under the wire-haired terrier's nose.

Almost every other word was a swear word and I felt embarrassed for Audrey. 'Here, Jimmie, have a wee dram,' and someone stuck a double whisky and a pint in front of me. 'We think ye are aw fookin' mad, gannin' awa' up yon fookin' hills when the fookin' pub is open – but Jimmie, your wee lady is a fookin' angel, she lent us some pans and showed us how to cook a fookin' dinner.'

I was released from his drunken embrace by Audrey, who asked, 'Have you had a good day love?'

'Oh, yes, it's been brilliant. How have you gone on?'

'Fookin' great!' said Audrey.

A COUPLE OF WEEKS LATER, after dodging boulders down Gavel Pot when one of our digs collapsed, I retired in a hurry to the Craven Heifer in Ingleton and explained the dangers of Pennine digs to a fellow caver, while leaning on the bar pouring some of Yates & Jackson's best bitter down my throat.

'Well, if we had been designed for digging down 'oles in the ground with Batty, I reckon we would have been shaped like kippers – flat, so we couldn't get squashed, and with both our eyes on the top of our heads to watch out for falling boulders and fuckin' crowbars,' I was saying, when in walked a couple of Northern Cave Club members with a harassed-looking Colin Davies.

Colin made a beeline for the bar and swallowed his first pint without breathing. He was halfway through the next before he stopped, belched and surreptitiously nudged me in the ribs. 'Psst,' he whispered.

'No,' I answered, 'I've only had three.'

'I need a word – it's important,' said Colin.

'Right, what's the problem?' I asked. Colin looked shiftily around the crowded bar, then lowered his voice and whispered in my ear.

'We've found her!'

'Who?' I asked.

'Rose!' I almost choked on my beer, which went down the wrong way.

'Where is she?' I asked.

'You know,' he answered, suddenly assuming the guise of someone involved in the Gunpowder Plot.

'When did you find her?' I asked, my voice a hoarse croak.

'Last weekend,' answered Colin, lighting up his pipe.

'Where is she?' I asked again.

'You know, me and my mate knows – but nobody else knows. We thought we would have a word with you first,' answered Colin, puffing like Sherlock Holmes on his bloody pipe.

'For Christ's sake tell me where she is – did she say anything?' Colin stared at me with a strange expression in his eyes, as though he was looking at a madman.

'*Say anything*? Bloody 'ell Jim, you know she can't say anything!'

'Why?' I asked, my senses reeling.

'Cos she's had about two tons of rock dropped on her, that's why. We've found her in our dig. It gave us quite a shock coming across her like that, just a skeleton with her hands tied. My mate, John, said, "Bloody 'ell, it's Rose!"'

'Two more pints, Jack,' I shouted above the hubbub as I tried to grasp what I had been told. I hastened to reassure Colin that I hadn't done my wife in, although the thought had crossed my mind – though if I had I wouldn't have buried her on a fell where cavers are digging like demented ferrets.

Colin seemed a little disappointed when I told him he could tell the police, and even more disappointed when a forensic examination revealed that the bound skeleton was very old, even older than Rose. It was a pity really, as not everyone has a skeleton in the cupboard. Even I felt a bit cheated, for her skull would have looked well on the mantelpiece and could have provided a good topic of conversation at dinner parties. As it was, I had to be content with police bloodhounds, which eventually unearthed her residing in Scunthorpe. I promptly divorced her – pity about the skull on the mantelpiece, though.

EXACTLY A WEEK AFTER THE DECREE my fair Audrey said to me over breakfast, 'What are you doing on Wednesday, Jim?'

'Er, dunno,' I answered. 'Nothing much – why?'

'We're getting married,' said Audrey, with a beautiful smile on her face. It's not given to many men, the chance to marry an angel, so I took it.

It's also not given to many men to live a life of bliss and utter contentment, especially if one is a member of the Northern Pennine Club. I had settled into a life of polished shoes, walking the dog around the park, doing jobs around the house, manicuring the lawn and generally being a dutiful husband, when Audrey said, 'I hope you haven't stopped caving. Why don't you go to the summer dinner?'

NPC summer dinners in those days represented a throwback to Pagan rituals. They weren't meant to be, for they always started off as quite respectable occasions where some members even wore ties (and some had even borrowed suits). All these nice Doctor Jekylls greeted each other in a very civilised fashion at the commencement of every dinner, little knowing that inside each one was a tiny, dehydrated Mister Hyde, who just needed soaking in three pints of beer before he became activated and changed the personality of his host.

The strange thing about this phenomenon was the fact that on the following day no one could ever remember what had taken place the night before, and this particular dinner was just the same.

I awoke with a dry mouth and a thumping head. Slowly, I recollected the landlord swinging on the hooks in the pub's ceiling and Karate Bill swinging after him, ending up impaled on a hook by one hand and swinging on the light with the other.

Soon, everyone was awake. Bleary-eyed bodies crawled out of tents, cars and vans and the aroma of frying eggs and bacon came from the tents of the hardier souls. Gradually, the village returned to normal.

Jim and Audrey
Photo: Norman Gunningham

When were Barker's hands run over by a vintage car, while he took 'classic photos?' Was that yesterday? Did we go swimming in the river? At some point, at some dinner, two of us had assisted Chester with his one leg to the edge of a small outcrop, before launching him into space – much to the consternation of two old ladies who were walking past. 'Oh, Ethel! Did you see those hooligans? They've just thrown a one-legged man off a cliff!' It was all a bit hazy.

The following weekend I turned up at Greenclose to lead a meet down Long Kin West. My team was a bit thin on the ground, which is another way of saying I was on my own apart from JJ, Karate Bill and another character who was going to help carry the gear. Then, coming up the road we spied a lonely figure and as he drew nigh we recognised the unkempt body of a sweating, cursing, limping Sambo.

'I've just walked fifteen bloody miles . . . Bloody Americans – no bloody wonder they messed up in Vietnam. Stupid sod!'

The 'stupid sod' in question was a black American sergeant who had taken pity on Sambo hitchhiking to the Dales after a slight malfunction of Sambo's van (the brakes were knackered). The sergeant had pulled up in a huge transport vehicle and opened the door. Offering Sambo a welcoming hand, the sergeant said, in the friendly way that Americans have, 'Hi buddy – welcome aboard. My name's Elmer.'

'Hi, Elmer,' answered Sambo, grasping the huge hand. 'My name's Sambo.' Within one second flat, Sambo was deposited in the gutter beside the grass verge and the transport driver heaped abuse on his head as he drove off.

'I don't suppose you fancy a trip down Long Kin West,' I began. I won't write down the reply, because it would take too long and would not be published anyway, owing to its extreme non-political nature. Needless to say, we ended up in the Flying Horse-shoes instead.

I never knew how Sambo had received his extraordinary nickname so, after mollifying him with a couple of pints, I asked him for the story.

'It's obvious,' said Sambo, 'Cos you're called Jim, some blokes call you Jimbo.'

'Well, not many, I generally get called something else . . . So, your name is Sam,' I said.

'No, my name is Kevin,' said Sambo.

I went for a long walk, alone.

ALL CAVERS HAVE A SPECIAL QUALITY that sets them apart from other mortals: eccentricity. It's built into the caver's make-up, for a person has to be odd or whimsical to want to crawl into dark crevices or hurl him- or herself down bottomless pits. With this eccentricity comes a camaraderie that is seldom seen in other activities, apart from among climbers.

There is none of this 'buddy talk' that takes place in American locker rooms, or the exchange of shirts and jockstraps or the kissing and hugging that goes on in football circles. There are no dirty deals made at the nineteenth hole, and no scratching balls behind the cricket pavilion – but as for 'bonding', we are as close as lovebirds when we find ourselves involved in a new discovery. Generally, this happens deep underground with your head almost up someone's bum, lying full-length in a restricted crevice while passing armfuls of mud and rubble to someone behind you who is in a fairly intimate proximity with your nether regions.

They don't come any stranger than the Northern Pennine Club's favourite mole, a certain Mr Batty who has one aim in life: digging holes. Unfortunately for the NPC, all

Mr Batty's holes led to dismal crawls, tight crevices, loose boulders or flood-prone death traps – but eventually, after a lot of work, nearly all later led into large, impressive cave systems. In the early days, the trouble with Mr Batty was that he had an unerring gift of picking digs that I, with Red Rose Cave & Pothole Club members, had recently abandoned because they were too dangerous, impossible or required lots of gelignite, which we didn't possess.

I would spend months working on a particular dig, suspending young cavers upside down by their braces so that they could either heave rocks out or try to insert their heads underwater to look through a letterbox crack to see if it would go. Gradually, for some unknown reason, I would run out of volunteers and end up in a Dales pub moaning about my clubmates' lack of faith. My woes were listened to, of course, by sympathetic members of the NPC – then several months later I would learn that one of my digs had 'gone', having been pushed by the NPC!

FOUNTAINS FELL, to the south-east of Penyghent, had been a forbidden area ever since I can remember. I had found this out on one autumn evening many years before when, as a young enthusiastic caver, I had pitched my tent on an obscure fell. The small tent creaked and flapped in the cold October wind. I shivered and rolled over to escape a pain in my right-hand side.

I dimly heard a gruff voice and the pain in my side increased as I moved. Reaching down to ease the irritation, my hand encountered something cold and hard. I hastily opened one eye and saw to my amazement the blue-grey steel of a gun barrel, which was painfully prodding at my body. Both eyes opened immediately and my shocked gaze traversed quickly up the barrel, through the open tent flap, past a gnarled finger hooked around a trigger and on towards an equally gnarled, large farmer who had the features of a sexually frustrated bull terrier.

'Right, get up! I've been after you buggers for years!' said the farmer in a rasping voice. 'You're one of them Blackpool Pirates – I've seen you afore,' he yelled. 'Out!'

I had been taught from an early age never to argue with a shotgun, so I presented myself outside the tent in one second flat and stood to attention in my father's borrowed pyjamas, looking up at the six-foot-six monolith before me.

'You must be mistaken. I'm not a Blackpool Pirate, or any other pirate, and I've never been here before . . .'

'*AND* – tha's not coming here again,' interrupted the farmer with his grizzled visage as black as thunder.

I was ungraciously hustled off the fell, with all my belongings hastily bundled into my dismantled tent and balanced on my petrol tank as I shot off down the rough track, skidding sideways and still clad in pyjamas. With the motorbike throwing up a spray of mud and smoke, a warning rang in my ears: 'I'll shoot thee next time!'

That was my first acquaintance with Fountains Fell. I later found out that there had indeed been a Blackpool Pirates Potholing Club, whose members evaded capture only by legging it across the fell and hurtling over a wall as shotgun pellets whistled round their ears, three lodging in someone's bum.

Already at risk from lead poisoning through using lead paint, I didn't wish to chance increasing my intake by having lead pellets injected up my backside by a trigger-happy farmer, so for a number of years I wisely stayed away from Fountains Fell. Then, over the grapevine we heard that the NPC had been allowed on the fell. Whether it was a case of blood relationships or there was a bitch the farmer wanted to mate with, or if he only wanted to mate his dog with one of the cavers, we never found out. For some time it was the only club allowed, until limited access was granted to other groups, and then only under strict conditions.

I hastily applied for permission to explore Gingling Hole and a few weeks later I and some clubmates descended this short, sporting cave. Moving along canals and traverses and down several small pitches, we gained Stalactite Chamber, an impressive fifty-foot-high, thirty-foot-wide chamber which totally and incongruously formed the end of the cave. Gingling Hole was a powerful, active sink and it was obvious that there was more to Gingling than met the eye.

We ferreted among the boulders, climbed part-way up the chamber walls and rooted under a waterfall which sank into rock debris. We began removing rocks and revealed a narrow rift, which was impassable. I then noticed a small annexe and what looked like an arched roof buried under the mud and fill. I had a rummage and then heard the sound of falling water – it needed a dig and we vowed to come back, as I was convinced that a major cave lay below.

Somehow, some NPC cavers heard about my intentions and, having found me standing at the bar in the Helwith Bridge Hotel, I was suddenly accosted by a very friendly Colin Green. He insisted on buying me drinks while telling me what a fine fellow I was, as he cunningly veered the conversation round to Fountains Fell. Soon, I was enthusing about the rushings and gurglings of falling water below Gingling's final chamber.

Colin bought more drinks and left me there, waving my arms about, still burbling about the 'caverns measureless to man' while he dashed off on his motorbike to warn his fellow clubmates of impending doom. The fact that another club could even contemplate digging in NPC territory brought Gordon Batty out in a cold sweat when he was told that 'Jim Eyre is going to dig in the bottom of Gingling.'

Several nights later, several shadowy figures went creeping across Fountains Fell. Within hours they were standing in the final chamber, looking at the place where my rushings and gurglings of water had been heard. After a tentative prod, Gordon pronounced that, 'Only a bloody fool would dig here – not even the Red Rose, but that bloody Eyre might!'

After much plotting and scheming, the NPC members secreted themselves in the cave and undertook a thirteen-hour marathon dig, which revealed a water-worn rift that dropped into a beautiful stream passage which they christened Fool's Paradise (I wonder why?). It led into a series of impressive passages and pitches and turned Gingling Hole into one of the finest caves in the Yorkshire Dales.

The breakthrough was accompanied by intense security, that made MI5 look like amateurs. A small group of trusted NPC members had to sign the equivalent of an Official Secrets Act, forfeiting all their wives and chattels if they leaked any sign of their nefarious activities. They went to extraordinary lengths to maintain secrecy. Colin Green was in his element as, acting like a sort of godfather, he would send out coded telegrams to the 'Secret Seven', who would assemble at a prearranged meeting place which would be changed every weekend, while telling other club members that they were going elsewhere.

The problem of caving club spies, which had already caused my downfall, was well known to Colin. He cunningly arranged meetings in pubs not frequented by cavers, such as the King William in Settle, or the Whistling Pig at Gisburn. His instructions were that cavers should dress like farmers or ordinary folk wearing suits and ties, and they should always arrive singly, as would a casual passer-by, and not recognise each other until Colin gave the signal. The team would later leave singly through different doors and make their way to Colin's house via different routes, taking care to park their vehicles in different locations before giving the secret knock and entering the 'two-up, two-down' on Constitution Hill in Settle.

A few hours' sleep would then be snatched, some cavers lying on the stone floor, four on the bed, two on the settee and one generally in the bath. The latter ceased to be a plum resting place when someone accidentally turned the water on, causing its resident, Bert Tucker, to suddenly leap up and cut his ear on the tap while a deluge of cold water shot down his neck.

At 3 a.m. Colin was awakened by his silent alarm clock (it was specially muffled with a caving sock, so as not to alert the neighbours) and everyone received a weak brew of tea before quietly creeping into Colin's van. This was pushed to the main road before he started the engine, then driven in the opposite direction from their destination, thus checking that the coast was clear before circling back and eventually parking the van in neutral territory adjacent to Fountains Fell.

The problem with writing a story such as this is that no one will believe the facts it contains. However, it becomes more unbelievable.

Upon reaching Fountains Fell, the group of cavers would walk in single file, carefully treading in each other's footsteps. On several occasions, where the soft, peaty ground left clear prints, Gordon would carefully walk over them backwards, thereby giving the impression to any passing Blackfoot Indians or gamekeepers that one person had walked off the fell, instead of seven going the other way.

Being winter, occasional snow caused problems, but this was alleviated by Cadge or Bob Hart bringing up the rear and brushing out the footprints with a hazel-twig broom, blowing the snow back to make miniature snowdrifts. Gingling Hole lies near to a recognised path, so any ladders hanging down the entrance pitch would give the game away, therefore our ingenious Batty and Green duo had, like Baldrick in *Blackadder*, devised a cunning plan.

Gordon would climb a few feet into the shaft and jam a plank across it from a ledge; hanging the ladder from this enabled everyone to descend, apart from the last man. He needed to be thin enough to squeeze into a tight cleft in the side of the shaft, from where he could drop the ladder to the others and pull the plank into the cleft out of sight, then climb down a tortuous rift to join the team. Anyone looking down the entrance would see nothing.

This major cave system took many man-hours to explore and survey. To accomplish this under conditions of absolute secrecy was brilliant, but there is no gain without pain – it meant being underground at four in the morning and not being able to surface until after dark the following night. However, these long, tiring caving trips were accomplished without incident – except, that is, when Chester's false leg was borrowed to use as a belay on a newly discovered two-hundred-foot pitch.

It was bad enough having a 'tin' leg, without his mates continually borrowing it to use as a stemple. This time, Chester was left legless at the top of the pitch, smoking a hand-rolled ciggy and slowly becoming colder during his protracted wait. The long hours underground, the enforced inactivity and less-than-adequate clothing soon reduced him to a shivering wreck.

By the time the men climbed back up the pitch after their explorations, they realised that Chester needed to be taken out of the cave as soon as possible if he was to avoid hypothermia. Helped by his mates and with his retrieved leg bent and suffering from metal fatigue, Chester was assisted to the surface. Colin's van was driven up a nearby track and secrecy was abandoned in the urgency to bring Chester's body temperature back to normal. He was placed in a hot bath, given lots of strong drinks and promised a new leg and a mention in the next newsletter.

'Oh, caving with the Northern Pennine Club can be so much fun,' he said.

Today, such cavers would be charged with discrimination against a mono-ped and classed as monophobics by the Politically Correct Brigade. It has not been recorded what Chester classed them as.

The NPC soon recovered from this escapade, as cavers do, and the exploration and survey of the Gingling extension was finished just in time for a club dinner. These were fairly decorous affairs and this one was no exception; someone had been sick inside the piano and we were just reaching the fifth verse of 'Cats on the rooftops, cats on the tiles, cats with the syphilis and cats with the piles' when the piano, unable to cope with the diced carrots, hiccuped and stopped completely, its keys stuck together. As chief guest I was doing my duty by trying to stay on my feet until breakfast and was singing along when the music stopped – I was then escorted to the bar by Colin and Gordon and asked about my latest dig.

'What dig?' I asked.

'You know, Gingling,' said Colin with a greasy smile on his face. 'You told me about it the other week.'

'Oh yes, we're just getting organised,' said I, slurping into my beer. It was too much. Colin, Gordon, Chester and the rest of the group standing at the bar, all burst out laughing.

'It's a brilliant place to dig,' said Gordon. 'Would you like to see where it went?' When I did see where it went, and how near I had become to being a famous caver like Batty, I grew very depressed and had to lie down in a darkened room for a week. Then I thought, 'What the hell. Who wants to be like Batty anyway?' and quickly recovered.

THE EXTENSION TO GINGLING HOLE, with its two sumps lying at a depth of 553 feet, left more questions than answers to the enigma of Fountains Fell. Close to Gingling Hole is a well-defined dry valley that in wet weather conveys a large volume of floodwater down the fell, to be swallowed by the 'wet sinks'. The water from both Gingling Hole and the sinks emerges at Douk Gill Cave and Brants Gill Head (in those days known as Bransgill Cave) near Horton-in-Ribblesdale, yet there is no sign of the water from the sinks in Gingling Hole, so another major cave system must exist nearby.

In 1949 the bedding plane at the bottom of the small pitch in the sinks was pushed by Dennis and Norman Brindle of the Craven Pothole Club, who found a further series of restricted bedding planes with another short, restricted drop before they were forced to give up because of the threat of flooding.

Northern Pennine Club members then took up the challenge and a year later Malcolm Riley and other club members made several forays into the miserable constraints of the sink, but were forced to give in. In autumn 1950, Brian Heys of the NPC dropped four pounds of fluorescein into the sink, and three days later Brants Gill Head turned green. This proved the existence of a major system and work intensified in an effort to push the cave.

In 1956 a serious attack was made on Gingling Wet Sinks (nowadays just called Gingling Sink) by the NPC. Brian, Dick Hylton and Jack Myers constructed a pipeline of heavy-duty, five-inch hose leading from a dam higher up in the surface valley to a sink lower down, thus bypassing the wet sinks, and this enabled further underground exploration by Brian, Gordon Batty and Bob Goodwin.

A junction beyond the crawls led to a high aven, but exploration was interrupted by a rapid increase in water levels when a sudden rainstorm proved that the pipe leaked like a sieve. To make an exit, the group underground had to fight against a strong flow of water; to add to their problems the dam collapsed, leaving only a few inches of airspace in the low crawls.

Luckily for me, I was a Red Rose member at this time – our life expectancy was much longer and our members were spared these traumatic experiences. Notwithstanding these minor setbacks, the NPC cavers, who have always had kamikaze tendencies, repaired their plumber's nightmare. Then, once more the young, slim and totally fearless were dispatched down the grasping, clammy, claustrophobic wet sinks while the more experienced stayed on top playing with pulsating pipes and fountains of water – until, inevitably, something collapsed and the underground team was flushed to the surface, coughing and spluttering.

It was back to the drawing board and the ever-inventive NPC strengthened the dam and laid eighty modified oil drums across the fell to a weird trifurcation of three large, rubber pipes, which sat on the moor like monstrous pulsating worms, spewing water from leaking joints while Batty and his group pushed and surveyed the wet sinks. Enthusiasm was finally extinguished when the team arrived one day to find a large, peaty lake slowly circling over the wet sinks, so the area was abandoned and exploration turned to other caves in the region.

Several years rolled on and the majority of the Pennine forgot about Fountains Fell, becoming interested in other projects. Not so Gordon Batty – he was a bit like Billy Connolly's 'wee scabby dog', a terrier that had buried a bone and had to return to dig it up.

The Secret Seven were resurrected and, armed with the survey of Gingling Wet Sinks, they began digging from the surface in an attempt to break into the high aven. Brief mutterings about Gordon's latest secret dig reached me on the grapevine. Referred to as 'Shush 2', when I asked him about it in the Flying Horseshoes he went very coy and said out of the side of his mouth so that no one else could hear, 'Shush, not so loud, we've left that and we're now working on Shush 3.'

Gordon's popularity waxes and wanes with the severity of his digs, so when he asked me to meet him in the King Billy the following Saturday, I realised that he was running out of volunteers and that his latest dig must be a sod. I was greeted by the others with deep suspicion for, although by then I had been a member of the NPC for several years, I was still classified as a Red Rose spy – such is the power of the Pennine mythology.

Eventually, after several pints, they became convinced that I was just another drunken bum, an ageing tiger with no teeth and well past my sell-by date. I was duly accepted into the Secret Seven, which brought it up to five members.

There is always an inherent risk in digging in caves, but Gordon seemed to have a charmed life. His group had been digging among unstable boulders over seventy feet down in a valley below Gingling, and while working under this creaking rock pile one of the lads had pointed out that a particularly large boulder was loose. Gordon had answered: 'Safe as a row of houses – you must be imagining it.' The following week their dig had gone, buried under tons of huge rocks.

A few years later he made a similar remark to me in Lost Pot when I realised that the rock bridge I was sitting on was held up by nothing but air. Given the fact that we were part of a rescue team hauling up a badly injured caver who had been struck by rocks falling from the bridge, it was not surprising that everything was loose. However, the rocks stayed in place for a few days more, avoiding our demise and that of the cavers below. The gods smiled on us that day.

HAVING BEEN ACCEPTED into the society of the Secret Seven, I became a member of Gordon Batty's digging team. The Gingling Wet Sinks dig (or Shush 3) had gone and another entrance now led into the eighty-foot aven beyond the flood traps of the surface sink. Unfortunately, the sides to the small entrance shaft kept collapsing, so the Thursday-night group was taking oil drums onto the moor to line the shaft.

Fountains Fell was still a prohibited area and ultimate secrecy had to be maintained, so we continued to cover our tracks and walk backwards in the dead of night. Thus, one night by the light of the silvery moon, three oildrums could be seen walking backwards across Fountains Fell. A local man who witnessed this strange phenomenon is reputed to have become white-haired overnight, after which he swore off drinking and is now the President of the Settle and District Temperance Society.

I have been on many caving expeditions and pirate trips in Britain and France, but have never gone to the extreme of deliberately walking backwards to the vicinity of a cave while carrying an eight-foot length of three-by-two on my shoulder, clutching a saw and a bag of two-inch nails, at three o'clock in the morning. It would have been hilarious, but for the hangover I had given birth to in the King Billy and which was now an adolescent. A night on Colin Green's stone-flagged floor hadn't helped, especially with blokes tripping over me as they went to the back to take a leak.

Suddenly, there was a sign from our leader (though how we saw this when walking backwards I cannot recollect) and we all dived into the nearest shakehole.

'Thought I saw something,' said Batty.

'What, there must be only us that's daft enough to go fell walking at three in the morning,' I muttered.

Our leader had a look at the pitch darkness ahead: 'Coast's clear,' he whispered and strode off (backwards, of course). Eventually, after more crouching in shakeholes, listening for the dawn chorus of insomniac gamekeepers, we arrived by a circuitous route at Shush 3.

'Well,' said Gordon with the proud proprietary air of a father showing off his new-born son, 'What do you think?'

All I could see was a shallow shakehole with a floor of slime, mud and stones and no sign of a sink or crevice of any kind. I was totally nonplussed, but Batty's face was creased by an ear-to-ear grin.

'Watch,' he said and lifted up a six-inch diameter round stone to reveal a hole the size of a saucer, itself part of a neatly camouflaged square iron lid. The mud and gravel were brushed off and the lid lifted to reveal a neat oil-drum-lined shaft, complete with a ladder.

Three oildrums could be seen walking backwards across Fountains Fell

This was better than any performance I had ever seen on telly – it was a magician's illusion par excellence: now you see it, now you don't. Anyone could have stood on top of the entrance without having any inkling of the cave underneath. I looked at the craggy face of Colin Green and the bland features of Gordon Batty, and realised that I was in the presence of genius.

We changed into caving gear, put our clothes into plastic fertiliser bags (supplied by Green Scavengers Inc.), lowered them down the hole and followed them into the darkness. A short ladder pitch took us to a small chamber, where a passage led to the aven. Colin, who is an expert in most things, was last in. He pulled the iron lid back into position, put his hand through the hole and scraped mud and gravel over it, then the stone – which had a bolt drilled into it – was pulled over the hole in the lid, a short rope was tied to it and fastened at the other end to the ladder, to prevent it from being dislodged.

It was brilliant. To all intents and purposes, the hole and the cavers it contained, didn't exist. We had been wiped off the face of the earth. No one else knew of its existence – not even our wives. No one!

I found this rather unnerving, because if by any chance a slight mistake meant that we couldn't resurface, there would be fell search and rescue teams combing the moors to this day. We would become famous as the Fantom Five of Fountains Fell, swallowed up in the mists of time, lifted off the earth by visitors from another planet. We would be the subject of countless documentaries and books with lurid titles such as 'the missing Jim Eyre was a closet sex maniac'.

However, this didn't happen. Instead, we hung up our clothes-filled plastic bags beneath an overhang, away from the water spraying down the shaft – a good idea until it rained and a small inlet found its way into one of the bags (mine!).

We rigged the eighty-foot aven, which gave a good ladder climb until I encountered a strange, half-finished structure jammed into a cleft halfway down. It tangled the ladder, interrupted my climbing and seemed about as much use as an ashtray on a motorbike. It was an artificial ledge being built for Colin to rest on when he was climbing the ladder; well, you can't be a genius and have the legs of a window cleaner. Batty didn't pay much, but he did look after his workers.

Once the team was down, Gordon and Colin were soon at work with a saw, hammer and nails, constructing a crude wooden ladder that wouldn't have looked amiss on the ark. I watched this operation with interest, because I had never seen a troll's joiner's shop before.

When the contraption was finished it was handed to me and I was pointed in the general direction of a boulder slope rearing overhead in the dark recess of the far chamber wall.

'There it is, get up it,' said Batty.

I looked at the tottering rock pile and my Heath Robinson ladder and realised why I had been invited along – something along the lines of: 'Who can we get who's daft enough to climb that? Why, of course, Jim Eyre.'

I staggered across the chamber like a candidate for a crucifixion, bowed under the weight of wood. I began climbing carefully as every block moved and, dragging my ladder up behind me, I looked upwards for the expected overhang or gap where I would need it. I eventually leaned the ladder against an overhanging block, which moved as soon as I began climbing again, so I hastily vacated the ladder for a chimney behind the boulder slope. After a sweaty struggle I found that I had reached the aven's flat roof, where a shale band had given way, causing the collapse.

A shout from the diminutive figures below: 'Does it go?'

'No,' I answered.

'Oh,' came a chorus.

'What am I supposed to do with this ladder?' I asked.

There was a long silence. After further poking around looking for any man-sized passages that might lead off behind the rock pile, I carefully made my way back down, dislodging two large chunks of rock in the process. They dropped like bombs onto the lights below, which dispersed between my first shouted syllable of 'Be' and my last, 'low!' Fortunately, no one was hit.

It was a disappointment for us all, because it meant the only way on was down in the claustrophobic, flood-prone crawls at stream level.

THE FOLLOWING WEEKEND the Secret Seven was again reduced to the three of us: Gordon, Colin and me. We intended to force our way through the low bedding planes that led downstream and Colin had elected to be our underground cook, so we left him setting up his kitchen near the stream, while we entered the low passage.

There is one sort of caving that I detest: in order to make progress, being reduced to lying prone in six inches of water and wet gravel with a solid roof, still dripping from the last downpour, bearing down heavily on your shoulders, forcing your body and head ever lower, until it requires you to remove your helmet and push it in front while wriggling like a large, cumbersome slug with your face and right ear submerged in the water.

I wriggled and thrutched as I followed Batty's behind and hobnailed boots, which scraped and kicked and grunted along an undulating bedding plane. I say undulating, because it went from bloody tight, to ''ang on, I can't breathe,' and these bits were generally semi-submerged for effect.

A really low section caused me problems as I tried to haul my body over a sandbank and stuck tight. I wriggled my way backwards and scrabbled out some shale and mud as I desperately twisted my neck to see what I was doing. In this position everything is magnified and, with one eye, I could make out a huge bank of muddy sand which seemed to be like the sand dunes of the Sahara, stretching as far as the eye could see. But, there was a giant hand, like a huge earth-moving machine, digging out a vast channel which was all of three inches wide. I thrutched forward again. 'Come on, Ers – you could get a bus through there,' grunted Batty from ahead.

After a frantic struggle, I slithered over the blockage and rejoined Gordon's right boot. 'We'll soon be coming to the tight bit,' said a voice up front. 'Fuckin' hell. What the **** do you call that bit I've just come through?' I asked, but the boot gave no reply and shuffled slowly ahead.

I followed it and we were soon lying full length in the stream, where the roof lowered even more until I had to scrape gravel out of the way to move. I could feel my hip bones, kneecaps and elbows clunking against the unyielding rock, and silently cursed the single-minded sod in front as we lumbered on. Eventually, Gordon stopped and I managed to crawl level with his waist. The stream followed the flat, black roof through a four-inch high gap. 'Ah,' I thought, 'even Batty can't follow that,' and had visions of a quick retreat.

But Batty possessed eyes like a hawk and had spotted a continuation of that bloody crawl over another sandbank. Once again I found myself cursing and sweating as we forced our bodies over the roaring stream and crawled over the banks of flood deposits against the roof, with the stream now out of sight somewhere below. After some distance the wide bedding closed to a narrow passage, which required modifying with a lump hammer – and we hadn't brought one.

The roof was covered in foam, so I didn't need much urging to back out. Having managed to turn round, I found my reverse gear much faster as I homed in on the smell of pea soup and carrots that wafted down the crawl. I emerged from the

There is one sort of caving that I detest

claustrophobic confinement of the bedding, to be confronted by flashing blue and yellow lights reflecting from the wet cave walls that illuminated Colin's rugged face as he bent over two roaring Primus stoves, which he pumped vigorously.

Colin was partially crouched under an overhang, almost obscured by clouds of steam which condensed on the low roof, creating a sort of equatorial microclimate with in the region of ninety per cent humidity. Drops of condensation would roll down the overhang to plop into the soup or explode on a hot stove. Our friendly hobgoblin crouched to his task, moisture dripping off his nose like snotty dewdrops as he peered intently into the mixture, ever stirring. The kettle began whistling and Colin became even wetter before he disappeared into the steam like a latter-day genie.

'Ah, you're back,' said Colin when he eventually saw us through the fog. 'How do you like your soup? It seems a bit thin.'

After our cordon bleu soup we felt equal for anything and, armed with the hammer, we returned to the attack, closely followed by Colin. After removing the restriction, we worked our way along a small passage which gradually became impossible, so we decided to lower the floor of mud and gravel. With Batty the human mole up front loosening the gunge, I passed it back to Colin, also lying full-length, who disposed of it in cracks and under the sides of the bedding – indeed, anywhere he could think of. In this manner we progressed slowly until we decided to call it a day.

'Back up, Colin,' I muttered. A few grunts and wriggles from the heaving mass behind me were helped by my feet on his helmet.

'I can't move,' came a strangled ejaculation. 'I think I've buried myself!'

After digging our way in, we had now to dig our way out. It took an hour to free the 'green man', who had packed enough rubble and mud around his body to turn himself

'How do you like your soup? It seems a bit thin.'

into a living mummy, wrapped in its own sarcophagus. We decided to leave him in charge of the kitchen in future.

GINGLING WET SINKS WAS NOT GOING to give up its secrets easily and the following weeks saw us working our way further into the cave, each time making me more nervous as examples of the sheer ferocity of the floodwaters were left in evidence. Finding froth on the still-dripping roof in the low beddings, and sand and shingle banks that moved from place to place, was unnerving enough, but when we saw some heavy fire hose (which had been used to divert the water) sucked down through the low beddings and pulled over the sandbanks further in, I started to become neurotic about weather forecasts and thought about the Mossdale tragedy.

On my weekend forays up to Settle I found that drinking till 11.30 p.m. and rising at 2 a.m. to creep across the fell and spend hours down Wet Sinks wasn't really conducive for good health and peace of mind, and so I felt distinctly uneasy as I followed Batty through the crawls, clutching my tools ready for more digging. The sound of running water seemed louder and, having deepened the crawl we were working on, we entered an unusual passage that dipped towards the stream below; this could be the break-through we were looking for.

I slid head first down the restricted tube and entered a mass of froth and bubbles. After about six or seven feet, it did a sharp U-turn, but I couldn't – I was the wrong way round and my body, unlike Batty's, only bends one way. I wriggled backwards, legs waving, and gradually managed to twist over in the slimy froth-covered U-bend and struggle upwards, completely demoralised when I realised that I had just been through what was only an hour or so previously, a sump.

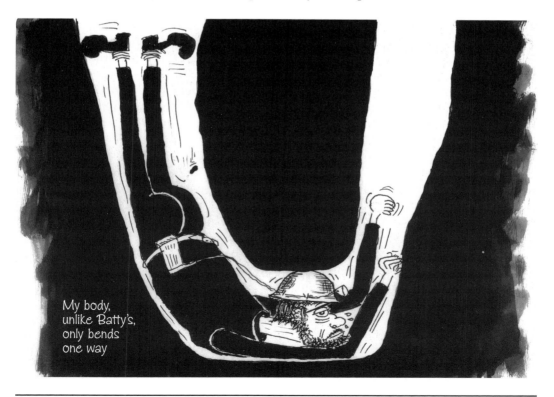

My body, unlike Batty's, only bends one way

I started thinking about insurance policies and my darling wife, my wee scabby dog and the sunlit uplands and blue skies of the great outdoors. I realised that there must be more to life than following Gordon Batty's hobnailed boots every weekend.

The cave ahead looked much the same when we retraced our steps, this time taking care to slide through the U-bend the right way round. Grunting and wriggling my way out I shouted to Gordon, who for a change was following my boots: 'Next week I'm going to go down a bloody big pitch and be surrounded by space.' He gave a non-committal grunt.

However, for the next month Wet Sinks was impassable and we sneaked up to the fell to watch a swollen torrent of brown water sluicing down the 'dry' valley into a small lake, where it swirled round and round like a giant bathtub being emptied until, with a horrible gurgling, it sank down into those low crawls below. Having a better imagination than Gordon, I could call to mind the noise of water under pressure and those flat roofs, now submerged under several feet of fast-flowing brown water.

Luckily for Gordon there had been a recent influx of young, starry-eyed, naïve cavers into the NPC. Some were on parole from Yorkshire correction centres and one or two were partially brain-dead, but they were soon co-opted on to Batty's digging team. I, of course, had just purchased a new house and had a garden to dig. What a pity!

I met Gordon's new recruits when they came staggering into the New Inn in Clapham ten minutes before closing time. They had ashen faces and rolling eyeballs, and their hands trembled as they reached for their first pint, which was downed without even touching their parched lips. One character, much larger than the rest, downed three pints without stopping for breath. He then turned to me, belched (which blew froth off his top lip onto my new sweater) and said 'That Batty! Ee's bloody mad!' There then followed a narrative about creaking bedding planes and loose boulders which made my beer go flat.

The exploration of Gingling Wet Sinks had been pushed beyond the crawls into a badly faulted area of loose rock and hanging death, a sort of underground whispering gallery. It was not like the real one, but it appeared to be, because the sheer sight of all that tottering rock reduced the lads to speaking in whispers. Batty found a way under the rock pile and, being a true leader, inserted his second in command, Dr Frank Walker, into a gap between the blocks and ordered him forward. The whispering rocks suddenly talked and slid down behind Frank, seemingly permanently separating him from his mates and the great outdoors.

The shocked silence that followed was broken by strange noises issuing from behind the rockfall, denoting that Frank was still alive but severely pissed off. An hour of desperate digging and scrabbling eventually released the trapped doctor, who vowed to go to church the following Sunday. The chastened band of gallant explorers hastily withdrew.

Kevin Millington (the narrator of this story in the pub) owed me a pint, so I nudged his memory and enjoyed the amber nectar. It felt wise to have it now, just in case.

'When are you coming with us again, Jim?' asked Kev.

'Well, I've got this bad back,' said I.

UNKNOWN TO US, the night-time activities of the Northern Pennine Club had not gone unnoticed. At that time several pirate groups existed, all descendants of the original Captain Morgan's lot, and the most notorious masqueraded under the name of the Northern Speleological Group. Somehow, they had breached our strict security and found out about Shush 3, Gordon's secret entrance to Gingling Wet Sinks.

During a walk with Gordon on a brisk winter's day, we wandered past Shush 3 and stopped dead. The site of a gaping hole where there should have been an innocuous shakehole was made worse by the circle of wellies, boots and trainers that surrounded it. 'Pirates!' gasped Gordon, before turning an ashen colour and swooning in a heap at my feet. It's the sort of reaction a house owner has when he's been told he has dry rot. I managed to bring Gordon round, fortunately without having to resort to the kiss of life. I held his hand until he recovered, then said, 'Never mind, Gordon, I'll teach these buggers a lesson,' and filled all the sweaty footwear with wet, gravelly mud and tamped it down, nice and hard.

My life is full of little happenings like that and, to make it even more interesting, there was another happening. It turned out to be the coldest night of the year and a Siberian frost hit Fountains Fell. It was magic; all the pirate's grotty footwear was instantly transformed into pretty Cinderella slippers, encrusted with lovely crystals of hoar frost that sparkled and glistened in the moonlight.

Unfortunately, not everyone appreciates the more aesthetic, artistic beauty of the finer things in life, and the delicacy of Cinderella's glass slippers was lost on these rough cavers – especially when they found their footwear had frozen to the consistency of reinforced concrete. Struggling back across the frozen fell in knackered, soaked caving boots, rapidly shredding neoprene socks, squelching caving wellies and with two unfortunates in woolly socks, this merry band of pirates was soon reduced to a mutinous bunch of cut-throats as their feet froze solid. And the throat they were going to cut was mine!

It's odd how rumours start in the caving world – a nudge here and a wink there, followed by a deadly silence when one enters a cavers' pub. Slowly the message came through that I was a marked man with a price on my head. Not much, though – I would never be a Jesse James as the poster only proclaimed: 'Jim Eyre wanted, dead or alive: £20 reward.'

I was offered Karate Bill as a minder from the NPC, but even though he was a black belt expert I didn't think he would fit the bill because, although willing, he was only five feet tall

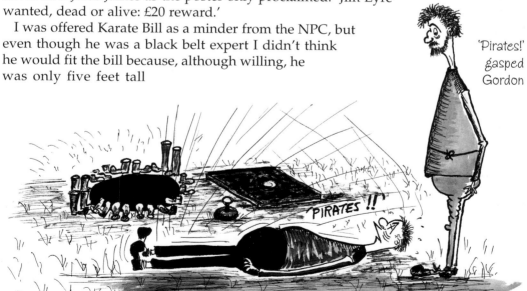

'Pirates!' gasped Gordon

and I would stick out above him for another totally unprotected eleven inches. Eventually, as in all the good westerns, came the showdown.

I heard that some pirate cavers were in the Craven Heifer, so I hitched my van to the rail, tightened my trousers and, in the best *High Noon* tradition, pushed open the swing doors and walked in. The talking ceased. The piano fell silent and the dancing girls screamed and fled the room. I made the long, lonely walk to the bar.

'Hi, Jack, give me a pint of bitter and a lager and lime – oh, and a packet of crisps.' (It was slightly different from the film script.)

I was immediately surrounded by a group of threatening cavers and accused of dark deeds on Fountains Fell. A steaming trainer containing an athlete's foot was thrust under my nose.

'Do you recognise this?'

'Yes, it's a trainer,' I answered, slurping my beer.

'I got frostbite. It's not funny walking across the fell in bare feet,' said one brute.

'I wore my wetsuit socks out,' said another; 'I've got chilblains and fallen arches,' said another.

'Well, how was I to know it was going to freeze – you shouldn't pinch digs,' I answered and, after promising them the address of a good chiropodist, I had the feeling that all would be well. Then, just as we were getting to the backslapping and 'ho ho' stage, it all went terribly wrong. As in all the cowboy films there's always one little sod that starts the trouble, and he crept outside and returned just as I was saying, 'Can't you take a joke?' Up he popped like a genie and deposited a load of frozen snow and crap from the road in my beer, yelling: 'Yes,' in a manic voice, 'can you?'

I am one of those unfortunate people who suffer from automatic reflex actions, and I immediately swung my glass in a circle, emptying the beer, ice and muck over my adversaries. Not a wise thing to do, I thought as I went to the floor under a veritable hail of blows. Things became rather vague after that, as pub fights do, and the next thing I remember is sitting in the van with Audrey examining my nose.

'It's bent,' she said.

'I know – it's always been bent,' I muttered.

'Yes, but now it's bent the other way,' said Audrey.

'Well, that would make it straight,' I mumbled, driving to the nearest street lamp.

'No, I don't like it,' said Aud after examining the offending proboscis. 'I think I preferred it the other way.' So, we drove to Lancaster infirmary to consult a nose-ologist and, surprise, surprise, there was one of my former adversaries, Derek Crossland, sitting in a wheelchair with a dressing around his neck and jaw. His arm was stuck out in a rigid splint, which also covered his hand.

'Bloody hell – what happened to you?' I asked.

'Bust my hand,' said Derek. 'What you in for?'

'I think I know what you bust your hand on – me nose has gone,' I replied.

All the participants are still around, older and wiser – except for Derek Crossland, a hard and popular caver whose life was tragically cut short in 1985 in a cave diving accident in Hurtle Pot, some time after these events.

Chapter 11

Turkish Delight

IT **STARTED WITH RUMOURS** that some French speleologists had simply walked into large river caves in southern Turkey – then, with an offer I couldn't refuse, came a telephone call from my old mate Reg Howard.

'Fancy a trip to Turkey, Audrey?' I shouted into the cloud of steam emanating from the kitchen.

'Oo, yes,' came Audrey's cry of delight.

It was 1974 and plans were made and plans were changed while the Turks and Greeks decided whether or not to go to war over Cyprus. Reg's new minibus conked out on a visit to the Dales and required a new diesel engine. We couldn't find enough cavers to take part and the Turkish–Greek border was closed. The omens weren't looking good.

'Sod it! We can always drive into Turkey from Bulgaria,' said Reg, and the expedition was on. Within a few weeks we were part of a crew ensconced in a bright yellow minibus, en route across Europe.

Since our trip to Iran, Reg and his wife Margaret had been running adventure treks into the Sahara and had once asked Audrey and me if we fancied a trip; Reg was most surprised when I told him that if ever I felt the need for sand, there was plenty at Morecambe. However, it seemed that their Saharan trip had been such a success that although we were now headed for a totally different country on a different continent, some of his customers were still on the bus – Reg had taken their money and declared them honorary cavers, thereby making up the rest of the team.

Martin Beverley was the epitome of an English middle-class gent abroad – clad in white tennis shorts, a white shirt and tennis shoes, he seemed to have stepped out of a Noel Coward sketch. Long, languid and lanky, with a thin bedraggled moustache hiding a stiff upper lip, Martin never complained when things or the food got rough. Everything was always 'larvelly'. Martin's sister and her girlfriend seemed to be two delicate English roses, but looks can be deceptive and they weathered any setback, as did Audrey who (until she met me) had led a fairly sheltered life.

The other non-caver was John Reilly, a quiet Irishman who kept amazingly calm while he suffered all sorts of mishaps with a stoicism not given to Anglo-Saxons. Even an ancient blow-up igloo tent hired from Reg failed to disturb his equanimity. Every night when we made camp, John would pump up his abode and, after two hours, the igloo would slowly collapse with an asthmatic wheeze, like a faulty Yorkshire pudding.

I only heard John complain once, at 3 a.m. in the middle of a horrendous

Audrey and Martin's sister walking beside the minibus

thunderstorm, when he paused in his pumping, turned a dripping face in our direction and said: 'Oi tink yor tent's knackered, Reg.'

Nearing the Turkish border, we became rather apprehensive when we ran across a giant traffic jam of vehicles heading out of the country, while our side of the road was completely deserted. Reaching the border we were surrounded by armed soldiers and, for a while, it was touch and go whether we would be allowed to proceed. Eventually, we were waved through.

There are several benefits, which are not immediately obvious, to caving in a war zone. It is, of course, imperative to pick the right war zone, as some caving buddies of mine once found out. They spent several weeks crouched in a small tent waving a pair of off-white underpants on a stick at the opposing Indian and Pakistani armies, which thought they were organising some sort of target practice and filled Jim Farnworth's underpants full of large brown holes – much to the horror of Jim's dear old mother when she did his washing on his return.

'It's a wonder you've any clothes left, our Jimmy, with the size of them Indian moths,' she said.

We were more fortunate and drove into a country bereft of tourists. Wherever we went, we were pounced upon with offers we couldn't refuse, almost running over Turkish salesmen who leapt out into the road, not realising the limited stopping power of a heavily laden minibus. In the hope of impressing whatever nationality approached him, one little chap dashed out wearing a Union Jack, the French Tricolour and the Stars and Stripes, whereupon we skidded to a halt mere inches from his smiling face.

'You camp here, Johnny?'

'How much?'

'One English pound.'

'Too much.'

'Half of one English pound.'

'How much is your beer?'

'Three bottles for one English pound.'

'Too much.'

'For you special price, five bottles for one English pound.'

'Done.'

As the country's sole tourists we received this special treatment everywhere we went and the bright yellow minibus soon became a sort of touts' collector's

They spent several weeks crouched in a small tent waving a pair of off-white underpants on a stick

item, as we stood out like a beacon of hope on the long, straight and almost empty roads where little men would materialise from nowhere every time we slowed down.

The empty tourist attractions were an added bonus and I had a magical, almost religious experience when we camped in the totally deserted ancient city of Ephesus. The white limestone steps and pavements, polished over two thousand years by bare feet and the sandals of ghosts from the ancient past, glistened as we erected our tents in the light of the moon, a shimmering silver orb in a black velvet sky studded with millions of bright stars.

I walked among the ruins of buildings with white columns, some still erect but most scattered like broken limbs, passing streets containing the faint imprint of ruined houses and the wraiths of humanity that had once lived and loved there. What were they like, these people from the past? Did they really see Saint Paul walking among them when the sea lapped the stones of the harbour? It now lay miles from the sea, drained by time that washed away the dust of their lives with the receding waters.

A headless, winged figure flickered and seemed to move as a thin wisp of cloud drew across the moon, and I detected a group of indistinct cloaked figures shifting silently over the polished stone steps below me; or was it a shadow cast by the moving cloud? Suddenly, the shapes were gone and I was alone with the ghosts of that white marble city.

For a while I stood in silence, looking over the ancient biblical port, before I joined my sleeping companions and crawled in beside Audrey who muttered, 'Where have you been?' and gave a non-committal grunt when I answered, 'In the past.'

After a night of strange dreams I awoke and found a small statuette of a barefooted, headless lady dressed in flowing robes standing by a pitcher outside our tent – it hadn't been there the night before. I kept it and often look at the figurine standing on my desk, wondering who carved the exquisite feet and flowing robes on my miniature 'Rebecca at the well'.

THE TAURUS MOUNTAINS consist of a wilderness of high peaks and foothills that extend from Antalya along the southern coastline before sweeping inland at Adana and reaching heights of almost 4,000 metres. The Manavgat Gorge cuts through several karst mountain ranges, forming an impressive series of deep clefts. Reg had travelled this way once before and had learned about the large resurgence cave of Düdensuyu (also known as Altinbesik Cave), situated three kilometres from the village of Ürünlü.

This was a picturesque mountain village where, on our arrival, Reg was greeted like a long-lost cousin.

These friendly mountain people were a complete contrast to the armed wild men of north-eastern Turkey and within minutes we were given keys to the village school to use as a base, and a party was arranged in our honour. Tables and chairs were set out in the cobbled village square and everyone gathered for the festivities.

Timothy, Jim and Reg drinking tea at Ürünlü
Photo: Margaret Howard

Sitting outside the local cafe-cum-shop, we enjoyed small glasses of sweetened tea as we waited expectantly for the belly dancers to begin. After some time, when the belly dancers had failed to materialise and I was being served my fifth drink of tea, a horrible suspicion began to dawn: Ürünlü was in a Muslim area and was 'dry'!

This was a disaster. Fortunately, we had brought some whisky for medicinal purposes and secretly kept our glasses of tea topped up, unobserved by our hosts – or so I thought, until I heard a fizzing sound in my right ear. I turned sharply and almost kissed a stubbly chin belonging to a flat-capped gent who had noticed the miracle of the self-replenishing glasses.

'Wheesky?' he queried.

'Er, no,' I said, but he gave me a crafty leer in the knowledgeable way that all drunks have.

'Psst,' he fizzed again, 'you like beer?'

Reg and I went into a quick huddle with him and struck a deal. Within minutes the local taxi (a pickup truck) was despatched to the next village, which was non-Muslim and 'wet'. Meanwhile, some local firewater was passed to us under the table and this, with the results from our booze-running friend from the 'untouchables', improved our evening. We were given tasty little saucers of goodies and held strange, broken conversations with our hosts in a thousand tongues – my Lancashire Esperanto of mangled German, French and Italian slang created a noticeable impression, and I heard one old boy ask another: 'What the hell is he talking about?'

Suddenly there was a lull in the conversation and we picked up the faint sound of weird music borne on the wind. Dusk began to fall and the surrounding mountains took on a purplish hue as the shadows deepened and the faint horizon turned a deep orange. As the light faded I noticed a faint flash along the brim of a distant hill, just before the sun sank in a blaze of red and golden fire.

The refrain of 'The hills are alive with the sound of music' came into my mind as twin headlight beams stabbed over the adjacent ridge and into the darkening sky and, with greater clarity, real music drifted across the valley. The villagers became more excited as, carried on the balmy evening breeze, the strangely oriental music grew louder still until a battered old truck came screeching around the steep, hairpin bend and pulled up in a cloud of dust. A crescendo of crazy music came from the instruments of four grinning characters perched on the back of the truck and, when they jumped down without missing a beat, shouts and laughter greeted them and they performed an impromptu dance.

It was brilliant – what an entrance! With everyone applauding and shouting greetings and the sound of exotic music conjured up by a banjo, a flute, drums and a funny-looking guitar, we were drawn into one of those magic moments in time that are hard to describe yet impossible to forget. The men took centre stage while the village females had to watch from the periphery, seemingly unconcerned judging by the happy smiles on their rosy-cheeked faces, lit by sparkling eyes and dazzling white teeth, as they clapped their hands and swayed their bodies to the music.

I was concerned about the men. Dressed in flat caps and what looked like old pin-striped demob suits, they were reminiscent of characters in old Mafia photographs and they were soon vying with each other as to who could perform the best dance. It was disconcerting for a lad with my sensibilities – they couldn't all have been to public school. I became a bit more perturbed when the local Boy George appeared. He flashed a gold tooth in my direction and began to sing in a wailing chant, which conjured up visions of a bad attack of flatulence as he advanced towards me with short, mincing steps.

Why do all these old farts always fancy me? I suddenly realised why I am not popular with the ladies – perhaps I'm a closet man's man!

Luckily, I was spared a fate worse than death when Boy George's boyfriend became jealous and slapped his wrist, before dancing him across the cobbled square to wild applause.

'Eh Jim, there's another old bugger fancies you,' said Reg as a nearby villager kept raising his glass of tea and giving me a gap-toothed smile. Naturally, I ignored him. We were joined by the local holy man, who spoke some English and, strangely enough like all the other villagers, liked British cigarettes. Our halting conversation was interrupted by a mighty yell as Fred Blinge, the local spoons man, took centre stage and he began beating himself vigorously with some large wooden spoons in a Turkish variant of a Cockney act, generally done with smaller spoons and less pain.

Fred managed a couple of encores of 'Singin' in the Rain' before sitting down to rapturous applause, then the band struck up again with a hauntingly evocative tune which brought forth visions of veiled brown women wriggling their hips and full of Eastern promise. But what was this approaching across the cobbled square? It was anything but a vision of sexual delight and I watched, dumbfounded, as my suitor approached. It was the old sod who had been smiling at me.

From beneath a flat cap his grizzled old face creased into an amorous smile, which revealed four gold teeth and a large gap as he came to a halt beside our table, grabbed me by the shoulders and said something in Turkish which was gift-wrapped in a breath that would have done justice to a long-dead pharaoh. As he hauled me to my feet, I pleaded to Audrey: 'Come and save me, tell him I'm married.'

It was hopeless. Everyone, including the villagers, curled up laughing as 'old grizzly' and I took to the floor. I can't dance properly with the ladies, so there was no chance I would improve with this smelly old fart, but I thought, 'Sod it – here we go.' I switched to my Fred Astaire and Ginger Rogers routine, turning us into the hit turn of the year – which delighted the villagers and filled my dance card for the evening.

The smiling holy man then asked us to do some English dances. After a great deal of thought, we realised that England has no culture of its own, so Audrey suggested that we dance the hokey-cokey. We got everyone up on the cobbles and sang and danced a very primitive version of this thirty-year-old number.

I watched, dumbfounded, as my suitor approached

His grizzled old face creased into an amorous smile

The musicians were quick to latch onto the tune and soon the villagers all joined in, even the ladies who danced by themselves until Audrey and Martin's sister joined them, much to their delight.

I STOOD IN THE SCHOOL PLAYGROUND the following morning and looked over a panorama of mountains that stretched away before me, range after range until they faded in the early morning haze. After breakfast we wandered through the village in search of a mule to carry our gear down to the gorge. Almost every person we came across said 'Hokey pokey' and laughed. It's at times like these when I wished I had been more diligent in learning foreign languages.

We soon found a mule and, after sorting out our kit, we followed the animal and its owner along a winding track that led us to a deep gorge. For three kilometres the track clung to the edge of a cliff before coming to an end on a broad ledge at the edge of a four-hundred-metre drop. Below, we could see the opening of a large river cave.

Unloading the mule, we carried the gear as we carefully worked our way down a loose scree slope to the river and the entrance to an impressive sixty-metre-wide resurgence cave. A strong river flowed out, forming deep pools which served as a swimming and bathing pool for most of the male villagers, and the waves caused by their splashing reflected sunlight far into the cave, lighting up the arched roof with moving dapples of light that danced across the rock.

We approached the bathers, small boys and old geezers – including my suitor of the night before, who shot out of the water like a grizzled Aphrodite almost losing his dodgy loincloth in his effort to embrace me.

John said, 'To be sure Jim, oi tink he wants to get his hands on your body again.'

'Well, tell him the engagement's off,' I said, as I dodged behind a smirking Reg to put on my wetsuit.

Reg and I left Martin and John, our willing novice cavers, loading up the rubber dinghy with equipment while Reg and I slid into the surprisingly cold water, where we were glad of our wetsuits as we swam into the semi-darkness. The impressive, wide entrance lake stretched on ahead until, after around 130 metres, the walls narrowed slightly as the roof soared out of sight over a marvellous natural rock bridge that spanned the cave. Beyond, the cave widened again and

The Manavgat Gorge

the dark waters of the lake ended, lapping against a massive wall of calcite which glowed in our lights as we approached.

I momentarily stopped swimming and looked up at a breathtaking wall of calcite draperies. It reared up, tier after tier, into the darkness of the roof over fifty metres above, effectively blocking the way beyond the entrance lake. Reg and I swam along the base of the flowstone looking for a way through at water level, but to no avail, so we climbed onto a large, mushroomed-shaped formation and unloaded the dinghy that by now had caught up. A strong draught blew from somewhere up high, which encouraged me to try to climb the flowstone.

At first sight this didn't seem too encouraging, as all the draperies and stalactites overhung one another, but as I made a tentative approach I spotted a weakness and managed to pull my way up under a steeply sloping, smooth flowstone formation to gain a precariously smooth traverse some ten metres above, with no footholds or handholds. I felt a bit like a doll on an iced cake – and the way on upwards was even worse, for I was on the underside of a lovely, large, mushroom-shaped bank of flowstone: smooth and pretty to look at but, as anyone knows who has tried to climb a mushroom, bloody impossible to ascend.

I stood there for a while, my fingers playing an imaginary piano as I felt for anything even remotely resembling a hold. Ah, at last I managed to place one finger around a small stal and, not wishing to take a header into the lake, yelled down for a rope. Having caught it I threaded an end around the small stal and clipped on. It was bloody ridiculous, really, but better than sod all as Nobby Hall would say.

Thanks to my psychological belay I gained a better position to attack the smooth overhang, which quickly led to a broader ledge. I found a slight piece of exposed rock and, hanging out under the overhang, managed to bash a peg into a small crack. I pulled on it and it moved, so I bashed it again and pulled – but not so hard. It held.

'Ladder, Reg,' I shouted, and was soon perched tiptoe on trembling legs on the top rung of a not-too-safe ladder as I felt feverishly for a handhold.

Suddenly, the ladder moved. I looked down and was confronted by a brown face and sparkling eyes peering up between my legs. I received a flashing smile from the owner, a small wet boy in swimming trunks who had swum across the two-hundred-metre lake, seen the end of the ladder dangling in the water and climbed up it, out of sight of Reg who was holding the line around a corner. The peg gave a sickening lurch.

'Bugger off,' I shouted. 'Sod off . . . imshi, allez, ladder kaput . . .'

The barefoot urchin smiled again and grabbed my leg. My desperate quest had produced a handhold and I lashed out with my free hand. '**** OFF!' I yelled.

The peg moved again as my visitor got the message and fumbled his way down the ladder to his mate below, where they remained for some time, unseen but noticeable by snatches of Turkish songs and whistles that came floating out of the darkness, before they eventually swam back to the entrance.

After this unnerving interruption, I managed to reach a small hole in the flowstone which was too large for a peg and too small for anything else. Having fiddled about for some time, I succeeded in jamming a peg and karabiner into the hole, then I pulled up the other end of the ladder, clipped it on, stood on it, made a tentative move and the whole contraption collapsed, leaving me hanging by one hand with my feet waving in space. Following another even more desperate attempt, I passed the overhang at last and, with a sigh of relief, fixed a bolt into the rock. It was the first safe belay.

Using the ladder, Reg joined me on my precarious perch. He clutched the underside of the smooth dome of calcite that towered above us, before gradually easing his body over the edge of the concave mass of polished limestone.

'There's no holds,' he grunted while defying gravity, advancing inch by inch in a kind of swimming breast stroke which steadily became more frantic as gravity threatened to win. I couldn't even offer assistance as his legs were thrashing about like the back legs of a frog experiencing an orgasm, and threatening to sweep me into space. Thankfully, Reg's legs finally disappeared from view as his breaststroke took him within reach of some huge gours, which gave us both access to a broad ledge.

A tremendous draught blew down and we were exhilarated as we examined our new position. However, after a close scrutiny of what lay ahead, we realised that we were faced with an insurmountable problem. Immediately overhead, the route was blocked by gigantic, overhanging stalactites the size of a cathedral's organ pipes, all tapering to sword-like points – beautiful, as smooth and pure as ice, and unclimbable. To our right lay a vertical drop to the lake, now far below. On our left, however, was a gap between the flowstone-covered wall and an enormous stalactite, which I chimneyed up for seven metres to find it was blocked solid by calcite.

I cursed. This immense, tiered wedding cake looked like it was going to beat us.

Standing on top of the massive gours, Reg and I could see the roof of this vast river cave continuing beyond the top of the pendants. There had to be a way.

There is nothing like the smell of a new cave to spur men to deeds of reckless bravery – or perhaps a better term would be 'foolishness'. I returned to the only route possible and once more scrabbled up the chimney until my helmet bumped against the solid mass of calcite. I looked across at the frozen Niagara and the mammoth pendants below and spotted a gap between them and the wall – if only I could reach it.

Desperate men form desperate ideas and I suddenly came up with a beauty: 'If I could fix a rope at the top of the chimney, I could pendulum across, swing into the gap behind the flowstone and jam myself on something or . . . er . . .'

The more I thought about it the dafter it became but, as I hung in space at the top of the chimney, I groped for anything that would hold a flying trapeze. I found a small slot in the stal and called Reg to bring up the rope and told him of my plan. 'You're nuts,' he said, then tied a karabiner on the end of the rope, dropped it down the slot and said: 'Pull on that while I keep my hand on it.' The karabiner held.

With Reg at the top of the chimney holding the jammed rope in place, I grasped the rope firmly and launched myself from underneath him, taking my weight on the rope. I made a fast tension traverse to a small stance on the left, gave a warning shout then ran like hell across the vertical stal before hurling myself into space, zooming past Reg like an out-of-control Tarzan. I just reached the gap behind the pendants before my momentum stopped and the force of gravity took over.

With knees, elbows, teeth and boots, I jammed myself across the gap, hanging there for two or three minutes, panting like a landed fish with glazed eyes, a pounding heart and a heady exotic mixture of sheer terror and exhilaration coursing through my mind. I was like a limpet, hanging on high above the lake.

A vicious tug on the rope nearly pulled me off my perch and I came back to reality as I realised that Reg, stuck at the top of the chimney, wouldn't know where the hell I had gone after my Mary Poppins act. For all he knew, I could have shot off anywhere! I shouted back before chimneying up

I could pendulum across . . .

behind the stal onto a sloping shoulder of smooth, polished rock. It was completely without holds and very exposed, with a forty-metre drop to the lake.

Beyond the stance lay a black opening which draughted furiously. My light flickered and began to fade and I realised that I had to fix a bolt before I could either go on or return so, straddled across the gap, I began hammering energetically. The bolt wouldn't grip – the powdered rock choked the hole and forced its teeth apart. I tried to clean the hole as my carbide light spluttered and extinguished. Switching on my trusty electric, I was bathed in a dull, yellow glow which rapidly waned as I hammered in earnest in the fast approaching twilight.

I couldn't make the bolt tighten, my light was almost out and I felt the old man with the scythe looking over my shoulder. I had no other choice: stay here in the dark until I fell off, or clip the rope onto the loose bolt, say a prayer and tiptoe softly down into space to rejoin Reg. His first words were, 'I'm glad to see you – my light's knackered!'

Together, we beat a hasty retreat in the orange glow of one flat battery.

Back in the village a delighted Audrey informed us that: 'You've missed a good 'do' – a circumcision party.'

'Not to worry,' I answered, 'we almost had one of our own!'

DISASTER! The box containing the extra carbide was missing; it was probably standing forlornly on Reg's drive in Southampton. The expedition was now lightless, so we scrounged around the village for torches, paraffin lamps or candles – anything that would glow. We were so desperate that we even manufactured a weird collection of oil lamps with floating wicks out of empty sardine tins.

We were saved by our friendly holy man, who volunteered to ride on his motorcycle for sixty kilometres over rough mountain tracks to a local bauxite mine to obtain some carbide. Late at night, while we were being entertained by the villagers, our saviour returned, hot, tired and dusty but triumphant with a large container of the acetylene-producing rock. I thanked him profusely and offered him a glass of whisky – which he hastily declined. I suddenly realised that one does not offer whisky to holy men and I apologised profusely, ordered tea and gave him some of the kids' toffees and three packets of cigarettes, for he wouldn't accept money.

The following day we made an early start. I was very nervous ascending back up the rope; rightly so, as I discovered that the bolt was literally hanging by a thread. When I took my weight off the rope, the bolt came out in my hand!

I hastily hammered in another bolt and clipped on the ladder for Reg while I free-climbed the last two or three metres to stand before the vestibule of a large, tunnel-like passage with a deep canal that stretched out of sight. The turbulent water, driven by a powerful draught from the dark caverns beyond, splashed against the lip of the calcite barrier and overflowed down the surface of this living sculpture of glistening flowstone.

It was an incredible find. We didn't quite know what to do about our two non-cavers, Marty and John. They were full of enthusiasm so, probably against our better judgement, we hauled them up the fifty-metre climb. Pulling up the dinghy was even worse as we managed to impale it on the end of a stalactite but, swinging on the ladder, Reg managed to free it and we dragged it to the top of the barrier for repairs.

Leaving the group crouched over the wrinkled rubber, I slid into the canal and swam through its clear blue water. The passage continued with a uniform width of nine metres until I rounded a curve, where my light reflected as dapples on the shallow arch of the roof. Another 180 metres stretched ahead to a calcite barrier, where I thankfully climbed out of the water.

Ahead lay a huge cavern which swallowed the feeble probings of my light. The timeless black space beckoned me on, but I returned to the canal to see Reg and John paddling towards me accompanied by a trail of bubbles, which denoted a sinking ship. They reached the barrier on one tube.

I hurriedly took over and, while the dinghy was still floating, returned across our River Styx to collect Marty. Long before he came into sight I heard his knees knocking together like a gypsy's castanets – when my light picked him out he was a dejected figure clad in a white shirt and tennis shorts (hardly the gear for caving), sitting on a rock looking like a whitewashed garden gnome. The poor bloke must have been frozen, but he wasn't downhearted.

'Isn't this exciting?' said Marty as I hove into view. Yes, I thought and it will get even more exciting if the dinghy sinks.

'Can you swim?' I asked my eager friend as he straddled the rapidly deflating dinghy.

'Oh yes, but I'd rather not,' answered my passenger.

I began paddling and could feel the vibrations of Marty's shivering through the rubber. 'Are you alright?' I asked.

'Oh yes,' he replied. 'This is larvelly . . . but I think we're sinking! My balls weren't in the water when we set off.'

I was relieved when we reached the end of the canal and, beaching the rapidly shrinking dinghy, I persuaded Marty to undertake some vigorous exercises to warm up his body before we rejoined the others. I then had a word with Reg who, being a

'I think we're sinking! My balls weren't in the water when we set off.'

hard man, didn't quite think on the same wavelength as I did with respect to the problems we could have with two novice cavers in an unexplored cave, especially when one was dressed for a game of tennis. We were in an enormous dry cavern, so we decided to let Marty and John do their own thing: 'Don't stray too far and try and repair the dinghy, while Reg and I have a quick look around.'

Reg and I pushed on into the massive passage. We were soon clambering over old calcite barriers which held back large gours set in black, polished limestone eroded into deep holes with razor sharp edges. A badly placed foot and that would be it. The walls of the cavern were now over fifty metres apart and the roof an indistinct thirty to forty metres above our heads. It was obviously a very old cave and could have extended into the heart of the mountain and onwards to somewhere in the wild karst, where the underground river began its journey.

Gripped by exploration fever, we pushed on past a large, fifteen-metre-high calcite boss which sparkled white against the left-hand wall where it stood on a tier of old, dried-out gours inset with pools coated with crystals. Our footsteps disturbed untold centuries of dried mud that caked everything in thick layers, throwing up fine dust as we passed holes which skirted giant blocks fallen from the shadows of the faraway roof. Below, reflecting our lights, the streamway continued under walls covered in flowstone.

We decided to stay in the higher levels and clambered over more fallen blocks as our lights picked out the black expanse of a large opening which overhung the main cavern. An easy climb past calcite formations, long dead and dry like the bones of some prehistoric creature, led us to a cascade of old gours, also dried out but covered in a dense mat of gypsum needles. They bristled and sparkled and stabbed our fingers as we climbed higher to the apex of the flowstone, where an easy climb down returned us to the lower tunnels. These began to subdivide into smaller passages, with holes that led to the active system below.

We suddenly remembered our two enthusiastic amateurs, who would by now be reduced to shivering wrecks, so Reg and I beat a hasty retreat. Marty and John were pleased to see us, but wore the worried looks of two beings longing for the great outdoors where the sun shines, the birds sing and everything is a blaze of colour. They had expended their energy trying to repair the punctured dinghy and even more energy trying to blow it up, only to watch it slowly shrivelling like a willy that's just had sex: they were both suffering from post-orgasm depression!

Reg and I sat our reluctant mariners on the last vestige of air remaining in the dinghy and, one each side, swam along the canal towing our shipwreck. We eventually regained dry land, even though it was dry land that was perched at the top of a fifty-metre drop with another painful dunking waiting for us at the bottom. I silently cursed Reg and his 'adventure seekers', for we would have been much better on our own. On the other hand, we couldn't have reached Turkey without them so, somewhat unusually, I kept my mouth shut. That is, I kept it shut until we had them dangling in space crying: 'I've got my foot through the ladder' and 'What do I do here?' and 'Do I get off here?'

'Stay where you are!' I yelled. Leaving Reg holding the lifeline, I shimmied down to guide our two buddies to the flowstone ledge beside the entrance lake. Reg lowered the wet mass of flapping rubber and Marty and John, then, half in and half out of the water, they splashed and swam their way out to the life-giving rays of the warm sun. The next day, much to our surprise, we found that the pair had no wish to further their caving careers, so Reg and I continued alone with a return to the high levels of Düdensuyu.

More large caverns and old oxbows were brought to life with our caving lights before the main, northward-trending larger caverns suddenly ended at a dry shaft with water below. We retraced our steps to an obvious junction at stream level, where an easterly passage branched off. It appeared to be a continuation of the canal, having flowed underneath the larger dry caverns; it obviously formed the main, active cave after deserting the high levels thousands of years previously.

In places the clear water was very deep and our route was occasionally blocked by large rockfalls, some of them very old, with the submerged boulders eroded into sharp, plate-like ledges with dark, jagged, corroded teeth that framed the deep blue depths. Crystal deposits and shallow calcite barriers made for good caving as we advanced, partly climbing and partly swimming, clambering over blocks and squeezing through gaps above the water.

It was too good to last. Eventually, after passing a couple of oxbows, the roof lowered until our final swim ended with us peering through minimal airspace at a cave roof that disappeared underwater. After what we estimated to be roughly three kilometres of good caving, this seemed to be the conclusion. As we made our way back through the dry caverns I dejectedly kicked at a mound of soft, dry mud. It burst open to reveal the dirty grey texture of spent carbide!

'Shit!' said Reg.

'Shit!' said I.

'It's the bloody French!' we said in unison.

The bloody French! We could have fought the Battle of Waterloo all over again. But how had they climbed the calcite barrier from the lake without leaving a trace? At that time French speleologists were the world's best, but I didn't know they could fly – apart from the spent carbide we found no evidence that anyone had entered the high levels before us.

It was a mystery that was only solved when I found out that the Spéléo-Club de Paris had undertaken expeditions to Düdensuyu in 1966 and 1967. Led by Claude

Chabert, the teams reached the upper levels by climbing onto the rock bridge just inside the cave entrance, where a traverse led them above the flowstone to the entrance of the high-level canal. So that was how proper cavers did it! Never mind, Claude sent me some nice photographs with compliments from his expedition.

Although the answer to that mystery had to wait till we returned to Britain, there was another puzzle to be solved.

This was our last evening in Ürünlü. The caving had been excellent, the hospitality marvellous, but for days we had been curious as to who had been cleaning out the school toilets. These were the stand-up variety and consisted of a couple of plaster casts of size ten feet plus a dirty great hole which, unless you were an expert shot, you often missed – and it is a notorious failing among Brits that they can't aim through their behinds.

Margaret therefore set up a 'bog watch' and discovered that our good Samaritan cleaning ladies were the village goats. We had just digested this interesting piece of information when the village headman appeared.

'Ah, Meester Jeem, Meester Reg, tonight we have a party. For you we kill a goat!'

WE WERE STILL BURPING when we reached Bulgaria – and so was the new diesel engine, for the cylinder head had worked loose. Reg tightened the bolts and managed to snap one off.

Bulgaria was probably the worst place in Europe for us to have had a breakdown and the next time Reg's ginger head disappeared under the bonnet I held my breath. A grunt and a 'Ah, bloody hell!' informed us that another bolt had gone.

That left us in a minibus proceeding at a very stately pace of 10 m.p.h. at full throttle, accompanied by strange noises from the engine. It suddenly gave another asthmatic cough and stopped. Again, Reg wielded his vicious-looking spanner in his noble fist.

'Shit!' A pregnant pause followed this expletive and then a very red, wild-eyed face reappeared from beneath the bonnet. 'You're not going to believe this,' he began. Somehow, Reg had gone for the hat-trick and snapped another bolt!

I am not much of a mechanic or very good at maths; nor am I hot stuff on Bulgarian breakdown services, but I did know that a Perkins diesel had only four bolts. Reg had snapped three, so that left one and the chance of having the engine repaired or replaced in Bulgaria was nil.

I smiled at Audrey, who had told me in a weak moment that she had some money secreted away in her underwear, and hoped she possessed enough for two single flights or bus rides to England. I studied the map, but I should have studied the Bible instead for, amazingly, the engine still worked – though only just – and we slowly progressed downhill at 8 m.p.h.

Rounding a bend, we were confronted by a compound full of lorries and men in blue overalls doing things to them. Quick as a flash Reg's crafty brain took over.

'Margaret, belt Timothy and make him cry, I'll drive in and stop and we'll dive under the bonnet and get the fags and whisky out, while you lasses flash your smiles and bodies.'

Oh, that we had a prime minister like Reg Howard.

His plan worked like a dream. Margaret nipped young Timothy, whose yelling set the other kids off as our yellow minibus lurched into the state compound, much to the amazement of all the comrades. They stopped what they were doing and stood, open-mouthed at what seemed like an American school bus full of screaming kids shuddering to a halt, disgorging two bearded, scruffy characters who immediately stuck their heads under the bonnet. The women and children looked appealingly at the stunned workmen and Audrey gave them one of her winsome smiles that could melt a heart of stone.

Gradually, a group of mechanics sidled over and joined us beside the engine; they garbled excitedly in a strange tongue when they realised that our cylinder head was only held on by one bolt. Reg started doing things with a hammer until one of the mechanics stopped him. Audrey produced the duty free fags and within a short time the state mechanics were obscured in a cloud of blue tobacco smoke as they discussed the technical problems of our sick diesel.

Just to jolly things along, Reg and I began shaking hands with everyone and talking in a strange language, then Margaret appeared with her youngest in her arms and a tearful Timothy clinging onto her dress. Audrey and Martin's sister also materialised, looking dutifully sad while clutching two bottles of whisky. Some plastic cups arrived and soon everyone became extremely friendly.

'Look out, here comes the foreman,' I heard one chap say in Bulgarian (it must have been what he said, as along came a portly gent in cleaner overalls than the rest, sporting a bowler hat). A whisky was thrust into his hand and a cigarette stuck into his mouth, before he too disappeared under the bonnet. He reappeared, red-faced and very excited, speaking very fast to me and Reg and waving his hands about in a manner that suggested that our engine was buggered. He popped his head back under the bonnet, took off his bowler then scratched his head, before emerging again and shouting at his men. There was much arm-waving and excitement before a man was dispatched into a shed – he returned with a complete welding outfit. Reg's face was a picture of anguish as he watched his beloved engine glowing red hot as the Bulgarian tried to weld a bolt head onto the broken shank of one of the cylinder bolts.

The look of anguish turned to despair when, to cool the weld, the mechanic splashed water on the hot metal. Everyone stopped talking and a tense silence ensued as everyone's heads went under the bonnet to watch the welded bolt being turned, followed by a communal sigh as it snapped off. Once again a bolt head was produced and the process repeated; this time it worked and the bolt was withdrawn to a loud shout of success and whiskys and fags all round. Slowly, they went through the routine again until all the bolts had been withdrawn, then a man was despatched to the workshop with the broken bolts where, it was explained to us, they would manufacture new bolts of the right length and thread to replace the originals.

More whisky and cigarettes appeared and the ladies even managed to supply our willing workers with a snack meal, while John handed out some 'girlie' magazines, which were banned in Bulgaria. Three blokes immediately hotfooted it to the nearest bogs clutching the erotic literature.

After several hours, with a repaired engine, we thanked our new-found friends; they refused payment, so we gave them the rest of our cigarettes and John's mags and departed, glowing with admiration for the communist way of life. This lasted exactly one hour, until we fell foul of a communist policeman who wanted to arrest us. Then a communist publican who refused to serve us . . .

Ah well, you can't win 'em all.

Chapter 12

Silly Rope Tricks

LIKE EVERYTHING ELSE IN MY LIFE, change seems to creep up on me. In the sixties a new technique was introduced that would, it was claimed, revolutionise caving – I knew little about it, apart from rumours that some American cavers had been descending vertical pitches on ropes. This seemed to us quite a natural thing for American cavers to do because, according to our knowledge, caves in the USA were large horizontal things that one could drive a bus through and American cavers, mere beginners at the sport, probably didn't know how to make electron ladders.

I launched myself into space and watched my best hand-knitted sweater unravel

One day I received a letter from some US servicemen stationed in Germany asking for information about Provatina, as they were organising an expedition to abseil into the shaft and prusik out on single ropes. Reading this over my breakfast caused my cornflakes to curdle – they were obviously mad or misinformed, so I thought the least that I could do would be to warn the poor sods of the dangers of the deepest and nastiest shaft in the world (as it was then). As I thought back on my own experiences with silly rope tricks, some of which had almost curtailed a promising life, I wrote them a long letter full of do's and don'ts (mostly don'ts) and promptly forgot about it.

My first attempt at abseiling took place in Scotland on some craggy mountain top where, as a mere youth, I launched myself into space and watched my best hand-knitted sweater unravel as it became mixed up with the rope. I arrived on a ledge wearing a kind of woolly bra, a brand new rope burn and a surprised look on my face.

My second attempt occurred on the top of Shepherd's Crag in Borrowdale in the Lake District, where I was about to jump off when a friendly clubmate pointed out that, even allowing for stretch, three feet of rope will not work on a one-hundred-foot pitch – as I had hold of the wrong end.

It was obvious that my technique needed perfecting, so my willing buddies chose the Ribblehead Viaduct as a perfect place to practise. For me to practise, that is – they were only going to watch.

'But what about the trains?' I queried.

'There's no trains on a Sunday,' said my buddies. However, there was one – and we had fastened my belay to the track. Swinging below the viaduct in the middle of the central arch, eighty feet above the ground, I watched the train coming, lights flashing, klaxon blaring, and felt the bridge vibrating as my rope began to bounce up and down.

A head appeared over the parapet: 'There's a train coming, Jim.' I couldn't think of an answer to this useless information, I simply clung to the rope and waited for the wheels to cut the end and hasten mine. Luckily for me, Frank, a very pessimistic individual, had altered the belay from around the railway line itself and hooked it around the fitting that holds the rail in place – just in case. Even so, the wheel flanges stroked the wire belay and my buddies, flattened against the parapet, reckoned that I was only the width of a midge's dick from being despatched to that great playground in the sky.

I decided that abseiling was strictly for the birds, until I came home late one night and found a long, lanky, unkempt figure sitting on my garden wall. As I approached he leapt to his feet and grabbed me by the hand.

'Say, are you Jim Eerie?' he asked, pumping my hand furiously. 'Great to meet you Jim – just got back from doing Provatina on ropes.'

His name was Wil Howie, a lantern-jawed character with John Lennon glasses perched on the end of a nose that jutted out of a straggly moustache and a sparse surrounding beard that looked as though it could do with some fertiliser.

Over the course of the next few days, Wil convinced me that ladders were old-fashioned and that 'single rope technique' (or SRT) was the only way to travel down big pits. We arranged a sort of educational exchange trip, whereby Wil would teach me the new American techniques and I would show him some English caves, teach him how to consume vast quantities of beer and introduce him to some of the more eccentric forms of English wildlife.

The following day Audrey and I threw some camping gear into the car and stuck Wil in the back, then I drove to Hubberholme in Upper Wharfedale to introduce him to some of the rarer species of flora and fauna – namely members of the Northern Pennine Club, who were undertaking a club meet at Birks Fell Cave, a newly extended and very sporting site.

The two-mile-long Birks Fell Cave had already achieved some notoriety, for it was liable to flooding and, coupled with numerous tight sections, crawls and strenuous moves, it had already been the scene of two protracted rescues. We were soon crawling through the restricted entrance series, where Wil experienced difficulties trying to force his six feet three inches round the tight bends. After several attempts and much grunting and words of advice, he reached a sort of double Z-bend, flat-out in the stream.

I watched Wil's brown boots thrash around for some time before his voice wafted back to me: 'Don't care much for horizontal caving, Jim,' he muttered as his boots gave a spasmodic twitch, moved around the next bend and stopped. The boots flailed about some more, this time without going anywhere, then a strangled voice, punctuated by bubbling noises, informed all and sundry: 'My arm's dislocated, my goddam light's gone out and my goddam leg's stuck. I don't think even Jesus can help me now!'

I thrust myself into a tight crevice above him and shone my light down onto the struggling victim.

'Jesus Christ,' blasphemed Wil.

'My arm's dislocated, my goddam light's gone out and my goddam legs stuck'

'No, it's me,' I answered as I talked him through the tight bit and eased his long legs round the acute bends.

Several hours later, after a good trip in the impressive cave beyond, we managed to extract Wil in one piece. We returned to our campsite and visited the George Inn, where Wil established a newcomer's record by consuming what seemed like twelve pints in two hours, I studied my guest closely and thought I should warn him that this stuff wasn't like Coca-Cola.

'Gee, Jim, I sho like yo beer,' said Wil.

I looked behind the steamed-up glasses at his glazed eyes and silly grin, which had been transfixed on his face since the fifth pint.

'Isn't that beer affecting you, Wil?' I asked.

'Nope, but I think it's afixin' to,' answered Wil, before collapsing across the table.

We took Wil outside and inserted him in his sleeping bag, erected a tent over the top and stood back in admiration.

'Anybody – *hic* – that can – *hic* – drink like that – *hic* – deserves to be a – *hic* – a member of the – *hic* – NPC! Bloody marvellous,' slurred Sambo before he fell over.

Two days later, when Wil recovered, he said: 'You English cavers are great guys. Your caves ain't much, but your beer sure is something else.' He then left for Germany, promising to return.

AFTER LISTENING TO WIL, I determined to learn more about abseiling and prusiking. Picking up my *Manual of Caving Techniques*, which no self-respecting caver was without, I turned to page 109, which said: 'except in unusual circumstances abseiling underground is not a good practice.' 'Hmmm, I wonder which bum wrote this?' I queried as I looked at the chapter heading: 'Use of Ladders and Ropes' by J. Eyre. 'Ah, hmm, er, yes.'

In spite of this excellent advice, I rushed to Greenclose (the Northern Pennine Club's headquarters) in search of further enlightenment and found that three of our less intelligent members had once taken themselves down Swinsto Hole using the club's best lifelines and the club's only bread knife. Several hours later two of them had emerged, triumphantly clutching a short, mangled, frayed piece of rope, two bandaged fingers and a knackered bread knife (the third man was never seen again).

Armed with this new-found knowledge and two assistants (one a keen young chap who read all the latest climbing books; the other couldn't read, but in the 1940s had been a member of an RAF mountain rescue team), I set off down Swinsto with my old manila sling and a couple of krabs I had once found during a rescue.

Swinsto offers cavers the chance of a through-trip from a higher entrance to a lower one, so that you can descend a pitch using only one rope doubled over so that you can then pull it down to rig the next drop, and so on. The first two small pitches were no problem, but my companions didn't like my technique, so for the third they readjusted my sling and twisted it between my legs until a change of sex seemed imminent. They flung the rope over a rotting branch jammed in the roof next to a good, solid-looking girder which, for some reason, wouldn't do, and I was despatched into space. As I juddered slowly down the pitch, I couldn't understand how the Americans had reached the bottom of Provatina without dying of old age, for even when I let go of the rope I hardly moved and eventually I ground to a halt.

Swinging in mid-air, I had a conference with my 'experts' up above, who solemnly informed me that there was 'too much friction'.

'How do I reduce it?' I asked, bouncing about on the end of the rope and getting nowhere.

'Can't,' said the experts. 'It's your wetsuit – you shouldn't have come down dressed like that.'

I jumped up and down until I jerked lower for another few feet and ended up standing on tiptoes on a small outcrop as I swore and tugged savagely at the rope. It suddenly released its grip on my wetsuit and I fell backwards into a pool at the foot of the pitch. It was about now that, my companions having joined me, the rope became stuck and refused to come down, so I stood back and watched with interest as the two 'experts' struggled to free it.

'What happens if we can't pull it down?' I asked. The well-read one, Eddie, put on a very knowing look and said: 'Ah, we could jumar out.' I breathed more easily.

'But,' continued Eddie, 'I've never done that before and we haven't got any jumars.'

The rope eventually came free and I found myself juddering down the next pitch, until a chunk of my wetsuit was pulled into my krab and I stopped with a jolt, suspended under a waterfall.

'Bloody abseiling, **** abseiling,' I ranted as, in desperation, I climbed up the wall and hung by one hand until I freed the jam, before descending to the head of the next pitch – a seventy-foot drop.

I really had the feel of the thing by now. I picked up speed, pausing every other second to yank more pieces of wetsuit out of the krab. Unfortunately, I became overconfident and, after a brief snatch at my billowing neoprene, I really began to fly.

Alas, my exhilaration was short-lived. I came to a sudden halt, surrounded by smoke and the smell of hot rubber from one side of my neoprene jacket, which had vanished in a molten mass in my karabiner. Sod's Law had dictated that I was again hanging beneath a waterfall, but as I struggled with fingers blue with cold I consoled myself that I wouldn't die of thirst or heat exhaustion. I tore off large pieces of my jacket and pulled out shredded neoprene from where it was wrapped around the rope within the krab.

With water drumming on my helmet and rapidly losing body heat, I had visions of turning into a cave rescue statistic, before I eventually managed to free the rope and dropped to the base of the pitch. Semi-naked, I half-climbed and half-fell down the next pitch, to eventually emerge from Valley Entrance, having learned that one does not do an over-the-shoulder abseil while wearing half-weight neoprene.

FORTUNATELY, BEFORE I WAS TEMPTED to try any more Indian rope tricks, Wil returned from far-off places. He arrived with a bottle of Old Crow American bourbon, a set of jumars and a wondrous flying machine called a rack. Jumars are metal clamps which grip a rope, sliding upwards but not down, while his rack was made from a U-shaped piece of stainless steel rod threaded with a series of movable alloy bars (his had six), each alternately slotted so that they could swing open, allowing a rope to be threaded through – once this was pulled taught, the tension would hold the bars closed. It was an efficient, high-friction braking device with a degree of control: by adjusting the gaps between the bars (or swinging one out of place), anyone using it could alter the speed of descent. In addition, the metal would dissipate the heat arising from friction with the rope.

This was the Americans' secret weapon, together with high-tensile ropes made from long fibres contained in a sheath. Using ropewalkers for ascending the rope (the system used devices attached to the foot of one leg and the knee of the other, while a roller wheel kept the rope against your chest; there were many variations), American cavers had been exploring newly discovered, huge shafts in Mexico. As demonstrated in Provatina, they were going well beyond the limits imposed by the logistics of wire ladders.

Under Wil's tuition, I was soon flying off railway bridges (disused), cliffs and gorges, plus I had one interesting experience off a bridge over a fast-flowing, deep river. This ensured that I learned to change over from abseiling mode to prusiking mode in mid-air – it concentrates the mind wonderfully when one is dangling a few inches above a river in spate while switching gadgets off and on a rope and sticking the unused ones somewhere else, all the time being sworn at by an irate American leaning over a parapet far above.

We descended a couple of caves and I became so intoxicated by my new powers that I toyed with the idea of leaping down Gaping Gill, a 360 foot drop from the surface of Ingleborough's moors. I was dissuaded by Wil, who pointed out that we were using some old Northern Pennine Club lifeline, which wasn't quite suitable – and anyway it was 250 feet short and I would probably slide off the end.

My old Whillans climbing harness upset Wil when he found out that it was older than he was, so he decided to make me a new harness of his own design to use for the new technique of ropewalking. Armed with lengths of broad climbing tapes and Audrey's sewing machine, Wil set to like a man possessed until he realised that, instead of stitching the harness together with strong nylon thread, he was using ordinary cotton. As Audrey pointed out to him, in her own sweet way as she snapped a piece in demonstration, 'It's only some cheap stuff from Woolies I used for Jim's shirt.'

'Jeesus Kerist,' said Wil and, having discovered there was no nylon thread handy, he went back over all the stitching and made Audrey and me swear that we would further overstitch the harness with strong nylon thread. 'Cos if yo' don't, Jim, yo' sho is gonna end up dead.' We both made a solemn promise and Wil returned to America.

Several weeks later I demonstrated my new skills to the NPC on the imposing face of Malham Cove. Before an appreciative audience, I leapt off the top of the limestone cliff and, with my wondrous rack, made an impressive descent. This brought gasps of amazement from my clubmates and a spontaneous burst of applause from a coach-load of tourists who had just arrived from Ilkley and thought I was part of the entertainment. Then, standing at the foot of the impressive overhanging rock, I prepared for my *pièce de résistance* – climbing back up the two hundred feet on a single rope.

I adjusted all my ropewalking devices and Wil's special sling, then set off. Well, not quite set off because, using an NPC nylon lifeline, I walked up the rope for several minutes while it stretched beneath my weight, before I left the ground in a sudden leap as the recoil took over. However, I soon lapsed into the rhythm of one step up on the rope, bounce three feet down, then six feet up – it was like climbing elastic or undertaking an upside-down bungee jump. Nevertheless, I soon stopped worrying about the rope breaking and concentrated on climbing, which was remarkably easy.

Just over halfway, I became aware of a faint popping noise, which confused me for a second or two. Then I suddenly remembered what Wil had said before he had departed for Mississippi: if I didn't overstitch the harness with nylon, 'Yo' sho is gonna end up dead.'

I had forgotten! The popping sound became more ominous.

'Yo' gonna end up dead!' Wil's words rattled round in my brain as I carried on climbing, not quite as nonchalantly as before. A close observer would have noticed that both hands were now gripping the rope, whereas before they were in my pockets. Pop, pop, pop. What was I going to tell Audrey? Mind you, she forgot as well – I could see her inscribing on my tombstone: 'Here lies Jim – his stitches pulled out.'

Thirty feet to go and the faces leaning over the edge were taking great interest.

'Something's ripping, Jim,' Bob Hryndyj (an NPC member with an unpronounceable name) shouted down with a malicious grin on his face. 'How's your trousers?'

'Mefuckinstitches!'

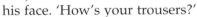

A different noise followed – the definite sound of splitting, of something giving way under stress. One of my ropewalkers came loose.

Twenty feet to go. With both hands clutching the rope, I was now pulling my body weight up as one foot stirrup hung useless and every time I put weight on the other ropewalker I could hear stitches parting company.

Ten feet to go, and my mates had stopped laughing. As I slowly worked my way over the lip someone grabbed me and hauled me in, away from the edge. 'Mefuckinstitches!' I gasped.

Back home, in some haste Audrey overstitched my harness with black thread – she wasn't really bothered about me risking my neck, but the dog would miss me.

I improved my technique and soon had my clubmates dangling out of trees, leaping off the edge of Trow Gill and hanging about in space in various open potholes, with me shouting instructions from the surface to the unfortunates below, transfixed as they were in the gloaming as they tried to use the unfamiliar gear.

Jim practising at Trow Gill
Photographer unknown

I lost many friends during my few short weeks as an 'expert' and was only saved from the threat of dire punishment by the fact that those who were threatening me were stuck, fastened to a bouncing rope and unable to proceed either up or down. They all said the same thing, though: 'I'll bloody kill you 'Ers, when I get out'. One in particular, a certain Steve Thorpe (who was built like a brick shithouse and rejoiced in the name of 'Thorpe the thug'), was one day dangling beneath me in the entrance shaft of Cow Pot. He cut an imposing figure with his pipe clenched in his teeth, blowing out blue smoke, clouds of ash and hot embers as he swore at me. His face was red, dripping with sweat and puffed up as he struggled to fix a ropewalker on his foot. Being a British home-made variety, this was causing him some trouble, but he eventually shoved all his attachments in place and began climbing. Then a ropewalker fell off one foot and the other one jammed!

I forget what he said, but it had something to do with my being born out of wedlock coupled with a warning concerning various facial adjustments – as though I hadn't had enough! Poor Steve – after he hand-over-hand hauled himself up the rope, he was too knackered to even intimidate a puffball.

My supreme moment of triumph came, however, when I had several members of the NPC dangling in unison from one of the highest viaducts in South Wales. Viewed from afar, it looked like a mass hanging, with Gareth Davies and me as the master puppeteers and our broken marionettes suspended in grotesque poses as they struggled to master the technique of changing over from abseiling to prusiking. One extremely large one promised to exterminate me if he ever reached terra firma again.

He cut an imposing figure with his pipe clenched in his teeth

SO BRITISH CAVERS BECAME SINGLE ROPE LITERATE; or not quite, because there was a sudden rush of rescues because some young cavers only half-learned the new technique. For a period there were some very tragic accidents because cavers used the wrong equipment and misjudged the depths of pitches, finding that they were unable to stop and sliding off the ends of ropes that were too short, or losing control on ropes that were long enough but were completely unsuitable.

SRT proved to be a blessing in disguise – it involves fastening yourself to the rope and this often proved fatal on Britain's short, wet pitches, for there is no escape when a flood pulse hits, or if fatigue sets in while hanging on a wet pitch.

The Cave Rescue Organisation was kept busy during those early days of British SRT and this change in caving coincided with the organisation taking over a new, purpose-built headquarters at Clapham in the Yorkshire Dales. It was conveniently adjacent to the New Inn where, after Wednesday evening sessions maintaining equipment, members would finish off with a drink or two. On one occasion one of the controllers, Ian Hopley, had enjoyed a pleasant evening drinking a pint or two while living up to his reputation as a raconteur, so he was not too pleased to be awakened at 2 a.m. by a phone call informing him that his services were required to search for a mentally retarded woman who was missing from the outskirts of Barnoldswick.

'You are going to make *me* mentally retarded, getting me out of bed at this time in the bloody morning,' muttered Ian. However, in the best tradition of CRO controllers, he and many others soon found themselves in the wilds of Barnoldswick, looking for an old lady wandering around in a distressed condition and clad only in a nightgown.

Several hours later, Ian found himself in a distressed condition as he had become separated from his fellow team members and discovered that he was wandering alone in unfamiliar terrain. He radioed back to base for instructions and was told to go along the canal, turn left at the sewage farm, turn right at the Rolls-Royce factory and head up the hill and over a stile, where he would find his team.

The wind was howling mournfully through the trees as our intrepid rescuer followed his instructions, creeping past an evil-looking copse of gnarled trees where at any moment he expected a demented figure in white, flowing, diaphanous flannel to leap out at him. He had the feeling that he was being followed and frequently stopped and looked behind himself, scarcely breathing as he listened for the slightest sound. He arrived at the top of the hill and sure enough there was a stile 'with a lid', as he later described it.

'Funny,' thought Ian, until he climbed over and found himself in an area of black polished slabs and serrated rows of white glistening marble. 'Christ! I'm in the bloody graveyard!' he cried. It was not a good spot to be in at 4 a.m. when life is at its lowest ebb. The sudden screech of a night bird made him jump. 'CRO One come in,' whispered Ian into his radio.

'CRO One to CRO Five. Receiving you – state your position,' came the reply.

'I'm in the bloody graveyard,' answered controller Ian as he saw something white fluttering behind a huge black mausoleum.

'Well, search it,' came the response. 'Over and out.'

'Over and out, I'll be over and out if I don't get out of here,' grumbled Ian as he hesitantly crept forward.

Suddenly, he heard an unearthly cry. 'It sounded like the wailing of a banshee,' he said afterwards. A white ghostly presence floated in space between two tall cypress trees

– and called out again with a weird cry sounding like the wind in the rigging of a ghost ship.

'I want yooooo.'

'Well I don't want yooooo,' said our unnerved controller. Blind panic took over as he set off in a four-minute dash, hopping over gravestones, flowerpots, stone angels, urns, edging stones and other graveyard encumbrances, pursued all the time by a little old lady in white who seemed to be gaining on him. 'Christ, perhaps she's been in the Olympics!' gasped Ian as he vaulted an angel with a harp and a surprised expression on her face, then did a hop, skip and a jump into a pile of earth and slid sideways into an open grave.

'Come in CRO Five, come in CRO Five,' bleeped the voice on the radio, which was lying where it had fallen. But CRO Five had gone, like a bat out of hell.

The little old lady was eventually found in a distressed condition – it seemed that she had seen a man running through the graveyard making strange noises. 'He didn't look right to me, and I should know because it takes one to know one,' she said with a knowing look.

BRIEF INTERLUDES LIKE THIS make it enjoyable to be part of a rescue team – there is always something happening to entertain the crew, like the small boy who became so excited in Great Douk Cave that he impaled his head on a stalactite and was taken to hospital with the inoffensive calcite growth projecting from his head (much to the amazement of the medical staff, who thought he was a unicorn). Even they were not as astonished as another member of our team who, in foul weather on Ingleborough, needed to send up a signal where a missing runner had been found in a state of collapse. We had just been issued with powerful new flares and, like most of us, Bob had not familiarised himself with the firing device, so here he was in a squall of sleet and rain and, in the haste and drama of the moment, he misunderstood the instructions.

'Hold with two hands in front of you with the arrow pointing upwards,' instructed the radio operator.

'Done that,' answered Bob.

'Cock the trigger with the thumb.'

'Hmm – done that,' muttered Bob, standing in the howling gale with rain dripping from his nose.

'Squeeze the trigger gently.'

'Right – here goes,' said Bob, and as the pressure of his finger increased his eyes registered something written on the side: 'First remove the cap'.

'Oh! Shit. I didn't do th—,' he said as a deafening bang and enormous flash preceded an Exocet-like fireball which shot out of the wrong end of the flare, whistled between his legs like a comet and hit a sheep a hundred feet away. 'Christ, I'm glad me legs were open!' he exclaimed as he stood there, half-deafened and half-blinded, gazing incredulously at the scorch marks on his trousers.

The sheep picked itself up off its scorched backside, gave Bob a baleful glare and seemed to say 'Sod you!' before buggering off.

LUCK PLAYS A MAJOR PART in all our lives and this is often illustrated in high-risk sports like caving. On one wet September evening in 1975, the team was called out to rescue a party in trouble in Lost John's Cave, a major system on Leck Fell, where a caver had gashed his hand. In very wet conditions team members descended the cave, to find that the casualty had cut his thumb on a sardine tin – not what one would call life-threatening – and consequently the rescuers were none too happy as they had been called out from a do. The stricken caver was feeling very sorry for himself, but recovered with amazing speed when one of the team told him: 'There's a lot of very drunk blokes being dragged away from a party to help you, and when they find you've only cut your hand on a bloody sardine tin they aren't going to be too pleased.' Within a remarkably short time the hapless caver regained the surface under his own steam.

Later that evening, towards closing time, word filtered round the pubs that there was another callout to Lost John's. 'It'll be the one we've just been on,' everyone reckoned, and took no notice. They were right: it was the same group which had caused the earlier callout, but this one was much more serious. The group had emerged from the cave under heavy water conditions – it had rained incessantly all day – and, after they had pulled out all their ladders, found that two of their party were missing!

Lost John's was well named, for the two cavers – both called John – had been mislaid somewhere in the wet, now-flooding depths of the cave and would be lost permanently without the intervention of the CRO. The six pitches in the cave were laddered in atrocious conditions while the day's heavy rain continued into the night. The pothole vibrated with noise caused by the thundering floodwater entering from numerous inlets all over the system.

It was by now midnight and five hours since the first callout to the caver bitten by the sardine tin. Some rescuers had to put on wet clothes and descend for a second time in dangerous circumstances. After a quick search of obvious routes had produced no result, more enquiries revealed that the missing men had last been seen heading downstream in the long stream passage that leads to the final sump, five hundred feet from the surface at the termination of two and a half miles of cave passages.

This long 'main drain' of the cave was notorious for building up localised sumps in wet weather and some cave divers were quickly alerted. Bob Hryndyj was woken from a deep sleep induced by several pints, imbibed as a celebration of the successful outcome of one rescue and secure in the knowledge that there wouldn't be another on such a foul night. It took the police constable twenty minutes to convince Bob that he wasn't dreaming and that there really was another callout to Lost John's, which he raced back to at 3 a.m.

The resulting rescue was astounding. Bob was joined by fellow cave divers Bob Cochran and Derek Crossland, and I helped to sherpa the heavy gear down the thundering pitches to the sump. Derek and Bob Hryndyj dived the flooded passage along a thirty-foot sump to reach the roomy Death's Head Inlet, where the missing cavers were found, cold and demoralised, but alive. They were given a five-minute lesson on how to breathe underwater and, separately, brought out safely – no mean feat against the powerful floodwater with frightened cavers. It was a job well done.

This very serious rescue formed the prologue to a spate of flooding incidents, which broke all records and stretched the CRO to its limits. In the space of eight weeks, the organisation was involved in nine callouts to rescue forty-nine cavers from flooded caves. An incredible six of these incidents happened in one night.

Saturday 15 November 1975 will go down in the annals of cave rescue history as the greatest 'nursemaid' operation of all time, with thirty-eight cavers trapped by floods through their own stupidity. There had been early snow followed by days of intermittent rain, leaving the moors sodden. The weather forecast for that Saturday predicted yet another depression bringing heavy rain, nevertheless – and unbelievably – six different groups of assorted 'cavers' decided to go underground.

At just after five in the afternoon the team received a callout to rescue twelve members of a recreation club from Stockport. The club was subsidised by the local council and was a good example of the trendy thinking of the mid-seventies, when Sport for All was the thing. During this period increasing numbers of youngsters were being taken over hillsides, up rock faces and down caves, apparently regardless of whether they actually wanted to do these 'macho' things or not. Some of us gained the impression that a lot of these activities were arranged more for the instructors' or teachers' benefit, and at least part of the problem was caused by the idea that anyone could become an outdoor pursuits instructor simply by attending a course. Without a background of hard-earned experience, this was a bad mistake.

In this case the youngsters were 'trapped' in cold, rapidly rising floodwaters in Long Churn, a fairly easy cave, a few feet away from an alternative dry, high-level route which would have taken the party to safety. Four young people were taken to hospital, with one sixteen-year-old girl suffering from exposure. The 'youth leader' in charge of the group later stated that: 'There is a calculated risk in all forms of adventure training,' and added: 'We took the maximum safety precautions to go to a cave which I have already visited fifty times. We would never see anyone go up Everest if we didn't do this sort of thing.' This chappie obviously needed to broaden his horizons; if he had already been down this small cave fifty times he was also in dire need of a visit to the opticians, having passed a very noticeable dry passage fifty times without seeing it. As for Everest . . .

Thirteen minutes after the first callout, a second team was despatched to Crystal Cave in Barbondale, where another party had been caught by rising water with one caver trapped in a small chamber beyond a flooded section. Bob Hryndyj and Phil Papard carried out a remarkable diving rescue by forcing their way underwater through rubble and loose rocks washed into the cave, then fighting to keep their underwater exit free from fill which the floodwater continually pushed back in. Eventually, while one of the divers kept the opening clear, the other struggled out with the casualty; Bob was almost trapped in the process.

This unique rescue, where both men showed great skill, endurance and sheer bravery in atrocious conditions, was later acknowledged when Bob and Phil were honoured with lifesaving awards from the Royal Humane Society.

A callout at 6.25 p.m. stated that five cavers, four of them schoolboys, were trapped by floodwater in Ireby Fell Cavern. Jack Pickup, the surface controller, organised a general callout for all outlying rescue teams as it looked like being a long night; a team from Lancaster was sent to help the overstretched local rescuers, along with two fire tenders to pump water away from the cave entrance.

It was a terrible, bitterly cold night with heavy rain sheeting down. As workers resolved one rescue they were immediately called to another and cold, wet, tired men were forced to climb into cars or Land Rovers and drive to deal with yet more groups.

Another emergency call was received from County Pot on Casterton Fell at 9.30 p.m., where three cavers were trapped in the flooded system.

'Hellfire!' said Jack. 'Who have we got?'

The Ireby team was nearest, so Jack grabbed a radio and arranged for a small group to drive to Bull Pot Farm, where they were to attempt to sort out the County Pot incident while others returning from the Barbondale and Long Churn rescues could supplement the depleted Ireby Fell team. It was fast becoming a game of chess, only instead of running out of moves the CRO was running out of men.

At a quarter to ten there was another call for assistance: nine Venture Scouts were trapped in Swinsto Hole. The surface controllers were now rather thin on the ground and the underground teams were becoming dangerously tired and needed more backup. In their desperate quest to save lives the radio communications team directed men hither and thither across the wet soggy moors, now flowing with floodwaters. Jim Leach grabbed a handful of men and they jumped into a Land Rover and departed for Kingsdale, to deal with the Swinsto call.

In the early hours of Sunday 16 November, at 2.20 a.m., word came through that eight cavers were trapped in White Scar Cave. The team held a quick conference: there was nothing we could do for them. White Scar is a resurgence cave and the only help that would have any effect would be to attempt a long stream diversion in Crina Bottom, where the stream sinks – and we hadn't the men to spare. The situation wasn't life-threatening, so the trapped cavers would have to sit it out in the high-level areas of the cave and wait for the flood levels to drop. If they didn't, we would rethink.

One by one the emergencies were brought to a successful conclusion; the rescued were fed, given hot drinks and sent home. The rescuers, meanwhile, stood around in groups, wet and miserable, until the early dawn because the White Scar situation was still unresolved. Eventually, those who had borne the brunt of the night's work went home, while a small group remained at White Scar in the cold light of a bleak sun.

As the rain stopped and the water began to drop, one of the divers – Phil Papard – decided to try to contact the trapped cavers. They were eventually found in the high-level passage beyond the Big Bertha rock pile, by which time the water level permitted them to exit via a small duck before it started raining again.

Oh, what a night it was. Twelve hours of sustained effort from over one hundred cavers, police, firemen and ambulance workers, had finally come to an end. Thirty-eight cavers lived to tell the tale, instead of becoming statistics as cave fatalities to be filed for later study. The press had a field day and the usual articles came from the instant experts and agony aunts Heart Throb Annie and Priscilla Ploops, who condemned all cavers as rampant lunatics. If some of today's politicians had been around then, they would have banned caving altogether and organised underground wardens with sniffer dogs to rout out the lawbreakers. 'Wet weather potholers rapped' and '"Cavers irresponsible" say rescue leaders' shouted the news headings, suggesting that reporters had caught some unguarded comments.

My finest hour came in the Monday's *Daily Mirror*, when my own unguarded comments were printed with my name just a quarter of an inch away from Maria Zuchowska's glorious breasts, as her lovely body hogged most of page nine. Oh Maria, to think we had been so close yet we never met – I wonder where she is now.

With publicity like this, who could go wrong? Settle Town Council granted the team the freedom of Settle (not literally) and put on a resplendent do at a local up-market hostelry. With the tables lined with sumptuous goodies, the term 'running buffet' took on a new meaning as the mayor delivered a longish speech, finishing with the words: 'Well, gentlemen, I expect you would all like to enjoy your meal,' whereupon he looked up from his notes to see the last of the trifle being licked from the bowl.

Chapter 13

The Hölloch

EUROPE'S LONGEST CAVE SYSTEM – the Hölloch in central Switzerland – is a veritable maze of passages on many levels and subject to severe flooding. It was not my first choice of where to spend Christmas in 1975, but I couldn't resist a bargain and I even managed to talk Audrey into coming with us. 'At last, our chance to join the international jet set and meet the beautiful ski people,' I said.

Audrey, who by this time was beginning to understand the working of an Eyre's brain, was not entirely convinced.

'I'm not sure about this travel company,' she commented. 'Dirty Frank's package tours – I've never heard of them.'

'Oh, they're only small, but wonderfully cheap,' I answered, and that convinced her. I posted a cheque to the company's office, via the Craven Heifer in Ingleton, and booked two seats on their luxury coach – which later turned out to be a small, vintage Land Rover.

The following weekend we met the rest of the team members – with names that could have been penned by Damon Runyon, they resembled a cast from *The Godfather*. The expedition leader was Dirty Frank (who was), next came Big Jane (who owned the Land Rover, who also was) and Mad Mitch (who wasn't – he was just strange). Then there were Kirk and Kos, who sounded like Albanian tap-dancing artistes but were, in reality, a pair of Lancashire piss artists, and finally there was Salford Phil, a Greek cockney.

After hearing of our plans to explore the second longest cave in the world, Audrey became concerned. 'Oh, Jim, won't it be wet and cold?'

'Yes,' I said, 'but we'll be alright when we get there,' knowing full well that with a crew like that we would never leave the *Gasthaus*.

After Dirty Frank received permission from his parole board, we were driven hot-foot across the Channel by a bionic Big Jane, who must have had a very strong bladder because we didn't stop until we reached Zurich at 3 a.m. By this time we were lost, so Mitch and Kos approached a lone taxi driver to ask the way. He took one look at the faces peering through his iced-up cab windows, locked all the doors and began frantically radioing for the police!

Later that day we reached our destination at Muotathal and the excellent Gasthaus Höllgrotte, which was run by the marvellous Frau Suter, whose hospitality was legendary. The *Gasthaus* was the unofficial headquarters of the Hölloch exploration group and, as well as being custodian of the cave, Frau Suter looked after us and the Swiss cavers who were also there like a mother – that is, with as much food as we could eat and as much booze as we could drink; it was a caver's dream.

The Gasthaus Höllgrotte was thereby voted the world's finest hostelry; you could keep your four-star Michelin guidebook hotels for the pampered rich! Where else would you find such a delightful lady whose one aim in life, it seemed, was to make cavers happy, where every meal filled the centre of a long table and, as fast as one course vanished, another replaced it?

As the wine and beer miraculously disappeared, so more appeared – all served by Frau Suter's beautiful daughter, Maria. Her breasts were barely contained in her Swiss bodice as she leaned over the table, smiling a beautiful smile as she plied us with goodies and drinks until, wearing vacuous grins, some of the weaker souls subsided into her arms, unable to articulate or move. The lovely Maria would then lift each one to his feet, swing him over her shoulder and carry him up the spiral staircase to our room. Now, that's what I call room service!

DULY RECOVERED, the following day we changed into caving gear. With Mad Mitch as our leader (he had been in the cave the year before, though he didn't tell us that he had been lost), we walked over the crisp, deep snow in bright sunlight to the entrance of the old showcave, almost a hundred metres above the rising in the valley below us.

The showcave had been abandoned for many years because frequent violent flooding had smashed the light fittings, steps and handrails and destroyed the cave formations. As we descended into the large cave mouth, the violence of this periodic flooding was evident: huge, fluted, organ-like speleothems lay broken and the old, grey flowstone had been scarred by rolling boulders.

In the lower reaches of the cave a heavy, barn door frame had been built into the rock and substantial two-metre-long baulks of timber were slotted into this and held in place by barometric pressure alone. Considerable effort was required to pull these away to allow us to pass and, once we were inside, the tremendous draught sucked the beams back in place with the ferocity of a slamming door. The inventive Swiss had found that this wooden barrier cut down on air currents in the cave, making the underground camps quite cosy, and floods washed the timber to one side rather than destroying a permanent door.

Now, that's what I call room service!

We soon decided that the Hölloch (or Hell Hole) is a strange, alien sort of cave. It was formed under pressure below the water table, creating an underground maze comprising around 130 kilometres of passages on several levels, with over eight hundred metres of height difference between the upper and the lower extents. The passages themselves are mainly featureless tunnels with floors of black, highly polished and almost marble-like limestone coated in slimy mud; coupled with scour holes and heavy fluting, in some sections this made getting around extremely difficult and caused many nasty falls. Walking was like skating on a limestone pavement (a karst feature containing deep erosion fissures) and within minutes I would have sold my soul for some tricouni-nailed boots to obtain a better grip.

The other (and of course the main) feature of the Hölloch is the angle of its bedding, which dips steeply towards the north-north-west and makes the use of fixed ropes and iron ladders essential in many places. A good description of the Hölloch would be to liken it to a London Underground system which had been submerged in the Thames for several years and then hoisted up to an angle of fifty degrees, with the lower section still underwater.

Into this complex we wandered, slipping and sliding, sweating and cursing. I had often suspected that Dirty Frank was a genius, because whatever it was that was broken or didn't work, he could fix it – and now I discovered that he had an unerring instinct which enabled him to see through solid rock, or so it seemed. Somehow, somewhere, Dirty Frank had obtained a survey of the Hölloch and had reduced it in size so that it would fit into his pocket. I watched in amazement as Frank unfolded his copy, which was not much bigger than a postcard.

'Can't get lost with this,' he said, proudly flourishing his postcard of spidery scribbles. 'There's over eighty miles on this,' he said.

'Where are we?' I asked.

'There,' said Frank, pointing a muddy finger at a little dot that looked like fly shit. 'In this chamber.'

It *was* fly shit, because the dot moved.

'Oh,' said Frank, 'perhaps it's this one,' and prodded his mucky finger at another dot on his master plan, almost obliterating it with mud. Not for nothing is he called Dirty Frank.

We headed further into the labyrinth, not holding a thread like Ariadne but clutching the end of Dirty Frank's sweater as he advanced boldly into the unknown, with his postcard of scrawled lines held ahead of him. We lost the reassurance of hanging onto Frank's sweater when we began to cast off surplus clothing – we were vastly over-dressed for strenuous activity in a cave with an almost complete lack of draughts. Even in the middle of winter, the Hölloch seemed quite warm and before long we were lathered in sweat as we slithered and staggered our way onward with queries of 'Do we go right or left?' or 'Is it up or down?' in the three-dimensional maze. Soon, Frank and Mitch were suffering from brain fatigue and the survey was totally covered in muddy fingerprints – then Mitch experienced sudden attacks of recovered memory syndrome as he thought he recognised a place from the previous year.

'Ah,' he shouted gleefully. 'I recognise this bit.'

'Well done, Mitch. Where are we?' I asked.

'I'm not sure – we were lost when we passed here, but I *do* remember it,' said Mitch.

We sorted ourselves out when we arrived at the first recognisable landmark, the Riesensaal or Giants' Hall, a large chamber with four converging passages and a visitors' book. This was a first for us, so we all duly signed it and I drew in a little cartoon of Dr Bögli, a very respected explorer of the cave (only my version had castors on his legs instead of feet, as I little realised that the distinguished gentleman was still active and would see the cartoon the following day – fortunately, he had a good sense of humour).

From the Riesensaal we descended into the lower levels, which during most of the year are submerged and are only safe to enter during the winter when surface water is frozen and the water level drops. We soon encountered the river Styx and the first of the many flood traps, which effectively seal cavers inside the cave as the river rises – and can continue to rise for a hundred metres! Dr Bogli and three other cavers were once trapped for ten days in the Riesensaal, before the water level dropped sufficiently to allow their escape. The group was extremely lucky, because within hours the floodwaters rose again and barred access to the cave for two months.

Crossing the Styx in a wooden dinghy, which had been left there by the Swiss cavers, made us think about flooding as we gazed at the mud-covered walls and roof of the low, stream passage. From here we worked our way up fixed ladders and thin, slimy ropes which were impossible to grip and we struggled up the steep inclines, back and footing, gaining a few feet before slipping down again. It was like climbing an underground greasy pole and by the time we reached the top we were all bathed in sweat and needed a brief rest before continuing along the largest of the drab tunnels that lay ahead.

All this time we had been climbing upwards, but now the passage suddenly dipped, forcing us to slide down several feet before confronting us with another greasy vertical section. The Hölloch is, indeed, not an easy cave to traverse.

We had just ascended one particularly slimy climb and were working our way up a large inclined tunnel when I heard a strange sound like a ruptured bagpipe. Every time we stopped to listen, the sound also stopped – and every time we moved off again, the weird, off-key wail echoed along the tunnel. After a great deal of detective work the mystery noise was eventually traced to Big Jane's bronchitis – being a big lass, she breathed heavier than most and emitted an extensive repertoire of off-beat accordion notes which ranged from 'Will Ye No' Come Back Again?' to 'Amazing Grace', played in an asthmatic wheeze which was amplified in the tubular passage. However, Salford Phil gave her the kiss of life and I gave her a Fisherman's Friend and a pat on the head, and she was cured.

Of course by this time we hadn't a clue where we were so we just continued following the larger passages. It all became too much for Big Jane for she suddenly announced, 'I can hear pop music.'

'It's your pipes,' said Mitch.

Poor Jane, she was cracking up – so I gave her another hot sweet and asked Salford Phil to give her another kiss of life.

'Bollocks,' said Phil in an ungentlemanly fashion. 'I gave her one last time – ask Dirty Frank.'

Alas, he couldn't reach so Jane had to struggle on.

'I can hear music again,' she said. Indeed, after some more time had passed we all began to hear faint music and came upon a thin wire pegged to the wall of the cave. Mesmerised, we followed the wire, which led us, like *Alice's Adventures in Wonderland*, straight into Bivouac No. 2.

This main underground camp looked like a film set and we gazed in wonder at the chamber's bright lights, whitewashed walls, curtains, shelves, tables, chairs and beds. The tablecloths spread on the tables and vases of artificial flowers, well-stacked shelves and the music were themselves mind-blowing, but when we were approached by a gentleman in a purple dressing gown and matching slippers, it was too much. We stood with our mouths wide open in astonishment – I half expected antennae to sprout out of his head as he said: 'Take me to your leader!' Instead, he said: 'Hello, would you like a cup of tea?' and showed us to a dirty table reserved for passers-by, where we sat down and enjoyed the Swiss hospitality, tea, schnapps and biscuits.

Our host was surprised at the short time it had taken us to get there from the entrance. 'How did you find the camp so quickly?' he asked. We showed him our survey and he gasped. 'With this,' I said, 'and that,' pointing at Dirty Frank.

'He must be very clever,' the gowned man remarked in awe, looking at Dirty Frank who was even dirtier than he generally was.

'Oh yes,' said I, 'he lives near a university.'

'Have a brandy,' said the Swiss gentleman.

While we sat talking another group of Swiss cavers appeared; they had been taking advantage of the holiday period to continue exploring the higher levels, and were spending a week underground. For our part, after staying awhile we returned to the surface to meet Audrey, Frau Suter and her family, and after a shower we got stuck into the festive season – not for us a troglodyte existence deep in the bowels of a Swiss mountain, of men dressed in purple dressing gowns and matching slippers!

AFTER OUR RECCE into the Hölloch we decided to do the winter sports bit. Kos started the ball rolling by taking Maria sledging down a one-in-three road which was covered in ice and overhung the *Gasthaus* like a miniature Eiger. Unfortunately, although Kos knew how to charm young ladies, he didn't know much about sledging and at the first Z-bend Kos and Maria became airborne and landed in a tree halfway down a gorge. The next run was accomplished with me using an ice axe to steer but, when I applied the brake by jabbing the axe into the frozen surface, I was yanked off the back of the sledge and Kos once again became airborne and returned to the same tree.

At this point we decided to join the winter tourists, because a funeral would spoil our holiday (especially so for the one in the box). Standing in a queue with the beautiful people at Andermatt, we soon discovered that looks can be deceiving as the skiers pushed and kicked in their efforts to get on the cable cars, shouldering lesser mortals out of the way. We brought out our secret weapons: Dirty Frank and Mad Mitch, whose après-ski outfits were indistinguishable from their caving gear with both of them looking as though they had recently been dredged from the bottom of a lake and badly blow-dried. Frank and Mitch marched boldly forward and the beautiful people, in their beautiful sparkling clothes, recoiled in horror, parting like the waters of the Dead Sea before Moses.

'Lovely day,' said Mitch, giving one of his leering smiles to a large blonde Fräulein, who emitted a yelp of horror and backtracked from Mitch as though he was Hannibal Lecter.

A similar procedure worked in the crowded restaurant, where people were queuing for seats. Frank suddenly decided to take a photograph. 'Excuse please,' he said to a smartly dressed group of Germans who were enjoying their Vienna schnitzel, and promptly plonked his ammo tin on a nearby stool and took out his camera which, for protection, was wrapped in a Dirty Frank vest. As any Dirty Frank fan will know, such a garment is never, ever washed, as it ruins the fabric.

Frank carefully unwrapped his camera and shook out the vest, covering the six Germans and their plates of goodies in a fine layer of three million years of glacial cave deposit. With cries of 'Was ist das,' and various other German phrases like 'Stupid English pillock,' they hurriedly departed the dust cloud, leaving six seats for us (a word of caution: this trick should only be tried on *small* Germans).

The holiday atmosphere was soon to be dispersed by a certain caver (me). Having been put suitably at ease in the convivial atmosphere of the *Gasthaus* by Frau Suter's excellent cooking, excellent beer, wine and free cigars, I began to wax lyrical about our caving prowess to the interested Swiss cavers. They soon realised that we were hard men – even Jane – and that we could easily reach the end of the Hölloch and make a return. The Swiss were suitably impressed, but did not realise that we had no intention of leaving the *Gasthaus* – and we were safe in our knowledge that no one in their right mind would give permission for a bunch of lunatic Brits to be let loose in 130 kilometres of very complicated cave.

Unfortunately for me, two of the group turned out to be Swiss 'tigers' and, after a quick discussion, they suddenly turned to me and much to my dismay informed me that they were going to explore some high-level leads in the Göttergang at the very end of the system. Not only that, they would guide us in. Warning bells immediately rang in the space where my brain should have been but, knowing that we could easily avoid becoming involved, I said: 'Great, which day are you going in?'

'In one hour's time,' they answered.

How do you tell a bunch of drunks that their Happy Hour is over and that they are about to depart on a round-trip comprising twenty-five kilometres of hard caving? 'Er, could you pack some food and your sleeping bags and extra lights – we're going caving,' is how I broached the subject.

'Sure, Jim.' Ho, ho. 'Great.' Chortle, chortle. 'Good 'ole Jim – always one with the jokes.'

'Er – I'm serious.'

'Bloody 'ell!'

ONE HOUR LATER, with a much diminished and not quite sober team, I followed the two nimble-footed Swiss cavers into the greasy confines of the cave, with my companions sweating, burping, farting and swearing at the weight of their bags and the silly sod whose idea it was to go caving in the middle of the night. The two guides never seemed to put a foot wrong and we came to the conclusion that they had suckers on their wellies, as they didn't seem to fall or slip with the same frequency that we did.

In a surprisingly short time, lathered in sweat but quite sober and in a state of shock, we arrived at the base camp. We were made welcome by the other Swiss cavers, some of whom had been underground for ten days while exploring the lower levels. Even in the dry conditions of midwinter, the cave was not totally safe, as evidenced by several wetsuited cavers who burst into the camp, having narrowly escaped from a low section of the Anubisgang where there had been a sudden flood caused by a temperature inversion outside that had produced a sudden thaw on the mountain slopes. One caver told of his hair-raising experience of clambering up a steep, muddy slope with the rising water gloop-glooping after him – he was given a glass of brandy to calm him down.

'What happens if the temperature inversion remains for several days,' I asked.

'Oh, we just stay here; we cannot get out,' answered a caver nonchalantly. 'And,' he continued, seeing my unease, 'if it stays warm, we all die here!'

Salford Phil asked if they had many accidents.

'Not too many,' answered the Swiss. 'We once had a man die, but he was very old – he was fifty!'

This caused a burst of laughter because someone had blabbed that I was fifty. There is no respect for senior citizens these days.

After a pleasant 'evening' – time being meaningless when living underground – we climbed into our sleeping bags and the Swiss in charge of the huge pressure lamp said in a loud voice, 'Goodnight cavers, the sun is going down.' He put out the light and we were plunged into the total Stygian blackness. I mused on the fact that I was comfortably tucked up in an underworld inhabited by crazy Swiss troglodytes in the middle of a Swiss mountain, and I fell asleep with visions of small Swiss gnomes working on some vast underground forge and Bing Crosby singing 'I'm dreaming of a white Christmas'.

I awoke from a restless sleep to find that the 'sun' had reappeared and we enjoyed a snack breakfast and a brew before visiting the bog. I collect unusual toilet experiences like some people collect stamps and the one in the Hölloch came next only to one high in the French Alps. There, balanced over a hole in a wooden sentry box that was perched over a glacier, I once looked down two thousand feet and watched with interest as the contents of my bodily evacuation fell into space – before a violent up-draught caught it and returned said contents with the speed of a rocket that was only exceeded by me as I hastily evacuated the toilet.

The 'toilet' in the Hölloch was located by following numerous arrows, which eventually took me well clear of the base camp area to a large chamber that ended at a steep drop with a chain bolted above it. Way down below lay the top of a Matterhorn constructed from years of crap deposited by thousands of bowel movements belonging to untold cavers frightened at being so deep in the bowels of the earth. The trick was to drop your trousers, grasp the chain firmly with both hands (a slip would be disastrous) and shuffle backwards until you were hanging over the brink, then do your stuff before shuffling forwards, letting go of the chain and wiping your bum.

A little plaque fixed upon the wall urged extreme caution. Written upon it was a little poem in memoriam to an early casualty, a certain Adolf Schizenblatt:

Poor Adolph, last seen swinging on the chain,
Oh dear, how sad, he's never to be seen again.
Not a cry, or a shout, or a gasp was heard,
And now poor Adolph lies below, in-turd.

Soon we were following our two guides further into the cave system, which as well as becoming more complicated became more interesting and I could well understand how Mad Mitch and his fellow cavers of the Northern Speleological Group had become lost the year before.

The trick was to drop your
trousers, grasp the chain
firmly with both hands and
shuffle backwards until you
were hanging over the brink

We were making good progress, but our group was becoming more spread out and
the stragglers were in danger of taking the wrong turning, so it was obvious that we
would have to either let our guides go on alone, or split the group. After a brief
discussion, Phil and I decided to tag along with the two Swiss, leaving the rest with
Dirty Frank and his micro-dot survey. Once we left, it seemed to give the Swiss the
incentive to increase their pace, and we soon passed the remains of the second base
camp which, even though it was high above the stream passages, had been destroyed
by periodic flooding.

Heading along the SAC Gang, I became uneasy about the many junctions and climbs
up and down; I was sure we would never remember the route back in all these tunnel-
like passages, each indistinguishable from one another. I thought, 'To hell with personal
hygiene,' and started dropping small pieces of bog paper at every junction. I mean,
what's the point of having a clean bum if you're going to die of exposure or hunger?

We soon saw signs, written on the cave walls with the soot of carbide lamps, which
proclaimed: 'NSG', each with an arrow which variously pointed in all sorts of directions
apart from the right one. These became more frequent and more frantic, some having
several arrows and some with the arrows crossed out and reversed. We half expected
to come across the skeletal remains of one of Mitch's mates after we found a final sign
which said 'NSG lost 3.30 a.m.', because Mitch is notoriously absent-minded and,

according to what he had told us, they had wandered about in this part of the system for twelve hours.

Leaving the Hoffnungsgang, our guides suddenly stopped, shook us by the hand, gave us some hasty verbal instructions and the address of a good undertaker, before pointing down a miserable-looking mud-covered tunnel: 'You go that way.' Then they pointed up a pleasant, dry passage: 'We go this way,' and disappeared.

Phil and I felt somewhat alone as we tried to remember what we had been told. We plodded on: 'First left, second right, traverse over two holes, go down the third, up in the roof at four-ways, ignore the next, go down the one after and pass the two on the left, then climb up and turn left at the cairn.' You know, simple stuff like that. It was no good looking for footprints or unusual pointers or formations, because there weren't any and the draughts were non-existent, so we just blundered on, working on instinct, with me surreptitiously dropping little pieces of toilet paper at each junction. These rapidly became smaller, as I was running out of bog paper.

After what seemed like three weeks and with my bits of paper reduced to the size of confetti, we came across a large, discoloured calcite formation and we slowly realised that we were looking at the Pagoda at the entrance to the Pagodengang. We had made it!

Turning right, we looked at the formations in the Reinacherstollen – formations are rare in the Hölloch and these were the only ones we had seen. Continuing, the passage eventually split into three small dead ends: we were at the end of the Hell Hole and as far as anyone could reach from the entrance.

We sat down to eat our sardine sandwiches and refill our carbide lamps, topping them up from a small pool. Phil lit a candle, stuck it on a rock, emptied both lamps and knocked the candle over, which plunged us into darkness.

Total darkness can be quite unnerving, but total darkness thirteen kilometres from an entrance at the other end of a maze of 130 kilometres of passages made the darkness, and our outlook, as black as it is possible to be.

'That was a bloody silly thing to do,' I muttered as I heard Phil frantically scrabbling about in his bag and among the gravel on the cave floor.

'Er, got any matches?' asked Phil.

'No, you've got them,' I said.

'Oh,' came his voice, followed by a pregnant pause (an expression I rarely use). 'Hmmm, that's funny . . . Ah . . . Oh, shit!' Phil's dismembered speech floated through the darkness with another noise that sounded ominously like a box of matches dropping down a gap in the rocks. 'I've dropped them.'

This statement had the doom-laden air of a virgin agreeing to sex with the evil prince for the first time.

I was a captive audience, trapped in a black box with a lunatic as I listened to the heavy breathing and frantic scrabbling in the water and gravel, interspersed with swear words I had never heard of. I also remembered that someone had borrowed the flint from Phil's carbide lamp and that mine was knackered . . .

'Shit,' said Phil. More scrabbling: 'Ah, got 'em – they feel a bit wet.'

More scrabbling, more obscenities.

'Can't find the fuckin' candle. Don't move – ah, got it.'

The longest moment of my life followed as Phil tried to light a match. The little scraping noises and faint blue flashes grew more feeble as the box became soggier.

'Try two matches together,' I suggested.

'There's only two left,' said Phil as another faint blue spark tried to turn into a flame. It spluttered and almost died before a weak flame was born; as I watched it being applied to a shaking wick by a shaking hand, I became religious.

'Give me the fuckin' candle,' were the only words I spoke as I watched Phil top up the lamps.

Our return to base camp was long and complicated and Phil was amazed at my route-finding, until he saw me picking up small pieces of bog roll at every junction. In the really complex areas where we didn't know whether to go up or down or left or right, we were both on our knees searching for minute pieces of tissue.

Arriving at the camp we spent some time with the Swiss before deciding to head for the surface and the loving arms of Audrey, Frau Suter and the New Year festivities. As it turned out this was an evening of free food, free booze and free cigars, which I enjoyed immensely while I thought, 'But for a pure stroke of luck, I could at this moment be sitting, cuddling a caver, trying to conserve body heat in total darkness at the end of Europe's longest cave, waiting for a rescue team that didn't even know we were missing.'

The evening ended when Big Jane and I became members of a religious sect, Mitch descended into an alcoholic trance (which is not much different from Mitch not being in an alcoholic trance), and Maria carried Kirk and Kos up to our room where, drinking Pernod and Southern Comfort, they swayed in unison singing 'The night the old brown cow caught fire', before collapsing in a heap.

All in all, it was a reet good do!

But for a pure stroke of luck, I could at this moment be sitting, cuddling a caver, trying to conserve body heat

Chapter 14

There's No Business
Like Show Business

THE CRAVEN HEIFER was heaving and we struggled to the bar, desperate for a pint. After a good day's caving, Jack's flat Yates bitter slid down our throats like nectar, washing away the cave dust we had swallowed in the higher levels of Lost John's Cave.

'Same again, Jack,' I said, as I leaned on the beer-slopped bar top and surveyed the packed, low-ceilinged room, looking to see who was in.

'Ah, Jim, just the man I want,' said Sid Perou, who had just materialised from the scrum around the dartboard. 'What are you having?'

Sid must have come into money. With three pints lined up and the promise of more, our diminutive film director explained his sudden wealth by the award of a BBC contract to make a documentary on some of the major British cave systems.

'We are thinking of making a film on the Lancaster–Ease Gill System – 'ere, have another pint,' said Sid, 'and I thought of George Cornes . . .'

'Ah, yes,' I interrupted, 'George will be great – he's just your man. Great character is George, he knows all there is to know about Ease Gill and he's very photogenic.'

'But, but . . .' Sid always stammered when he became excited and I noticed a shifty look come into his expression. 'Yes, but he's having trouble with his knee, and – ah, here comes Lindsay, have another pint.'

Sid's mate Lindsay Dodd, ace sound man, sidled up and explained that although George was to be the main man in the forthcoming epic, he and Sid would like me to be a stand-in for George on some of the more difficult bits. I gasped, completely overcome, for George – the discoverer of Lancaster Hole – was my hero. It was like being asked to be a stand-in for Queen Victoria.

'Will I be made up to look like him?' I asked.

'No, there's no make-up good enough – and anyway, we're only using your legs,' said Sid. 'George will do the talking and you will do the walking.'

'Actors will be paid,' said Lindsay. 'The equity rate is eighteen pounds an hour but, being a leg double, you will receive slightly less – about fifteen pence an hour at least, which isn't bad considering that you won't have to learn lines. We might even make it fifteen pence a leg.'

After several more pints I was convinced and signed on the dotted line, then promptly forgot all about it.

After an absence of several months, in 1976 Sid and Lindsay began frequenting the Craven Heifer again, generally just in time for last orders. About then, Bob Emmett and Kenny Taylor began to miss their regular drinking hours and they too would come staggering into the pub just in time to slurp some beer before closing. I noticed that they didn't seem as young and carefree as they used to, and commented on this to Bob.

'Been on a hard trip, Bob?' I asked.

'Hard? It's bloody hard,' he answered, staring morosely into space. He suddenly turned to face me. ''Ere, are you going to make a film with Sid?'

'Yes,' I answered.

'You must be bloody mad!' he exclaimed, and walked away from me in disgust.

It later turned out that our intrepid film crew had been working in Pippikin Pot, a tight, restricted, and now famous cave that several years previously had

Sid filming in Long Churn Cave for Beneath the Pennines, *while Lindsay records the sound. Photo: Ian Plant/BBC*

defeated my attempts to dig it out. Pippikin was now part of a large and complicated network of cave passages that linked the Ease Gill System to the caves of Leck Fell.

For four months, using every weekend and half the North's caving fraternity, Sid and Lindsay had been filming, with Bob, Kenny, Eddie Edmondson and a lady named Gillian as stars. It seemed that each trip was an epic, for even manhandling the equipment down the restricted entrance series was an expedition in itself – and when things went wrong, they really went wrong.

The cavers had taken a portable generator down, but once it was in position they found it wouldn't work, so that day's filming was abandoned – and when they finally did get it going, everyone was almost overcome by fumes. Someone dropped a tin of petrol down a twenty-foot pitch next to Kenny, who was using a carbide lamp; they say that Kenny moved so fast he became a blur. Sid later filmed a controlled explosion and discovered that it wasn't controlled enough, as it blew over his camera and blasted apart a very expensive lens. These were, however, minor setbacks in Sid's world.

The highlight of the Pippikin saga came when Sid was filming Gillian, the female star of the show, as she was climbing down a rift towards him. With Lindsay on sound and Bob holding a light, Gillian, with legs stretched wide apart, chimneyed slowly down the rift towards Sid, who was lying directly underneath.

With her long, lissom legs at full stretch, Gillian's neoprene wetsuit could take no more and, slowly, the crutch split open, revealing her crutch. Sid was unaware of this vision of a small furry creature desperately trying to escape from the restraining confines of black rubber, because his eyepiece was steamed up – as of course were Lindsay and Bob, who were by now utterly mesmerised until Bob, being a farmer, asked Lindsay: 'Is that what I think it is?'

Lindsay didn't know, because he had never seen one, and they both fell about laughing. Sid eventually finished his sequence – both he and Gillian remained completely oblivious to what had been captured on film.

The amusing sequel to this tale came the following week, when two VIPs from the BBC visited the Leeds studio where some of Sid's rushes were being studied. The pair listened with great interest to the editor and casually viewed the rushes until one suddenly observed something rather strange.

'I say, Tristram, could you run that bit back?' There was a long silence. 'Is that what I think it is, Hubert?' (He hadn't seen one either.)

'I say, how did that get in there?'

'I don't know, but it seems to be escaping.'

'Ho, ho, very good, excellent stuff – what a pity we can't use it.'

AFTER ANOTHER ABSENCE Sid and Lindsay reappeared and I was informed of a change of plan. The 'star' of the show was suffering from arthritis and George said: 'You can let that 'Ers take my place as long as you make 'im look as handsome as I am.'

After some discussion about modifying my nose with make-up as it interfered with the camera lens, Lindsay reckoned it wouldn't be too bad once underground, because it's dark anyway and with a bit of mud smeared on it my nose would look sort of outward bound and rugged. Sid eventually agreed, as long as he didn't do close-ups on the surface, because the programme would probably go out before the 9 p.m. watershed and he didn't want to frighten the kids.

The following weekend they took me to the Marton Arms in Thornton-in-Lonsdale for 'background information'. This meant plying me with drinks and letting me talk into a microphone, which I thought was a great idea, so I filled a tape with verbal rubbish while they filled me with beer. Then, having secured what they wanted, the duo took me home and poured me through my letterbox before driving back to deepest Yorkshire to work out a plan.

I soon found myself walking up and down Ease Gill beck, pointing out the various sinks while Sid and Lindsay recorded every move. This was the first time that I had faced a movie camera and I found it difficult to take it seriously, especially with Sid's vague instructions.

'Talk about the sinks,' he said, so I did – but when I mentioned the caves below, he stopped me. 'George has said that bit. Don't forget that we are starting in the middle.'

'We are?' I answered. 'But what about the other bit I've just done?'

'Oh that's for the end,' said Sid.

'Ah,' I said, completely confused.

I soon got the hang of it and started talking with great gusto, waving my arms about like the blokes on the telly.

'Cut. Er, don't wave your arms about, Jim.'

'Right.' So the next take saw me completely immobile, staring fixedly at a sink – a gap between two boulders – saying that 'The water sinks here' while pointing at a large pile of sheep droppings. I suddenly burst out laughing at the incongruity of it all.

'Cut.' Sid was not amused.

'Scene one, take seven.' Neither was Lindsay.

Off we went again and eventually I managed to present a good semblance of a dialogue before stopping and looked fixedly at the camera, which still whirred while Sid and Lindsay waited expectantly for more.

'Er, that's it,' I said.

'Oh, er, fine, but perhaps I should have told you, don't just stand there when you're finished, walk away,' said Sid.

'Scene one, take eight,' said Lindsay. There's more to this filming lark than meets the eye, I thought as I followed them down to the rising.

Lower in the valley, just below a small gorge, the combined waters of the Leck and Casterton Fell systems emerge into daylight after traversing many miles of subterranean passageways through some of Britain's finest caves. The main rising is generally an impressive volume of water that swells up from the ground in a dome of raging, swirling liquid several feet high that gives birth to a large stream. Today it was a dismal trickle that barely struggled out of a crack in the rock. Such is Sid's genius that he had chosen the middle of a drought to film a rising. The three of us stood there, looking at it.

'I can piss better than that,' said Lindsay.

Sid then filmed Lindsay eating a harebell and Lindsay putting some salt on a slug, before discovering that he had left a camera lens a mile back up the valley. When he returned much later, he couldn't find his tripod and slowly realised that he had left it near Cow Pot, a mile in the other direction.

Filming with these two was going to be fun and I recalled Bob Emmett's words: 'You must be bloody mad.'

Soon, the big day dawned. A crew of volunteers had been recruited by Sid while sitting under a sign in the Craven Heifer, which stated alluringly: 'Do you want to be a star?' For this part of the film, with unerring skill, Sid had picked the weekend that the drought broke – it was pissing down, thus ensuring that Lancaster Hole (which is normally a good wet-weather bolt-hole providing sport when everywhere else is inaccessible) had a queue of wet, impatient cavers waiting to descend the entrance pitch.

Two clubs were involved, both supplying cavers who were barely past the novice stage. I gradually became so upset by their pathetic performance that I took over and organised some blokes to pull up the lifeline while I tied a caver on the other end and despatched him down the hole. This speeded things up tremendously and, after twenty cavers were sent into the depths, we began to lower the filming gear followed by the camera crew. We were just getting organised when three of my clubmates appeared out of the mist and offered to help. As we were short-handed, I lifelined them down along with the rest of the equipment.

A portable generator remained on the surface to supply Sid with power, so a couple of volunteers were left in charge. It was not a pleasant job; we were being lashed by gale force winds and soaked by driving rain, but at least I was at some point supposed to head underground. The telephone was rigged and Sid rang from below.

'Start the generator . . .'

'Great, generator working, lights working.'

Everything was ready for the big scene where I was to climb down Lancaster Hole's 110 foot entrance pitch towards Sid's camera, then greet my fellow cavers. We rigged a double lifeline so that I could be roped from below, but as I was tying on my end, the rope was nearly dragged from my grasp.

'Up, up,' came a muffled cry from below – some clown was climbing the ladder, instead of someone lifelining me from the bottom!

'Sod off!' I shouted. 'Go down again!'

'Pull, take up the rope,' and then after a brief pause: 'Help, I'm going to fall off!'

'Well, bloody well fall off, you silly sod,' I muttered as I was forced to pull up the slack lifeline (although some cavers are pathetic, I wouldn't like to kill one).

I hauled up the rope in the driving rain – and what was on the end but bloody Karate Bill, one of my mates who had offered to help. I was furious.

'Why don't you take up another hobby, like knitting?'

'If you think I've come twenty-odd miles just to stand in the pissing rain and lifeline silly buggers like you up and down all bloody day . . .'

Next came Tiger: 'Why don't you take up another hobby, like knitting?' I enquired of the red, perspiring face blinking at me from behind steamed-up spectacles. Then I hauled up Brandon: 'You're like the bloody three stooges, only you're not making me laugh!' I went on and on as Tiger said: 'No need to loose your cool, Jim,' and they slunk away in disgust. I tied on the lifeline and disappeared down the hole, leaving the generator men alone on the surface, still laughing after being thoroughly entertained.

A star is born. This well-used phrase soon became 'a star is bored' as weekend followed weekend of slogging through the cave with two ammo tins each and the interminable waiting and hanging about as we shot this and double-taked that. I now know why film stars end up on drugs! And it made it worse when Wil Howie and his luscious girlfriend appeared from the States and came down the hole to watch me 'act'.

Wil said, 'Yo sho ain't no Marlon Brando, Jim, so stick to yo painting and decorating.'

Later at home, I got my own back for that slur on my acting ability by waiting until they were taking a bath together and chucking in the dog. I was told off by Audrey for frightening the dog, while Wil commented: 'Yo caint act like Marlon, but yo sure is a mean hombre like he is.'

GRADUALLY, SID AND LINDSAY became a way of life and I slowly became immune to things going wrong as well as the fact that we had no script and no storyline, which didn't seem important. One day we arrived at Bull Pot Farm – the caving club head-quarters – to find that we had no helpers.

'Did you tell the York lads, Sid?' asked Lindsay.

'Er, no, I thought you were going to,' answered Sid as he made a slight adjustment to his camera by bashing an adjusting screw with a small rock.

Sid's camera was an incredible machine. It had been underground in Canada, France, Mexico, New Guinea and various other parts of the world; being battle-scarred and covered in neoprene, with odd bits attached with adhesive tape, one could be forgiven for thinking that it was a load of junk. In Sid's hands, however, it became a magic wand that transformed the mundane into works of art.

We managed to collect a couple of helpers from the farm and set off across the fell, when we saw some cars coming down the road and recognised our crew. Sid gave me his camera to carry while he and Lindsay rushed back to organise things. With the camera slung on my shoulder I walked across the heather-covered fell, taking in the scenery and the occasional skylark when I became aware of a strange, metallic whirring noise which seemed to be coming from my left ear. For a second or two I became worried that my left cerebellum was becoming detached from my right and was relieved when I discovered it was only the camera running.

What! The bloody camera's running?

I whipped it off my shoulder and pressed various knobs and turned everything that would turn. Of Sid and Lindsay there was no sign and three other members of our party, including Ron Bliss (who was a photographer), were somewhere ahead.

'The bloody camera's running – what should I do?' I shouted.

'Point it at something,' answered one bright spark in the distance. Eventually, when we had regrouped and we had all had a go, Ron found the trigger, which was conveniently tucked away under the handle and hence had been resting on my shoulder.

'Yo sho ain't no Marlon Brando, Jim'

Thus we went through a hundred feet of film of grass, sky and a large nose (mine) peering into the lens. We decided not to tell Sid.

We survived shooting our set piece for the day and had just returned to the surface to find that we had a portly gent and his family for company. It transpired that he had seen one of Sid's signs in the pub, so after a meal he had dragged his wife and two daughters to Bull Pot Farm where he expected to discover BBC vans, technicians and film stars like Glenda Jackson and Michael Caine to be littering the place. He was most disappointed when he found out that *we* were the BBC.

'Is this it? You mean to tell me I've come all this way and there's no famous actors?'

'Yes there are,' said Lindsay. 'This is Harry Blogs from York and Billy Harrison from Leeds, both famous bit part players, and Harold who has a walk-on part, and . . .'

'But we expected to see stars,' interrupted the portly gent.

'Look no further,' said Lindsay, and with a grand sweep of his hand he pointed at me and said in a very reverential tone: 'This is the star of the show, Mister James Eyre.'

'Oo, I've 'eard of him, we're doing 'is mother at school, Jane Eyre,' said one of the daughters. 'Is she with you?'

'Er, no, she's down the hole,' I replied, stretching the truth just slightly.

Our new acquaintance began regaling us with tales of his youth and how he was once a potholer. 'Brought the wife to show her this hole,' he said. 'I once fell thirty foot down there and broke an ankle,' he added proudly.

AS THE WEEKS WORE ON, I became convinced that Sid and Lindsay were jinxed. No matter how meticulously they checked their equipment on the surface, it could be guaranteed that as soon as we were underground something would go wrong. The lights would suddenly fade or the electronic clapper bleep wouldn't bleep, or Lindsay's bag of tricks would start acting peculiar.

The amazing thing about these two characters was the casual way in which they overcame seemingly insurmountable problems. The delicate mini-mike which was threaded into my helmet developed a fault; Sid fixed it using his belt buckle as a tool. Lindsay did some even more high-tech electronic engineering on his tape deck, using the bent nail which I used to keep my accumulator top on. I suggested a few tools would be handy – a screwdriver, for instance.

'Ah, yeah, yeah,' said Lindsay. 'We used to carry tools, but we kept losing them; besides, it's more fun this way.'

I expect it's the sort of answer anyone would obtain from a bloke who held the world record for walking backwards from Leeds to Ingleton, so I didn't make any more suggestions. However, the words I came to dread were, 'He's gone out of sync again.'

A brief word to the uninitiated: as the film carried no soundtrack, Sid had adapted a special unit to synchronise the sound and vision running through the many wires that trailed between Sid and Lindsay like a spidery umbilical cord. When I went out of sync, it meant I would come over like one of those actors in a foreign film that had been dubbed with an English dialogue. This is alright for spaghetti westerns, but not for a Sid Perou epic and such an occasion always ended with us having to re-film the sequence at another time, generally when one of the key personnel couldn't come. The annoying thing about losing a sync piece always seemed to be that the original was better than the final version.

Lindsay and Sid in Long Churn Cave
Photo: Ian Plant/BBC

By this time I had begun to refer to Sid as Sir Alfred, with reference to Alfred Hitchcock. This was not because of his skill, but because the film was fast turning into a mystery – for me, at any rate, as the plot seemed to only exist in Sid's head. I must admit that there were times when I threatened to lose my cool and even the imperturbable Lindsay occasionally showed signs of cracking, but Sid was impervious to insult and sarcasm and seemed to be in a different orbit from us lesser mortals.

Lowering equipment down the entrance shaft of Lancaster Hole was always a nerve-racking business. Expensive gear clattered and ricocheted off snags on the rough walls as the metal ammo boxes dangled precariously on the end of ropes. Once, a bunch of containers fouled on a ledge, the men above pulled and yanked savagely at the rope, and swung them free. One box had a faulty catch, which suddenly flew open and rolls of film and other expensive-looking pieces of kit rained upon our heads as the containers were lowered towards us, then we watched, horror-struck, as teetering half out of the open ammo tin was Sid's prize possession, a £700 lens. As it came within reach it slowly fell from the tin, and I grabbed it.

Once the telephone was rigged we ordered the surface team to start the generator and, for the first time since they were formed, the vast caverns above Fall Pot were illuminated by our powerful film lights. I stood looking up in awe as the innermost recesses were lit up and the dark shadows dispersed to reveal a huge passage over the other side of the cavern.

'Jim? Jim? Where's Jim gone?' asked Sid when he realised that I had vanished. I was, at that moment, traversing above a wide, hundred-foot drop, past the cascading waterfall that tumbles from high in the roof to splatter on the rocks far below.

Sod the filming, exploration comes first . . . As another 'actor' and I gradually worked our way across and up into the mysterious passage, we found that the floor of dried mud bore the imprints of a solitary set of footprints ending at a cascade of pure white calcite that glistened and sparkled in our lamplight. Standing there, I slowly realised that I was looking at my own footsteps made over twenty years previously, when I had made the same climb and found the same calcite flowstone blocking the way forward.

Not many people have the privilege of looking at the footsteps of their youth and I hope they are still there, recording the passing of a young, enthusiastic caver in his quest for the ultimate discovery. If so, they will match further footprints of mine, left in other barely accessible parts of the Ease Gill System to upset the young explorers of the present when they come across them after some demanding climb to produce comments such as: 'Some bastard's been here already!' Until, of course, they make their own discovery and experience the thrill of seeing sights no man has seen before, leaving their own footprints for posterity.

Clambering down again we were brought back to the real world by an irate film crew, who told us to 'Stop pissing about and get over here.' Oh, the mundane life of commercialism – what it is to be a celebrity!

We continued filming for several hours, until the film lights suddenly went out. 'Sid, did you fill the petrol tank on the generator?' asked Lindsay. Sid couldn't remember, so that was filming finished for that day.

Nearing the entrance pitch, we met a couple of cavers who said that they had seen lots of sparks coming from our ladders. True – their lifeline had sawed through the generator cable!

Climbing out was even worse than getting in, and heaving stuff up and returning the line for the next load was very time-consuming. Then one of the lads from York was looking up the pitch when a drop of water hit him in the eye and flicked out his contact lens. Have you ever tried looking for a contact lens in semi-darkness in a muddy, gravelly pool under a spray of water and debris falling from 110 feet above?

We eventually set up some battery-powered filming lights and four of us spent an hour or so crouched on our hands and knees, going through the contents of that grotty pool and its immediate surroundings. It was like looking for a marble in a gravel pit: we found several sardine tin keys, bits of glass and what looked suspiciously like the end of a condom, but no contact lens.

In the meantime, the youngest of our volunteers was trying to climb the pitch, but the lifeline was threaded through a rung and he was having trouble. We shouted him down and I tied on and climbed up to the problem, untied the lifeline, pulled it through the rungs, retied and continued climbing to find, much to my delight, that the lifeline was threaded through another rung! I clipped onto a rung with my karabiner and sling, untied and repeated the process – then, as I climbed onwards, found that the idiots above had managed to thread the rope through the ladder a total of another five times! This takes an inordinate amount of skill and I congratulated them on breaking the world record for being prats.

THE FILM WAS SLOWLY TAKING SHAPE. Sid had seen the rushes and, although he was way behind schedule, the ever-optimistic man thought we would scrape through. It was still a mystery to me, especially as we had done the end and some of the middle, and now we were doing the bit where the cave was discovered.

I was to illustrate a breakthrough in my own inimitable fashion – I still had no bloody script! All I ever heard from Sid was: 'Five, four, three, two, one – Action!' or a long pause and then a 'Say something Jim, even if it's only goodbye.'

I yelled from halfway down the hole: 'The bloody wire's stuck!' just before he landed on top of my outstretched leg

I had to walk across a chamber, talking as I moved, crouch down beside a gap in the boulders, look intelligent as though I was about to discover a huge cave, then dive into the gap and disappear head-first down a forty-five degree slot and emerge into the passage below, which Sid would capture in another take.

Lindsay dressed me for the part, sticking a mike inside my helmet and running the wire down my inside leg and out past my ankle – I'm sure he got a kick out of this! After a couple of dummy runs, we ironed out the snags and it was: 'Scene fifty-four, take one. Action!'

I walked across the foot of the boulder fall saying something intelligent, followed by Lindsay and some volunteers with a battery of lights, then I stopped by the hole in the boulders, said something else intelligent and, as planned, dived head-first down the hole – forgetting that Lindsay and I were wired together like Siamese twins. Lindsay, complete with his tape recorder around his neck, was jerked off balance as I yelled from halfway down the hole: 'The bloody wire's stuck!' just before he landed on top of my outstretched leg, which was still sticking into the chamber.

'Cut,' said Sid with a look of abject pain on his normally cheerful face. 'Scene fifty-four, take two.'

Later in the week we received a frantic telephone call from Sid.

'Hello, Audrey, could Jim come and do another sync piece in Lancaster Hole?'

'No,' said Audrey, 'you're driving him mad.' Then she added: 'My dog's stopped speaking to him.'

Eventually, duty-bound, I agreed and spent the rest of the evening being looked at by four accusing eyes – two soulful ones from Tara our wire-haired terrier, and two neglected ones from Audrey.

WE FINALLY REACHED THE PART where Sid was filming the connection from Ease Gill to Lancaster Hole and one weekend the BBC sent two reporters to write an article as advance publicity for the *Beneath the Pennines* series. They would be going underground with us.

One happened to be a nice young lady dressed in the height of fashion. I explained to her that caves and cavers are nasty things and nice young ladies need overalls to keep clean and to protect vulnerable young bodies from rock projections and cavers' knobbly fingers. 'You also need boots,' I added.

'Oh,' said the young dear, 'I've got some boots.' She rushed off, to reappear in a pair of thigh-length, stiletto-heeled, tooled Moroccan leather jobs which would have looked great in a sexual fetish magazine. 'Do you like them?' she asked.

'Very nice,' I said. 'Awkward on ladders, but very nice . . .'

The young man who accompanied her was the photographer and he was obviously an expert because he didn't use flash equipment. When I queried this, he explained: 'I've got a very fast film in here, which will take all the pictures I need with the aid of a normal caving lamp,' so I loaned him one of mine.

Exactly one hour later the poor bloke was stumbling about underground trying to take photographs in a dull yellow gloom, which gradually deepened as the bulb filament was reduced to glowing like a cigarette end. After some time, he approached me and spoke: 'When I said that this film was fast, I didn't mean it would work in the bloody dark!'

I apologised about the lamp and told him it probably needed more tap water in it.

It's hard being a 'star', for every time I took the young lady off to show her some marvellous formations, I was brought back by Sid who made me get on with my acting. By the time I had finished she had gone off with Ron Bliss, who really was showing her formations!

Ron was required to describe how he had made the connection between Ease Gill and Lancaster Hole, while some weeks previously Sid had filmed George Cornes, the discoverer of Lancaster Hole, talking about his part in the exploration. Then there was me with my stand-in part.

For the film, Sid had acquired several sets of semi-waterproof overalls for all the main actors. These came in a variety of bright yellow, blue, red, green and orange to make us stand out against the drab background of the cave. This was a brilliant idea, but when Sid filmed the end before the beginning and the beginning after the middle, with several weeks in between, some of the cavers forgot which colour they had used.

'What colour overall did you wear when we shot the end sequence, Ron?' asked Lindsay of Ron Bliss.

'Er, I think it was yellow,' said Ron.

'No, it was blue,' said I.

'Er, I'm not sure, perhaps it was red,' said Ron.

'It wouldn't be red,' said Lindsay, 'because I wear red, and it would have clashed.'

'Well, perhaps it was green,' said Ron, becoming even more confused.

On the surface we asked Audrey, who was the original clapperboard lady. 'Blue,' she said.

The result of this confusion caused yet more confusion at BBC Leeds, where the editor became very excited when he noticed one of his stars had entered the cave in a blue overall and exited at the other end in an orange one. It was almost as though

Doctor Who had dropped into the wrong programme and almost as big a gaffe as when Rob Palmer was being filmed at Alum Pot for another programme in the series.

Rob had to abseil down the two-hundred-foot entrance shaft while Sid filmed the bottom section so that Rob sailed majestically down the rope and into vision, wearing a lovely bushy beard.

It was several weeks before Sid could film there again, to produce the top-of-the-shaft scene, but when the day came and Rob was required to start his abseil, he arrived smooth-chinned as his current girlfriend had given him an ultimatum: 'No shave, no sex!' It made caving history when Rob set off down Alum clean-shaven and landed at the bottom with a full beard.

As an American buddy of mine remarked: 'It must have been a helluva long abseil, Jim!'

Mind you, knowing Sid as I do, it could easily have been the other way round – setting off with a beard and arriving clean shaven. Now, *that* would have amazed the American: 'This hole's so big, it's got a barbers' shop halfway down!'

At the last minute Sid decided to film me in the original entrance to Ease Gill, part of which consists of a narrow, twisting passage aptly called the Snake. It is a sod of a thing which used to cause us anguish in the old days as, lying full-length in icy water without waterproofs, we had to struggle round the acute bends or undertake a traverse when the lower route became too restricted.

Somehow, Sid and Lindsay managed to jam themselves above me while I thrutched below. This was to be a sync piece, but I didn't need to act as I grunted my way through the narrow confines, trailing my wire behind me. My dialogue suddenly became disjointed as I slowly realised that I was stuck.

Trying surreptitiously to free myself, I continued, 'These sharp bends in this passage make it' – pause and struggle – 'extremely difficult to' – stop and try to free leg – 'make any progress, and' – longer pause while I thrashed about madly – 'sometimes you get stuck' – I was now involved in a desperate battle to free myself – 'and you find that . . .' – desperate wriggle – 'bollocks! Sid, I'm stuck.'

'This is brilliant, keep it up Jim – you'll win an Oscar for this,' Sid said from above.

'I'm not bloody acting, I *am* stuck.'

'Oh, well, try and free yourself while I keep filming. If you get stuck permanently, it should be worth a bit. I'll give your share to Audrey,' said Sir Alfred.

When the BBC proudly screened *Beneath the Pennines* in 1977, Sid hired a TV set and for the next five Tuesday evenings the stars of the caving world assembled at Skipton and, looked after by Alison, Sid's charming wife, we settled down to watch each other attempt to act in the five different caves. These were hilarious evenings and after we had been reduced to hysterics at each others' performances (I came across like a working man's David Bellamy, talking down my nose), we all adjourned to a nearby pub to be entertained by Sid, Harry Long and their trad jazz band.

The series was a great success and the telly has seen many repeats over the years. My finest hour came when the Cup Final was postponed because of a technicians' strike, and in an obvious panic the BBC picked up the nearest thing to hand – the Lancaster–Ease Gill film – and broadcast that to millions of unsuspecting viewers patiently expecting to see the event of the year. Instead, they got me and a warning flashed upon the screen: 'Please do not adjust your set – this nose really is bent.'

Chapter 15

I Join the Jet Set

NOW THAT I WAS A FILM STAR, I patiently waited for offers to come rolling in – but the nearest I had was a mention in the *Radio Times* from the young lady in the Moroccan thigh-length boots. It wasn't very complimentary, so it was back to work painting and decorating while fate worked on a change in my lifestyle.

One day, when I was working at my favourite stately home, I was approached by Richard Reynolds who introduced me to a fellow climber, Derek Wigget. He was an expert in every aspect of the building trade and all things electrical, as well of being in the top echelon of climbers.

Derek's small, gold-rimmed glasses gave him a studious air, which was offset by an explosion of frizzy hair that sprang from his head, producing the appearance of an absent-minded professor who had simultaneously had a bad trip on LSD and suffered a violent electric shock. However, I soon found out that looks can be deceiving, for underneath that mild exterior lurked – not a tiger, but a very impressive Spiderman. The work at Leighton Hall, in which we were both engaged, dropped behind schedule as we dallied on nearby quarry faces and rock outcrops, and it was only natural that Derek should be introduced to the joys of caving.

I decided to take Richard and Derek down Gingling Hole. This turned out to be not one of my best decisions, because I almost lost my favourite customer and, in due time, it would have guaranteed that his charming wife Suzie would never have spoken to me again.

Gingling is a spectacular cave with splendid formations, big pitches and lots of acrobatic moves. One of these involves inserting your body down a very narrow, eighteen-foot drop and, more importantly, getting that body back up again.

Richard was a well-built chap but, aided by gravity, he just managed to wriggle his way down until we eventually reached the bottom of the pothole. Together we then began our arduous return up the two-hundred-foot pitch from the sump and along the passages leading to the eighteen-foot pitch, where I made sure I was in front.

As I fought my way up the pitch, I instructed Richard – who was standing below me – to do exactly as I had done and dropped a short line to him to tie on. He set off and immediately jammed in the narrow space; he tried again and again, but to no avail. 'Go down and take something off,' I instructed.

Richard did as I requested and, being a strong, determined sort of individual, launched himself up the ladder again, only to become stuck higher up. He hung there, struggling, and tried and tried again . . .

'Get off the ladder and put your left foot in that crack and your right elbow in that recess, then try to lever yourself up,' I said, outwardly calm but inwardly panicking. Richard struggled and struggled, but in the end his red, perspiring face looked up at me from his rocky prison and he said, quite seriously:

'Jim, if you don't get me out of here, you'll never work for me again!' I thought this was a fair comment, because it wouldn't be much of a customer who was stuck permanently in a crack in Gingling Hole; think of the trouble I would have discussing colour schemes and delivering the bills.

Meanwhile, underneath Richard's struggling body, Derek was becoming rather uneasy because he also didn't fancy becoming a permanent resident. In the end, after a great deal of manoeuvring, with me pulling on the rope while Richard threatened to split the rock and Derek pushed from below, we extracted Richard from the crack's loveable embrace; Derek followed and we made our way out of the cave.

IT WASN'T LONG before revenge was enacted – the pair soon had me clinging to even smoother rock, suspended in space and time and frantically searching for holds that weren't there, as I grappled with the giant black crags of Wales.

Derek turned out to be an interesting character who, due to his climber's love of Wales, had left his native Wolverhampton and relocated to a remote hillside near Deiniolen. There, he had rebuilt a derelict house, taught himself to speak Welsh and bought a large, scrap chapel organ which he reinstalled in his house after building an extension for the organ pipes. He then set himself up as a sort of a Welsh answer to Captain Nemo who, instead of playing his organ in a submarine, played it in fine isolation on a wild Welsh mountainside.

It was one of life's strange experiences when Audrey and I and our wee scabby dog stayed at this unusual house on the hill, and found we were sleeping on a sort of musician's gallery above the organ. Imagine being suddenly blasted out of a wine-induced coma in the early hours of the morning by a demented figure in mauve-and crimson-striped pyjamas, frantically pulling out the stops as he bashed out Bach's Sonata in G minor, joined by a panic-stricken wire-haired terrier howling its head off! Narrowly avoiding a well-aimed climbing boot, Derek looked up at us with his owl-like expression and said, 'Ah, you're awake. Do you take sugar in your tea?'

'If you don't get me out of here, you'll never work for me again!'

A few weeks later I was working with Derek again when he asked how I felt about working in France. He explained that he did jobs for other climbing friends in France, one of whom had just bought a house in the Jura – and they would need a decorator. Always ready for something different, I told him I was willing and promptly forgot about it, until the following month when I received a phone call – if I was still interested in the job, I should hop on the next available flight to Geneva and 'Bring your

Derek Wigget playing the organ

climbing gear.' So began the French branch of 'Monsieur Jacques Eyre, *décorateur'*.

Derek and Jen met me as I arrived in Geneva. Jen was a striking, raven-haired beauty accompanied by a miniature 'Shirley Temple', her daughter Chamouni, who was extremely bright, precocious and sophisticated beyond her tender years. Peter Stone, Jen's husband, worked as an editor for the United Nations while Jen had graduated through the zany world of *Private Eye* to work very efficiently at numerous freelance causes – this was a very busy couple who, apart from going skiing, climbing and having a heavy work schedule, also seemed to support an army of local craftsmen, gardeners, Derek and babysitters, although in Chamouni's case a lion trainer would have been more appropriate.

I found myself an integral part of 'Chez Stones' and was soon working in beautiful surroundings on their lovely house in Crozet at the foot of the French Jura, within spitting distance of a ski lift. Well supplied with good French wine and food, with Jen rushing to fortify me with large glasses of whisky every time I looked like slowing down, and with dinner parties every night enlivened by political chit-chat, it was an exhilarating time as I discovered how the other half lived. This was especially the case when, on a very formal occasion, little Chamouni became annoyed with a fly that was buzzing around and took a swing at it, saying in her charming way: 'Oh, piss off fly!' Peter's boss was most amused.

I soon found that, while at Crozet, it was a case of one day's work and two days' playing in the French, Swiss or Italian Alps, either climbing or walking. After two or three weeks Jen insisted on paying me much more than I was worth, reimbursed my airfare home and insisted that I come again and bring Audrey next time.

Back in Lancaster, after fighting off disgruntled customers who didn't realise that I had been working on a better offer, I managed to catch up on my backlog of work. Then Jen rang . . .

'Oh, Jim, I've got this lovely wallpaper and I don't want to spoil it, so could you and Audrey come out?'

Jen had the sort of voice that made grown men wilt at the knees and within a few days Audrey was being introduced to the delights of Chez Stones, and the Stones family was being introduced to Audrey. This brought forth comments such as, 'Oh, Jim, I didn't know you had such a beautiful wife,' and 'How do you put up with him?' to Audrey, who was immediately adopted by Chamouni and whisked away down to the village to be shown off to Madame Chaprese, who ran the village shop. 'This is Audy,' she proudly announced (it was some time before she could pronounce 'Audrey').

With the paperhanging soon disposed of, it was 'all hands secure ship' (Peter was in the Royal Navy) and everyone would scuttle round, fastening the numerous window shutters, bolting doors and stacking three cars with everything bar the fridge. Soon, the entourage hit the road, bound for the Alps.

The Stones didn't camp, they moved house – and when we eventually found a campsite large enough to fit us in, to anyone watching it would have seemed amazing that so many people, children, animals and a complete canvas village could be disgorged from only three cars.

There were bundles, bedding, boxes, brollies, blankets, books, boots, buckets, bowls, barbecues and material for the use of, tents, windshields, chairs, tables, an icebox, a mountain of food, several crates of wine, two suitcases of maps, another mountain of rucksacks, ropes, climbing gear and an inflatable boat, and oars, and lifejackets . . .

Gradually this mountainous pile was transformed by Jen into a small canvas settlement – she seemed to know what was in each mysterious package and where it went, and with Peter she marshalled the scurrying minions of babysitters, gardeners, relatives, friends, itinerant travellers and Chamouni into a coherent workforce. Eventually, order was achieved out of chaos and everyone sat around watching Peter, in his baggy climbing trousers and red socks, preparing the barbecue.

'Anyone got a match?' he queried.

No – we had forgotten to bring them.

IT WAS EARLY AUTUMN when Audrey and I returned to Cosy Crozet, as Audrey called it. Once I had worked out that there was no difficulty in aligning the pattern in the expensive Korean grass wallpaper that Jen had bought, and dealt with the intricacies of papering around an iron spiral staircase, the job was soon done and it was again heigh, ho and away, this time for the ski slopes of Val d'Isère. The 'heigh, ho' soon turned into 'Hey! Oh!' when I found that skiing isn't as easy as it looks, especially in climbing boots that kept coming detached from the skis.

Derek had loaned me his old skis, which were made of wood, about fifteen feet long and had first been used by Saint Nicholas. I spent some time entertaining the beautiful people as they watched this eccentric character in climbing breeches and an ex-army anorak falling over, until one chap took pity on me. He sat me down on a bench and crouched over the skis while saying something in French, which roughly translated meant that only an English pillock could try to ski on skis from a museum while wearing climbing boots that didn't fit the bindings. He tightened all the straps and screwed in the toe and heel clips, then said, still in French, 'Now, you stupid sod, see if you can fall out of those.'

Whatever he had done, it worked – wherever I went, those planks of wood on my feet went with me, and after several rather painful falls I began to get the hang of it. I was soon cruising majestically down a gentle slope, but as I gradually picked up speed it slowly dawned on me that no one had told me how to turn or stop. It wasn't like riding a motorbike; there's no handles and no brakes, and I was going faster and faster in a dead straight line down a hill that was becoming steeper and steeper.

I was fit in those days and I reasoned that if I kept my balance and didn't try to turn, and if nothing got in my way, sooner or later the mountain would stop going down

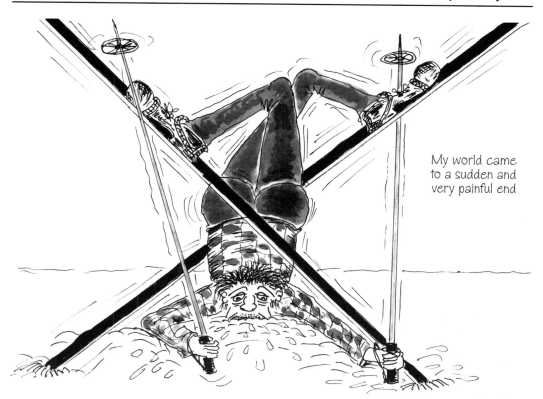

My world came
to a sudden and
very painful end

and I would come to a gentle stop. Then, I thought I was seeing things at first, but no – the ends of the skis, which seemed an awfully long way off, were slowly coming together. No matter what I did, they were beginning to cross over one another . . .

I was going to die a dreadful, mangled-up death. I imagined the pain as my left leg went over my right shoulder and my right leg went over my left shoulder. The skis crossed and I employed the emergency brake – I plunged my ski poles before me, in the middle of the big wooden cross of my out of control skis. The effect was instantaneous: my world came to a sudden and very painful end as I hurtled over the tips of my skis, which became embedded in the snow and formed a black cross in the air with my feet still attached, while the rest of my body was contorted below, facing uphill.

I lay there, shouting in agony, partially hanging onto my throbbing ankles like an obscene crucifixion as other skiers unfastened my boots then helped me back up the hill to the restaurant and Audrey's loving arms. Both ankles had swollen up like balloons and I was convinced that the left one was broken. I cursed Derek and his antique skis and cursed myself for being so stupid, mollified only by Audrey ministering to my every need and pouring bottles of very expensive beer down my neck to alleviate the pain.

I was examined and told that neither ankle was broken, though both were badly bruised. However, as is generally the case with me, several years later I discovered that I had permanently damaged one ankle and broken a bone in my left foot.

The 'damage' ruined my career as a ballroom dancer, but not – it seemed – as a would-be skier, for in spite of my protestations Peter kitted me out in proper ski boots (which would act like splints, he said) and modern skis with quick-release grips. Under his expert tuition I learned the rudiments of skiing and the following week we travelled to Flaine where, after being introduced to Anna, a family friend and the wife of a Dutch ambassador, we went up a mountain and people shot off in different directions down various runs. This left me uneasily looking for an easy way down while being watched by Anna, who, sensing my plight, said: 'I shall take you on an easy run, Jim. Follow me and do exactly as I do.' Then, with a couple of swishes and swirls, she was gone.

Up there on a round dome of a mountain top, surrounded by the snow-covered peaks of the Alps under a dark blue sky and a hot sun, I carefully followed the dot in the distance, until Anna suddenly disappeared over a precipice – the start of a red run. I painfully snow-ploughed to a halt underneath the sign that warned of this more difficult route.

What was I doing on a red run, when I wasn't even safe on the nursery slopes? There must be some mistake. I looked down what seemed to me to be the north face of the Eiger, and there was my guide patiently waiting two hundred feet below.

'Come, Jim, it is easy. Take wide sweeps and if you have trouble, turn uphill and you will stop.' This woman exuded such confidence that I took my life, placed it in her hands and steadily set off down the steep slope, doing twice as many sweeps as anyone else and still managing to go completely out of control as I picked up speed. 'Turn,' she shouted. 'Turn your skis uphill.'

Desperately, I did as she instructed and found to my relief that I stopped. It felt great – I was in charge. Then, slowly, I started to slide backwards and again picked up speed. As I was no good at going forwards, I was bound to be completely useless at going backwards. A flood of instructions was followed by a panic-stricken cry: 'Sit down! Fall sideways!' Which I did, bringing fresh pain from my abused ankles.

After a struggle to regain my feet I found that I was facing the wrong way and hadn't been shown how to turn round, so I sat on my bum again and swivelled around before beginning the painful progress of rising to my feet once more.

Eventually, I reached the patient Anna. She must have been very annoyed to be saddled with this strange painter and decorator that Peter and Jen had imported, who was dressed in out-of-date climbing gear and spoke 'Andy Capp' English.

'That wasn't too bad,' said I, thinking that we were at the bottom.

'Oh, it was not too bad,' said Anna, 'but the next piste is a little bit more difficult.' When I glanced over her shoulder, I saw that far below lay something that looked like a white tablecloth crawling with ants. I gulped and wished I had taken up hang-gliding.

'We go down there?' I asked.

'Yes, but we go this way – follow,' said Anna, who launched herself into space before turning sharply to traverse beneath a steep, limestone face which contrasted with the brilliant white of the snow as grey and gold. Constantly zigzagging, my patient guide shepherded me down onto less perpendicular slopes before stopping.

'Ah, Jim, you do very well,' she said, smiling. 'Would you like a beer?'

I looked at her with my mouth open. 'Er, yes,' I answered.

'Well, if you can reach that,' she said, pointing into the far distance at a stamp-sized chalet, 'I will buy you a drink. Come.'

She gave me a wicked smile and leapt onto the piste; I followed, eventually reaching the restaurant where she was sitting on the balcony with two beers. I took off my skis and found that I could hardly climb the staircase – I slumped onto a seat with relief, then slurped the beer down in one go.

'There's no gain without pain,' I quoted, and the delightful Anna waved the waiter over. 'More beer for my friend,' she said.

BACK AT CROZET, I found that I was in demand by a French builder who was constructing a large ranch-style house nearby. He was desperate for a paperhanger, so Derek did a deal which had me perched on high on a one-inch-thick plank while trying to paper a sloping ceiling. As I advanced towards the apex, the plank bent and the high point of the roof became unreachable, even on tiptoes.

'This is barmy,' I said to Derek, 'we need a better plank.' However, after a scout around we hadn't found anything suitable, so we raised the legs of the trestles on bricks to make up for the dangerous sag in the plank. This meant proceeding along the plank with a folded length of pasted paper, starting off on my knees and advancing until crouching, then standing and reaching the apex on tiptoes at full stretch, listening to the thin plank creak ominously beneath my feet.

I didn't trust that plank, which wasn't even a plank – it was just a piece of fascia board – and on my third length of paper my fears were justified. With both arms at full stretch while wielding my scissors overhead, I heard a loud crack and the plank snapped in two. I hurtled down with my scissors still waving in the air and a sixteen-foot length of pasted paper following.

Fifteen feet isn't normally too far to fall, but it is when you're not expecting it. I landed heavily on my already badly injured left foot but, fortunately, my cry of pain was muffled by the length of wet, sticky paper that wrapped itself around my head and shoulders. One half of the broken plank hit the pasteboard, causing Derek to stagger back and knock the paste bucket over, and this made him slip and thus inadvertently saved him from being harpooned by my long paperhanger's scissors, which narrowly missed his left ear as he went over backwards.

'I told you that fuckin' plank was no fuckin' good,' I moaned as Derek surveyed the upturned paste bucket, the broken pasteboard and the sticky, paper-wrapped individual at his feet.

'I didn't know it was so dangerous, being a decorator,' said Derek.

'I didn't know it was so dangerous, being a decorator'

Work was abandoned for the day and I hobbled back to Jen's house, where Audrey poured us a stiff drink, sat me on the terrace and surveyed my ankle, which was going through another colour change.

'You should have seen him, Audrey. He was trying to use the ceiling paper as a parachute,' chortled Derek.

COMMUTING BETWEEN LANCASTER AND GENEVA became a regular part of our lives and I managed to play with Peter and Derek, who were both good climbers, on big mountains – which set my adrenalin flowing – as well as on lower, four- to five-hundred-metre high, exposed rock faces like Le Salève and Le Miroir de'Argentine. I paid for my education in entertainment value and, of course, by an occasional bit of decorating, although there was one bit of education which I narrowly avoided.

Derek and I had been walking in the Jura and poking about in a few caves. On the way down we came across a group of people watching a local expert demonstrating his skills at the new sport of hang-gliding and, after his display, we discovered that for twenty francs we could have a go. We were on the side of a steep mountain, but there was no instant drop-off or cliff and we presumed that we could land safely without getting into trouble.

'Fancy a go Jim?' asked Derek.

'Yes, why not,' I answered , so we stood in a queue of young French adventurers.

The first chap was given brief instructions and told to run down the steep ground before him. We watched with interest as he gave a loud yell and raced away, then suddenly soared into the air like a bird.

'Wow,' I said, 'look at that. Just like a b . . . bloody 'ell!' as Icarus suddenly fell to earth.

The lad wasn't too badly injured and his friends dragged him away while the next volunteer stepped forward. He ran like fury down the mountainside, shot into the air, then shot down again, still running, then shot up again, higher – then, for some inexplicable reason, he turned sharp left into a tree. His friends rushed to console him as the next youth stepped forward, again to receive hasty instructions. Off he went, running like hell. He made a perfect take-off but, unfortunately, when he swung his legs into the sling the hang-glider came within two feet of the ground and went sailing down the mountainside, dragging its 'pilot' through a large area of gorse bushes.

'Poor sod,' said Derek, as the pilot's mates rushed to pick up the tattered remains.

The hang-glider was undamaged and, just as I noticed that the queue in front of us had vanished, I received a whiff of garlic and a voice in my ear: 'Monsieur?' It was the hang-glider owner gesturing me to his magnificent flying machine.

'Er, what do you reckon, Derek? Fancy having a go?'

The answer was a definite negative.

'Yeah, I'm with you. Let's go and have a beer,' I said.

Jim and Peter Stone climbing on Le Salève near Geneva
Photo: Derek Wigget

THE FOLLOWING YEAR Jen gave birth to another daughter and, as she had recently been working in Africa, she agreed with Peter to name the new arrival Seiriol, an African word for 'peace'. We soon received a request for Audrey's calming influence and, after seeing Audrey off on the plane, I returned home to my humdrum existence of working, caving, climbing, boozing and writing a book, which my misguided buddies had insisted upon, not realising the consequences that an uncontrolled pen can have on a peaceful life.

After two weeks Audrey returned and life returned to normal. I put in some overtime to earn the extra cash required for a holiday to Corsica, which we had booked with two friends. However, owing to the activities of a certain Gordon Batty, I nearly didn't go.

Gordon dragged me into the creaking confines of a cave that was in imminent danger of collapse and had a name that summed up anyone who was daft enough to enter it. Crackpot Cave in Swaledale has long been an enigma. A large rising, with the source of the stream many miles away, it had defied all attempts to extend the known cave, which is large and impressive and ends in a dangerously loose boulder fall.

A way was once forced through the boulders, but henceforth deemed unsafe. Batty and I had both been there before and, with cavers' optimism, when we returned we reasoned that it didn't seem too bad and we made our way to the bottom of a high-level chamber that bristled with loose blocks overhanging an opening. I popped my head through and looked up at a black expanse surrounded by unstable blocks, each weighing several tons. I hurriedly withdrew my head.

We decided to use science to remove some of the more obvious dangers and constructed a thick wall under a good, sound, flat roof – a sort of air raid shelter from anything falling on us. Crouched inside it, Gordon and I took turns with a long iron bar at prodding the loose rocks overhead: it was generally a quick prod and a quicker duck into our refuge as the large blocks came tumbling down and rumbled past us.

This might seem like a dangerous operation to normal people, but cavers who think they are on the verge of a big discovery don't think like normal people. Crash, bang – more blocks came crashing down and more of the cave above was revealed. Then I struck lucky when, with a tentative poke, I brought down a huge rock which was barring progress.

Unfortunately, it was also holding up most of the cavern and there was a tremendous crash as several rocks moved at once. The solid, safe ceiling of our air raid shelter collapsed and a huge block of limestone fell between Gordon and me. It was almost an out-of-mind experience as this three-ton rock slab landed and in slow motion toppled and rolled towards Gordon, who backed away as I tried to grapple with it from behind.

It was all over in seconds as, with an ominous grinding noise, the slab ended up against the cave wall – with Gordon behind it. I could only see his face over the top of the rock. His eyes were staring and his mouth was opening and shutting, but no words were coming out. Luckily, he had been forced into an angle in the cave passage, where the fallen block had pinned him without crushing him, and after a mighty struggle he was able to wriggle free and force his body over the top. Only then was he able to speak.

'I'm not cccoming dddown this ffffuckin' cccave aaagain!' he said, yet within three weeks he was back to help free a caver who was almost buried underneath another rockfall.

With only enough room for two rescuers, Gordon and Bob Emmett built a retaining wall to hold back the creaking rock pile as they steadily worked towards the trapped caver, whose only visible parts were his legs sticking out of the mass of fallen rock. After many hours of nerve-racking work, using car jacks and stemples to lift the slabs that trapped the victim, the injured caver was eventually dragged free by Bob and Jack Pickup; he was badly injured, but alive.

'YOU SHALL HAVE TO STOP going out with that Gordon Batty,' said Aud, as we busily packed for our bargain holiday. This entailed driving to Dudley to meet Frank and Carol and stay the night, then taking Frank's car to Gatwick and flying to Corsica. It was a 'mystery holiday' – Frank had spotted a 'three weeks for the price of two' extremely cheap, off-season bargain in some magazine he had been reading and, having always wanted to tour Corsica, I persuaded Audrey that it would be brilliant. It was!

When we eventually arrived at our destination, we were shown some rows of little wooden huts set back from a glorious beach. Frank said they looked like 'Bloody dog kennels!' but they were clean, contained twin beds, a fridge and all the other essentials; they were a bit spartan, but cosy. Looking out of the window as Audrey unpacked, I noticed that several very brown people were walking about without clothes. Ah well, the French are very casual about that sort of thing, so I didn't think any more about it. Audrey hung up her nice dresses and beach outfits in the wardrobe while I wandered outside and discovered that the only people wearing clothes were us! I hurtled into the hut next door.

'Eh, Frank, which magazine did you find this holiday in?'

'Dunno, it was one me daughter's boyfriend left lying about,' he said in his broad Black Country accent. 'Why?'

'I think you've booked us in for three weeks on a naturist holiday!' I answered, as Audrey came bouncing in all of a dither.

'Jim, Jim, there's a big German out here walking about with no clothes on. Come and do something about it!'

It was hilarious. As we stood there laughing, a glorious young blonde German Fräulein, naked and golden-tanned, appeared in the doorway.

'Hello, you are English? I heard you talking, do you mind if I come in? We are your neighbours,' she said as another young, naked, golden goddess appeared. 'Hello, would you like to join us for – how you say – a velcome drink?' Vich we did.

Sitting around the trestle table outside, we told these young ladies and their boy-friends of our plight and they had fits as they excitedly retold the story in German to their friends, who also roared with uncontrolled laughter.

'Vell, vot are you going to do about it?' asked one.

'If you can't beat 'em, you might as well join 'em,' said Frank, and to a huge cheer he stripped off. We all did likewise and so began one of the best holidays we had ever had.

By a sheer stroke of luck, we were in a very expensive naturist resort on one of the best beaches in Europe. There were windsurfing facilities, numerous beach bars and restaurants, and we discovered that naturists are not oddballs or perverts but some of the nicest people that one is likely to meet – even the strange little Italian who liberally hung gold jewellery from all sorts of peculiar parts of his body, set off by a large, gold bull's head around his neck to draw attention to what was swinging below. This caused Carol's eyes to widen in disbelief and Audrey told me not to stand next to him.

It was surprising how soon we became accustomed to walking about totally naked and within a very short time we all felt that we belonged to an ancient tribe of brown-skinned people. After swimming and exploring the place, we quite naturally gravitated to one of the beach bars where, after consuming a large helping of mussels cooked in wine and several large steins of very strong German beer while surrounded by gorgeous naked young ladies, Frank and I thought we were in heaven.

This was where I met Lisalotte Lot, who promised to teach me German, and her husband Hans, who didn't speak much English, but who promised to run the lasses down to the butcher's shop in the village: 'For tonight, we have party.'

In fact, every night was party night. All the trestle tables were joined together between the huts, everyone contributed samples of their cuisine and loads of wine and spirits appeared. Oh, and contrary to common belief, everyone would dress for dinner. By the time the ladies had put on their finery and applied a little make-up, they could easily have been the most beautiful women in the world. These were great, candlelit evenings, with the sound of the rolling surf in the background and pleasant and jolly Esperanto-style conversations. The gatherings ended in the small hours and began again in the morning, when we shared outdoor showers and compared hangovers or went for an early morning swim.

I had always fancied windsurfing and, after several beers during our midday snack, I mentioned this to Frank. Soon, a small crowd of bystanders had gathered at the water's edge to watch Frank and me climb onto then slither off what was suddenly a ducking and diving surfboard. It was obvious that our approach to the sport was wrong, for learners don't generally tackle windsurfing in a rough sea while semi-inebriated and smothered in sun oil. Frank, who was holding the board, gave up after I managed to stand on it for ten seconds, but then did a trembly and flew through the air, giving him a karate kick in the face.

It was too rough, so the next morning when the sea was flat calm and there was only a light, offshore breeze, I struggled and struggled until there I was with the sail erect, standing in the proud posture of a captain in charge of his ship as I slowly went where the wind took me. Tentatively, I executed the manoeuvre that the windsurfer owner had demonstrated – I turned the sail, which suddenly collapsed on top of me, causing a capsize. Ho, hum, back to the drawing board. I tried to force the board the right way up again and the sail back in position; after my sixth ducking I finally succeeded in putting the sail up, but I was completely knackered. I stood, motionless, hanging onto the sail while I got my breath back.

The wind had freshened slightly and I was soon enjoying the exhilaration of the sun and spray on my body as I bowled along at a steady pace. A faint shout from the faraway shore alerted me to the fact that I was a long way out and it was time to turn around, so carefully I walked around the sail and waited for the board to follow suit. Strangely enough, although I turned round, the board didn't.

After several attempts, holding the sail in different positions, I did manage to turn the board around. Success? No, for I was still proceeding in the general direction of Sardinia, stern first.

Looking back at the fast-diminishing shoreline and lots of ant-like figures rushing hither and thither, I heard a faint shout borne on the wind: 'Turn.' So I walked around the mast again and the board turned the right way round, but it still proceeded towards Sardinia. Whatever I did, and whatever I did I did it very carefully so far from shore, nothing made any difference – the windsurfer kept going in the same direction.

I began to wonder what would happen when a naked man speaking a foreign language arrived in Sardinia without a passport.

Meanwhile, back in Corsica, there was consternation. Audrey borrowed a pair of binoculars to take a last glimpse at her disappearing husband, while the owner of the windsurfer hastily prepared his inflatable for a lengthy sea journey. At long last I heard the sound of an outboard motor and an irate German appeared.

'Turn!' he shouted.

'It won't,' I replied.

'Turn!'

I demonstrated by walking round the mast and continued heading for Sardinia. He swore at me in German and became very excited, until I went through the whole procedure again and fell into the sea. As I endeavoured to lift the sail he shouted: '*Nein, nein*! Sit!'

I straddled the board while he dismantled the sail and placed it in his dinghy, then threw me a length of rope and began to tow me back to shore. What ignominy – everyone, it seemed, was standing on the beach, waiting for the shipwrecked mariner. A great cheer went up as I waded ashore.

'You silly sod,' said Audrey.

However, it was all part of life's rich pattern and later, at the beach bar, we were all laughing about the incident. The Germans bought me drinks with much '*Prosit*,

'Turn!' he shouted

gesundheit' as they toasted the sailor home from the sea. I replied, 'Bollocks,' as I raised my glass to them. Unfortunately, thinking this was an English toast, they raised their glasses in return and solemnly said, 'Bollocks!'

Frank, who was a real comedian, did this every time we had a drink, looking at the Germans and French and raising his glass with an innocent smile, saying: 'Bollocks.' After a week this had become the general toast among the community and it was hilarious to see groups of solemn Germans raising their glasses to the sound of 'Bollocks.'

Sitting behind an upturned boat, I was receiving German lessons from Lisalotte when she suddenly said, 'Here is a word you must learn, Jim. It is "Kugeln" – you know, like your English bollocks!' and we both fell about laughing.

WHATEVER THE MERITS are of lounging around in glorious weather on a glorious beach with glorious naked ladies who insist on buying you beer, they eventually pall. I began to get itchy feet and was determined to see what lay beyond a distant headland, so one day I mentioned that I was off for a casual stroll and wandered away.

It was pleasant splashing along in the surf with the sun playing on my body and I soon passed like-minded people until I was on my own, scrambling along the rocky headland, keeping a weather eye open for any unsuspecting holidaymakers who could be thrown into a traumatic shock at the sight of my naked body. I didn't know how far the naturist beach extended, but I needn't have worried for the holiday season had finished and the coast seemed deserted. I strolled along the wide sweep of a bay with its backcloth of jagged limestone peaks partially obscured in a blue haze, enjoying the scent of mountain herbs borne on the breeze, mixing with the tang of the salt spray.

This was real freedom. I hadn't a care in the world as I approached the other end of the bay and eyed up the steep, rocky spur that barred the way on. I wondered what lay beyond; I had plenty of time and it would be an easy climb in boots. I approached the foot of the rock and made one or two tentative moves, finding it quite a novel experience for I had never climbed in bare feet before – or in bare everything, for that matter. I was balanced on one big toe when it slipped and down I came – not far, fortunately, and more annoyed than hurt I picked my wet bum from out of the sand. I then discovered that I had damaged the big toe that slipped and that, although I always thought the odd toe was dispensable, they are all integral parts of one's foot and I found it difficult to put my full weight on my left foot. Cursing myself, I began limping back along the beach, trying to work out how many miles I had walked.

The pain soon became worse. A large black cloud came rolling down from the mountains, obliterating the sun. The wind suddenly increased, whipping the beach into a miniature sandstorm. The temperature plummeted as it began to rain.

I was in trouble. I hobbled as quickly as I could with my arms folded over my chest in an effort to conserve body heat and, after what seemed ages, reached the second headland. The clouds had thickened, the wind had progressed to a gale and, unbelievably, it began to hail. With the ice stinging my back like so many needles, I headed inland, looking for shelter in the lee of the cliffs. There was nothing, so I had no choice but to keep going. As I rounded a bend I could see a small beach cafe and I limped towards it; the place was closed for the winter and it had no overhanging roof to shelter under, but some old-fashioned oilcloth was fastened to a table which had been left outside.

Rapidly becoming an exposure case, I tore the cloth free from the drawing pins and draped it around my head and shoulders. Wow, was it cold! The oilcloth's clammy embrace against my already cold flesh really made me jump, but it kept the wind and hail off and within minutes I could feel my body warming up as I stumbled painfully along the beach, picking up a broken branch as a makeshift crutch-cum-walking stick on my way.

My fellow holidaymakers, ensconced in the glass-fronted covered cafe, watched lightning fork from the black, glowering clouds and looked along the deserted beach as the rising surf sent spumes of foam blowing in the hail. Sand thrashed through the air and rattled against the windows. Suddenly, Audrey shouted, 'There's someone out there,' and all eyes tried to focus on the frail, hooded figure of an old man stumbling along the beach, clinging to his gnarled stick and partially obscured by the driving hail.

'Poor old bugger,' said Frank. 'Look at his thin legs, the poor old sod can hardly walk. And his nose is just like Jim's!'

I stumbled painfully
along the beach,
picking up a broken
branch as a makeshift
crutch-cum-walking
stick on my way

Chapter 16

The Magic of Mexico

WITH THE MEMORIES of Corsica fading along with my all-over tan, I was reduced to flashbacks of dicing with death on narrow mountain roads and visions of blue skies, rolling surf and young, golden people, when the letterbox rattled and Audrey made a sudden dive to reach the post before Tara the terrier could destroy it all. She came back into the room, looking at the mail.

'Oh, we've received a card from Hans and Lisalotte – I think she fancies you. Eh, and we've an invitation from Carl, that little Italian, to stay at his hotel in Southsea. And here's one from America for you; it's probably from Wil.'

Audrey handed me the envelope, neatly tattooed with Tara's teeth marks. I opened it and read the letter.

'You're right, Aud, it's from Wil – and he wants me to go caving with him in Mexico at Christmas. What do you think?'

'Oo, is that where those big holes are? Do you think you're up to it? You can be a pain in the bum sometimes, but I don't want you to kill yourself.'

I eventually convinced her that, like the proverbial bad penny, I would return to her loving arms. 'Right love, you go, for you may never get another chance. I can always have Elsie [her mother] up here for Christmas.'

The trip was on and I began to imagine the sheer immensity of those huge Mexican shafts. I stood at the foot of Blackpool Tower, trying to conjure up a picture in my mind of two towers on top of one another, thinking of the inescapable fact that I would soon not only have to abseil from that great height, but also prusik back up. It seemed incredible.

The weeks went by quickly and a parcel suddenly arrived out of the blue. It was the latest purple Karrimor rucksack with, tucked inside, a note from Peter and Jen: 'Couldn't bear to think of you among those flash Americans with your awful, mud-stained rucksack.' What a pleasant surprise.

THE LAST TIME I had spoken to Wil Howie, he had given me the impression that he lived in 'hillbilly country' where his daddy did the 'layin-on of hands and healin' people'. He said: 'If'n yo ever calls round, make sure yo stands at the gate and hollers, otherwise yo might get yo head blown off.'

Full of apprehension, in December 1978 I arrived at Jackson in Mississippi and, to my relief, found that Wil – still as scruffy as ever – was there to welcome me. He drove me to meet his parents and sister, who were very nice, respectable people and not at all like he had painted, then after a meal we left for Wil's abode. There, to my amazement, was Gareth Davies (affectionately known by his buddies as Gareth the Gob because he became a bit garrulous when he had downed a few), who was courting Wil's lovely sister.

I had caved with Gareth several times and he greeted me with: 'I know you, boyo – wasn't you the drunken sod with the varicose veins that was stood upside down on the table in the Ancient Briton?' Ah, the price of fame, gained from drinking in a Welsh cavers' pub!

With the van loaded, we drove to Baton Rouge in Louisiana to pick up John Sevenair, then into Mexico via Laredo in Texas to continue into the hills behind Linares, where we met Louise Hose and Tom Strong, Wil's friends who had motored from Los Angeles to bring a 1,500 foot rope, enough to handle the 1,345 feet depth – 410 metres – of El Sótano de El Barro. We tested the gear and checked out the ropes on the 260 foot deep, dry gypsum shaft of a giant artesian well, which also gave me the chance to familiarise myself with American techniques.

During the rope check, Wil made the rather unpleasant discovery that there was a problem with the 1,500 foot rope. He walked over to where I was coiling another length.

'Hey there, Jim, I've some bad news – the long rope is damaged.'

'Oh, that's a sod – it means we can't do El Sótano,' said I with disappointment tinged with relief.

'But, Jim lad, I've got some good news: we can still do the drop if we tie two ropes together. It just means that you have to pass a knot,' said Wil with an evil grin on his face.

'Oh,' I answered. My bowels gave a lurch as they reminded me that they had passed all sorts in their time, but never a knot. I reached for the tequila and took a long swig.

The following evening, while camping by the dried-out río Santa María, 150 miles north of Mexico City, Wil put Tom and me through an intensive course on knot passing using a nearby road bridge.

In the morning we drove to a nearby village, loaded our bodies with sixty-pound packs, includ-

Louise Hose (top) and Wil Howie testing the gear at Pozo del Gavilán

ing drinking water, then divided the rope into three coils and began the long hike up to El Sótano, which involved a round-trip of about thirty miles and a vertical gain of nine thousand feet. By the time we reached the second ridge and made camp for the night, I was no longer a male chauvinistic pig.

Louise was responsible for the transformation because, with her short shorts that seemed to have been sprayed onto her bronzed thighs and a red headband holding back her long, fair hair, she was turning into a caver's dream. She was a superwoman capable of not only carrying the heaviest loads, but when we collapsed she also dished out extremely pleasant back massages to the weaker male sex. As I lay under her ministering hands, I groaned with delight.

'It ain't meant to be erotic, Jim, so take that silly smirk off your face,' she said. 'Gee, you Brits are all the same!'

'Right, now do the front,' I said, 'then I'll do y—' but she had gone. A bit touchy, these Americans, I thought. I wonder why I'm no good with women.

Reaching Rancho El Barro, we found the little *refrescos* stall closed, so we topped up a couple of water bottles and dosed them liberally with chlorine, because although Mexico is a beautiful, fascinating country, its water supplies at that time contained all sorts of weird creatures ranging from liver fluke cysts to things that affect your brain cells (even mine).

We camped above the village – well, we bivvied, just kipping on the floor around a smouldering campfire where some of the others smoked cannabis – at that point I understood why they call it shit. It looks like it and smells like it and it will remain one of life's mysteries to me because, after my compatriots insisted that I join them in sharing joints, I lay back listening to them burble about how 'the stars have become bigger and brighter' when all I could think about was that I would sell my soul to the Devil for a pint of Newcastle Brown and that they were talking a load of bollocks.

After – to use the term loosely – breakfast, two local lads appeared and led us through the wilderness of plants to the edge of El Sótano. Mist shrouded the bare limestone edge and we sensed, rather than saw, the vast dimensions before us. Wil cleared some loose rocks from the lip before we began rigging the shaft with five hundred feet of PMI rope tied onto nine hundred feet of Bluewater, both being high-tensile, abrasion-resistant ropes. By the time Wil was ready to make the first descent, the morning mist was beginning to disperse and shortly over half an hour later a very faint shout echoed from the depths, informing us that he was down.

I clipped into the rope and, under the watchful eyes of Gareth and Louise, double-checked everything before easing myself over the sloping edge. Looking down between my legs as I braced against the lip, I could see the rope going straight down, melting into space in the biggest hole in the world. It was awesome and quite beyond anything I had ever imagined, with the slightly undercut limestone face dropping down and down into a giant funnel where trees, looking like green dots, clung to a massive slope of boulders overhanging a further drop. Everything was so vast, it was mind-blowing.

El Sótano is situated on the side of a mountain. To my left the high side of the shaft towered over me, with its large, grey slabs fringed by trees. To my right, around fifteen hundred feet away and framed by a panorama of distant hills spreading out to the blue horizon, the lower rim dropped into a huge, overgrown gully, a dark crease in the white limestone which suddenly plummeted out of sight. Behind me, about seven hundred feet away, the opposite wall dropped sheer to join in oval symmetry above the elliptical green well, 1,345 feet beneath my feet. I had been fascinated by big holes ever since I started caving, but this one was the grandaddy of them all and was about to gobble me up!

I carefully eased the rope through the bars of my rappel rack and, maintaining a steady, slow pace to keep the rack cool, I abseiled into the depths while ignoring the exposure, because it was unreal. The plants hanging on the facing wall gradually drew further away as I descended and looking down the rope was like peering out of the window of a plane. I was surprised at my almost fatalistic calm as I watched the knot progressively making its way up the rope.

The knot that I had passed on the practice bridge was a friendly, tail-wagging sort of knot – it had smiled at me in the soft sunlight – but the knot that was edging its way towards me from the grim depths of El Sótano looked mean and vicious. It growled evilly at me and seemed to swell in size as I approached, ready to do battle in my thick welding gloves.

It is not for nothing that Audrey calls me Fumble Fingers Fred and I have known for some time that I will never become a concert pianist or a brain surgeon. The thick, protective gloves were a mistake and by the time I fiddled with a very small catch on my jumar and clipped it onto the rope, I was too close to the knot. I came to a halt with the knot pulled into my rack, along with my sling, camera strap and safety cord. If that was not enough, the two main karabiners on my Whillans harness had, somehow, twisted together and also jammed into the rack.

It was a bit of a balls up. The first thing that entered my head was that the hot rack would immediately melt the main rope, sending me hurtling to my death, so I hastily poured my valuable drinking water over it. Luckily, I was using a Howie system on my rig, so I was able to place my shoulder jumar high on the rope and lean back in 'comfort' to survey the problem and try to think my way out of what seemed to be a serious situation.

The knot growled evilly at me and seemed to swell in size

Taking out my trusty knife and watching the main rope very carefully, I cut my camera free and tried to untwist the two karabiners which were forcing their two knots into the rack. When this failed, I rigged a knee-mounted ropewalker and tried several times to force my foot-mounted ropewalker onto the rope, but rapidly came to the conclusion that either I or my climbing system was not designed for hanging in space while trying to lift nine hundred feet of rope and assembling a ropewalker which was fastened securely to my boot. Using the knee cam and a spare Petzl ascender, I tried to prusik up, but was held back by the weight of rope pulling at my waist.

After more struggling, I tried lifting up the nine hundred feet of Bluewater and anchoring it to the rope above me using the Petzl ascender to remove the dead weight, but by now I was becoming tired and had to rest. I couldn't understand it – it wasn't this hard when I passed the knot on the bridge. Swaying gently on my airy perch, I looked down and could just make out the minute blue dot that was Wil's helmet – and two curious grey objects that fluttered like two moths. I realised I had lost my gloves.

Securely anchored in permanent orbit, almost in the centre of the world's largest hole, I realised that my situation was unique – I could become famous.

'Wil,' I shouted.

'Yes Jim?' came his faint reply.

'I seem to have a bit of a problem.'

A long, uneasy silence followed and I could almost hear Wil's brain ticking over. Eventually, a distant shout drifted up.

'Hang about.'

During a career that now spans over sixty years of caving, this must rank as one of the finest pieces of advice that I have ever been offered. I was at a loss for a reply.

Then came another shout: 'I'll come up.' It was followed by a word of warning: 'The rope is going to bounce.'

Dangling five hundred feet down and nine hundred feet from the floor in El Sótano could be the ultimate experience that television game shows are always searching for, but that paled into insignificance when Wil started climbing.

The rope began to bounce, gently at first and then more violently, before beginning to gyrate as well. I have never felt so helpless in my life, hanging like a broken puppet held on a slender cord by the unseen hand of fate. To take my mind off mundane things like how long it would take for me to hit the bottom when the rope broke, I started taking photographs – of the sky, of my boots – until the Wil Howie 'bring 'em back alive' service popped into view between my legs. His homely features seemed to me like those of James Bond.

The face studied the conglomeration of metal and rope and smiled a weak sort of 'Christ, what a bloody mess' smile. I waited for words of wisdom.

'Y'all seem to have got yo'self into a bit of a tangle, Jim lad, but we'll soon have you out of that.'

We started to do a sort of daring young men on the flying trapeze act as Wil, suspended below me, handed me various ascenders and tapes which I clipped onto the rope above the knot. Showing great expertise, he then gradually worked his way over the knot and the useless lump of humanity that was fastened to it, only standing on my balls once. We had one nasty moment when, face to face, there was a sudden loud retort of a cord snapping and I threw my legs around Wil in a vice-like scissor grip, as I didn't want to lose him at this stage. Checking our gear, we found that it was the safety cord on the top ascender that had snapped; I released my grip and Wil gradually moved into position above me.

Acting under Wil's instructions, I pulled up the dead weight of the Bluewater and Wil clipped a loop onto the rope above us, thus taking off the strain and allowing me to free the knot from my rack. I worked upwards for a few feet and mounted my ropewalkers on the top rope, then Wil freed the loop of rope from above and handed it to me to lower back down. Fortunately, I did this slowly, for as the weight came gradually onto my foot-mounted ropewalker, I became painfully aware that my leg was being twisted. When I had placed my ropewalker I had clipped into the loop leading up to Wil – which was now reversing its direction as it was lowered. I was extremely lucky not to have released the last few feet, for the resultant jerk would have either broken my ankle, damaged my knee or even twisted my leg free from its socket.

I very carefully heaved up the heavy rope again and handed it back to Wil. I was now very tired and both hands kept knotting with cramp, but eventually we succeeded in putting everything back in place and, after shouting words of encouragement, Wil set off up and I followed. I began to warm up, but with only a hundred feet to go my foot cam felt odd. Looking down, I saw the metal sheath splaying open and the cam pin which held the thing together was slowly being pulled into the sheath, safety wire and all. It was within a fraction of an inch from total collapse.

This was the last straw. I stopped and cursed this useless British-made device as I fixed my trusted Petzl hand jammer on the rope and climbed the last hundred feet on one knee and one hand – after swinging on a rope for three hours, this was all I needed! As I dragged myself over the edge the bloody ropewalker fell off. Gareth picked the cam from the ground with a look of amazement. 'Fuckinell!' he said.

Gareth and Louise later made the drop without incident, but when they returned to the surface we found that we couldn't retrieve the rope – it was snagged around some obstruction, probably one of the many fallen trees at the base of the shaft. After a lot of struggling we left it and made our way back through the forest in the dark, constantly losing our way, until we smelled woodsmoke and heard John Sevenair, our camp guardian, shouting to attract our attention.

We were short of water at the camp, so Gareth and I volunteered to find some – but instead we became lost. After struggling around in circles we heard the distant sound of dogs barking and realised we had descended on the wrong side of the mountain and had to retrace our steps. When we eventually reached the village well, Gareth discovered that he had forgotten the chlorine tablets, so we had the choice of either drinking the water and developing amoebic dysentery, or spending the night dying of thirst. We settled for the latter after standing in a bucket of the stuff, longing but unable to drink it though hoping that we could perhaps draw it into our dehydrated bodies through some primeval roots in our toes.

Have you ever had one of those days?

Back at camp the following morning, with tablets dissolved, we were still supposed to wait for twelve hours before the chlorine became effective. We were so parched that some of us drank it anyway, reasoning that the chlorine would work just as well in our stomachs.

Louise volunteered to return to the bottom of El Sótano to free the rope. 'No, no,' I said, 'Let me.'

'No, no,' they all replied in unison. 'You're far safer up here,' and the gallant Louise put all these hairy-arsed cavers to shame by abseiling down the biggest drop in the world, passing the man-eating knot, freeing the rope and prusiking back up again without a hair out of place. She wasn't even breathing heavily, but looked just as delightfully seductive. I was convinced that she was an extraterrestrial.

THERE MUST BE BETTER PLACES to spend Christmas Eve than a back street in an insalubrious quarter of old Mexico City. However, there we were, being greeted by a slightly more salubrious Mike Boon, who offered to share his pre-cooked Christmas dinner of very old, very burnt Mexican beans. Such generosity is hard to resist but, thankfully, we did and, after a visit to a nearby supermarket, we spent a pleasant evening building hangovers and burping our way through T-bone steaks. Clutching all his worldly possessions in two polythene bags, Mike, caver extraordinaire, adventurer, freedom fighter and a latter-day Mark Twain, accompanied us to Cuetzalan in the state of Puebla.

Leaving behind the teeming millions of Mexico City, with the broad highways bursting with an overload of traffic spewing noxious fumes, we headed east towards the Gulf of Mexico. There was a complete contrast between the buzzing, frenzied activity of the city and the beautiful country of rolling green hills, coffee plantations and pleasant

Tom (left), Jim and Wil returning from El Sótano de El Barro
Photo: Louise Hose

people. The women were dressed in colourful costumes covered with complicated embroidered patterns the origins of which stretch back for over a thousand years, to before the conquistadors left their legacy of old Spain.

At the top of a hill we passed a road sign: 'Beware of fog at 2 p.m.' This strange local weather pattern was caused by the sun's heat producing midday evaporation over the nearby Gulf, which almost daily rose over the more temperate Cuetzalan climate and turned into dense fog. Mike was a regular visitor to this part of the world and, with Pete Lord (another British caver) had set up in a house just outside the town. Here they could live very cheaply while exploring miles of caves in the area.

This is one of the joys of caving, for there are still lots of places in the world where caves can be found by youthful enthusiasts, without being burdened by permits and the great cost and logistics of large expeditions that affect the mountaineering world. Caving then and now is a Cinderella sport that avoids glamour and commercialism, yet allows its participants to enjoy the thrill of original discovery, without fuss and in a light-hearted manner, which to me is the true sporting ethic.

We pulled up at Casa Carmen, a house rented by American cavers from a lady called Carmen. The rent was low and it was packed with cavers – indeed, as we were talking a van from Ontario pulled up and disgorged yet more – they almost needed the kiss of life to bring them round.

With the arrival of Pete Lord and a couple more British cavers, Casa Carmen was soon bursting at the seams, so groups went off caving to create more floor space. The reason for the popularity was that winter remained the only safe time to explore the huge river cave systems in the area; torrential rain falls during summer, and the Christmas break was a good time for North Americans to travel.

I was soon introduced to Wil's American buddies and Bill Liebman, Joseph Lieberz and Rick Rigg invited us to join them exploring a new cave they had found. Cueva Piloztoc was presumed to be an inlet into one of the larger known river systems, and Rick had been stopped by a 300 foot pitch – about one hundred metres.

The next morning I packed my caving gear, ready to move off, not realising that the Americans do things differently from us Brits. By the time they had looked at several maps and surveys, packed their 'all conditions' survival kits, spare lights, medical chests, compasses, clinometers, candles, cameras, stopwatches and computers, it was teatime.

I guess you could never catch an American caver with his pants down (not that I would wish to), for they always have everything with them, even spare braces. If I ever have the misfortune to become trapped underground, I hope that it will be with an American (preferably female), for they could supply drinks, feed you with goodies, supply you with toilet paper, mend your light, pat you on the head when the going gets rough, and no doubt would even wipe your bum if the going got rougher. They are so

Casa Carmen

methodical that, for someone like me who had once negotiated his way underground between two caves 400 feet apart using three cigarettes and two matches as my only light source, it made my brain hurt.

The caves in the Cuetzalan area are extremely humid, with temperatures averaging around sixteen degrees Celsius, so caving in wetsuits can be a very sweaty experience. Drinking water bottles were a necessity for, though we were surrounded by and often swimming in water, it was highly polluted from the villages above. By the time we had travelled a quarter of a mile in Piloztoc we were really steaming as we thrutched and pushed our way along a narrow passage formed in a washed-out shale band. We stopped for a much-needed drink where the crappy passage ended above an even crappier drop, which was overhung by an underground slag heap of loose flakes produced by the compressed clay and schist that was peeling off the walls.

This was Rick's 300 foot pitch. I chucked a rock down and pronounced it to be 'about 250 feet.' Rick then used science in the form of a pocket computer and stopwatch, producing a figure of 245 feet. This estimate was then reduced by fifteen feet so that we could use Bill's 250 foot rope, from which Joe Casson had already cut twenty feet. They were still arguing when I grabbed the rope and abseiled down in a shower of falling debris, one hefty piece hitting my shoulder. It did, indeed, reach the bottom.

Below the pitch a steadily descending passage formed on a chert band had nodules of black, polished rock projecting from the clay and schist. After several hundred yards of crouching in a crab-like fashion in the low, twisting passage, we suddenly broke into a flat-roofed cavern that was over 200 feet wide.

I stood, dumbfounded, peering through the gloom at what appeared to be three-foot-high white lilies. They were growing on a sandbank which jutted out of a wide, swiftly flowing stream that flowed into the darkness. In the opposite direction I could make out a faint luminosity and hear the roar of falling water. Heading upstream with Gareth and Alejandro, a young Mexican caver, we reached the foot of a daylight shaft that resembled a miniature Gaping Gill. About 200 feet high, with a similar ledge and waterfall, the shaft spiralled to the surface through the filtered sunlight.

We retraced our steps and began splashing our way downstream in the spacious, flat-roofed passage, which widened until we had difficulty making out the walls. As we progressed the open joints of the thick roof slabs became jammed with litter that had been forced in by summer floods, and it was weird walking under joints and rifts festooned with plastic bottles, packaging, footballs, car tyres and all sorts of odd material that hung down like so many streamers of festive decorations.

It was obvious that we had entered Sima Zoquiapan, a large cave that takes the effluent and rubbish from the flood drains of Cuetzalan, previously partially explored by Mike and Pete. The cave became lower and filthier and my interest rapidly waned, even more so when the Americans decided to survey the cave on their way out. In spite of my protests that 'I am just an explorer,' I was conned into helping. I grabbed the right end of the surveying tape (which meant I only had to hold it) and did my bit for the lightning fast survey back to the pitch; Rick later confided this was the fastest survey he had ever done.

The 230 foot climb was hairy, to say the least, for the rope was some old lightweight stuff that should have been condemned. I fastened onto the flimsy rope, said a few words to Jesus, and began climbing. It bounced up and down and within seconds a rain of shale came down. I tried to remember what we had tied the rope to – yes, it was a bloody great lump of shale and instinctively my climbing became more gentle as I tried to avoid the see-sawing motion that the elasticity of the rope produced.

Suddenly, a chunk of conglomerate came whistling past my left ear. I tried to pull my head into my shoulders but, alas, I am not a tortoise, and another slab hit me on the helmet. I continued climbing until I reached the lip of the pitch and found that the rope had sawn its way into a foot of shale. Giving a warning shout to the others below, I heaved the rope outwards and a mass of clay and rock fell off the wall. I thankfully dragged myself over the edge, which I cleaned off as best as I could before calling to the others that it was their turn to come up.

It was 4 a.m. when we arrived back at Casa Carmen.

THE FOLLOWING DAY Mike organised the Canadians for a long push into Atepolihuit de San Miguel, another significant river cave. They were going to camp underground while tying up several loose ends and hopefully joining the cave to another in the extensive Cuetzalan network of caves – 85 kilometres had already been explored in the area, with many outlying systems hardly having been looked at. Eighteen cavers left the house and we had the place almost to ourselves, so after a good sleep and a wash we enjoyed a tour of the area.

The terrain consisted of low-lying, rounded hills interspersed with shakehole-like depressions containing a variety of plants in a profusion of colour, broken here and there by the broad leaves of banana trees, fronds of palm trees and the deep, glossy green of cocoa plants. It was a beautiful, verdant countryside with ancient trails coloured in the red ochre of the underlying clay, threading their way across the undulating landscape, passing shingle-covered dwellings that were barely discernible in the surrounding foliage.

On the wider trails we met locals sitting astride their horses, white eyes and teeth flashing from beneath their broad-rimmed pointed sombreros and leading heavily laden mules by a tatty piece of rope, like so many friendly 'bandits' from my boyhood days spent watching films. Occasionally, we came across little *refrescos* stalls where we had a bottle of beer and watched the locals drinking tequila, some incongruously dressed all in white. Short, squat men carrying enormous loads would stop for a rest and a hard-earned drink, giving a friendly greeting to the 'locos gringos' before continuing on their way.

Down at the market in Cuetzalan I marvelled at the lovely Puebla Indian women in their dazzling white costumes covered in intricate embroidery and their skirts that swirled in a blaze of red, black and gold. The high cheekbones of their healthy brown faces, their sparkling dark eyes and short stature indicated their Toltec ancestry, as with chubby little babies tied onto their backs they waited patiently by their stalls of nuts, earthenware pots or clothes for customers in the throng of colourful locals to stop and make a purchase.

I shall never forget the bright sun beating down on Cuetzalan's marketplace, the bright glare reflecting from the dazzling white of the stall covers, the dresses, the bangles and baubles and flashing smiles of these happy, colourful people. In fact, I became so carried away by the scene that I bought Audrey a purple and white poncho.

'Just what I've always wanted,' she said later.

SUMIDERO DE JONOTLA, our next objective, was a caver's dream. A substantial cave entrance stood out among the lush foliage of a beautiful valley, where an impressive stream meandered through the trees before crossing the sunlit, grassy landscape and gently falling down a series of low outcrops into pools where women did their washing. They spread the clothes out to dry on the grass, creating a colourful picture of contrasts, with the peaceful scene ending abruptly as the stream tumbled down a huge boulder slope into the dark opening of the cave mouth, set dramatically against the white limestone scar.

Standing on an adjoining hill, I took a photograph before following the Americans into the valley. We clambered into the darkness of the cave over boulders and rocks as big as houses, slipping and fumbling our way downwards yet incredibly still being within the cave entrance, which had assumed massive proportions. Some of the group became separated in the rock-strewn maze.

Reaching the underground river, I looked back up at the largest entrance I had ever seen, with ant-like figures illuminated by a strange green light, broken by the sun's rays slanting through vapour clouds rising in the heat. And I had left my camera in my rucksack, outside!

For some reason, only three miles of Jonotla had been explored and our group's objective was to push further by climbing up through an eyehole before the terminal sump. As my eyes adjusted to the darkness, I was amazed at the size of the cave passage and the amount of water flowing, even in this dry Christmas period. I could only think what it would be like during one of the frequent summer storms that transform the steep, cobbled streets of Cuetzalan into waterfalls and it didn't need much imagination to reason how those giant rocks had been forced into the entrance of the cave.

The bustling market in Cuetzalan

With passages two to three hundred feet wide and the roof generally out of sight, we crossed the streamway from side to side, balancing on the rims of deep, submerged scour holes and old gours as we progressed downstream. The two cavers in front stopped before a wide lake, then floundered into the water and swam to the other side. As we followed we made out an immense bank of flowstone that stretched from wall to wall, ending in an outstanding ivory-coloured beehive formation overhanging the lake. There was just sufficient airspace to allow us to swim underneath the barrier; we emerged in a high cavern with a mountainous slope of calcite-covered rocks leading upwards to a vast black space and enormous, high-level passages festooned with flowstone and rock sculptures. This was super caving and made British caves seem like rabbit holes.

Moving on through large, dry caverns, sometimes traversing over the unseen river far below, we split into two groups. A gigantic branch passage, liberally decorated with stalactites and gypsum crystals that flashed in our lights, remained unexplored and Joseph Lieberz and his team said goodbye with smirks on their faces. They simply walked into more than three miles of fantastic passage that was a hundred feet square, and was still continuing when they had to return.

Our party had drawn the short straw. We prepared to abseil to the river, from whence came a fierce draught that blew the belay tape sideways in the wind. We hadn't seen Wil since we entered the cave, and by now I was becoming a bit concerned. However, someone said that there was yet another group in the cave and that Wil had probably joined them.

Bill Liebman and I made the forty-foot abseil into the narrow river canyon, followed by Mike Cowlishaw and Pete Robertson. They had volunteered for the unenviable task of surveying the river passage, which contained long swimming sections offering no respite. Bill and I left the two surveyors heading upstream, while we swam downstream into the teeth of a wind strong enough to ripple the surface of the water. Some sizeable stalactite curtains, discoloured by thousands of years of periodic flooding, came to within inches of the water and a howling gale whistled through the narrow gap.

I asked Bill to stay clear and keep his carbide lamp shielded from the draught while I ducked through backwards to protect mine; having my light suddenly extinguished in such conditions could have spelled disaster, as – unwisely – I had no electric backup.

A short canal section lay ahead. I was taken through by the strong current into a colossal cavern with rocks the size of two-storey houses jumbled in three unstable pyramids. Shining my light back, I picked out a lightless figure floating towards me. Bill relit his lamp and we climbed out of the stream, working our way along the left-hand wall of this monstrous cavern towards the sound of falling water. Then we experienced one of the most impressive sights I have ever seen underground.

The cavern ahead formed a huge rectangle, with walls so cleanly cut they could almost have been quarried; they towered into the darkness overhead, out of reach of our lights. A large hole in the smooth wall emitted a powerful waterfall that thundered out in a powerful arc, almost at right-angles to the rock.

Faced with this tantalising challenge, we forgot about our main objective – according to my companion, this powerful inlet was unexplored. I managed to find a traverse that led me directly below the waterfall and I climbed higher to a broad ledge. With water showering over me, I could see a passage beyond but, in spite of having good handholds, I couldn't pull myself into it against the pressure of water, which hit me in the chest like a water cannon and forced me back. However, a few yards to the right another, less-powerful waterfall allowed us to gain a steep, twisting passage and, climbing beside the waterfall, we passed two junctions before reaching a high-level chamber where a jet of water entered from a hole in the roof, twenty-five feet above our heads. This would need scaling equipment, so we turned our attention to the side passages, which led into a high rift running parallel to the main cavern and covered with unusual crystal formations.

Not wishing to damage the crystals we climbed back down and returned to the main cavern where we clambered down a rock pile at its far end. From there we abseiled back into the water and swam along the steadily narrowing streamway until the roof closed down, leaving only one inch of airspace at a large formation overhanging a small, bell-like chamber.

I took my helmet off and submerged until I could see beyond, but after a few feet the wall ahead descended beneath the water – it sumped. Above the flowstone lay an eyehole that looked fairly easy to reach, if we could force a way past the overhanging walls. After two attempts, which ended with me falling back into the water, we decided to put a bolt in. Bill stuck the bag on a rock and opened it, to reveal two tins of spare carbide and some sandwiches. Wil had the other bag, which contained the climbing gear!

'Bollocks!'

I persuaded Bill to stand on my shoulders and have a go. He fiddled about until he gave a cry that sounded something like 'Geronimo!' then fell off.

Bill and I made the long swim back against the current and retraced our route to the entrance. After thirteen hours of caving, we found a very cold, very disgruntled Wil bivouacking near the entrance. He was 'dying of hunger' and had been plunged into the 'Stygian gloom' of permanent night when he ran out of carbide.

'I opened the goddam bag and what do I find? Mother fuckin' climbing gear! Yo caint eat the fuckin' stuff, and it won't light. Jeesus Kerist, where yo' two bastards been?' He was most upset, was our Wil. We had eaten all the food, so we gave him some carbide.

Later, working our way back over the surface in the pre-dawn half-light with some of the others, I noticed one of the group behaving very oddly. He seemed to be looking for something and when I investigated I discovered that he was picking up some strange, reddish-coloured fungi.

'Magic mushrooms,' he said.

'Ah,' I said, 'are you going to have bacon and mushrooms for breakfast?'

He looked at me very oddly. 'I don't eat the fuckin' things, I smokes 'em!'

Coming from a bloke who had been known to shoot firework rockets at police helicopters, I suppose this was a reasonable answer.

I THINK THAT IN ANOTHER LIFE I was a Toltec or an Aztec, for I discovered that I had a strange affinity with the Mexicans – possibly because, like them, I was always broke or pissed and here I was, on New Year's Eve, gaily swinging off a seventy-foot 'maypole' in Cuetzalan's churchyard, with Mike Boon and fellow inebriates festooned aloft with me. Considering that the 'rungs' on the pole were bits of orange boxes held on by one-inch nails and that there were two bodies on each rung of the madly swaying structure, it's amazing that no one came to grief.

We originally thought that we would aim for a British version of the famous *voladores* ritual where five men climb a pole, four of them coil their ropes around the top section of the mast then launch into space from the four arms, spinning and circling from the revolving pole as they slowly descend. However, we didn't have any instructions and only one rope, with which Mike seemed in danger of hanging himself, so we were working on Plan B.

The natives below had never seen anything like it and were shouting: '*Vivan los gringos locos*,' when the local drunk – having fallen off during a previous attempt – came clambering back up the pole, dusted himself down and gave a stupid grin to his 'amigos' before trying to jump off again. For a minute or two it was touch and go whether Mike strangled himself doing a classic abseil or was thrown off by the Mexican – who eventually stood on top of the pole waving his sombrero until he dropped it. The Americans simply looked on, numb with astonishment.

For a minute or two it was touch and go

AFTER A FEW MORE DAYS CAVING,

we headed north for Cuidad Valles with an extra passenger, Martin Cannon, and found our way to the Condesa restaurant, a caver's meeting place. Here we were given a message informing us that Louise had tried to drive her Toyota upside down, which had removed the roof. Fortunately, nobody was hurt and the vehicle was still mobile, so Louise and Tom would be joining us on the trek to the magical Sótano de las Golondrinas, which translates as Pit of the Swallows even though the birds that live there are white-collared swifts.

The eleven-mile walk to Golondrinas followed an old, paved Aztec trail that meandered through beautiful countryside. The profusion of bushes was full of exotic flowers, only ever seen as house plants in Britain, and strange orchids clung to trees in sun-dappled clearings. With the rope stretched between us in three coils to spread the load, we walked past an occasional ramshackle dwelling, where we became the objects of fascinated attention from barefooted women, their black hair held back by coloured, plaited woollen headbands, who clutched babies to their breasts or held young children by the hand.

This ancient route was over a thousand years old and the flat stone slabs were worn smooth by the passage of people and horses. We frequently met other travellers, who raised a hand as they gave us a friendly greeting. Gareth offered to swap his kit with a man much shorter than he was, struggling as he was under an enormous burden, balanced on his back by a headband. Light-heartedly the man dropped his pack and gestured to Gareth, but he couldn't even lift it off the ground.

As we approached the top of the first ridge, the trees became smaller and giant cacti raised their bulbous, spine-covered fingers through banks of brilliant red and gold poinsettia. The trail broadened on the crest and the hazy blue outline of the sierras was framed by a stream tumbling down the valley by the side of the trail. On the opposite side, under the shade of the trees, stood a *refrescos* stall.

With horses tethered to a rail, men in sombreros leaning against the bar and a jovial, red-faced, moustached gentleman waving us over, it was impossible to walk past and, after welcoming us like visiting royalty, he insisted on giving us free drinks. This naturally led to us returning the favour and in what seemed a remarkably short time we found that our soft drink amigos had gone on ahead, leaving Gareth, Martin and me with the Mexicans, propping up the bar.

'Just like old times, boyo,' said Gareth. 'Get 'em in again.'

Reluctantly, after many 'Grassy-arse *señores*,' we said *adiós* and galloped after the others. After an hour or so, we caught up with them by another stall, drinking lemonade. Ugh! We had to have another beer.

Our magical mystery tour finally came to an end after we left the main trail, took out our trusty machetes and hacked our way through some unruly undergrowth to reach a ploughed field, which Gareth said was the campsite.

A short distance away through the trees lay Golondrinas. Gareth insisted that I see it so, in deepening dusk, we thrashed our way through the jungle to emerge on the bare limestone blocks that fringed a large, ominous hole, 200 feet long and 160 feet wide. It was a sight that took my breath away.

Gareth, looking more evil than ever with his unkempt covering of facial hair, heaved a bloody great rock down the hole, mentally timing it and looking at me at the same time. A deep, sonorous boom eventually welled up from the depths, striking terror into my soul. Gareth grinned an evil Welsh grin: 'What do you think, Jim boyo? I'll bet you don't sleep tonight.'

By the time we returned Martin had rigged his little green tent and was sitting, cross-legged, under his poncho and wide-brimmed hat beside a small fire, over which he had suspended a small kettle. He looked more like a native than the two

Louise and Tom at the start of the walk to Sótano de las Golondrinas

small boys who were watching him. We wandered over and I gave the boys a couple of sweets each (I always carried sweets, to impress small boys' larger sisters in case I ever met one, which I hadn't because small boys' sisters can't stand the little sods and keep well away from them). After a while the pair tired of watching us struggle to make something edible and they wandered off, to return within minutes with armfuls of ripe, juicy oranges, which they gave us. They had evidently reached the conclusion that we were starving.

The next morning we all spent some considerable time rigging the 1,100 foot drop – a full 333 metres. Wil showed me the damaged rope from El Sótano and told me not to worry, because the damaged bit would be near the bottom – if you can call sixty feet from the ground 'near' – and warned me to treat the rope gently. After looking at a tear in the plaited sheath that exposed the filaments inside, I promised to coax it through my rack with care.

'And don't go fast, or your rack will get too hot and melt the exposed filaments,' said Wil before disappearing from view.

Before following Wil, I diligently checked that the five bars on my rappel rack were correctly placed, then I pushed out over the edge. I hung there, suspended in a bush – my life is full of anticlimaxes. I relieved some of the tension from the rope and cleared the short overhang before looking down at seven acres spread between my feet, eleven hundred feet below. I slowly and carefully adjusted my bars to regulate my speed, before beginning my serendipitous flight into inner space.

Golondrinas is not a hole, it's an experience. I gazed in wonder as, after the first fifteen feet, the walls receded further and further until I left the white glare of the sun and hung in the centre of a giant vault. Thousands of birds circled in small groups, flickering shadows against the vague background of the distant walls, now softly coloured grey-green.

Indeed, moving steadily down the rope I had the feeling that I was descending into an illusion and I would soon become part of it as the distances seemed entirely unreal. The small flocks of green-and-yellow parakeets, wheeling and turning like multi-coloured dots, only served to heighten the sensation I had of hovering in a vast pleasure dome.

El Sótano had an open-air vastness, but here in Golondrinas I felt that I was truly inside a hole, floating into a netherworld of half-light. In the words of Coleridge's *Kubla Khan*, I was descending 'through caverns measureless to man, down to a sunless sea.'

I hardly seemed to be moving, but the faraway map of the floor slowly began to take on contours with angles and sharp lines at the base of the walls, and smaller rocks came into relief as large boulders became apparent. I saw a dot move among the boulders and heard a shout; it was Wil, still a long way below. I glanced at the rope whistling through my rack, faster than I had realised, and slowed myself as I suddenly became aware that I was indeed descending into a huge pothole, with steep slopes of debris suddenly rushing up to meet me.

I hit the floor, staggered back and sat down, quickly unzipping the hot bars of my rack from the rope. 'Wow!' I yelled.

Wil stood there wearing a broad grin: 'Well, what did you think of that, Jimbo?' he asked, patting me on the back.

'Wow!' I replied and stood there with my mouth open, completely mesmerised.

I wandered about this verdant world of moss, lichen and ferns in the strange, greenish half-light, exploring a subterranean Lost World. I scrambled down between the blocks that led to lower depths, choked of course by the tremendous heaps of debris that had fallen in over time. I noticed strange tracks along the bottom part of the walls and wondered if spacemen had landed here after leaving von Däniken's site of the *Chariots of the Gods*.

Looking up the giant shaft, I imagined it as an ideal launching pad into outer space, until I saw a faint dot which seemed to be singing in Welsh and I took a photograph of a flying Welsh gnome. I was most impressed by the sound of Gareth's voice, echoing from the walls as he descended.

Then came Tom's cautious descent, followed by 'Superwoman' who, making strange noises that only American women can make, came zooming down, bronzed muscles flashing and thighs threatening to burst out of their tight confines. I'm sure she didn't need the rope, just blue tights and a red cape.

At long last came the moment of truth, the return. Wil rigged in and climbed past the damaged section of rope and, after adjusting my climbing aids, I eventually followed. Reaching the damaged section I was amazed to see that the outer sheath had parted company with the filaments inside, and I very carefully eased my ropewalkers past. Once clear, Wil established a good rhythm, twenty steps then wait for me, then twenty steps again – one waited while the other climbed, avoiding conflicting bounces, then every six cycles or so we would sit back and rest. The Howie system is perfect for climbing in tandem like this and I felt completely at ease, once I was far enough up the rope to kill myself if it suddenly broke. I mean, there's no point in worrying about the drop when you're that far up, so I enjoyed the view and the general enthusiastic chit-chat that Wil produced from above. The swifts were preparing for their evening flight and we watched their increased activity as we climbed.

Slowly, I became aware of a pain in my right side where the continuous pressure of a karabiner was making itself felt, and by the time we reached the white limestone near the surface I was beginning to breathe heavily. Wil leaned down and shook me by the hand.

'Been great climbing with you, Jim. Only a hundred feet to go and you're making good time, you old sod.' For a minute, I thought he was going to cut the rope . . .

Another few moves and we were fighting through the bushes on the lip of the shaft. I heaved myself over the edge after 53 minutes of climbing – one for every year of my life – and lay there, more than slightly knackered after a fine experience.

Will Howie at the bottom of Golondrinas

Chapter 17

The Perils of Publishing

THE **ADVICE GIVEN** to Mrs Worthington, that she should not put her daughter on the stage, should have been extended to Mrs Eyre telling her not to allow her number one son to become a writer. In that manner, I could have saved myself a lot of grief.

Returning from Mexico, I promised Audrey that I would never leave her again, consoled Tara the dog and threw myself into work. Then, after a hard day slogging over a hot paintbrush, I spent many evenings in the spare room, slogging over a hot pen as I finished the book that I hoped would transform my life. It did, but not quite in the way I expected.

Peter Thompson, publisher of *Caving International* magazine, decided to print my epic tales as a book and so *The Cave Explorers* was born. Unfortunately, Lachesis was still busy and when she heard of this, she laughed so much that she knocked over the spool of thread that measured my life, which severely kinked it. Turning to Clotho, she said: 'We'll get the bastard this time.'

The Cave Explorers was published in Canada under the Stalactite Press imprint and sales began well: the exchange rate was favourable and prepublication offers brought in lots of advance orders. However, the promised publishing date came and went as the book was delayed by the bookbinder, which was having financial problems. Peter bailed them out with an advance, but the bookbinder used this to pay off a previous debt and so the majority of the books were left unbound. Meanwhile, the exchange rate altered dramatically, putting more pressure on Stalactite Press.

Luckily for me, I was unaware of all these problems – I was bathed in the glow of a soon-to-be published first-time author and had received requests to appear on television and radio to promote the book. Then I received a letter from Peter, informing me that he intended to launch the book at the forthcoming Eighth International Congress of Speleology being held in the USA in July 1981 – and could I come over? Life seemed good.

There are much better ways of spending time than going to cavers conferences but, as this was in the line of duty, I swore to Audrey and Tara that after this one more time I wouldn't leave them again, and I was soon hotfooting it to Bowling Green. All I knew about Kentucky was that it was supposed to be full of child brides and hillbillies brewing moonshine so, with great expectation, I boarded the plane, hoping that every day I would become severely inebriated when young ladies queued up to offer me moonshine and marriage. At John F. Kennedy International Airport in New York my dreams were abruptly dispelled by the burly, uniformed armed men, who all had their eyes on me and my large purple rucksack.

I flashed my visa and passport at the man in control, who was a cross between Humphrey Bogart and Mike Tyson and was glaring at me as though I had some sort of foul disease.

'This you?' he asked, looking at my passport photo (my face isn't kind to cameras).
'Yes.'

'What is the purpose of your visit?'

I wondered what the hell that had to do with him, but answered: 'I'm going to a conference.'

'Where?'

'Bowling Green.'

'Where's that?'

'Kentucky.'

'What sort of conference?'

'It's an international conference on speleology.'

'Ugh?'

He turned to his mate with: 'Say, George, what's speeleeolology?'

'Search me, Todd; sounds like one of those touchy-feely things,' answered George.

Todd turned to me and asked, 'Say – what's speeleeolology?'

'Well, it's basically about going down holes in the ground,' I replied.

'What sort of holes?' he asked.

'Well, holes of speleological interest,' I replied as I watched him kicking my rucksack. He seemed to have gone off 'speeleeolology' as he lifted my rucksack and grimaced at its weight.

'What's in the bag?' I toyed with the idea of saying 'drugs', but decided against it 'cos I didn't like the look on his face.

'Speleological equipment.'

'How you getting to Kentucky?'

'I was thinking of going into New York and catching a bus.'

Todd suddenly turned friendly and said, 'Listen buddy, if you go down to the bus depot dressed like that and backpacking, yo' sure as hell is going to get robbed. If I was you, which I ain't, I would go out that door there and see Harry on Delta Air Lines, and he'll fix you up with a flight as cheap as the goddam bus.'

He then waved me through and glowered at the next passenger.

I eventually found Harry among a massive semicircle of airline booking offices and told him that Todd had sent me.

'Bowling Green? Now where the hell is that? Ah, Kentucky – now, your best bet is to have a word with Homer over on Southern – desk fifteen. Tell him Harry sent you.'

'Hi – Homer, Harry sent me,' and within seconds I was booked onto a flight to Louisville.

I was soon aboard the plane being wished 'Have a nice flight' by a smiling air hostess, who presented me with a packet of nuts and a Coca-Cola. In no time at all I was being wished 'Have a nice day' as, late at night, I stepped off the plane.

It was strange wandering on and off planes without the hassle of passport control and customs, and I felt quite guilty as I walked outside, half expecting an armed guard to chase after me as I approached a lone taxi.

'Hello, I'm trying to get to Bowling Green.'

'You won't get there tonight buddy, the last bus has gone.'

'Oh. Is there anywhere round here I could kip out for the night?' I asked.

He looked at me very strangely. 'Waddya mean, kippout?'

'You know, roll up in my sleeping bag till morning.'

The driver burst out laughing. 'You can roll up in yor sleeping bag any place, but yo' sure as hell won't see mornin' around here,' he said and burst out laughing again.

'Say, are you a Brit? Look, hop in and I'll take you to a cheap downtown hotel – it'll only cost you a couple of bucks, and you'll still wake up with yor head on,' and he burst out laughing again.

Louisville was much larger than I expected. The taxi passed most of the flashing lights and the hustle of a thriving city centre and eventually pulled up in a much quieter area. When the driver said 'Downtown,' I looked out and thought that you couldn't find a more down town than this.

A large, seedy-looking building that had obviously seen better days was the hotel. I climbed the worn steps, went through the swing doors and entered a marble palace. It was 1920s again – the place was luxury clad in Italian marble and, at the far end of the entrance hall, beyond the huge, tarnished chandelier and almost submerged behind a huge desk, stood Sammy Davis Jr, or what looked like him.

'Hello – I'm looking for a cheap room for the night,' I said to the man.

'We start at two bucks.'

'Brilliant, that's just the job,' I said.

'But I wouldn't recommend it.'

'Why not?'

'Taint got no air conditioning and you'll probably die in the night,' he said.

All my life I have tried to avoid air conditioning for, where I come from, it means howling gales, shivering under extra blankets or draughts that freeze pipes, so I answered that it didn't matter.

A large, fat lady appeared from behind a curtain.

'For an extra buck he can have thirty-three, we jest don't want the sheets all messed up with sweat.'

So I paid my three dollars, was given an enormous key and motioned towards the lift: 'Third floor, lock your door, stick the bottle cap in the conditionin' to stop it rattlin'.' The faded air of opulence continued from the mahogany-panelled lift, along a wide corridor of threadbare carpet and flock wall coverings, to room thirty-three.

I opened the door and stepped into the sticky heat of a sauna tainted with old cigar smoke and cheap perfume. I hastily opened the window and was assailed by noise and blast furnace heat from the street outside, which made the room even hotter. I hastily slammed the heavy window shut and tinkered with the large, galvanised iron box that took up half of the lower pane; suddenly, with a noise reminiscent of my old New Hudson motorbike, the thing started shaking and rattling and a blast of Siberian air came howling into the room. I hastily fiddled with the controls and just managed to turn the thing down before I developed frostbite, then my eyes alighted on a beer bottle cap lying on the windowsill. After careful consideration, I wedged the cap between two vibrating pipes and the noise stopped. With this technical level of American know-how, I understood how they had reached the moon.

The large room was furnished in a style that would make the experts on the *Antiques Roadshow* cry with envy. It was like being in a time capsule – the bed itself was as big as a London bedsit and the bathroom was made entirely of marble, with ornate fittings, shower, a separate toilet and a bath where I could imagine illicit gin being made.

After a shower I felt the need to explore and as I passed 'Sammy' I said: 'The room's great, I'm just going for a stroll round.'

The cigar fell out of his mouth as he went slack-jawed with horror. 'Say buddy, be careful, it's a war zone out there!'

Leaving the cool interior of the hotel, I stepped into the heavy, sticky heat of the brash, noisy, rundown centre of old downtown Louisville, vibrant with life and flashing neon lights, even though it was past midnight. I headed for a bar and suddenly realised that I seemed to have stumbled into a sort of thieves' den – where I was the centre of attraction.

The beer I ordered went down in one and I hastily left, but back on the street I became aware that I was the only white man in town. I also noticed that there seemed to be an awful lot of ladies hanging around – and that they wore extremely short skirts and possessed extremely large breasts which tried to burst out of their skimpy bindings. Right next to my hotel was a large sign of flashing bulbs which delivered a message to my startled brain: 'Sex show, twenty cents'.

There is something perverse about the male of the human species. You know damn well that you're not going to get much value for what today is fifty pence, but I crept slowly past the open door into a passageway lined with curtained cubicles. A large, dark gentleman suddenly appeared and gestured me past several cubicles which, judging by the strange cries of 'Go, go baby' and 'Oh man, I'se gonna blow ma top!' that came from within, seemed to be occupied. A curtain swished aside and closed behind me. Apart from a coin machine and a full-length mirror on the end wall, which was surrounded by coloured lights, there was nothing else and I had the feeling that I was about to be ripped off.

I put twenty cents in the machine and the lights went out, to reveal a young lady on the other side of the mirror. She had no clothes but, only inches from my mesmerised gaze, she was doing incredible things to her body, rocking and squirming to loud pop music. I could hear the occupants of the other cubicles shouting encouragement.

Then the lights came on, the clear glass was transformed back into a mirror and I was alone in my little cubicle. It was almost as though I had imagined it so, just to check, I put another twenty cents into the machine – and lo and behold, there she was again, smiling at me through the glass and asking me if I would like to do things with her. I was about to reply when the lights came on again.

I realised that we were never going to achieve first name terms at this rate, so I crept out and almost bumped into the resident of the next-door cubicle. He rolled his eyes and shook his head and said, 'Say man, did you get an eyeball of dat pussy – hey man, it was almost purring!' I gave a non-committal answer and sidled outside, then up the hotel steps past Sammy (who appeared amazed to see me alive) and finally flopped into in my enormous bed, which seemed redolent of the last time that Bugsy Malone slept here with his moll.

AFTER A RESTLESS NIGHT dreaming of being chased by Elliot Ness and his law enforcers, I caught a bus to Bowling Green.

The university where the conference was being held dominated the small town and, after meeting several cavers that I knew and talking to several that I didn't, I looked for Peter and the bar. Wandering through the corridors, lecture halls and cafeterias, I was struck by the number of soft drink machines that littered the place. Americans were queuing up to guzzle the stuff – it was almost as though Western Kentucky University was an alien breeding ground for Coca-Cola addicts. I asked a caver for directions to the bar – he looked at me and howled with laughter. 'Bar! There ain't none, buddy – this is a dry county.'

For several seconds I stood there, numb with disbelief. Somewhere along the line my education had been neglected, for I was unaware that any Western civilised country prohibited selling and drinking alcohol. And this was America, the land of the free! My acquaintance could see that I had suffered a culture shock and told me not to worry, 'Because jest down the road is the Bowlin' Green city boundary.'

I hastily thanked him and walked down the road for a couple of hundred yards, until I came upon salvation in the form of the Brass Ass Saloon. I entered the bar, stood for a second as my eyes became accustomed to the gloom, and heard a raucous shout: 'Why, it's Jim – what yer 'avin?'

It was Phil Rust, whom I hadn't seen for years, and we were soon reminiscing from behind two very large cold lagers. The barman appeared with two more, which we hadn't ordered.

'Ah think yor lovely'

'Have these with the young ladies' compliments,' said he.

The two young ladies at the other end of the bar were blonde, blue-eyed and gorgeous, and they soon joined us. They were also very young, but within a very short space of time we were becoming very well acquainted indeed. I knew I had devoured enough lager when the beautiful Lolita locked her arms around my neck, looked deep into my eyes and said in a husky southern drawl, 'Ah think yor lovely.'

'Ah think yor short-sighted,' I answered.

'No, ah mean it honey, let me buy yo'all another drink.'

What could a gentleman do in a situation like that? It would be an insult to refuse.

THE FOLLOWING DAY a lot more cavers appeared at the university and I met Peter and Mike Boon, his co-editor on *Caving International*. They informed me that a load of *The Cave Explorers* had been flown down for the conference, but the whole lot had been impounded at Louisville airport to check that there were no illicit materials inside the packages. This meant that a customs official would have to assure himself that there were no undue sexual references or anything to cause offence within the text.

Bloody hell! What a country! You couldn't buy a drink and you couldn't read a book unless it'd been vetted by some bloody customs officer!

After a day spent meeting people, attending boring lectures and beginning to experience the onset of Coca-Cola poisoning, I found myself shepherded onto one of a fleet of buses, which took us to Jesse James' hideout in Lost River Cave. What seemed like two thousand people were packed into the large cave mouth, given 2.15 glasses of wine and some 5.4 inch cubes of cheese while I watched a barbershop singing group comprising fifteen pink-jacketed gentlemen mime something or other. As I was standing at the back, I couldn't hear anything over the general hubbub, but it looked good – their mouths opened and closed in perfect unison, like so many goldfish in a bowl.

The matriarchs who controlled everything then ushered us back to the bus convoy and returned us to the campus for more Coca-Cola and the evening's highlight, a lecture on the effect of 'Gallstones in the Tertiary Rhinobladt' by Professor Isopod Whelkenstein (or some such thing). Unfortunately, a group of like-minded British cavers and I couldn't stay, for we had a more pressing engagement in the Brass Ass Saloon where my young, blue-eyed blonde was waiting, along with a group of her friends and several large jugs of beer.

After a while, one of the local youths turned to me and said, 'Howdy ther Jim, we'all seem to have a problem.'

'What sort of problem?' I enquired.

'Well, we have these two kegs of beer – could yo'all help us drink them?'

Being stout English gentlemen, with years of experience at this sort of thing, we accepted his offer and were taken to a wild party in what seemed to be a derelict house. I don't know what the occasion was, but 'it sho went with a swing'. It ended with Mike hanging on a window ledge high above the street, while a well-known professor threw dead bats at another well-known professor, who was hanging from a picture rail above a very deep stairwell.

As for what came next, I have a blank period in my life as my brain took a rest, until I came round sitting in a large American car being driven by Phil in an erratic manner on the wrong side of the road. The vehicle eventually decided that it didn't like being driven by a drunk, so it carefully parked itself in a ditch on a sharp bend. Phil and I fell asleep on the grass verge with the car headlamps angled into heaven, evidently trying to beam down a ministering angel.

Ministering angels, it seemed, were scarce in Kentucky, but traffic cops were not. I was brusquely awakened by a threatening figure with a gun, who kept kicking me in the ribs. 'On yor feet, buddy,' he snarled. American police are well known to us Brits as being trigger happy and, not expecting this one to be any different, I jumped to my feet with alacrity. As requested by the kind policeman I stood there, next to my drunken mate, with my hands in the air.

'This yo car? Yo drunk? I'm a-takin' yo in,' the man said.

I've always known that Phil was a crafty sod, but was unaware that his brain could work at lightning speed.

'Oh officer, thank heaven you've found us,' he began, and went on to explain that I was an eminent English professor who had been invited to address the congress at the university and that, being unfamiliar with the controls on the American car and driving on the opposite side of the road and suffering from jet lag, I had become confused and misjudged the corner, because English cars are smaller . . .

'What you a perfessor of?' snarled the cop, turning to me.

My mouth opened and closed but no sound came out.

'He's in shock,' said Phil, 'that's why I made him lie down and go to sleep.' Seeing the next question coming he continued: 'He's a famous author and he's here to promote his book.'

'What's it about?'

'Speleology,' said Phil.

'Speeliolology? What the heck is that?' asked the cop.

'A study of karst and speleothems and related features,' said Phil.

'Oh,' said the cop. 'Yo been drinking?' he asked, turning to me.

'Just a drop,' said I.

He helped us push the car back onto the road and said to Phil, 'Yo better drive this time,' then waved us on our way.

PETER, MEANWHILE, HAD DRIVEN TO LOUISVILLE to retrieve his books from customs, where he was told that they were obscene owing to a passage someone had underlined in red ink which read, 'I sucked on a wet fag.' Peter patiently explained that the author was not performing oral sex on a damp homosexual, but trying to light a wet cigarette in the confines of a very wet cave.

After a hurried meeting with other officials, Peter promised to add a footnote to the offending passage and the books were released. Soon, I was surrounded by groups of adoring American cavers as I put 'witty' comments in the books before I signed them. This seemed to be a must in the USA, or perhaps it's just among American cavers, for they are just as barmy as their British counterparts.

I found the book signing quite challenging – the conversation generally went like this:

'Could you sign it, Jim?'

'Certainly.'

'Could you make it personal?'

'Yes, what's your name?'

'No I don't mean that – I want you to write something in it about me.' So I wrote, 'From Jim Eyre to Harry Bloggs, the best caver I ever met.'

'Gee, Jim, that's brilliant – wait till I show it to the kids!'

From there on it became sillier: 'From one tiger to another' was quite popular, until the requests became more demanding, like: 'Ah want somethin' really special, Jim.' At a loss, I wrote in bold letters: 'This book is stolen', which brought the house down.

I HAD NOT REGISTERED at the congress, because I didn't know I would be there for long enough; I didn't need accommodation, I said, and I didn't need to pay camping fees because I didn't have a tent – and I didn't intend to go to any lectures, or have any meals. In other words, I was a non-person and the nice American ladies who were running the show didn't seem to like it. In spite of the impression that the *Easy Rider* type of films gave that Americans were laid back, it didn't seem to be so: they were highly regulated and, because I was outside the system, these dear ladies became excited and confused (an effect I seem to have on a lot of people).

During my nomadic existence at Bowling Green (my rucksack was in someone's tent, my money and passport locked in someone else's car), I more or less existed on the hoof and the nearest thing I had as a permanent residence was a place with some Texans at the bottom of the campsite, under an old oak tree which I shared with their Alsatian dog. We seemed to get on fairly well – not me and the Texans, but me and the dog, which used to wake me every morning by hitting me with its tail or cocking its leg over my recumbent body. There were consolations – we shared the dog biscuits and every morning I staggered to the showers, which always appeared to be full of nubile young women. It seemed to me that this was the best way of getting rid of a hangover, but that was before I discovered an interesting creation that had been brought from Texas on two pickup trucks.

Wandering around the campsite, I noticed a lot of activity in a small copse behind some large plastic screens. On a small sign hanging on a branch were painted the words 'Hot Tubs' and an arrow pointing directly at a naked young lady, who was smiling at me. 'Hi there, Jim, you come to see our hot tubs? Come in.'

In the screened-off area were several bench seats, a shower and, dominating the scene, a fixed ladder fastened to the first of what looked like two giant cooking pots of the sort that African cannibals used for boiling missionaries. Underneath the scaffolding that held these in place was a maze of pipes with two gas burners roaring away, trying to cook the naked cavers simmering nicely inside the pots. I took my kit off, had the obligatory shower and followed the young lady up the ladder to plop into the first pot with lots of medium-rare pink people. Then I became really adventurous and, climbing more steps into the second pot that was on gas mark six and going for the full boil, I joined the rest of the crowd.

I had never before been parboiled and I sympathised with the numerous shrimps and lobsters that I had dispatched in this manner, although – as far as I am aware, not being a shrimp – they never had such delightful company. It became even more delightful when I felt something gently touching my willy . . .

I looked at the two ladies on each side of me and they both produced angelic smiles. Nobody could smile like that while stroking my willy so, as I was sure there were no

We discovered that he could make one ball jump up and down

fish in there, I reached down and grabbed a foot. It turned out to belong to the bearded Texan opposite: 'Got you goin' for a minute thar, Jim,' he said, grinning.

Somebody making a video came along.

'Hello people, I vant you all to look at ze camera,' said the man, a naked Hungarian caver. When no one showed the slightest interest, he shouted again and said: 'Look at zis!' When we looked at 'zis' it grabbed our attention all right, because we discovered that he could make one ball jump up and down.

'Zis' went down a bundle with the ladies and brought smiles to their faces that an old-fashioned 'Watch the birdy' could never hope to achieve.

One American, realising that he had a captive audience, rigged up a projector and began showing his caving slides. I have never been surrounded by naked, well-washed, glowing pink, young female bodies while having any desire to watch caving slides, so I crept away.

BACK AT THE UNIVERSITY the culture vultures were still avidly swallowing the three-thousand-words-a-minute that were being spouted at the numerous lectures and the Coca-Cola machines had all dried out. I bumped into Ben Lyon, who was clutching a fistful of pink tickets and had an offer I couldn't refuse, so I left him with a smile on his face and a ten dollar note in his sticky fingers. With my newly purchased ticket I searched for the coach that would take me to Cumberland Caverns in Tennessee, which Ben assured me was the second largest cave in the world.

I had already 'done' the largest cave in the world, on which occasion I had watched one of the world's largest cavers (a woman with a vast behind, suitably encased in what looked like tights made out of flowered curtains) become stuck in Mammoth Cave. Walking through a large, dry passage which momentarily narrowed to three feet, I had watched in astonishment as the obese figure in front, who was wearing a bunny hat, came to a sudden stop, halting the flow of two coach-loads of people. The bunny quivered and one of its ears went loppy as the owner turned her head and said, 'Hell, ma butt's stuck. Could yo'all give me a push?'

'Hell, ma butt's stuck'

I had looked at the red per-spiring face (or what I could see of it behind her thick glasses, hat and a large pile of candy floss held to her mouth in a massive fist) and peered over her shoulder at two enormous breasts which threatened to explode out of a red top. Assess-ing that the cave ahead was clear, I sunk my hands into that huge pliable behind and kneaded her through this Mammoth squeeze like a over-size piece of dough.

'Gee – thanks, buddy,' she said before waddling into the distance.

Finding a coach for Cumberland Caverns, I hastily looked around to see if the world's largest caver was on board: she was and she saw me. 'Hi there, come and sit with me,' she yelled, pointing to the adjoining seat and the three spare inches next to her over-flowing body. I waved and muttered something about being allergic to candy floss before I fled to another coach.

After a three-hour drive the coaches pulled up at the cave, where we discovered that there would be several hours' delay before we could enter. This gave us the opportunity to be entertained by some orange-coloured Indians, Davy Crockett and a charming performance from the gentleman who owned the cave but who 'didn't hold with hard licker!'

That meant hanging about in the hot sun existing on cold tea, the inevitable Coca-Cola and water melons for another three hours. To while away the time I made a cardboard cut-out of Ben Lyon and threw stones at it.

Eventually, we were all shepherded into the cave where, in the chandelier-lit main chamber, we were provided with fried chicken, pecan pie and, yup, you've guessed it, more Coca-Cola! However, the day was saved by some brilliant clog dancers and Tennessee's finest fiddle player, who provided us with some great entertainment.

Being the British caving scene's finest fiddler, I rapidly rounded up all the characters who liked beer, forced them all onto one coach, fixed a fiddle with the driver and persuaded him to take us to the nearest honky-tonk, where we stacked up with beer then sang filthy songs on the journey back.

THE CONGRESS ORGANISERS realised that many cavers were succumbing to Coca-Cola poisoning and they had received special dispensation to open a bar, but you could only obtain the beer with tickets previously obtained from one of the official congress organisers. Mike, Peter and I, plus a few others, wandered across and, after having a word with the barman, came to an agreement whereby we paid him with cash.

Several pints later, I found myself entertaining two dear, middle-aged ladies with drinks. With my usual charm, I was getting on extremely well and I had just told one that her eyes were like Elizabeth Taylor's, when she noticed that my uninterrupted flow of beer came without the use of yellow tickets. Immediately, she was transformed from Elizabeth Taylor into Girda Shizahouse from the SS.

'How did you get zat beer vissout der yellow tickets?' she demanded.

'I bought it,' I replied.

'It is verbotten – it is against ze rules. You must buy ze tickets for ze beer!' yelled Girda, slapping her jackboot with her riding crop.

'It's easier just buying it,' I explained.

'You vill be disciplined for zis – ve haff means of making you buy yellow tickets,' she wept, then broke down and said: 'Vy, oh vy are you English so different? Vy vont you obey orders?' Poor woman! I consoled her with a little hug and bought her another drink, still without a yellow ticket.

Unfortunately she was one of the Kommandants. The following day, after doing my duty at the bookstall, a group of us were sitting at a table that was groaning with beer when I was approached by the two dear ladies. I offered them a seat, but they preferred to stand.

'We have had a committee meeting about you,' said the one with Elizabeth's eyes.

'Ah,' I said.

'But we don't know what to do,' she said with a sob in her voice.

'Never mind, ladies – sit down and I'll buy you a drink.'

It's surprising what a few drinks can do to a couple of upright ladies and, being surrounded by unruly Brits, they were soon experiencing fits of giggles.

'You know, Jim,' she said, solemnly, 'you're right about this beer – it does taste better without those goddam tickets. Do my eyes really look like Elizabeth Taylor's?'

Americans like talking and at the closing ceremony the speeches droned on and on and on. Sitting a few feet from the closed bar, we asked when and if it would ever be opened – whereupon several cavers suggested that I did it myself. Within minutes, the grille was raised and two of us were pouring pints. As soon as we were noticed, we became inundated by thirsty Americans thrusting yellow tickets at us.

'Don't need tickets,' I muttered. 'Just leave 'em on the bar.'

Eventually, Elizabeth arrived. 'I wondered who had given permission for the bar to be opened – somehow, I had the feeling that you would be involved.'

'What yer 'avin? We've got bitter, lager and Guinness,' I said, bathed in sweat. 'You wouldn't like to take over, would you?'

WITH THE CONFERENCE OVER Louise Hose and Tom Strong invited me to stay with them in Denver, so I arranged a lift with a friend of theirs on a 'share the driving, share the petrol, pay your own fines' basis. After a week or so in the Rockies I returned home with a fistful of dollars, leaving behind a successful book launch, some notoriety, more friends and some very confused Americans.

The curse placed on me by the Greek gods seemed to be working overtime, for the delay in bringing finished copies of *The Cave Explorers* to the British market was stretching the publisher's finances. The book seemed to be jinxed – as soon as Stalactite Press had a load of books packaged and crated for transit, the Canadian railways went on strike. I received a frantic phone call from Peter telling me that he would have to freight some copies by air – it would be a costly business, but he felt that prepaid customers should receive their copies quickly, and the book needed reviewing and more publicity.

I was in charge of sales and distribution and I soon discovered that book retailers and distributors are the people who make the profit and hold the power. Fortunately, though, I had many friends in the caving market and this eased the situation.

A week later two huge canvas bags of books appeared, which I delivered individually or posted. My telephone became very busy and, daily when I came home from work, a delighted Audrey relayed congratulations from the cavers who had received their copies.

Within days the strike in Canada was resolved, so things were looking up – but not for long, because the Liverpool dockers went on strike almost as soon as the crates were unloaded. The book reviews were good, even one from an American reviewer who, it was said, had never given a good review before and, as the word spread, orders began flowing in.

The strike eventually ended and the crisis seemed over. One sunny morning Audrey and I read through various witty comments from the pile of correspondence, including one which stated: 'Bloody awful book – kept me awake all night because I couldn't put the fuckin' thing down.'

I was still chortling at this when Audrey said: 'You've got one here from a solicitor. What's an injunction?'

As this was 1981 it was fairly unusual for a painter and decorator to be served with an injunction. In fact, serving injunctions was a rarity reserved for the extremely rich to prevent peasants complaining when the lord of the manor had his evil way with the peasant's wife, or to stop some scribe writing nasty things even though they were true. It seemed to me that, in effect, the laws of libel were a rich man's weapon to ensure censorship and, as I discovered, they cannot be challenged in a court of law without the aid of lots of money. It is an anomaly that the defendant must prove that he or she is innocent of libel charges, instead of the right enshrined in English law that it is up to the plaintiff or Crown to prove him or her guilty.

That fateful morning, as I dived into my eggs and bacon, I was aware of none of these things and it just felt like a huge joke that someone was trying to put *The Cave Explorers* into the same category as *Lady Chatterley's Lover*. I therefore ignored this legal threat, wherein the plaintiff had applied for an injunction to restrain me and my agents, servants or otherwise from distributing copies of the book or publishing any statements referring to the plaintiff.

I had just read and digested the letter when a partial eclipse of the sun darkened my lounge as a huge articulated lorry pulled up in our quiet avenue.

'He must be lost,' I said to Audrey as we watched the driver talking to Les, our next door neighbour. He kept gesticulating in our direction and after a while the driver walked purposefully down our drive where, armed with a sheaf of papers and invoices, he rang the bell.

'Mr Eyre? Could you sign here?'

'Er, what for?' I asked.

'I've some books for you.'

'Ah! How many?'

'Two thousand, five hundred,' said the man.

I am not easily shocked but, taking in that huge transporter and its load of wooden crates, each the size of a hen cabin, I merely stood there with my mouth open.

Audrey looked at me, the driver and Les and said, 'I suppose I had better put the kettle on.'

After lots of sweet tea we all set to and, with a gangway of planks rigged against the deck of the lorry, we began crowbarring the massive crates open and unloading load after load of bloody *Cave Explorers* into wheelbarrows. We wheeled them across the garden, filled the garage, filled the porch and then used the crates to floor the loft and filled that as well. Les looked at me in a new light.

'Bloody 'ell, Jim,' he said, 'you mean to tell me that you wrote all these? What are you going to do with them?'

It was a good question . . .

THE NEXT MORNING, after a restless night, I spent a long time on the telephone, informing Peter of the threatened injunction and then telephoning my numerous friends in the caving world, who were all amazed that anyone would want to see a caving book banned. To a man, they offered to help by removing the books from my house, and quite a number offered to remove the plaintiff. At one stage I found myself being introduced to a nefarious Mancunian character, who gave me a 'shopping list' over the phone which illustrated the varying degrees of grievous bodily harm he could inflict at my behest. I had never before heard of a price list for face realignment, broken limbs or long hospitalisation, and I felt a chill run down my spine as the gruff voice explained what he and 'the lads' would do for the cause of literary freedom and a few quid. I thought about the caver who had made the introduction in an entirely new manner as I made my excuses to the hit man and said 'I'll let you know.'

I soon discovered that an injunction is a serious matter and can be granted over the most trivial cause – and if the defendant cannot afford to contest the charges, he or she is liable to pay the other side's costs plus any damages that may be awarded by the court.

I was in a Catch-22 situation. I did not have enough money to contest the claims, but if I didn't I would be deemed to have lost and become liable to large damages. In extreme cases the law could make a claim on any assets, for example my family home.

I determined that no one was going to put me (and especially Audrey) in this position, so I hunted for a legal eagle. However, Lancaster is not a hotbed of high-flying eagles and I ended up with the bloke who had helped us to buy our house.

'An injunction!' he exclaimed. 'Ee, I've never been asked about that before. I only do house conveyancing.' He rifled through his law books for a few minutes and said, 'What you need is a barrister.'

'Right, give me an address or phone number and I'll get one,' I replied.

'Oh, you can't do that,' the man said. 'You're not allowed – only a solicitor can approach a barrister.' I felt that I had stumbled into the world of Pooh-Bah!

'You mean I can only employ a barrister if I employ you first?'

'Well, I wouldn't put it quite like that. "Employ" is not a word we use in the legal profession,' he said, considerably miffed. 'We offer our services.'

The more one learns about the law in this ancient land, the more one becomes aware how bloody unnecessary it all is. After I learned that legal aid is alright for burglars suing householders whom they have just robbed, I found that it's not alright for some poor sod like me to defend himself against actions that could ruin his life.

THE WRIT OF SUMMONS duly arrived at about the same time that I became ill with a debilitating stomach complaint, but I set off for the high court in London armed with all the necessary facts to prevent an injunction being granted – that is, to show that everything I had written was true. Everything was against me. The weather was foul, with snow and ice blocking the railway lines causing the train to be several hours late. There were no vacant seats, the toilet was blocked and I had the trots, which became worse as I realised that I was two hours late for the hearing. I grabbed a taxi, which deposited me at the court and then, once inside this gloomy edifice, I had to ask several gowned figures for directions to the right chambers. Eventually arriving at the right place, I was informed by the group that was representing the plaintive that I was lucky, because the judge had been detained as well.

The judge finally arrived and sat on his ornate seat on a dais that placed him ten feet higher than the rest of us. After a lot of mumbo-jumbo and watching the other side confer, flocking like bats in their black cloaks and horsehair wigs, it was my turn.

'Is anyone representing the defendant?' asked the godlike figure from on high.

'Er, I am,' I said and, standing up and in my best Perry Mason manner, I spread all my relevant bits of paper across my desk. 'Er, your honour,' I muttered in an attempt to escape from the appalling possibility of not addressing the great man correctly – which only increased the tension as everyone else had addressed him as 'my lord.'

I launched myself into defence mode, quickly demolishing all the plaintiff's accusations as I fired off proof of the facts as written and dates and other witness' notes to corroborate everything that I had said as being true. With an imperious wave of his hand, his lordship stopped me in full flight.

'Mister Eyre, have you proof of justification? Learned council state that you have demeaned the plaintiff in the eyes of his fellow men.' Then, leaning over to peer at my pile of evidence, he suddenly asked: 'Are those newspaper cuttings?'

'Yes, my lord,' I replied.

'We don't accept newspaper reports as evidence in a court of law,' he boomed in a loud voice.

'Ah,' I said.

'So you are not represented, Mister Eyre.'

'Er, well, no, I'm doing it myself . . .' I began.

'I suggest that you find representation, Mister Eyre,' and with that he dismissed me with another even more contemptuous wave of his hand. 'The injunction is granted,' said his lordship.

'Bollocks,' said his Jimship (under his breath, of course).

The next move in this legal game of chess was for me to sign a formal document stating that I would contest the injunction in a court of law, where I would attempt to have it lifted. Failing that, a date would be set for a trial by jury.

A kind young lady in a cockeyed little wig took me under her wing, produced the relevant documents and guided me through a labyrinth of dull corridors to have them signed, sealed and deposited. She also explained that the injunction was not valid until it had been handed personally to me and suggested that I engage a barrister.

Once again I contacted my legal eagle, but it seemed that the only places that can support the lifestyle of barristers are big cities, and Lancaster was not big enough. However, by a sheer stroke of coincidence he had a barrister friend with chambers in Manchester. After a warning that his fees would probably make me bankrupt, my solicitor squeezed me into his natty little sports car and we duly met my barrister to be. He had been forearmed with a copy of the offending paragraphs in *The Cave Explorers* which seemed to have caused the upset and, after studying this and a copy of the entire book for some time, he suddenly changed from being a nice, pleasant chappie with a good sense of humour into an interrogator intent on forcing a master spy to reveal his secrets.

'Is this true?'

'How can you prove it?'

'What does this mean?'

After a while I became sick of this interrogation and said, 'Look it's all true – it's just a light-hearted account of what happens on caving expeditions. It's supposed to be bloody funny! Are you making me out to be some sort of criminal because someone didn't understand the humour?'

'Are those newspaper cuttings?'

I was really annoyed, having to explain every dot and comma and nuance of a chapter that to me was highly amusing, harmless fun – especially in the context of the 1960s and the circumstances in which the account took place.

'Calm down, Mister Eyre, I was merely putting you under the sort of pressure that you will probably receive in court. I had to ascertain that everything you had written was true. I have decided to take your case.'

DURING THE DARK, snowy winter evenings of early 1982 I became aware that I had a stalker for, every evening when I came home from work, I noticed a small man in a shabby raincoat and trilby hat seated in a car opposite my bungalow.

For several days he had appeared at my front door with a brown envelope clutched in his hands, and kept asking for me. Every day Audrey told him I was at work and when he suggested that she could give this brown envelope to Mister Eyre when he came home, Audrey suggested that if the envelope contained a legal document it should be delivered personally as she couldn't be held responsible.

It is perhaps better to draw a veil over the intrigue and subterfuge that took place throughout those cold January days. The small man in the shabby raincoat almost froze to death outside my house, little knowing that, unlike the rest of the avenue, we had a rear entrance.

One night I took pity on this poor emissary of the law, who was only doing his job, and we invited the small and now quite blue man in. Tea and the injunction were served and *The Cave Explorers* was then effectively banned from sale in Britain.

It requires quite a feat of imagination to visualise a caving book, even one which a reviewer said was 'definitely not for caver's mums', nestling cheek by jowl alongside such classics as *Naughty Nymphos*, *My Life and Loves* and *Fanny Gets Laid* in some dingy back street sex shop, being sold to nefarious-looking characters in dirty macs who talk from the side of their mouths: 'Psst, got a *Lady Chatterley*, a packet of French letters, a *Cave Explorer*?'

Were my literary below-the-counter endeavours to be classed with the likes of Anais Nin or Henry Miller? Would *The Cave Explorers*, concealed in brown paper bags, be sold to perverts who, by reading their illicit contents, be corrupted into starting caving?

Having paid a large sum of money to my barrister, I received his learned advice. This explained in some detail what is considered defamatory in law and the difference between defamation and making someone merely appear ridiculous. If my statements were true and I could prove they were true, I could plead a Defence of Justification. However, my barrister was more concerned about my use of the word 'con', as he felt that this might be the weak point in any jury trial, especially as these trials tended to take place in London where the usage of the word 'con' is different from that in north-west England (where it doesn't have fraudulent connotations). He also pointed out that the cost of such trials was usually *huge*.

I needed an expert in the English language. By chance I was decorating the house of a university professor and over morning coffee I mentioned my dilemma. He asked for a copy of the book and contacted a colleague, a senior lecturer in English who had a PhD in dialectology.

Mr Peter Wright, to whom I am eternally grateful, put the spring back in my step when, on 1 March 1982, I received a detailed breakdown of the word 'con', which stated that it is derived from the Latin *conducere*: to conduct. In 1896 it meant merely 'persuade', though in the nineteenth century it assumed two meanings – to cheat in a financial sense (confidence trickster or con man) or 'to persuade a reluctant person'. In all four instances referred to in *The Cave Explorers*, no money is mentioned or implied, and in all four instances Mr Wright and another specialist came to the conclusion that the word 'conned', as used in the book, in common parlance meant 'persuade'. This meant that the main plank in the plaintiff's action for defamation had been kicked from under him and my barrister immediately applied to have the injunction lifted – which cost us £600, but it was worth it.

The onus was now on the plaintiff to drop all charges or proceed with the court case. Instead, I received more affidavits, one of which showed a barely legible photocopy of a picture of a caving shop window advertising the banned book, exhorting customers 'to buy now, while stocks last'. Then, in the next post, I was informed that the plaintiff's solicitors had put forward proposals to settle the matter, which were basically for me to pay the plaintiff's costs to date and to distribute the remaining books with an agreed insert.

I agreed to put in an explanatory addendum, but refused to pay any costs. Peter Thompson, meanwhile, pointed out that it was *his* prerogative to claim legal costs and to sue for lost sales caused by the injunction. Letters continued to be bandied to and fro with suggestions that further large sums of money might be spent in continuing actions, then I received a request that the plaintiff might visit me in person to talk things over, which he did. This turned out to not be a good idea, because I had to be restrained by Audrey – she later explained that an assault would have hurt our case a lot.

Eventually, the saga died a death. To pursue further action the plaintiff would have had to deposit a large sum of money with the court and his legal advisers would have informed him that when our injunction had been lifted it had weakened his case, plus which the added defence notes from my barrister made his chances of winning a very expensive suit look very slim. The threatened action was withdrawn – I don't know how much it cost him and I don't care; I only know that the action was totally unnecessary and all that unpleasantness could have been avoided with one phone call, which would have produced an addendum for insertion into every copy of *The Cave Explorers*. It would have been cheaper, too.

Audrey threatened to leave me if I ever wrote another book. 'Or at least, if you do, make sure the people you write about are either broke or dead!' These were words of wisdom from the lovely Aud.

AUDREY MUST ALSO HAVE BEEN GIFTED with second sight because, at the next committee meeting of the Cave Rescue Organisation, some character who lives life on the edge had worked out that, just after his granny's golden wedding anniversary, the CRO would be fifty years old. This caused great excitement – and it's not often that committee meetings throb with excitement. Listening to some of the suggested ways of celebrating our golden jubilee made me wonder why all these stalwarts were not television producers – they evidently had the right sort of space between their ears.

When everyone had calmed down, someone proposed that 'we' write a history of the CRO, publish it and make lots of money to breathe life back into our financial deficit of £1,350.86. After lots of voting and showing of hands, I realised that 'we' had been changed to 'me' – 'Because you can write proper, as proved by *The Cave Explorers*.' After another exciting half-hour discussing what to call it, a certain doctor of medicine suggested *The 'Dead' Cave Explorers*, which I and John Frankland thought was brilliant but which others thought was not quite politically correct.

Ben Lyon had a momentary lapse of memory about my recent court case when he generously offered to publish the book and donate all proceeds to the CRO, and so the project was born. The rest of the committee promptly forgot about it for a while, whereas I, always serious about the job in hand, mused on the fact that the CRO had brought 250 rescues to a successful conclusion. I soon had reason to hope that I would be success number 251, for I was about to become stuck in Dale Head Pot.

Chapter 18

Through Caverns Measureless to Man (almost)

BATTY HAD DONE IT AGAIN. Some people solve crosswords, some take up gardening or golf – Gordon Batty digs 'oles. Unfortunately, all Batty's 'oles lead into 'orrible caves, which means that he eventually runs out of cavers 'sound in wind and limb' to explore them and he invariably ends up with me. The voice on the phone said: 'Now then, Ers, fancy a good caving trip?'

'Who is it?' asked Audrey.

'It's Gordon – wants me to go caving.'

'Tell him you're ill,' which I was, one step from pneumonia.

'Dale Head's gone,' said the voice on the phone, indicating a major caving break-through.

'I've got a temperature and a stinking cold!'

'Be reet,' said Batty, 'see you on Saturday.'

'Did you tell him?' asked Aud.

'Yes.'

'Are you going?'

'Yes.'

'You must be mad!'

That is how I came to be stuck fast in a very unnatural position, crouched in a sitting position over a flake of rock somewhere between a canal and a sixty-foot wet pitch, with my bum in the canal and my head jammed solid against an arched roof. But, I had better start at the very beginning, as Julie Andrews used to sing.

GORDON BATTY AND MIKE WARREN had been working on and off for four years at Dale Head Pot on the southern flank of Penyghent in the Yorkshire Dales. The work was mostly 'off' because of the problems they encountered, but eventually they gained access to a promising pothole in a good area. By the time I joined the team in February 1975 hopes were high for some great exploration.

At the bottom of the entrance dig lies a low, fifty-foot-long bedding crawl, which in wet conditions takes a lot of water and makes the tight, twisting flat-out 'heartburn crawl' a flood trap that causes water to back up in front of any caver unfortunate enough to be making an exit while the stream is running. It has since caused the death of one caver by drowning, as it is extremely difficult to reverse around the tight bend in the middle section.

Fortunately, on this occasion there was very little water running and, taking my belt off and pushing my helmet and battery in front of me, I forced my protesting body, face scraping against solid rock, into this abominable crawl. Reaching the bend I found that the opening ahead diminished yet further and the rock pressed down on me from all sides. I struggled and squirmed, trying to ignore a feeling of claustrophobia and the fact that my legs, which are long, are only designed to bend one way. I was solidly stuck.

A voice from ahead wanted to know what I was doing. I answered: 'At this time, bugger all – I'm stuck!' After an almighty struggle I backed out of the crawl, turned on my other side (which enabled me to bend my legs around the corner) and I joined the others in a slightly larger section. With more grunting and groaning, this led us after 120 feet to a junction with another passage, where the cave became bigger as it took on the form of a rift.

There was an obvious change in the nature of the cave's development here; the rock bedding gave way to shale and holes in the floor provided promise of an extensive development. We traversed over them to reach the first pitch, a 45 foot descent into a roomy chamber where a stream cascaded out of a narrow opening in a side wall, before falling for another fifty feet.

Dropping the next easy pitch in the stream, we found that the route below split into two – one roomy, cold, very wet and 130 feet deep, the other a series of small pitches which led to an abomination of muddy traverses and small muddy pitches that gained an adjoining rift.

Gordon has never been a lover of pitches, especially those of the wet and exposed variety, so not unnaturally, I suppose, I found myself following him on the latter route, together with Bob Hryndyj and a few others. Being a cave diver (and therefore only happy when surrounded by water), Bob couldn't understand this either, but we struggled and slithered along the mud-filled rift that Batty's detour had led us into via an eyehole in the pitch wall.

After clambering through a pool of liquid mud, we slid down a short slope into a high, narrow rift. Looking along the only man-sized bit (the bottom two feet, which were filled with gunge), we could see another pitch.

Finding a belay point in all that mud was quite a challenge and we ended up using a long belay anchored around a dubious chockstone, then sat on it for good measure as Bob squeezed his way backwards, unravelling the ladder behind him and pushing a small tidal wave of mud before him. The sludge suddenly disappeared into space with a satisfying 'plop' before Bob followed it with a cry of: 'Wotafuckinole!'

Sitting above the rift, I watched my companions become transformed into chocolate soldiers as, one by one, they wallowed in and were almost obliterated by the mud. Soon, it was my turn and, as I forced my way backwards, supported on one arm and slithering armpit-deep in liquid mud while my feet tangled with the buried ladder, I cursed loudly until I was silenced by a slab of mud which slid gracefully off the wall and settled like a chocolate blancmange on my helmet and face.

My probing feet suddenly encountered space and, accompanied by a load of gunge, I slopped over the edge of the pitch. The gunge fell in a rather satisfying way directly onto Eddie Edmondson who, 35 feet below, was holding the end of the double lifeline. When I arrived in another welter of falling mud he looked at me with a hurt expression; well, I presume it was a hurt expression, for all I could see were his bloodshot eyes peering out of a wobbly mud statue.

The rift continued down. We climbed onwards, cautiously, as a slip on the greasy surface would have sent us out of control and into the narrow, water-filled section below. When I reached a small, semi-submerged hole carrying the sound of running water, I attacked it with a hammer and chisel while the others struggled along the rift.

After enlarging the hole slightly, I was amazed to hear voices on the other side, telling me to come through. I looked dubiously at the three-inch airspace in the six-inch hole, but a distant voice informed me that it had been bypassed and that I should climb the rift. I only did so with great difficulty, for trying to traverse on mud while wearing a wet wetsuit is to defy all the known laws of physics. Three times I slipped down again, before finally reaching a mud bridge and, thankfully, I slid (fell) down the other side into a large passage.

Down to the left I could see the stream and a way on, while coming from the right was a sound of distress. After thrutching my way up through a corkscrew passage I came across Batty trying to persuade one of Bob's wellies to go onwards into the unknown, but the wellie, which was peering out of a small hole, refused the request and returned along with its owner. I patiently explained to this gruesome twosome that they had missed the obvious way on and, once back at the junction, we dropped into the water through a partial duck. This brought us to a powerful waterfall, which poured from another inlet overhead before spraying down a magnificent forty-foot pitch.

I climbed up the inlet but found it became a bit tight so, surmising that it connected with the big wet pitch we had bypassed, we were forced to beat a retreat as we had run out of ladders. The forty-foot pitch, and any that lay below, would have to wait for another trip.

All cave exploration is full of surprises and the exploration of Dale Head Pot was anything but boring. The following week, ready to do battle, we thrutched our protesting bodies through the crawl with two objectives in mind: to bottom the cave and to forge a connection between the bottom of the 130 foot wet pitch and the inlet over the as-yet undescended forty-foot pitch.

One group laddered the wet pitch in the main rift, while four of us slithered along the muddy rift, which we had now christened SRT (Shizen Right Through). We soon arrived at the forty-foot pitch, a pleasant climb under a waterfall which washed the mud off us. Below the pitch the cave closed in again, but a narrow canal led off through two low sections. I splashed my way onwards to find a crouching Batty peering at a small, nasty opening where the roof descended and vanished underwater. It looked as though the cave might sump.

'What do you reckon?' I asked.

'Dunno,' said Gordon, 'stick your head in.'

I crouched and started to drift inwards until only my head remained above the water, but it wouldn't fit through the small airspace.

'Take your helmet off,' said Batty. He snatched my helmet from my head, spilling all my fruity polo sweets.

I eased my way through the duck, but directly ahead lay another one. I approached it carefully, making sure there were no rock projections below the water as I partially submerged and went through. The resulting canal ended at a small passage where water spilled over a knife-edged rib of rock and dropped through a round borehole on my right.

Lying full-length in the canal, with no headroom, I struggled to look down the borehole without falling into it. I was in an odd situation – imagine a man lying in an open coffin which someone has placed on the brink of a cliff below a large, overhanging rock; he can't climb out of the coffin because of the overhanging rock, yet he needs to see how deep the cliff is before he rolls over.

With Batty shouting burbled queries through the ducks, at last I managed to contort my body into a series of strange positions, ending with me being perched like a humpbacked crow with my bum in the canal and my legs and a severely bent body leaning over the drop, while my head was jammed tight under the low cave ceiling. I could see down a magnificent spiral staircase where water sprayed into more than sixty feet of space, but, but – *I was stuck*!

I was stuck!

I bent my body as far as it would go but, given my exertion and resulting situation, I was knackered.

Batty kept shouting: 'What are you doing?' I kept replying: 'I'm stuck.'

'Well, I can't help you,' he said. 'I'll get wet!'

'Bastard,' I muttered as I began an almighty attempt to escape, which meant forcing my head even lower while trying to wriggle my bum sideways without falling down the pitch. I was keen to be the first down, but not dead – and I imagined an even more horrifying scenario: what if the cave flooded? Wriggle, wriggle, panic, panic . . .

After dislodging several vertebrae, I plopped back in the canal and rowed my broken body backwards.

Bob and Eddie, both considerably younger and more pliable, eventually managed to descend the Pool Pitch and another after it to reach a final sump at a depth of 540 feet, making the pot the third deepest in the north of England.

Another member of the Northern Pennine Club, Iain Crossley, who had not yet learned the rudiments of exploring water-filled passages (that is, not to go through a duck with your head underwater and your backside breathing air), almost came to an untimely and watery end when he became stuck. There was some discussion about fixing a pipe to his bum and blowing in air before his pale, blue face surfaced and said those immortal words:

'Sod this for a game of chess!'

THIS WAS THE TIME OF FRENZIED ACTIVITY among northern cavers, as the Ease Gill System was being extended under Ease Gill beck towards the promised land of Leck Fell and the new extensions of Pippikin Pot and Gavel Pot. Numerous caving clubs showed renewed interest in Lost John's Cave and Notts Pot because they realised that a master cave there could extend under three county boundaries. The fictitious Three Counties System slowly changed from being a dream to a possibility as cave divers began to push back the frontiers of world caving, having been shown the way by Oliver Statham and Geoff Yeadon with their epic dive from Kingsdale Master Cave in January 1979. They undertook a 6,000 foot 'Underground Eiger' dive through twisting and restricted underwater passages in cold, murky water, to emerge after two and a half hours at Keld Head. Their dive shattered the world record for an underwater traverse and established cave divers as the new underwater astronauts.

Other dives at Keld Head had found flooded passages heading towards Marble Steps Pot and Ireby Fell Cavern on the shoulder of Gragareth. Underwater connections between Ireby and Notts were already known, and the Notts water was presumed to enter the Lost John's master cave, which flowed towards Gavel, which headed towards Pippikin . . . which went where? The combined water from all these caves, along with water from Lancaster Hole, was known to emerge at Leck Beck Head risings, so the possibilities were endless.

Modern high-tech cavers, with their high-tech gear, studied the problems and, keeping their bodies pure and physically fit, worked long and hard to solve them. Surveys were studied and excavations undertaken, some resulting in dangerous holes that were abandoned or quickly collapsed, such as at Peg Leg Pot where a member of the Red Rose Cave & Pothole Club was almost crushed.

This is another of the joys of caving – solving age-old geological problems is a bit like playing three-dimensional chess while blindfolded, so can you imagine the frustration these dedicated cavers felt when the survivors from a Northern Pennine Club dinner came staggering up the dry Ease Gill beck one day, trying to clear their booze-sodden brains with a gentle stroll, and – like cavers do – they pulled a few rocks from the stream bank. In doing so they discovered the key that unlocked the mysteries of Leck and Casterton fells. Dedicated diggers threw down their crowbars and wept.

'That bloody Batty! Ee must 'ave X-ray eyes!' moaned a Red Rose member that saw this miracle.

If cavers were like footballers, Gordon Batty's transfer fee would be astronomical because he didn't do anything – he just pointed and said: 'Dig there.'

LINK POT WAS AN INCREDIBLE FIND, back in October 1978. The fifty-foot entrance rift dropped straight into a large passage approximately fifteen feet square and 250 feet long with, at first glance, three passages leading off.

We almost ran down the impressive entrance hall – with excited shouts and sparkling eyes, we were like a bunch of kids who had just been given the keys to a toffee shop. Three of us took the natural route downstream but, disappointedly, we were soon stopped by a large rockfall. However, several ways led under and through the unstable mass, though all of them were a bit dodgy. I soon found out just how 'dodgy' when a large boulder I was embracing suddenly moved and gave Derek Brandon a playful nudge, which knocked him down a twelve-foot hole before trundling past. Fortunately, he wasn't injured, for when we were exploring we hadn't time to stop for squashed cavers. It's a matter of priorities!

While everyone else was poking about in the other obvious passages, with pretty formations and solid roofs, we followed the cavers siren that lures men to their doom – a draught that enticed us to creep under huge rocks, a form of 'hanging death'. Being with Batty (who has no sense of the hereafter), Derek (who had just been knocked senseless) and Kev Millington (who has no sense at all), I wondered if I was doing the

I froze and waited for my end as it swung above me

right thing as, lying flat-out on my back, scarcely breathing, I inched my way under a huge, pointed boulder which hung suspended among a mass of creaking, angular rocks. I brushed against it with my chest and it moved, swinging on an unseen pivot. I froze and waited for my end as it swung above me, living the horrors of The Pit and the Pendulum until it stopped.

Looking at the hundreds of tons of rock which were apparently held up by this finely balanced keystone, I continued with my limbo dance macabre until, with a sigh, I pulled clear into the passage ahead.

Working our way carefully through the unstable rocks, we breathed easier when we entered a clean, stream-washed passage which led us after 150 feet to an eighty-foot pitch. Looking down, our lights picked out a rope hanging from a bolt in the wall twenty feet beneath us.

These remains formed a mute reminder of some caver's desperate attempt to scale the shaft from the passages below, which had to be Echo Aven, part of the Earby Series in Ease Gill. We quickly laddered the pitch and I climbed down to verify this and make the connection official – we had forged another link in the chain.

At the other end of the entrance hall our fellow cavers had been running amok like a pack of demented ferrets as they explored a complicated maze heading south towards Pippikin, but they were becoming increasingly frustrated when the passages led them everywhere except into the Hall of the Mountain King in Pippikin. The excitement was so intense that, after a night celebrating, five enthusiasts decided to do a night trip down the cave. Thus, the Night Shift Series was born and Keith 'Tiger' Langham discovered the way to Pippikin, although he didn't know it and retired to bed, disgruntled, while the day shift carried on.

The exploration was intended to be the fastest of any cave ever, because, having such an easy entrance and being in such an important area, the Northern Pennine Club members didn't want any pirates pinching it. However, the exploration of Link Pot wasn't to be as straightforward as we thought – indeed, what cave is?

Early in the exploration I remember being with Tiger and pointing out a small stream trickling from an insignificant-looking passage above The Canyon (part of the main passage running parallel to the entrance hall) and telling him to 'Stick your head up there and see where it goes,' while we all galloped off in a different direction, hence its name as Tiger's Inlet. Nobody else seemed interested and, two weeks later, Tiger and Derek returned. Tiger felt he had a duty to thoroughly explore the inlet, so he was the one to have the last laugh when the pair entered a series of low, decorated passages leading to a roomy chamber and a series of small phreatic tubes.

As they progressed, both men became aware of a low murmuring intruding on the oppressive silence. They were baffled, for the network of old tubes they were exploring had not seen running water for centuries, but gradually the murmuring turned to the sound of a powerful stream and the crawl suddenly broke out above a 25 foot deep stream passage where the water hurtled over a pitch. It was a truly magical find. By accident, they had made an unexpected discovery, like two of the three princes in the Serendip fairytale; Tiger and Derek demonstrated their academic prowess by naming it Serendipity and baffling the rest of us (because we didn't even know they could read).

The discovery was the equivalent of Eureka Junction in Ease Gill and the following day a supporting team of excited cavers followed Tiger down the eighty-foot wet pitch into an easy, four-foot-wide walking-sized stream passage that went on and on, soon causing us to run when we thought that we were going to race each other all the way to Pippikin.

It couldn't happen, of course, and Easy Street soon lowered to a restricted sump. It was time to call out our own proteus, Bob Hryndyj, an outstanding cave diver, who entered the eighteen-inch-high sump and found it 'swimmable'.

The dimensions of the underwater passage slowly increased to three feet wide and two feet high. After a dive of 175 feet, Bob surfaced in a flat-out crawl with, after he thrutched forward for ninety feet in full diving kit, another sump – whereupon Bob had to return for his reel!

By now cold and tired, Bob retraced his route and entered the second sump, which was roomier with an airbell that allowed him the luxury of standing up to fix his line on a flake of rock before continuing – then after only another ten feet his line ran out. In front he could see a rise of shingle, gaining what appeared to be an air surface. Severely frustrated, Bob returned from this remarkable dive to find that he was over-due by half an hour and that, in his words, 'my epitaph had already been written, with my car and my new sleeping bag auctioned among my fellow cavers.'

On 16 December Bob returned and entered the sump wearing a special harness holding two fifty cubic foot cylinders of air and another 400 feet of line. Crawling between the two sumps with two bottles strapped to his hips was hard work, but it paid off as Bob passed two airbells and reeled out a further 150 feet of line before emerging, at last after a dive of 260 feet, in a low canal. He dekitted and crawled for 300 feet into a large waterfall chamber and – he was in Pippikin. It was a fine achievement.

THE CONNECTION HAD BEEN MADE between the Casterton and Leck cave systems, and the cave divers, who were at the new cutting edge of cave exploration, began working on connecting the other nearby caves. This was a task not given to normal men, although, as one given to studying cave divers as one would an alien species, I could never make out how they differed from ordinary, air-breathing cavers like me.

Cave divers were all crazy, did strange things, drank a lot, chased each others' girl-friends and, in a police line-up, anyone would have experienced difficulty in picking out the divers from any less harmful members of society. However, there is something that lurks beneath their psyche, as I found out one day when I found Bob measuring my roof rack.

'Can you come to Huddersfield and pick some stuff up?' he asked.

The following weekend I returned from Bob's house in convoy with two vans loaded with mysterious black metal boxes, all padlocked and bearing skull and crossbone symbols, while my roof rack was filled with what looked like torpedo tubes and the boot was chock-full with round objects the size of turnips. These all had high explosive signs plastered over them and had been carefully arranged around a giant pan of stew which took the place of my spare wheel.

'Drive slowly, very carefully and don't have a bump,' said Bob.

Something was up and I didn't know what it was. Soon, I was shepherded to the Flying Horseshoes at Clapham Station, where we became slightly inebriated before staggering along the road back to the club's accommodation at Greenclose, 'Cos, my tiddly mates said we're 'avin' a party.'

A huge bonfire was blazing and what seemed like all the caving world was there, diving into huge bowls of hotpot and other goodies dished out by the smiling lasses, while two of the lads stood over two large barrels of beer, dishing it out to all and sundry.

'Ee,' I said. 'A-hic-party – 'oose is it?'

'Yours,' said Audrey. 'It's your birthday – you're fifty!'

It seemed that after living a dull, mundane existence on the fringe of the caving world's nonentities, I was about to be made famous by Bob. His day job as a presenter of precise pyrotechnic displays for an international fireworks company had given him the idea that he would transform me from what he saw as a sort of ageing Eliza Doolittle into something grand and glamorous, like Queen Victoria – because, said Bob, 'She had a firework display for her golden jubilee, so I don't see why you shouldn't. Besides, I like making bangs.'

Aided by his inflammable mate Steve Thorpe, who also liked making bangs, Bob put on a fireworks show that will go down in the annals of Craven

'My granny once saw the vicar with a rocket up 'is arse'

history. 'Yorkshire had never seen 'owt like it,' said Rabbity Fred, 'it fair rattled me roof tiles.' There were bangers and fizzers and wailers and whizzers, and the sky was lit up for miles around with a magnificent kaleidoscope of cascading fire from the thousands of bright jewels that exploded from huge rockets. Large explosions from maroons and bombs seemed to shake the very ground we stood on as, illuminated by the bonfire flames, we watched in awe while the shadowy figures in the background flitted about with hand flares, igniting this and that.

Suddenly, after a brief pause, a fountain of brilliant white light at the bottom of the garden turned into two facsimiles of army tanks, which fought a fierce battle with balls of fire shooting from each vehicle to explode against the other in deafening explosions. As these outlines flickered and faded another set piece burst into life, which proclaimed in letters of fire: 'Jim Eyre is Fifty'. I was stunned.

Luckily, I was saved the embarrassment of being overcome with emotion by a figure with long, black hair wearing a red, flowing gown. With arms outstretched, Richard Ellwood appeared through the smoke and flames as if walking towards us through Dante's Inferno, seemingly unscathed.

What a night! It was fantastic – an experience I shall never forget. It only needed a band to strike up with 'God Save the Jim' to outdo Queen Victoria's celebration. But, of course, being cavers we made an attempt to extend the festivities when some of the lads tried a spot of fire-walking – and learned that one does not do it with one's socks on.

Later in the night, Rabbitty Fred turned to me and said, 'My granny once saw the vicar with a rocket up 'is arse which 'ad gone wrong – ee was running like 'ell to get away from the explosion of stars wot you get when it stops fizzin'!'

THE LINK POT CONNECTION gave added incentive to the cave divers as they tried to push underwater exploration under Leck and Casterton fells. The risks involved in this, one of the most dangerous of sports, were brought home to the caving world when, in an attempt to find the underwater connection between Aygill Caverns and Bull Pot of the Witches, Ian Plant lost his handline in very restricted visibility and took a wrong turn among the maze of submerged passages. A very proficient diver and a popular member of the Dales' cave rescue organisations, Ian sent his last radio signal at 3.30 p.m. on Sunday 16 March 1980.

Everyone who knew him and his lovely wife, Sally, was stunned – more so as Sally and Ian had worked unceasingly to help rescue other cavers – but at this fateful moment there was nothing anyone could do. Conditions underwater were so difficult, with poor visibility in the low, wide passages, that the search continued all night and into the next day. Ian's body was found at 1.40 p.m. on Monday and a further thirteen hours' struggle took place before Ian Watson, Geoff Yeadon and other divers and friends brought his body to the surface.

Ian didn't die in vain, for the connection between Aygill and Bull Pot was eventually established, thus extending the Ease Gill System into Barbondale and giving rise to future debate on the origin of the caverns.

As the network of passages slowly extended across Leck Fell, interest was renewed in the age-old debate of whether Notts Pot and Lost John's Cave could be connected. In the 1950s and '60s I and my reluctant press gang of Red Rose 'volunteers' had started a series of surface digs in the shallow valley above the shooting hut on Leck

Fell Lane. Two of these digs possessed howling draughts, denoting vast caverns below, but one collapsed and the other one – Committee Pot – was nearly a DIY grave. Here, after digging around and under a huge slab of rock that we christened Big Bertha, she suddenly decided to move when I reached a small chamber beneath her. Not wishing to simulate the hero in Aida, I scuttled from underneath before the whole thing slid down with a grunt, thus effectively finishing our dig until, several years later, I sold it to Gordon Batty – but even he was defeated by the man-eating rockfalls and demanded his money back.

Back then in 1967 I was convinced that a large cave passage connected Notts to Lost John's and I organised a team of sherpas to carry in diving gear for Mike Boon and John 'Oggie' Ogden. At that time cave diving kit was fairly primitive and, as he perched over the sump, Mike had to ease on his wetsuit with the aid of washing-up liquid. Both divers reported passing from a tight rift through an arch, but the passage eventually became impassable. The memorable thing about this expedition came when Mike was taking off his wetsuit, for he accidentally knocked his bottle of washing-up liquid into the sump. A powerful waterfall soon turned the final chamber into a vast washing machine and the whole place filled up with soapsuds, which chased us up the ladders like a thing out of Quatermass, threatening us with death by bubbles. Only a few weeks later Oggie was one of the six cavers who perished in the Mossdale tragedy.

Still sure that there was a connection between the two caves, we started rooting about in the higher levels of Notts Pot. However, in those days members of the Red Rose club were determined to become old age pensioners and, after I had nearly clobbered one with a falling rock, I received a rebuke: 'Bugger you, Ers, you're dangerous,' and my team quit. I therefore joined up with some cavers from the Happy Wanderers Cave and Pothole Club, who were involved in similar acrobatics in Lost John's with some desperate scaling led by Pete Livesey, which had taken them into a high-level series above Lyle Caverns.

I watched Pete undertake a spectacular climb on overhanging, smooth, muddy walls, which was quite unbelievable. At the top he secured a ladder so that us mere mortals could follow, but these high-level passages, although leading towards the newly discovered Acrobat Series in Notts that had been explored by members of Lancaster University Speleological Society, were unfortunately blocked by stalagmite and rock.

In February 1982, the Northern Pennine Club's 'hole hound' took to sniffing around Leck Fell like a mangy old terrier as he rummaged among the loose rocks of an old British Speleological Association dig which even Bob Leakey had deemed unsafe. A caver with the initials G.B., which should mean Grievous Bodily Harm but in reality meant Gordon Batty, thereby decided that the BSA's Lost Pot would make a worthy Thursday night dig whenever his wife Maureen let him out to play. Batty and his trusty lieutenants, Glyn Edwards and Frank Walker, aided by other club members and one-legged Peter 'Chester' Shaw (in case they needed his artificial leg for an extra stemple) managed, after several nights' work, to gain access to several pitches which led into Lyle Cavern in Lost John's. Descending these seemed to be a dangerous undertaking from the word go.

Working among the loose boulders involved extensive shoring and the first true pitch, a ninety-foot-deep shaft, posed a particular problem as an extremely unstable slope of large loose rocks overhung it. The team attempted to stabilise this with scaffolding poles and with some apprehension, Glyn eventually made the first descent while kicking down loose boulders before him and eyeing the precariously perched boulders above him.

The following week the group, joined by Kev Millington and others, descended the next pitch of seventy-five feet, which took them to a thirty-foot climb which dropped them into the Lost John's master cave. Chester, our secret weapon, made up for his missing leg with durability and enthusiasm and, using a technique borrowed from Johnny Weissmuller, he had managed to descend the two pitches by swinging on his hands, aided with support from the lifeline. Climbing back up was going to be harder – but Chester had the bright idea of taking off his artificial leg and leaving it with Glyn, then yelling to his stout comrades above for a pull up. Unfortunately, the loss of the artificial leg also caused Chester to lose his equilibrium and, as an almighty tug came on the lifeline, he found he was completely unbalanced – not only mentally, which is usual, but physically as well. A couple of rocks jammed in his pocket would have done the trick, like muleteers who balance a load on their beasts of burden, but it was too late. Chester was airborne.

Swinging all over the place, Chester gave his unprotected stump a nasty bang before he was pulled off the ladder and yanked up the pitch like a broken puppet. He ended up sitting on his arse on the edge of the pitch, unable to move because his leg was still with Glyn. Chester sent up the gear, then he was hauled bodily up by the NPC tug-of-war machine.

The next weekend a larger group of NPC and Red Rose cavers descended Lost Pot, the former to tie up some loose ends and the latter to take photographs. Heavy rain had fallen during the night and Frank felt uneasy about the state of the rocks above the first pitch, especially when he saw how the water was washing out the fill and exposing gaps between

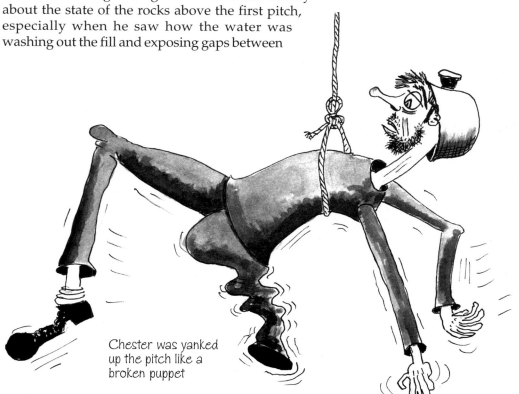

Chester was yanked up the pitch like a broken puppet

the overhanging boulders. His concern was confirmed as Kev, the last man to climb down, was on the ladder when he was struck by a stone falling from the unstable rock bridge.

Later in the day the NPC cavers began to make their way out, leaving the Red Rose taking pictures. Frank was first up the pitch but as Kev was climbing two stones fell from the base of the fill, one hitting him on the head and cutting an ear. The rock jam could collapse at any moment and after two of the Red Rose group had climbed up, they were warned and the NPC cavers left. Jim Newton had tied on the lifeline and was just about to start climbing when a large part of the jam suddenly collapsed with a roar like thunder, raining what Andy Walsh estimated to be one and a half tons of rock onto their heads.

There was no appreciable cover to protect them. Andy cringed into a tiny alcove as he watched Jim struggling to remove his foot from the ladder before he was obliterated by falling rocks. The bulk of the avalanche just missed Jim, but one large rock hit him on the helmet and he fell forward, to be struck again on the shoulder and foot.

It seemed ages before the fall of stones stopped and Jim lay motionless, face down in the debris with his feet suspended on the ladder. Andy, who had medical qualifications, scrabbled across. His first impression was that 'as his major cuts did not even bleed, it was obvious that he had died instantly'. Then, after a numbed interval, he slowly realised that Jim was breathing and he shouted up the pitch for a doctor and a stretcher.

Up above, beyond the precariously balanced remains of the rock pile, the thunderous crashes of falling rocks and cries from cavers produced a confused picture. The Red Rose cavers scrambled out, to inform Frank and Kev, who were changing in the car park, that: 'Just as the third man was climbing the pitch, the rock bridge collapsed and as far as we can tell only one person is alive at the bottom of the ninety.' Frank made a quick trip home to nearby Westhouse to collect some scaffolding poles and timber, and the cave rescue team was called out.

Below the rockfall, Jim's fellow club members had no choice but to move his unconscious body from the bottom of the shaft, where stones were still intermittently falling. He was lowered down a fifteen-foot gully and placed under an overhang, which afforded some shelter, but it was not ideal – Jim was resting on sharp rock in the cold, wet draught from the nearby Lost Pot waterfall. Communication between the two groups was difficult and, with a rock still dropping now and then it was understandable that no one below came near the bottom of the pitch while Frank tried to stabilise the remaining rocks.

The small fill had been washed away completely, leaving some large, black, gritstone boulders jammed across the rift, which still (just) held up the rest of the bridge. If one of those moved, the whole lot would collapse. Frank gingerly manoeuvred a scaffolding pole into position under the large boulders, then jammed it across the rift and wedged it in position with a smaller, angular rock.

The fine limitations of this sort of engineering were demonstrated when, with a tremendous clatter, the pole suddenly shot into space; it ricocheted from the shaft walls and shot past the frightened men below like an Exocet missile.

Having been called out from Lancaster, I arrived to find a team above the ninety working to shore up a safe platform to work from, while Frank and two others had descended the pitch with a first aid kit and a body harness. Being a doctor, Frank would assess the situation then wait to assist with hauling the casualty and his minder up the pitch.

I glanced around at the group perched on boulders, which seemed to have no visible means of support, with the rescue workers' lights shining up through gaps in the rocks, revealing a latticework that barely touched. I said a silent prayer as I realised that everything could collapse beneath us, resulting in at least eight deaths if we and the rocks fell ninety feet onto the men below.

I hadn't time to dwell on such morbid speculation as I was soon engaged in pulling up the semi-conscious Jim Newton, helping to manhandle him through a restricted passage to where men above could pass him back to others. We then lined up every-one from below and cleared the top of the pitch before I suggested that we block the entrance to Lost Pot as it was totally unstable.

'Oh, we'll soon sort it out,' said our underground Brunel in the form of Batty.

Jim Newton was rushed to hospital, where the doctors became slightly puzzled when they discovered an impression in the top of Jim's skull that looked astonishingly like a car key. Not familiar with Jim's habit of keeping his car key in his caving helmet, they were even more puzzled when they discovered the car key itself, so they put it in the indentation, turned it and Jim's brain started working again. He must have been the first bionic man!

The mighty blow that he had suffered had also knocked out Jim's glass eye, so it says much for the thickness of his skull that he eventually made a good recovery.

THE THURSDAY NIGHT TEAM returned to do battle with Lost Pot, armed with stemples, poles, planks and other sundries. A scaffolding platform was soon erected twenty feet down the ninety-foot pitch and Gordon and Glyn built a retaining wall, while Frank and Steve Webb assisted by carrying in cement that was mixed by Chester. According to Chester, who was higher in the entrance rift:

'I had just made myself comfortable and was rolling a fag, when a crashing, rumbling noise came welling up the rift and the whole place seemed to tremble – though not as much as my knee; I swear adrenalin flowed up my tin leg!'

Frank and Steve came scrambling up the rift with rumblings and crashes following them, though by the time a white-faced and frightened Steve reached Chester, the last of the bangs had stopped.

After a minute or so Frank elected to climb back down to see what had happened to Glyn and Gordon. He found them on the opposite side of the shaft, still shaking. The retaining wall had held back some of the collapse as they clung to their perch like frightened budgies, but the rest had gone down the pitch. Steve, who had been on the other side, had the unenviable experience of feeling the floor suddenly disappearing from beneath his feet – he survived by sitting on a couple of wall stemples.

The intrepid diggers decided to call it a day. They blocked the entrance to Lost Pot before going to the New Inn in Clapham for a well-earned pint.

AFTER THIS DISASTER, with Lost Pot now truly lost, efforts to forge further links in the Three Counties System turned elsewhere. Some years previously, Martyn Farr had confirmed Mike Boon and John Ogden's findings that the Notts Pot downstream sump didn't go, so the cave divers concentrated their efforts at Gavel Pot, Pippikin Pot, Lancaster Hole and the rising at Witches Cave. John Cordingley began to push the Lancaster Hole Downstream Sump. In 1964 this had already claimed the life of a diver when Alan Clegg failed to resurface, in spite of a gallant attempt to save him by Mike Boon, who brought him out and tried to resuscitate him.

As John and his team pushed towards the risings, so Geoff Crossley, Ian Watson, Geoff Yeadon and others began pushing back the boundaries of Gavel and Pippikin, while us air-breathing mortals could only stand and wonder as the watery tentacles of Ease Gill Caverns began to extend to the south-west towards the risings and across Leck Fell towards the Lost John's master cave.

With the desperation born out of frustration, I ended up with fellow NPC members, risking life and limb in the very dig that I had sold to Batty, Committee Pot. We were soon reminded that the place was potentially lethal and gave it up in disgust, although we remained convinced that a large cave lay below. I didn't wish to become one of my own statistics and realised that it was much better to sit in my back room, writing about cave rescues than being one.

I had been working on the book about the history of the CRO and, eventually, *Race Against Time* was born in 1988 with the assistance of John Frankland, Dave Hartnup and others. And a lovely, glossy book it was that went on the market – with exploding pages, a device that ensured that each book was only read once, for as the pages were turned they fell out! Poor Ben Lyon, our publisher, went up the wall. There was a fault in the binding and the books were withdrawn while another batch was produced.

Ben gave the suspect books to some cavers, who were asked to dispose of them – which they did, by selling them at half price to other cavers. Soon, Ben was flooded with complaints about leaves falling out of books, which put Ben off publishing for life. He didn't actually blame me, but one day over a pint he asked me if there was any truth in the rumour that I had upset some Greek gods.

Once properly printed and bound, *Race Against Time* was a great success for everyone concerned and made a lot of money for the CRO, guaranteeing that Ben's name was put forward for either a knighthood or a sainthood. I wasn't sued again (although I was threatened), so the curse of Provatina must have been lifted, I thought.

'**FANCY MAKING A BROADCAST?**' It was Ben: 'They want to interview you on the John Dunn Show on Radio Two.'

'Er, well,' I said, 'I'm not sure.'

'Great,' said Ben, 'they'll be in touch.'

When I told Audrey, she said, 'John Dunn? Oo, my favourite programme – *everybody* listens to him.'

The thought of sixty million people listening to me was too much, until I realised that not everyone would be listening at once.

'I'll get you a new shirt,' said Aud.

'It's radio,' I said.

'Well, you'll sound better with a new shirt – it might stop you sniffing,' she replied.

After a few days and several phone conversations with the BBC producer, I presented myself at the broadcasting link-up at Blackburn radio station. I was to make a live broadcast with John Dunn, who was in London. I was escorted to a studio, seated behind a table in front of a microphone, and told that John would speak to me before the broadcast – and not to be nervous. With that the nice lady who had tried to soothe my nerves vanished.

I hastily scribbled some answers to the daft questions that I knew I would be asked, then a light on the table in front of me lit up and a voice came through my headphones – it was another nice lady, who tested the sound level, asked me a few questions, told me to stop sniffing and said that John was ready.

The familiar voice of the most popular broadcaster of the time soon had us chatting like old mates and, with an introductory recording of a song about working down a mine (which went 'I owe my soul to the company store'), I was launched on the unsuspecting millions of British listeners. After a couple of nervous stutters, I relaxed and the interview was a success.

The young lady came back in, gave me a cup of tea and said, 'That was marvellous – could I have a copy of the book, and will you do another broadcast for Radio Lancashire?'

Back home I was met by a jubilant Audrey, who was quite proud of the fact that she had made two recordings of the broadcast: 'Oo, didn't you do well, you didn't mumble and you only sniffed once.' Several phone calls followed, all offering congratulations; one was from my brother, who said 'I didn't recognise your voice – you sounded quite intelligent,' while my mates said it was a load of rubbish.

I had just put down the phone from such a call when it rang again. It was Liz from BBC Belfast, who wondered if I could do another interview for Radio Ulster. It meant that I headed back to Blackburn to chat to a very jovial Irish character, who started by saying that he thought all potholers were barmy. A really laid-back interview ensued, with me telling him funny stories and him offering to take me caving in Ireland.

Yet another interview, this time the Radio Lancashire one, had just been finished when Ben Lyon, who must be the world's best book promoter, said he had booked John Frankland (my co-author) and me to appear on Russell Harty's television programme *Now* – and could I do an interview on Radio Cumbria, then take a reporter down a cave for another local radio broadcast?

I informed Ben that I had an old lady's bedroom stripped bare and I had some work to do, so he said he would do the Cumbrian interview if John and I did the rest. It was a good job that the 'celebrity' culture hadn't been invented, or we could have ended up on one of those mind-numbing shows like *Big Brother*. Instead, we struck lucky and were sent our

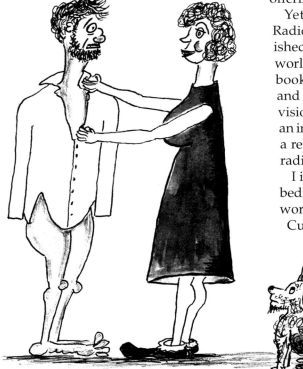

'You'll sound better with a new shirt – it might stop you sniffing'

own equivalent of 'Little Sister', a charming, very young, very innocent lady reporter, who had been sent without a bodyguard to interview John and me in a cave.

We explained that before going caving we had to be interviewed in a typical Dales pub, where we soon had a steady supply of drinks on her expense account. We thrilled this young lady with stories of caves and cavers, which she dutifully recorded, not realising that she was listening to one of the world's greatest bullshitters as she gazed enraptured into John's eyes. When we eventually took her into Yordas Cave, an easy, walk-in site, John went into overdrive as he re-enacted several rescues, complete with sound effects. It must have been the beer.

I thought I was good at the ancient art of bullshitting, but Frankland made me look like a novice. Like a sort of sex-changed Scheherazade in a yellow oversuit, he spun tales of derring-do which almost had *me* believing him, hitting a karabiner on the wall to produce the sound of someone driving in a peg, and splashing water with his foot to illustrate a rising flood, as he produced his own version of an underground *Archers*. What a thespian!

The young lass came out of Yordas clutching her tape, already rehearsing her acceptance speech for best reporter of the year, while – completely mesmerised – I looked at John. If he hadn't been a doctor, I'm sure he would have been snapped up by MGM.

We soon came into contact with some real thespians and arty types when it came time to record *Now*. Several days after the Yordas escapade, John and I arrived in Chapel-le-Dale where, grouped outside a cave rising below White Scar, a motley group of individuals was crowded around a BBC outside broadcast van. The director was a tall man clad in an oversize waterproof with extra shoulders; he was almost unrecognisable under a large, floppy hat. Being a mate of Sid Perou, he knew me from my appearance in his blockbuster *Beneath the Pennines* television series.

Telly people are very strange. If the programme to be recorded has anything remotely connected to buildings, sewers, caves, monuments, planting a tree and cutting the first sod with a silver shovel, or standing on top of a mountain, the participants must wear a yellow plastic safety helmet. We were to be no different – we were told to put on overalls, wear a helmet and look like cavers, even though we were standing near the main road and the only thing likely to fall on us would be the Harrier jet that was buzzing about.

My caving gear at the time was unwearable, so I had borrowed Jim Newton's red overalls, which didn't fit and left me hunched like a budding Quasimodo. I didn't mind putting on my helmet, as I knew the way that Jim – or perhaps his overalls – attracts falling boulders. Standing there like two pillocks, we awaited the star – the local boy made good, Russell Harty, who eventually arrived half an hour late having enjoyed a meal and beverage at the Gamecock Inn in Austwick. He bounced up to us, shook my hand and called me doctor, until we pointed out the error of his ways. The interview was brilliant – the Harrier came whistling over our heads and the heavens opened with a mighty hailstorm, with lumps of ice rattling off our stiff plastic suits like machine gun bullets.

Russell asked us questions in his own, eccentric manner, only becoming excited when I told him a tale of a caver with his trousers down becoming trapped above me, and me being face to face with his spotty bum.

'And what did you do?' he asked breathlessly.

'Put a match to it,' I replied.

'Oh,' he said. 'How cruel.'

I nearly asked him what he would have done, but thought better of it.

THE TREMENDOUS CHANGES that had taken place in caving were illustrated in July 1985, when two Northern Pennine Club divers, Rupert Skorupka and Barry Sudell, laden like pack mules, staggered onto the fell intent on doing battle with the Notts Pot sumps.

It's not often that anyone comes across cave divers lost on a barren moor and the lone walker who was accosted by two chaps attired in wetsuits, carrying fins and heaving an array of cylinders and ropes, was quite concerned when he was informed that these two eccentrics were going diving but they couldn't find any water. 'Nearest water round here is down yonder,' he answered, pointing to the faraway River Lune. When he was told they were looking for Notts Pot, the walker stretched out his left arm and pointed up the fell, little knowing that his gnarled finger was directing the two cavers into history.

Over the following days, Rupert passed the previous limit in the downstream sump, leaving the way ongoing after a dive of 110 metres when he was forced to depart for a trip to Mexico. In his absence two more divers, Chris Danilewicz and Rick Stanton, joined Barry and continued pushing the dive until they came to a massive bank of silt blocking the passage – it was a cave diver's nightmare. For several weekends they dug underwater, until they began to wonder if they were at the correct site. Rick was provided with the answer while investigating a low bedding and almost lost his mouth-piece when he came face to face with two yellow plastic ducks!

It is extremely difficult to laugh underwater and even harder
to hold a conversation with two plastic ducks

It is extremely difficult to laugh underwater and even harder to hold a conversation with two plastic ducks, but they told him that he was now on the right route because they used to live in a sump in Ireby Fell Cavern. Ever since Phil Papard had made the connection from Notts to Ireby Fell in 1976, they had always wanted to travel downstream and experience the big, wide world.

With the downstream route clearly identified and after a dye-test in December 1985 confirmed it, Barry Sudell was soon scrabbling at an underwater, shingle-blocked archway which duly collapsed on top of him, revealing a passage one and a half metres in diameter that headed upwards towards a silvery ceiling of airspace. Moments later Barry broke the surface and entered a virgin cave, his light penetrating millions of years of stygian darkness to illuminate a passage about six metres high and almost two metres wide that receded into the distance. When Rick joined him, the pair dashed into the Notts Pot II master cave, finding massive avens, waterfalls and cascades. Notts Pot had 'gone'!

It was the start of a huge series of discoveries, where caves were joined and sumps were broken to reveal yet more passages to the divers. When Bob Mackin's electronic wizardry pinpointed one of the avens in Notts II as lying beneath Committee Pot, it only needed a troglodyte with no imagination and a firm believer in immortality to start poking again at that creaking rock pile. Soon, the suspicious figure of Colin Davies could be seen creeping across Leck Fell, hiding under the cover of an evil-smelling smokescreen from his ancient pipe. No one knows how many men deserted him or how many times he narrowly averted being buried alive, and no one knows how many months he laboured in the creaking confines of Committee Pot, but in the end, enmeshed in a corset of scaffolding poles, Colin and his band of helpers dropped their 'dry' route into the Notts II extension in November 2000.

It was forty years after I had pulled out the first rock from the Committee Pot dig and felt the cold dank breath of timeless caverns blowing on my face while clad in woolly sweaters and hobnailed boots. There had been months of dicing with death with loose rocks, months of digging channels in the moor to divert streams, months of conning my diminishing band of helpers that we were about to enter 'caverns measureless to man', until only two Red Rose members – Mike Bateson and Tom Sykes – were left. Eventually, in spite of my bribes and entreaties, they also deserted me and the project had been shelved to await the coming of the divers and Colin Davies.

Learning of the breakthrough I felt some sort of perverse satisfaction, for in a way the story of Notts Pot, first explored in 1946, illustrates how the story of cave exploration is never-ending. The explorers may change and the techniques used may differ, but caves around the world will always remain dark, enigmatic places of mystery, beckoning and challenging the adventurous to solve the secrets of the great untamed barren wilderness under the earth.

The timeless caverns of the earth can never be fully explored, but successive generations have and will continue to enjoy plenty of fun and excitement pitting their wits against the cold black spider that chuckles its watery laugh while waiting patiently for the unwary to make a wrong move.

So far, I have escaped.

Chapter 19

A Short Walk in the Himachal Pradesh

BEING A MEMBER OF A CAVING CLUB is a bit like being related to a dys-functional family of harmless, amiable lunatics and whereas in normal society some people are allowed to grow old gracefully, I find that this is impossible in the Northern Pennine Club. Here, whenever caving palls, someone will come up with a new challenge like running a marathon or organising an assault course, or some other silly suggestion that is guaranteed to risk life and limb. All cavers are natural adventurers and most are involved in other outdoor sports such as climbing or skiing, and unfortunately many of our fellow club members have suffered accidents, some fatal. When Mike Thomas, one of our most popular members, suffered a horrendous skiing accident that changed him from being a cave diver and climber into a paraplegic, Kev Millington designed a specialised wheelchair that enabled Mike to be assisted to the summit of Ingleborough. Standing on the top with the victorious group and an exhilarated Mike, I said: 'That was bloody marvellous.'

'Yes, not bad for a training run,' answered Kev. 'We're doing the Cuillin Ridge in Scotland, next!'

He had to be joking.

Hadn't he?

No, he wasn't . . .

A few weeks later the campsite at Sligachan was invaded by hordes of NPC cavers and an extra lorry-load of beer was ordered for the mad northern sassenachs. There was a second load for the bloke in the wheelchair, who didn't need to go to the toilet and who appeared to

A man in a wheelchair had been found on the Cuillin Ridge, apparently unharmed and with a broad smile on his face

the locals to be completely mad, because he was telling all and sundry that he was going onto the ridge.

The following morning over twenty volunteers collected around Mike and his winged chariot, and we began the 3,000 foot climb through the wilderness of steep scree and boulder-strewn crags. The weather was perfect and the spectacle of two lines of vivid T-shirts and shorts, straining on ropes or lifting poles and slowly crawling up the steep mountainside, must have stood out at a distance like a giant, multicoloured caterpillar.

Several ruinous hours later, Mike was deposited on Bruach na Frithe. Grinning like a Cheshire cat, he produced a bottle of whisky, which we drank before I suggested that we leave him there. It would certainly have caused some confusion among the climbers who found him, and even more confusion among the Air Sea Rescue lads when they were informed that a man in a wheelchair had been found on the Cuillin Ridge, apparently unharmed and with a broad smile on his face. Unfortunately, I was outvoted.

SOMEWHERE DURING THE COURSE of one of these NPC 'happenings', I realised that my slide down the razor blade of life had increased and succeeding in my lifetime's ambition of climbing in the Himalaya was looking distinctly distant. Ruminating on my looming demise while slurping beer one day, I mentioned my fascination for the last blue mountains.

'Your wish shall be granted,' said my small, sunburned companion.

I looked closely through the fog of smoke and beer fumes and recognised Colin Hall, the NPC's answer to Rudyard Kipling. He was an old India-hand and proprietor of a fairly downmarket travel company: NPC India Tours Inc. Colin had travelled extensively in the subcontinent and spoke a Peter Sellers type of broken English which was fairly indecipherable in Yorkshire, but went down well in the Punjab. Before I knew what I was doing I had signed on for an expedition to the Himachal Pradesh in northern India in autumn 1995.

Some months later we were organised into two groups and, after packing, unpacking and repacking a large rucksack several times, I arrived with Team A at Colin's house in Settle. His first act was to declare my rucksack too heavy and he emptied all my carefully prepared kit onto the floor. He removed my high altitude gear, my arctic survival thermals and long johns, a stove, spare boots and various other items, all of which I considered essential for survival.

'You won't need that lot,' said Colin, throwing out some waterproofs. 'The monsoons have finished and it won't be cold – I only wore shorts the last time I was there.'

As soon as he turned his back, I hastily shoved as much as I could back into the rucksack and stuffed my anorak pockets full of dehydrated food and socks. All too quickly, Colin returned from his rummaging to stand before me clad in shorts, a T-shirt and sandals, while clutching a small, lightweight rucksack containing less than I would take for a Sunday afternoon picnic.

The taxi arrived with Pam and Mike Neill and we were soon at the airport in Leeds, where we met with Roy Roebuck, a hard mountain man sustained only by a carrier bag full of Newcastle Brown ale. He had recently returned from attempting to climb the Matterhorn: 'We would have done it, but for the guides throwing rocks at us,' said Roy.

At the airport in Amsterdam, just as we were about to embark on the flight to India, we discovered that Colin had lost his ice axe and Mike had lost all his money and passport. They dashed back into the concourse and returned with Mike's bulging wallet, which he had left on a seat. Colin was clutching not one ice axe, but two, both of which had been left unclaimed on the carousel.

We had more trouble with the airline stewards as they bandaged all the sharp edges on the axes before stowing them away, all the while muttering dark Hindu curses against climbers in general and our bunch in particular.

Once we had settled down for the long flight ahead, our leader enquired after our comfort and well-being before amazing everyone by insisting on buying us drinks. This he did several times, amazing us even more – it was not until we disembarked in the hot, sticky sauna of Delhi that we discovered the drinks on the plane had been complimentary.

Colin led us with unerring instinct to the darkest confines of the terminal, where we exchanged cash for carrier bags of Indian currency, which was old, grubby, falling apart and stapled with metal strips into large blocks, making the banknotes almost impossible to separate. Marching us outside, Colin metamorphosed into a native: his skin became darker and he began speaking a strange language, a sort of half-Yorkshire and half-Hindu pidgin as he harangued taxi drivers until he found a suitable one to transport us.

I was overwhelmed by the teeming multitudes, the stagnant, humid heat, the noise and the traffic all going in different directions – even on the same side of the road. Millions of people were trying to commit suicide by wandering haphazardly among the lorries, cows, unlit cyclists and taxis being driven on the pavement. All this took part in the blackest of black nights, enclosed in a thick, evil-smelling fog produced by cheap diesel fumes, the people illuminated only faintly by headlamps that resembled candles as we tore along while our driver often took both hands from the wheel when he turned around to talk to us. He also appeared to take us twice round Delhi before making his claim for the journey and depositing us at a hotel.

Nirula's Hotel, even in the early hours of the morning, was a magnet for climbers and backpackers. After a meal and a few hours' sleep, we followed our Pukka Sahib Colin down a dingy street and watched in amazement as he tried to do a deal with several taxi drivers at once. After shouting something that seemed vaguely obscene, he eventually walked away, to be shouted at to return by two of the youngest drivers who, after much gesticulating, agreed a price to take us northwards. How far north depended on their boss, so we trooped into a rather smart office where we watched Colin make another deal. We handed over wads of currency – some to the drivers, the rest to the boss – and loaded our gear into two fairly new white taxis, then headed out of Delhi on a journey that was an adventure in itself.

Travelling in India was magical – you needed a magic wand to negotiate the hazards of highways that suddenly turned into dirt tracks, or to allow you to brake suddenly as a large, iron cowcatcher emerged from trees at the side of the road, followed by the rest of a giant locomotive hissing steam and pulling a mile of wagons which disappear in a cloud of smoke and clattering of wheels. Stops were frequent and inconsequential: two lorry drivers are having a chat, someone is selling goods from a roadside stall, a mile-long traffic jam is caused by a bony cow chewing its cud while lying in the middle of the road. Travelling through roadside villages was an excuse to wonder.

Modern road surfaces often finished at the entry to any village or small town and one was instantly transported back into time as the red, sun-baked soil took the place of asphalt and deep muddy pools and iron hard ruts slowed traffic almost to a standstill. The roads invariably widened, leaving room for vehicles to casually come to a stop while their occupants emerged to buy food or drinks, have a puncture mended, or just stand and chat. Women wearing exquisite saris were surrounded by healthy-looking brown children, all smiling; what beautiful people – they existed on practically nothing, yet had something that we in the Western world seem to have lost: the ability to smile.

I could understand Colin's fascination with India and after only a couple of days I felt myself falling under its spell. We kept the sliding doors on our taxi open, so we travelled in air-conditioned style while staying in close contact with this colourful, busy world and our fellow travellers on the road. At one point we followed a lorry containing two platforms packed tightly with women, all smiling and waving at us with several diving for cover when I raised my camera, to emerge seconds later, laughing, when I put it away.

Our drivers were cheerful, friendly characters and nothing was too much trouble. They would stop when we required a meal or a drink and, there being five of us, we frequently swapped around in the taxis to prevent life becoming boring and the drivers soon became a part of our group. We were all on first-name terms and everyone chipped in when both drivers were fined, twice, for some traffic infringement or other. Passing a bus at a bus stop was one.

At Ambala they telephoned their boss and asked if they could go on to Chandigarh; more money exchanged hands and we headed northwards again. Suddenly, the lead taxi shot off along a cart track, so we followed across the fields, hemmed in by high stalks of sweetcorn, up and down a rollercoaster of dried-out ditches, to eventually pull up in a small, primitive village of grass-roofed dwellings where the driver in front leapt out to embrace his sister, whom he hadn't seen in years.

After drinks of tea, we continued cross-country to a minor road which took us to the busy town of Chandigarh, one of the most modern towns in India where, unfortunately, our drivers had to leave us and return to Delhi.

We were now in the Punjab with different religious customs – the bad news was that the locals didn't drink alcohol, but at the smart hotel we booked into I soon discovered that beer was obtainable if we were discreet.

Colin brokered a new deal and we were duly met by two turbaned and bearded Sikhs, who loaded our gear into their taxis and away we went again, to be stopped almost immediately and fined for driving through traffic lights. Once out of town we were treated to a display of driving that convinced us that they were quite mad, as they raced each other down the narrow roads until we almost collided with a bus and the other taxi went into a ditch. However, no one was hurt and the taxi was only dented, so after a bollocking our drivers proceeded at a more stately pace. We eventually left the hot, sticky plains and drove up the steeply ascending roads of the Himalayan foothills towards Dharamsala, where we paid them off and booked into a dark, damp guest house. We could feel a difference in the chill air and in spite of Colin's insistence that the monsoons had finished, it was raining.

We called to see the Dalai Lama, but he was out so we spun the brightly coloured prayer wheels outside the palace walls and looked at the devout worshippers in the inner temple. This contained a giant prayer wheel, partially obscured in the blue haze of incense smoke, while tinkling bells marked a procession of people with strong Tibetan features – rosy cheeks and brown faces – who were dressed in garments patterned in intricate mosaics of vivid red and green. They made their way solemnly along the raised walkway outside, spinning the wheels as they advanced towards the inner sanctum.

I ENVIED THESE SIMPLE PEOPLE with their beliefs, for I have none and am the poorer for it. The curious mixture of different religions and the multiplicity of strange gods that are worshipped in India left a deep impression on me.

Soon, Roy and I found ourselves walking up a steep hill to visit another deity – a monkey god. We had barely started before all thoughts of religion were rapidly dispelled. I suddenly felt two small hands gripping my right thigh under my short shorts, one very close to my erogenous zone and I looked down in horror at a pair of dark, luminous eyes, a Beatle haircut and bared, vicious fangs. The monkey clung to my stick-like leg with one hand and both feet, while with

I suddenly felt two small hands

its free hand it delved into my pocket – it pulled out a handkerchief in its search for nuts, leaving me in a cold sweat in case it found mine. I didn't dare strike out, for seven of its mates were jabbering and screeching and showing me their awful teeth as they cavorted around my feet, one undoing my boot laces as I stood stock still.

After being thoroughly frisked, my assailant and his gang ran off. Mobbed by bloody monkeys! Who would ever believe me? I made sure that I bought some nuts from the next nut-seller I came upon.

My respect for these primates increased when I rounded a corner and found Roy busily engaged in photographing a large family group – we assumed they were rhesus monkeys or baboons. I was not aware that Roy was a pervert but, to give him the benefit of the doubt, I don't think he realised that while he was taking pretty pictures of the young babies and mothers suckling their young, he had neglected to observe that a giant of a male was also doing what he was supposed to do: copulate. Just like people would, he took great exception to being filmed on the job so, with a mighty snarl, he went for Roy. I have never seen a man run so fast up a one-in-three gradient. Roy's legs were a blur as, with vicious fangs snapping inches from his bum, he ran for his life while I made a detour through the trees in case this outraged animal, with its slavering jaws and hair standing on end, attacked me next.

We came across several people on their way to the monkey temple as we continued up the steep path. Everyone was dressed in their best clothes; none were molested by monkeys, although I noticed they always fed the animals as they passed – it was probably a case of 'never bite the hand that feeds you' and it implied that Roy and I were tight bastards.

Reaching the temple in a clearing near the crest of the hill, we were surprised at the many couples that had made the steep climb. The men were dressed in light, linen suits and polished shoes, while the women looked cool and composed with well-manicured, painted toes peeping from slender sandals, looking as though they had walked straight from a film set. They were also immaculately dressed in colourful saris with not a hair out of place; their beautiful faces were dappled by sunlight filtering through the trees and it flashed from their gold necklaces, bracelets and dark eyes.

We watched as everyone went into the temple, which was crawling with monkeys, and waited until they left before we entered the small, moss-covered building, handing a few rupees to the attendant monk. Inside were lots of painted saints with the faces of monkeys and real monkeys scampering everywhere – it was an animal liberationist's delight. We never found out what the monkey god represented, so we dashed back down the hill to find the others ensconced in a tea room, drinking Indian beer.

THE NEXT DAY we went for a long walk in thick cloud, stopping at various tea houses and viewpoints where Colin pointed into the thick fog to indicate where one could see certain Himalayan peaks on a clear day. He still couldn't understand why it was raining, 'Because the monsoons always finish on the eighth of September.'

'Never mind, Colin, someone's forgotten to put the clock back,' I said. Our pukka sahib seemed a little sad, with rain running off his T-shirt and down his short, hairy legs into his squelching sandals.

We travelled along the banks of the Beas river up the Kullu valley to Manali, where we met Chas and Fran, two more of our group. Together, we booked rooms at the Hotel Jupiter and explored this busy, colourful little town that formed the starting point for many climbing and trekking expeditions, as well being as a sort of Mecca for hippies, junkies, dropouts and Buddhist monks. Large, garish signs advertised treks, exotic meals, tours, ponies, guides and hot springs, and multiple stalls with local produce intermingled with clothing. There were knick-knacks for the Indian tourists who disgorged from the numerous buses in a happy, expectant throng, for this was the Indian equivalent of Blackpool.

Telephone shops were abundant too, so I surprised Audrey with a phone call, which certainly made her day, then we had a Tibetan meal and several bottles of Kingfisher beer before making arrangements with our mountain guide, Tikam Thakur. He was a fit-looking chap with a fine black moustache who had been on two successful expeditions to K2.

We went for a long walk on the following day for, even though Manali was only at an altitude of about 7,000 feet, the surrounding hills would prepare us for higher things – though we did use a taxi to ascend the 13,000 foot Rohtang Pass. The long, twisting road was set against a backcloth of giant, snow-covered mountains that stretched into Tibet, but was blocked by two massive landslides where we were forced to wait until a handful of workers moved the worst of the rockfall. Three more were using a hammer and a long chisel to drill a hole into a rock the size of a bungalow, while cars and old lorries skidded and stalled as their drivers, assisted by their passengers, tried to force the vehicles over the steep boulder slope. In Britain this would have been a major disaster, but here it was an everyday occurrence that was treated as a useful stop for a smoke or an excuse for a good laugh.

The smartly dressed couple who waited beside us formed a complete contrast to the wretched family we encountered on the next bend. Here, the snout of a small ice field had been carved out to make a temporary summer dwelling while the family brushed stones off the battered road surface. The futility of it all saddened me, but they still smiled as we drove past.

We found a more incongruous sight on the summit of the pass, where some high-caste Indian women were waiting patiently. A strong wind blew from the ice-covered summits across the valley; we were dressed in sweaters and anoraks, and we still felt the cold – yet the women were only wearing pretty but very flimsy saris. They were given mangy-looking hats, fur coats and fur-lined boots before being assisted onto Himalayan ponies to take them to another ice field, where a miniature shrine decorated with painted icons had been cut into the ice. A young lady wearing high heels and clad only in a gold sari, which left her arms and stomach bare, walked daintily past, balancing cautiously on the thick ice. You don't see many sights like this at 13,000 feet.

Later that day Team B arrived, unkempt, knackered and still shaking from the flight between Delhi and Bhuntar. We were now an expedition – I use that term loosely, to match the state of some of Team B's bowels, for they had not been very prudent with their food. After we enjoyed a night on the town celebrating our reunion with our rougher clubmates, we realised that our sightseeing days were over.

A BLEARY-EYED CREW climbed aboard our hired bus and we proceeded to Manikaran, with its quaint temples and hot springs steaming alongside the foaming Parbati river. Colin showed us a very smart hotel, then took us to another, much cheaper one. We settled in before discovering to our horror that Manikaran was a very religious Sikh town and, as such, was beer-less. In no time at all we hired two taxis, which took us five miles back down the valley to a hotel that also became beer-less when we consumed its total stock. The proprietor, realising that he was entertaining Yorkshire's prime beer-suppers, rapidly sent two runners down the valley to purchase the only liquor store's total supply of Thunderbolt beer which, together with a fine meal, went down extremely well.

Our two Sikh taxi drivers, who had stayed on as our guests, rapidly became two sick taxi drivers after they also consumed large amounts of beer. They were not only sick, but severely drunk and we almost ended up in the Parbati river on the way back to Manikaran.

After sleeping three in a bed with an ice axe prodding me up the bum, we met Tikam and his cook, a wiry little man named Ram Singh, and began to load our Himalayan ponies with the expedition's kit. We were at last ready to set off over a narrow bridge and begin climbing the steep, zigzag trail, leaving the town and civilisation behind.

Working our way along precarious paths high above the river, we followed the sure-footed ponies across recent rockfalls and almost vertical scree, always with a cautious eye on the crumbling cliffs which overhung us. We later discovered that in this area of the Himalaya all the foothills consist of a giant jumble of loose rock and shale, inter-mingled with blocks of crystals and conglomerates of all descriptions, as the mountains are continually moving and reforming.

Passing a couple of villages, the trail became more defined as it wandered through trees and seven-foot-high cannabis plants, which brought a smile to the faces of our two resident junkies. Continually climbing, we reached another, smaller village where the members of Team B, feeling the effects of the altitude after their quick transition from sea level, collapsed thankfully by a tea stall, where we all drank gallons of sweet Indian tea provided by a sweet Indian lady. These stalls are an integral part of Indian culture and can be found in the most unexpected places on the lower trails.

At the next village we stopped for the night, sleeping in our bags on the veranda of the local school, and awoke to blue skies and brilliant sunshine. As we progressed ever higher, the scenery became magnificent with the stark white of snow-covered mountains glistening through the upper branches of tall spruce trees. Our ponies threaded their way through sunlit clearings, past giant ferns and rhododendrons where the brilliant red flowers contrasted with the dappled grey of the passing horses.

Tikam was a good leader and waited for anyone who was flagging, and in this way we made a steady pace up the wide valley until, after two steep climbs and a long traverse through colourful alpine meadows, we reached an isolated farmhouse with some farm animals. Just beyond it we made camp and Ram Singh murdered two of our pet chickens, which had been caged and slung on the back of one of the horses. We were sorry to see Hetty and Doris go, but it was either them or us and they made an excellent meal with rice and all sorts of mysterious ingredients – I don't know what Ram Singh did with them, but they tasted good.

Crawling out of my tent in the morning to greet another glorious day, I looked at the jagged peaks of the Manikaran spires which dominate the Parbati valley, now far below. Ahead, snow-covered peaks appeared above swirling clouds, masking the high ground we had yet to traverse. No one was stirring and sitting in complete silence I drank in the crisp, pine-scented air. A nearby torrent formed an integral part of the land, where water streaked the hills and valleys with white ribbons and the sound of falling water was as permanent as the mighty grey mountains and high snows from whence it came.

Ram Singh lit a fire and shouted to the camp; the magic was broken. Looking down the steep bank at the cataract, I noticed a back eddy protected by large granite boulders. I climbed down, stripped off and gingerly entered the water – it was bitingly cold, but after several attempts I immersed myself, gasped for breath and leapt out, my skinny body looking like a frozen fish finger. However, after the initial shock it felt great, so I got the soap working and washed my gear as well as my body, before another quick immersion was followed by a yelp of pain. This produced a cheer from the spectators lining the bank above and a few more hardy souls enjoyed a wash before we broke camp.

Everyone was now fit and we made good progress as we climbed higher. As we left the treeline behind, the ground became steeper and was strewn with loose rock, which made it hard for the ponies. A few of us walked on ahead, aiming for the peak of the next hill where Tikam had told us to wait.

Suddenly, the skies clouded over, the temperature plummeted and it began to rain – not rain as we know it in Britain, but heavy, freezing-cold rain that came down in a deluge like icy rods that felt as though they were piercing my skin. Within minutes, the skies darkened further and a icy wind blew from the mountains as we struggled to reach shelter among the large boulders littering the skyline.

Eventually, numb with cold and clad only in shorts and vests, we staggered over the brow of the hill and Chas spotted a huge, overhanging rock with a dark opening below. Chas, Fran and Colin scrambled in on hands and knees, closely followed by Kev Millington and me with cries of 'Shove up.' Being cavers, we were used to tight places – but this was a shepherd's dog kennel, fortunately unoccupied by the dog. Five in a dog kennel wasn't bad – it was a bit rough on Kev, though, for he sat in the dog's water basin and gave us a good imitation of Pluto swearing.

When the horses arrived we rapidly unloaded our gear; mine was easy to reach as my rucksack had been ripped open when one of the horses had taken a fall. Piling on warm clothing and waterproofs, I looked at Colin. He stood there in a lightweight cagoule, shaking with the cold while his short, hairy legs turned a shade of blue.

'Why don't you put your trousers on?' I asked.

'I didn't bring any,' said Colin. 'It wasn't like this last time and the monsoons should have finished by now.'

We hastily erected the tents and gift-wrapped Colin using loaned gear, then put him to bed with Pete, who had enough gear for three men. The weather closed in with a vengeance and on the coldest, wettest night of the trip, I, who had previously shared a tent with almost everyone except the three women, suddenly found myself alone in a pink 'Punch and Judy' tent which I had borrowed from Tikam. It was not a mountain tent – it was not even a picnic tent and, as I hung onto the pole and surveyed the pink mass of wet cotton that was blowing in the wind (it was impossible to peg it down with only three guy ropes and a bootlace), I realised I was in for a rough night.

After struggling for some time with my rucksack weighing down one side and several loose rocks holding the other, I used two spare bootlaces to secure the flaps then sat on the folded groundsheet and dolefully watched a stream flow past my feet. I clung to the swaying tent pole, which threatened to jerk free at any moment. It seemed a better idea to share some accommodation with my dear friends in their high-tech mountain tent. I politely knocked on the zipped-up door.

'Hello Kevin,' I said .

'Piss off, Ers,' came the reply. 'No, you can't borrow a cup of sugar,' came from Chris 'Nesbit' Raison, the other occupant. Aren't friends fickle.

Somehow, I survived the night and we made the last leg towards what was to be our base camp. The weather began to clear as we walked into a wide, high-level glacial valley, where we splashed along a flood plain and crossed numerous, fast-flowing streams which ran from the glaciers ahead. The clouds lifted, revealing a vista of snow-covered peaks that curved around to our right, ending with Christmas Peak and the awesome Pyramid Peak, a giant monolith of steep rock and ice.

Tikam led us to a meadow beside one of the glacial streams almost under the shadow of Pyramid Peak. While the others put up their tents, I could only stand and stare at the sharp, triangular mass that reared above my head against the backdrop of the deep blue Himalayan sky and the glistening snowfields and ice seracs. Our objective, Christmas Peak, lay on the other side of a massive glacial moraine and appeared more accessible and less vertical, but it was covered in thick snow and ice cliffs like an extremely large Ben Nevis.

Both mountains seemed so near and were just below 20,000 feet high; not big by Himalayan standards, but giants to us. I found myself planning a route up onto the ridge of Christmas Peak – although that snow did seem awfully thick and fresh . . .

I felt exhilarated. Here I was, a few weeks from my seventieth birthday, surrounded by Himalayan peaks – and with a bit of luck I would manage to climb one, even if only a small one. I could almost see the gods smiling.

With camp set up and a meal inside us, we had a recce and realised that our first job would be to build a Tyrolean traverse over the fast-flowing river. Chas volunteered to wade across with the rope at a shallow point, where three hardy shepherds were already crossing to reach their sheep and goats. Their boots around their necks, the trio were leaning on their sticks against the current, while pulling a reluctant dog on a piece of string.

Everyone shouted words of advice and laughed at his struggles, until Chas joined the shepherds; they patted him on the back and shook his hand before helping him rig the rope taughtly across the water. These people, who come the lowest in life's pecking order, are in my mind higher in human values than any politician or shallow being that graces the pages of 'celebrity' magazines.

Several of the team road-tested the Tyrolean with varying degrees of success. Roy discovered that, although he always fancied himself as Tarzan, his physique wasn't right (his arse was dunked in the icy torrent) and Mike's physique, although perfect for swinging through trees, didn't do much for him when he stuck his finger into the pulley wheel.

After an enjoyable meal of curried goat we sat in the mess tent making ambitious plans for the morning, convinced that we were about to bag our first Himalayan peak.

AS THE EARLY MORNING SUNLIGHT struck my tent, I leapt outside and was just in time to see the sun being obliterated by dense cloud. It began to rain and hail as I retreated, to watch the hooded figure of Ram Singh's assistant stagger across with a mug of tea, well-laced with hailstones – a sort of tea-on-the-rocks – on which the expedition could founder if the weather set in.

A bit of light relief came as the adjoining tent was unzipped and what appeared to be a half-plucked chicken emerged. It was a not-too-happy Roz, whose ex-army sleeping bag had burst in the night and covered her and John Frankland in feathers. As she peered at the thick cloud she screwed up her face in misery, before vanishing back into her nest.

After breakfast, the cloud lifted slightly and a small group of us made a recce up the Tos glacier, a massive jumble of boulders – some as big as houses – balanced precariously on the creaking mass of the glacier. It was hard work threading our way through this two-mile-wide rock pile as, teetering on moving blocks and squeezing between giants that could crush us like flies, we made slow progress towards the ice cliffs where the Tos river burst from beneath the moraine.

We watched from a safe distance while rocks crashed into the stream, before the dark clouds lowered and the rain began again, making our faraway tents look like dots surrounded by water. After sheltering under an overhang, we returned to camp and dolefully realised, when the rain turned to sleet and snow and the wind strengthened, that we would not be 'bagging' any peaks.

That evening, with almost everyone jammed into the mess tent, leaving three to take turns sitting outside, we cheered ourselves up with Fran's home-made hubbly-

What appeared to be a half-plucked chicken emerged

bubbly pipe. However, the only person affected was Pam, who amused the rest of us by talking about sex toys and other strange subjects.

The weather grew steadily worse and after three days our team of jolly mountaineers turned into a wet, soggy pile of humanity as we huddled together for our evening meal. The snowline now lay just outside, mutiny was in the air and I was thankful that our base camp was only at 13,000 feet, rather than higher as we had originally planned. Asked my opinion on whether we should sit out the bad weather or cut our losses and break camp, I opted for staying.

'There must be numerous people my age, stuck in nursing homes with other boring old farts watching crappy telly programmes, and I'll bet they'd sooner be up here,' I said.

'Bloody 'ell, the daft old geriatric's been on the wacky baccy again,' said Nesbit.

'I knew we shouldn't have brought him,' said Kev.

We decided to see what weather the morning would bring. Later, sitting alone in my tent, I heard a voice: 'Can I come in?'

It was Roy, coming to keep me company and stretch his body, for he was sick of lying down. 'And I've brought this,' he said, holding forth a bottle of genuine Scottish whisky (brewed in Bombay) with a flourish.

Life immediately took on a rosy glow. We sat up for half the night until we had demolished the bottle's contents and most of my brain cells, for Roy, being the gentleman that he is, insisted that I drank more than he did.

I was roughly awakened the next morning by Kev and Nesbit banging on my front door, shouting: 'Wake up you silly old bastard, we're going!'

Fumbling about in a daze as I tried to pack this and unpack that, I realised that whisky, geriatric brain cells and 13,000 feet don't mix and I was still scrabbling around as the others left. Snow lay on the ground and the boisterous streams were now torrents when I tottered after the team, slipping and staggering from rock to rock as my badly packed rucksack pulled me off balance. At the main, deep channel, with white water breaking over the rocks, I made the first jump. While I was wobbling unsteadily on a pointed rock, something flew from the top of my pack – it was my sleeping bag, which was borne away by the current.

I galloped downstream and caught it – but perching on a shingle bank in the middle of a fast-flowing river, repacking my rucksack while suffering a thumping headache and fighting back an urge to spew up, was grim. However, all was not lost for my saviour, in the shape of Nesbit, waited for me and threw over his walking sticks to help me cross the deep channel.

We plodded after the others. The journey back down the valley seemed to be never-ending and it transpired that our retreat, which was fast turning into a rout, had been planned by Kev with military precision. We would carry all our own gear and Colin, Roy, Kev and Nesbit would try to make it to Manikaran in one marathon slog. John, Roz, Keith, Pete and I were to take two days, while Chas, Fran, Pam and Mike would descend with the horses, Tikam and Ram Singh, taking three days.

The heavy, incessant rain and driving winds ensured that everyone was soaked to the skin, and my rucksack, which I had neglected to cover, increased in weight as everything inside became saturated. Heads down, our group slithered and slid on the greasy track and across fresh landslides, often falling as we stumbled through quag-mires and waded thigh-deep through floodwater.

Staggering up a steep climb, we met two natives sheltering under an overhang. John asked how far it was to the nearest village – with big smiles, these two slightly built men heaved our weighty, sodden bags onto their shoulders and gestured us to follow.

If my bag had contained all my worldly possessions and my assistant had run away with it, I couldn't have cared less – I was so relieved to have that weight removed from my shoulders. We quietly followed our helpers to Busheni and shelter for the night.

The five of us were given floor space in an ancient, wooden house – we soon trans-formed that tidy little dwelling into a swilling mess of wet, soggy garments, boots, sleeping bags and semi-clad bodies as we tried to wring the moisture out of our clothes. The good lady of the home brought us large saucers of hot tea, which returned some heat to our starved bodies and we collapsed into our bags like survivors from a ship-wreck. I listened to the loud drumming of torrential rain on the galvanised iron roof before slowly succumbing to a fitful sleep.

IT HAD TO HAPPEN. I, the only one who had not suffered from Delhi belly, had an attack of the trots – and trot I did, stepping on Keith in the process. I blundered blindly across the darkened room and galloped down the exterior staircase in the pouring rain, then ran up the steep, slippery track that left the village, a wet, naked figure on a mission. It was the first time I had ever had a crap and a shower at the same time and, shaking with cold, I staggered back to the house thoroughly cleansed inside and out. I stumbling back across the room, standing on Keith again, as I sought the refuge of my sleeping bag.

'Where, where?'

When the cold, grey light of dawn broke, I stirred and awoke to hear the monsoon still hammering on the roof and something else hammering on my lower intestine. I hastily grabbed my shorts and dived outside again, followed by Keith's trodden cry of anguish. I flew down the staircase to find that villagers in the Himalayas get up very early.

Three small boys stood under the dripping eaves – in desperation I gestured to them by crouching and pointing at my bum. This brought big, beaming smiles to their faces and they pointed up the village to what looked like a communal tip. As I galloped up the hill, they followed; it seems that not much happens in an isolated mountain village in the middle of a monsoon downpour, and I had made their day.

'Where, where?' I shouted with my legs crossed.

They pointed at the large pile of brushwood and straw, so I walked towards the centre of the pile to find that it covered a huge pile of shit. My bare feet and legs sank in with an oozy, squelching sound.

I couldn't smell anything because I was in shock. I dropped my shorts and my bodily contents in front of my interested audience, which was joined by two little girls and their mother. They all smiled broadly and I half expected them to applaud when I had finished. Chastened, I made a shitty journey back to terra firma, where I was instantly swilled clean by the rain and nodded at by the lady, who said something which I took to be: 'I'll bet you enjoyed that. We did!'

WHERE WAS THE BLUE SKY and warming sun of a few days previously? After a bowl of porridge, we thanked our hosts, gave them some rupees and assisted each other to put on our now seriously heavy rucksacks full of wet clothing for our trek down the Parbati valley alongside the thundering river.

We felt as though nothing would ever be dry again and we became immune to the incessant rain running off our bodies. As we descended out of the clouds the rain stopped and, splashing our way almost knee-deep in water around a bend on the washed-out trail, I was amazed when we came across a man and two women in flimsy, brightly coloured saris. From the well-brushed hair on their heads – on which they balanced large baskets – to their sandal-encased feet, they were spotless. The watery sunlight sparkled from the gold thread in their dresses and they smiled as they glided past. I greeted the man and asked how he and his companions kept so clean. He laughed and replied: 'The women are graceful, they have natural balance.'

Clambering across loose rock on a recent landslip, we eventually came in sight of Manikaran, far below. Clouds of steam were rising from the sacred hot springs, where the goddess Parbati had her earrings stolen by Sesha the serpent.

I was telling Keith the legend when we noticed a bright blue bundle bouncing its way down towards the river. It was Keith's sleeping bag and I spent a pleasant half-hour watching him struggle down, followed by his agonising climb back after retrieving it.

We eventually regrouped and spent the time waiting for the remainder of the team on rest, recuperation and rehydration, before moving back to Manali. The team was becoming depleted: Mike and Pam had to return to England, while John and Roz were being attacked by a bug, so they decided to stay and recover in Manali then meet up with us again later. The remaining members planned to head onward to Tikam's place at Solang Nullah.

Manali was awash with climbers and trekkers who had been driven from the mountains; one group had been stuck at 20,000 feet on Dharamsura for six days, held there by fierce blizzards. Another group that passed our camp had turned back from Animal's Pass, so we had been right to leave the mountain.

Tikam ferried us to his climbing and skiing centre, which was in a magnificent setting overlooked by a snow-covered mountain rejoicing in the name of Friendship Peak – our next goal. We were already best of friends with Tikam, Ram Singh and his team, so we ordered several crates of Kingfisher beer and Ram Singh did us proud with the banquets he concocted in his tiny kitchen.

I HAD REACHED THE POINT where I was sick of sleeping with blokes – they fart and belch and their socks stink. I know some women are like that, but at least their skin is smoother and the rewards are greater. Keith and I had now become so close that we were wearing each others' underclothes – when at last we made the trek up the valley, I had visions of a high-altitude camp where I could sleep in comfort away from Keith's trainers, which had begun to lead a life of their own.

Alas, how wrong can you be?

We were self-contained on this part of the expedition: we carried all our own equipment (tents, stoves, food, climbing gear . . .) and as a consequence our rucksacks were even heavier than before. However, the weather was glorious and the scenery was magnificent as we started our long walk towards the foothills, which we intended to do in one day. We soon left the trail and, guided by Tikam, we crossed the Solang Nullah and struggled up some steep ground, which led to even steeper ground that in places reduced me to hands and knees.

I had just burst through my second pain barrier of the day and was being succoured by Fran (women always have a nice thing about geriatrics) when the skies turned black and it began to rain heavily. Why does it always rain above 12,000 feet in the Himalayas?

Our team was reduced to a soggy, miserable, mutinous band – especially Keith, who is an old-time philanthropist and leaves gear behind him wherever he goes. He was now without waterproofs, having left them in Manikaran to join the list of a sweater in Manali, a T-shirt in Dharamsala and his underwear in Chandigarh. He wasn't becoming fitter, either; it was his rucksack becoming lighter. Standing in the pissing rain wearing a sweatshirt and shorts, Keith looked so dejected that I took pity on him and gave him an old plastic flasher's mac. He looked even more unhappy – like a refugee from a Great Yarmouth postcard who has been retrieved from a drain, the mac didn't fit, he could only fasten one button and the sleeves finished at his elbows.

He looked like a refugee

'ONLY ANOTHER THOUSAND FEET,'
said Tikam. 'It is very steep.'

Coming from him, the master of understatement, that meant that it would be perpendicular. We splashed across the knee-deep torrent of a mountain stream, having long given up any pretence at keeping dry, and I naturally looked for a route following the water.

'No, Jim,' shouted Tikam. 'Up.'

I looked in the direction his hand was pointing, but all I could see was a vertiginous wall of dense vegetation receding into the thick cloud base. Wearily, I plodded upwards, soon resorting to using my hands as well as my feet and stopping occasionally for a breather before continuing to climb this green, overgrown treadmill. The hill levelled out slightly, though ahead it rose even steeper as the wind strengthened, lashing us with hail and sleet.

'Camp here,' shouted Tikam.

Through a break in the clouds, we saw the impressive, sheer, Eiger-like walls, jagged ridges and pinnacles of the 20,000 foot Hanuman Tibba, then the clouds closed in again and we erected our tents, which grew like lopsided mushrooms on the steep ground. After more brief instructions from Tikam, he headed back down – we were on our own.

Wet and soggy, we crouched in our four mountain tents. As the cloud of vapour from our bodies slowly cleared, I realised to my horror that I was sitting between Kev and Nesbit – what had I done to deserve this?

When the rain eased, we made the campsite more habitable on the fifty degree slope and the capable hands of Fran and two helpers soon coaxed the stoves to work behind a huddle of rocks as she began cooking our food. The light faded, the clouds started to thin and we had the promise of a clear night, so a lightweight team of five decided to try for an alpine start. It was therefore early to bed, but not to sleep . . .

Three in a mountain tent is not much fun, but when said tent is perched on a steep slope it is ridiculous, especially when I was sleeping in the middle on my bargain basement self-inflating mattress. In spite of the earnest salesman's entreaties, I had scoffed when he tried to sell me the more expensive 'non-slip' variety, replying that: 'You can't slip off one of these.' On my third trip through the tent flaps, as I went sailing down the hillside, I realised that you can.

Kev and Nesbit soon became disgruntled by my frequent vanishing acts, and even more aggrieved as I climbed over them on my return. Then I discovered that by putting one leg in each of their sleeping bags, I could remain in situ. I finally fell asleep, only to be awakened by my bladder!

Expletives rained back and forth regarding my age and common sense as I left then clambered back in after my sojourn, and it was with a combined sigh of relief that Kev and Nesbit crawled out of the tent at 2.30 a.m., swearing to throttle me on their return. Keith and Fran made porridge for the gallant summit team, which also included Chas, Pete and Roy, so I gave the chaps a stiff, upper-lipped farewell before I told them to sod off and let me go back to sleep. I cursed my age as they set off, but I now had the whole tent to myself and slept blissfully – until I again slid out of the tent door.

The five climbers flogged up in the darkness, reaching the glacier at first light. The day looked promising, but clouds soon enveloped them as they climbed onwards and, as the temperature rose, the snow and ice beneath their feet turned to slush. Nearing the top of the glacier, an immense serac collapsed, sending blocks of ice hurtling past the team. Through a break in the swirling clouds they briefly saw the summit ridge before another serac fell and, although there was only a thousand feet left to climb, the deteriorating conditions dictated their return.

Back at the camp we had awoken to an incredible view of Hanuman Tibba soaring into the clear sky, with the first rays of the sun creeping over the distant twin Gyephang peaks. As the rays struck the pinnacles and needle-sharp ridges, they painted the massive rock wall with golden fire, then we watched the slopes slowly become alive with thundering avalanches and listened to the sharp crack of unseen cannons reverberate across the valley as the ice released its iron grip.

Wisps of cloud floated across the face then a thick veil drew over it like a huge curtain, hiding the sight from our eyes – the gods had deemed that we had seen enough. It was unbelievable – the

On my third trip through the tent flaps

huge cliffs which moments before were full of warmth, were now a cold, barren and forbidding precipice, shrouded in grey snowfields and dark, swirling clouds.

Leaders are not born or made, they just materialise like genies out of jam jars. I don't know what started this process in Fran – perhaps it was the porridge – but she was suddenly transformed from a quiet, unassuming woman into a Lagerplatz Führer and decided to make our 'campsite' into something fit for returning heroes. Keith, Colin and I were soon moving tents, building a cookhouse and landscaping a flat area; we laid out wet clothes to dry and no doubt Fran would have had us ironing if there had been a handy electric socket.

Being older and more experienced at this sort of thing, I made an excuse about making a pictorial record of the expedition and left our budding Hausfrau from Hell with her willing assistants making a meal for our intrepid mountaineers while I set off up the steep, slippery scramble behind the camp. Even without a heavy rucksack I was soon struggling, pulling myself up using the roots of the tough plants that covered the loose rock, which ended in a sharp ridge – it was a sort of Lake District high-level Striding Edge, along which I advanced carefully in the thick cloud.

After a while a break appeared and I saw the ridge converging to a flat area covered in small yellow flowers and patches of short, wiry grass – the col would have been our campsite if the conditions had been better. I realised that I would be stupid to wander around in a fog, so I sat on a rock until the wind pulled back the torn grey curtain again, revealing the rock slabs, snow and ice of Friendship Peak. I hastily scanned the lighter patches and thought I could see some figures, then the cold wind and driving rain signalled my return to the camp.

Later that day we watched a lone man struggling down the steep terrain towards us; it was Roy, who had not adjusted well to the altitude and had returned before the rest. Fran brought him round with a hot drink and at four in the afternoon the others appeared, grey-faced and staggering with tiredness – all apart from Nesbit, that is, for nothing seemed to affect him. 'It was hell up there,' said Chas. 'He never stops talking.'

THE FOLLOWING DAY we removed all trace that we had ever been there and, in heavy rain and sleet, we retreated down the valley with Keith in his flasher's mac and Colin with his blue, hairy legs muttering about the 'fuckin' weather and fuckin' monsoons.' Reaching Solang, we found that Tikam had replenished his stocks of Kingfisher and little Ram Singh was busy making us a giant meal. A good night ensued and everyone became inebriated. Sod's Law seems to work better in the Himalayas than anywhere else, for we woke to cloudless blue skies with Friendship Peak mocking us in the brilliant sunlight.

'Sod it,' said Kev, 'let's go to the bath house at Vashisht.'

By the time I had sorted myself out they had gone, so I hired a put-put and asked the driver to drop me at the hot springs in Vashisht. I walked up the wooden staircase and entered the old temple, where there were separate bath house doors for different sexes, these being well marked behind two large shoe racks. I looked for boots or climbing sandals and even sniffed for Keith's trainers, but no – all I could see were flip-flops and curly-toed footwear, but I left my boots and wandered in.

The hot water flowed from a small cistern surmounted by a carved head, before entering something that was the size and shape of a small swimming pool. There the resemblance ended, for the water was dark green and contained what looked like lots of small poached eggs, gently steaming. On closer inspection the eggs turned out to be the eyes of a number of brown gentlemen who were floating in the water, several of whom flashed me a welcoming smile.

I couldn't see Millington and Co. anywhere, so I presumed they either had done their thing or were quietly drowning in those opaque, dark-green depths. Whatever misgivings I may have had, I thought I should at least make one quick trawl to check.

Being in the land of the Kama Sutra and in a chaps-only situation, I presumed that skinny-dipping would be de rigueur, so I smiled at the small brown attendant who came scuttling across and gestured to my undercrackers. 'Okay, I take them off?' I asked. 'Okay,' he answered with a big beaming smile which abruptly vanished when I did.

I sauntered to the pool, where the poached eggs took on looks of horror as they saw this scrawny apparition with a broken nose sidling towards them with his willy swinging in the wind. Several eggs sank in embarrassment. The attendant, showing valour far beyond the call of duty, hurtled towards me clutching a small towel and his face, grey with fright, clutched me to his bosom as he held the towel round my body. He looked up into my eyes with all the fervour of a devout Christian peering into the eyes of Old Nick, expecting at any moment to be vaporised.

'Oh, not permissible, sir,' he said, trembling. 'Not permissible naked willy.'

'Oh, sorry, is it because it's white?' I asked.

'No sir, not white, not brown, not permissible,' and he led me back to my undercrackers and insisted that I put them back on.

'I want to wash them,' I said.

'You wash here,' he said. 'Bum, undercrackers and willy, all together in one place,' and he demonstrated under a hot water tap which flowed into the pool.

It's quite an experience washing undercrackers while wearing them – and even more interesting trying to wring them out in front of a large audience of poached eggs.

'Not permissible naked willy.'

THE ATROCIOUS WEATHER in the mountains gave us time to take taxis to Shimla and travel back to Delhi on the train. Shimla, spread over two wooded hills against a backcloth of snow-covered mountains, carries ghosts of the old British Raj – with British churches, a cricket pavilion, half-timbered buildings and a statue of a young Queen Victoria gazing serenely down on the broad expanse of the esplanade, it was a fascinating place. I felt like Dr Who after returning from one of his time travels to discover that he had pressed the wrong button and alighted at the wrong stop. Where were all the Victorian ladies in their voluminous dresses and large, ornate hats, shading their delicate features with dainty little parasols as they walked arm in arm with their escorts? Where were the smart men in red uniforms with gold braid and medals glistening in the early morning sunlight?

We felt that we were part of an illusion as we passed the officers' mess with its polished brass cannons and wooden soldiers standing smartly to attention behind a painted fence. Just down the road the Playhouse was advertising Gilbert and Sullivan in glass-fronted boxes on the wall; I entered the foyer, all brass rails and red velvet, and could smell the cigar smoke and perfume while the faint sound of ladies gossiping murmured in the background.

Shimla is a pretty town, plucked from Sussex and deposited here, with all the best British values. The railway, too, was British – it wasn't running. Well, it had been the day before when we took turns at standing in a queue to buy the tickets, but now it seemed that although the train was waiting in the station, we could not board it because a computer had failed in Delhi.

'Does the computer drive the train?'

'No, the driver drives the train.'

'Well, what does the computer do?'

'It tells him when he can drive the train.'

'Ah, so that he doesn't collide with another train.'

'No, there is only one train and one set of lines.'

We had to reach Delhi on time for our flight home, so we came up with the bright idea of hiring a minibus.

'Sorry, no minibus sir.'

'Oh.'

'But for you, special price, I hire you a coach.'

'Done.'

And we were, because I think the coach was last used to take Shimla's bandsmen to play at the Delhi Durbar, when George V was on the throne. We first had a clue that things were not quite what they seemed when we had a puncture and found that there was no spare wheel and no tools to put one on if there had been one.

A visit to a nearby blacksmith saw a group of Northern Pennine Club international motor mechanics returning with tools, only to find that the jack wasn't big enough to lift the coach. Large, flat stones and pieces of timber were called into play, as was a group of strolling players who entertained a crowd of onlookers with music, in spite of threats from Kev (who said he would do things with the sitar which were not included in its teaching manual).

The original tyre rubber was buried under several layers of Indian remoulds (whereby six-inch-wide strips of old tyre were glued on top of each other) so, once we had the puncture repaired, we understood why there was a small temple and a holy man at every steep hill. It was essential that we stopped at every shrine, for the holy man was the Indian equivalent of the Automobile Association. The driver's mate would leap out to be blessed and have a large dab of red paint placed on his forehead – another was smeared on his thumb, to be pressed to the driver's forehead when he returned to the cab. This was the Indian driver's equivalent of 'God bless all who sail in her'.

Driving up the steep passes wasn't too bad, but going down the other side was unnerving when the coach seemed to go faster and faster while the driver vigorously pumped the brake pedal. At the next temple we *all* got out and received a dab of red paint on our foreheads.

Having just freewheeled to a halt after 'rock and rolling' down one particularly vicious pass, the driver and his mate began fiddling under the bonnet, then the driver informed us that they couldn't go on because, 'The engine not good.' They would, apparently, 'need more rupees' to fix it.

'The only thing that would fix this fuckin' coach is a crusher,' I answered, but – concerned that we would miss our flight –– we promised him more money if he could persuade his sick vehicle to trundle onward to Delhi.

Sitting behind the driver I had grown aware that, for some time, the brakes were becoming worse. The diminutive driver was by now literally jumping up and down as he furiously stamped on the brake pedal when he wanted to slow down, but this being India – where everyone drives by the seat of their trousers – I didn't worry *too* much, but merely made sure that he kept his spot topped up with red paint. However, when we reached a system of dual carriageways near Delhi the roads became busier and the driving grew more erratic.

Suddenly, the coach left the road and hurtled down a steep bank before crossing another busy carriageway, going through the traffic heading in the other direction and ending up by the side of the road. It all happened in seconds and for a minute no one spoke, until John, who had been asleep, said: 'Ah, are we there?' If he had been dreaming of heaven, he was almost right.

The driver and his mate dived under the bonnet again and talked very excitedly as they tried to screw two brake pipes together. It was too much for our resident engineer, Kev, who grabbed each small man by the scruff of their necks and heaved them out of the way.

'Bloody hell, these brake pipes are knackered.'

'Yes,' said the driver, 'but I fix.' He waved his only tool, some ancient pliers, as though they were a magic wand. Kev took the pliers and removed a section of pipe, then marched off with it into a village. An hour later he returned looking extremely frustrated but carrying some more pipe – which didn't fit. To prevent Kev from killing the driver and his mate, who were now industriously fastening wire around a cloth-covered leaking joint in the hydraulic brake system, I suggested that we should pool our remaining money and hire taxis to take us into Delhi.

The problem was, before leaving we neglected to have our foreheads daubed again with a holy man's red spot.

If anyone reading this account ever feels depressed or suicidal and thinks that life is not worth living or is totally boring, and has reached the nadir of despair, take heart – for there is an instant cure. Take a taxi ride in New Delhi at the peak of the rush hour; it makes school runs in Britain seem like a visit to the public gallery in the House of Commons.

'Bloody hell, these
brake pipes are
knackered.'
'Yes,' said the driver,
'but I fix.'

We piled into three taxis and headed into the war zone. This began twenty miles outside Delhi with a haze of diesel fumes. It was dusk when we joined the stock-car race of overloaded lorries, put-puts, cars, taxis, lunatics on bicycles, cows and beggars lying in the gutter. As it became dark we found ourselves inches from the back wheels of a lorry, one of four driving abreast and belching thick, hot clouds of fumes while motorcyclists on unlit bikes threaded their way between them.

Suddenly, the lorry swerved to reveal a cow lying in the centre of the road. The reflexes of our Indian driver were amazing: brake, clutch, a quick twist of the steering wheel and we missed it by a fraction of an inch.

'Bad karma if you kill cow,' said our driver, flashing me a beaming smile of white teeth.

By now it was obvious that no one could see any other road user, because most of the vehicles were unlit and Indian diesels created their own thick fog. Everything appeared to work on horn blasts. One was a warning, two meant that you were thinking of passing, while three meant that you were doing so and frightening the passengers to death.

With everyone busy sounding their horns, it was a mystery how this system worked – but every time our horn was sounded, we received a response from the driver in front. His skinny brown arm would wave us back or beckon us on, sometimes deciding otherwise as the fingers did a quick wobble when something suddenly thundered past in the opposite direction. At the same time our driver would be waving down a put-put driver intent on committing hara-kiri, or swerving to avoid a family sitting around a fire in the gutter as they cooked their evening meal.

The traffic suddenly slowed and veered around a dead cow which had been left lying in the middle of the road surrounded by large stones, an Indian warning sign meaning 'if you suddenly run into a large rock which wrecks your steering you will shortly be encountering a dead cow'. Why can't we Brits have such a common sense approach to motoring?

BACK HOME IN THE ARMS of my dear Audrey, my Indian experience seemed like a strange dream. Then, a week later, I received an official-looking document with the address of the Government of India Tourist Office emblazoned under its logo and signed by the Promotions Business Manager.

Dear Mr Eyre,
On behalf of my colleagues at the Tourist Board of India, I would like to welcome you back to the U.K. and hope that your recent excursion to the Himalayas was enjoyable and successful. Our organisation aims to guarantee that all travellers to India and the Himalayas fully benefit from the opportunity to visit.

In your particular case, however, it has come to our attention, through our local agents, that you were held in very high esteem by the members of the local community in Manali. As such the local community has chosen to bestow upon you the title of 'Supka' – which roughly translated means 'the Old Man of the Mountains'. Apparently, the community was most impressed by the enthusiasm you displayed towards the local culture, and speak very highly of you.

Our organisation is most keen to promote Anglo-Indian relations and we have been asked by our principals if you would consent to a portrait of yourself being included in the next issue of our special mountain range stamps.

Audrey looked at me in amazement. 'Oo, fancy you on a stamp, I'll have to tell our Betty and Norman, and Ron and Marge, and . . .'

As Audrey rushed to the telephone, I hadn't time to tell her that 'supka' is another name for the yeti, a large-footed, hairy beast of low intelligence.

But I don't have large feet . . .

Postscript

THEY SAY THAT YOU SHOULD NEVER GO BACK to relive old memories. It's never the same: where once was all blue skies, it is now grey and gloomy and raining heavily. Several good friends made just a few years previously are recently bereaved or have developed a debilitating disease, and the 'good 'ole buddy' from the last caving trip you went on died six days ago leaving a grief-stricken wife. All the good memories one had of that paradise on earth are obliterated never to return.

It seemed so to me, at least, as the second millennium saw me approaching Epirus – the last wilderness in Europe – in a hired car, only to discover that the dirt tracks that once threaded the region had all been replaced by first-class roads that would put British motorways to shame. Looking across the vista of mountains and gorges, my eyes were dazzled by silver ribbons of new, galvanised iron crash barriers that twisted and writhed into the distance. My wilderness had gone.

I almost turned back, but around the next bend Astraka reared up, its white and gold cliffs unchanged and unchangeable, like a crenellated Gibraltar beckoning me on through the evening mist. The Zagori region of Epirus was now a national park and, thanks to the activities of British cavers, Provatina had become a tourist attraction. It was mapped and signposted in a variety of publications and guidebooks on sale in the numerous twee restaurants and guesthouses which were springing up very tastefully as lower Papingo and upper Papingo's old stone houses succumbed to the attention of rich speculators and Greek craftsmen, who were transforming the stone-slabbed buildings without losing the character of the place.

Jim standing outside the church, cloisters and the Greek Alpine Club hut in Papingo in 2000. Photo: Kath Alty

We booked in at the schoolhouse and crossed a circular, stone-flagged courtyard to sit under the shade of a huge plane tree and enjoy a few glasses of beer as we took in the dramatic backcloth of the limestone buttress rising like an ancient fortress to the top of the first gully. Then my companion noticed grizzled, elderly, weather-beaten faces appearing from the edges of an archway leading to a narrow alley, along which heavily laden donkeys clip-clopped their way up steep paving to gain the age-old mule tracks winding across the mountains. Another grizzly, who had been lurking half-hidden in the shadows of the restaurant, brought two more bottles of beer.

'Hello, meester Jeem,' he said as he grasped my hand. It was Dimitrios, who had been one of our 'donkey boys'. It was a rare moment, full of emotion as the veil of thirty-seven years parted. I took out some shabby black-and-white prints of actors on that faraway stage and within minutes the courtyard was filled with wizened villagers shaking me by the hand and I met their children and their children's children. Sounds of delight echoed in the clear air as each picked out relatives and former acquaintances from the grainy photographs. Bottles of beer kept appearing and toasts were drunk to all my Greek contemporaries who were 'sleeping', and to many more who had emigrated. The other tourists were told that that 'Ee was the bloke that first went down that bloody girt hole on the mountain.'

Sometimes, returning to relive old memories is exactly what you should do.

*Jim at the entrance to
Provatina in 2000
Photo: Kath Alty*

By the Same Author

'Lancaster Hole and the Ease Gill Caverns, Casterton Fell, Westmorland'. *Transactions of the Cave Research Group of Great Britain*, Vol 9 (2), March 1967, pp61-123 (with Peter Ashmead)

The Cave Explorers. Stalactite Press, Calgary, 1981, viii+264pp

Race Against Time. A history of the Cave Rescue Organisation. Lyon, Dent, 1988, 208pp (with John Frankland)

'The Ease Gill Cave System'. *British Cave Research Association*, Speleo-History Series (1), 1989, 48pp

Right In It. Mendip Publishing, Castle Cary, 1992, 80pp

It's Only a Game. Wild Places Publishing, Cardiff, 2004, 256pp

References and Further Reading

The following sources are recommended for further reading or have been mentioned in this book.

HRYNDYJ, Bob. 1976. '(Cave Rescue) Lost Johns Pot'. *Northern Pennine Club Bulletin* (2) [the *White Bulletin*], pp31-2

JUDSON, David. 1973. *Ghar Parau*. Cassell, London. viii+216pp

LIVESEY, Pete. 'Abseiling – 101 Golden Rules.' *Crags*. (19), June/July 1979, p30

   'Travels with a Donkey.' *Crags*. (21), October/November 1979, pp19-20

CULLINGFORD, Cecil (ed). 1969. *Manual of Caving Techniques*. Routledge & Kegan Paul, London. x+416pp

The quotation on p81 is from: THOMPSON, Frank. 'Journey to the Depths.' *Daily Express*, 29 June 1968

Publisher's Notes

In *It's Only a Game*, the first part of Jim's autobiography, two pictures showing George Band descending Rift Pot appeared on p118. These were credited to Ron Bliss, but new information shows that they were taken by an early Red Rose CPC member, Arthur Woodall. Arthur has identified the 'unknown' caver as Chris Riley from Blackpool.

Details of the series of six rescues that occurred on 15 November 1975 appear at the end of Chapter 12. It was widely reported in newspapers of the time and within subsequent caving articles and references, that 47 people were rescued that night. However, adding up the numbers of individuals rescued in the separate incidents (12, 1, 5, 3, 9 and 8, using the CRO's data) produces a total of 38. Some reports mention sixteen people rescued in the first of these callouts, making a total of 42.

It seems likely that the oft-quoted 47 people rescued is a mistake, perhaps based on the number of people in the combined parties, some of whom gained the surface on their own and made the callout. The account in this book uses a total of 38 rescued individuals.

Glossary

bedding plane	a wide but low cave passage
jumar	device used to ascend a rope in *SRT*
krab	karabiner or snaplink
master cave	a major cave system with many tributaries, sometimes known to exist but not yet discovered
SRT	single rope technique

Index